Ethics for Our Times

Ethics for Our Times

ESSAYS IN GANDHIAN PERSPECTIVE

Second Edition

M.V. NADKARNI

OXFORD

UNIVERSITY PRESS

OXFORD
UNIVERSITY PRESS

Oxford University Press is a department of the University of Oxford.
It furthers the University's objective of excellence in research, scholarship,
and education by publishing worldwide. Oxford is a registered trademark of
Oxford University Press in the UK and in certain other countries

Published in India by
Oxford University Press
YMCA Library Building, 1 Jai Singh Road, New Delhi 110 001, India

© Oxford University Press 2011

ISBN 13: 978-0-19-945053-4
ISBN 10: 0-19-945053-6

Typeset in Minion Pro 10/12.6
by SPEX Infotech, Puducherry, India 605 009
Printed in India at Rakmo Press Pvt. Ltd., New Delhi 110 020

To,
my grandchildren
Hansa, Pranav, Nandan, and Ved,
and their generation,
with love,
and hope
that they will be more ethically concerned
than their seniors
with issues of environment, poverty, and injustice

Contents

Foreword

The world is in turmoil. Disaffections like terrorism are spreading widely and hitting headlines day after day. The continuing degradation of environment seems to have become an irreversible process. While the nations forming the global community should come together and cooperate to build a new world order, conflicts and disputes are more common than agreements and joining of hands in a common endeavour for the benefit of all. Programmes, like Millennium Development Goals (MDGs), which bring together the global community for removal of poverty and deprivation in the developing countries, do not quite live up to their promises. The shadow of excessive consumerism hovering over developed countries and the trap of poverty, in which many developing countries including India find themselves, give rise to serious apprehensions about the future. While economic growth and development are crucial for achieving a breakthrough, these need to be part of a wider agenda based on concerns for human development and welfare, with full commitment to working for achieving them.

This book by M.V. Nadkarni makes an admirable attempt to explore the building blocks needed to construct such a wide agenda. He is uniquely qualified for this task as a leading ecological economist, who has worked extensively and in-depth on the developmental issues relating to the poor and marginalized subsisting in locations with degraded resources and vulnerable to frequent disasters, such as droughts and floods. He realizes that the plight of these sections of the society is an inevitable consequence of the lifestyle and the growth-cum-development priorities of the elite forming the creamy layers. Consumerism and poverty-trap are the two sides of the same coin! It is this recognition with deep conviction that has led him from ecological theories to Gandhi's approaches, values, and philosophy. Gandhi's dictum that there is enough in the world to meet the needs of all but not their greed, and the primacy he gave to 'antyodaya'—lifting up the lowest and the most miserable—are widely known. Nadkarni pursues these dicta to their roots, going deep into Gandhian thought and vision for mankind. What distinguishes his approach is that he is a social scientist turning to Gandhi for guidance and not a Gandhian, who is usually prone to accepting Gandhi as an authority on all issues and problems.

It is not an accident that the literature cited by him has as frequent and numerous references to Amartya Sen, the Modern Western and other thinkers, as to Gandhi's writings. I have seen few books taking such an approach that Gandhi himself would have heartily commended.

I welcome this book as a timely and useful addition to the current debates among academics, activists, and policymakers on the present status and the emerging prospects for the globalizing world. The first part, containing four chapters, is the core of the book, presenting Gandhian ethical approaches to deal with current crises examined from the criteria of social science research. The second, covering three essays, places these approaches in the broader context of debates among the modern philosophers on basic concepts like social justice, equity, and harmony across different sections in human societies. As Hinduism is the main source of inspiration and ideas to Gandhi, the last part, with two chapters, deals with the ethical foundations of Hinduism. Laypersons and even academics tend to confuse between the foundations of Hinduism and the features of Hindu society, such as orthodoxy, superstitions, and perversions of organized religions, which are also common in other religions. A look at the foundations of Hinduism is of help in understanding Gandhi as a thinker, activist, and philosopher. Philosophy originates in the religious quest for the vision of the ultimate reality and its implications for human societies. Thus, the book is comprehensive in its analyses of ethics as a conceptual framework, and as a guide to action in tackling the problems of modernizing societies, particularly of the developing ones. The style and the flow of ideas and arguments are smooth. Jargon, which is inevitable given the theme of the book, remains within limits. I recommend the book to all those who are worried about 'Today' and wish for a peaceful and prosperous 'Tomorrow'. Gandhi can help if and only when we are willing, and even eager, to help ourselves.

V. M. Rao

Preface to This Edition

I am happy that Oxford University Press is bringing out a second edition of this book. In addition to updating, where necessary, and correcting the typos, this edition has added a Part IV on 'Some Contemporary Concerns', with two new essays. Some contemporary concerns or dilemmas in pursuing economic development, such as environmental destruction and displacement of people, were already discussed in Part I in the first edition. Some specific issues like abortion, capital punishment, and preferential treatment of historically disadvantaged social groups were explained in the essay, 'Holistic Approach to Knowledge' in Part II. The second edition now has added two more areas of urgent concern in Part IV—'Ethics in Business' and 'Gender Justice'. I hope that this has added further to the value of the book.

Earlier, ethics was considered simply a matter of personal character, cultivated since childhood by parents, shaped by culture and circumstances, and came naturally to an adult without any special training or study, but not any more. Ethical dilemmas, already as old as the epics, have grown manifold in the complicated contemporary civilization, and have to be dealt with not only by individuals but also by organizations, business enterprises, and policy makers. To face and resolve them, ethics has to be taught, studied, and contemplated upon. That is why many professional schools such as law, medicine, and even sports have included ethics in the courses offered by them. Ethics has to be a part of any training of administrators, managers, the police, the army and other professionals, to make them sensitive to ethical concerns in general and human rights in particular.

Hopefully, this book will be useful not only in such specialized courses, but also to any ethically concerned general reader and organization. A special feature of the book is that it is relevant particularly to Indian conditions, though it also has a universal appeal.

I am grateful to Saraswati Naimpally, Kishore Nadkarni, Subhashree Banerjee, and S. Subramanian for helping me in various ways.

M.V. Nadkarni

Preface to the First Edition

A friend told me that he finds a book on philosophy most useful. When the mind is burdened with problems and the spirit is restless with worries that haunt you, especially when you go to bed, all that you have to do is to reach out for a book on philosophy. And lo, before you go to the second page, you are fast asleep! I hope that my readers will find this book more useful than that.

Ethics is the philosophy of good and bad, right and wrong, or moral philosophy. The task which the book sets for itself is not to preach morals—there are better people to do that than me—but a much less ambitious and risky one of reflecting philosophically on morals. Instead of simply being told what is good or bad, it is better to be philosophically equipped to think over and be capable of judging for oneself what is good and right, particularly in complex situations. This book aims at stimulating holistic-cum-analytical reasoning on ethical concepts and issues. However, discussions about morals cannot be avoided in ethics any more than discussion of plants can be avoided in botany. But I hesitate to call ethics a science. I am more content with it being considered a branch of philosophy. Anyway, ethics is not simply a bunch of 'dos and don'ts'. Relying simply on moral instructions, especially pronouncing 'don'ts' one after another, has its risks. A child was behaving, to the horror of its mother, exactly opposite to what it was being told not to do. 'Don't throw food on the floor!', and it throws food on the floor. 'Don't pinch your baby brother!', and it pinches him. 'Don't go to play before finishing your food!', and it does exactly that. The distraught mother told her neighbour about it. The neighbour observed the child's behaviour for some time and then asked the child, 'Dear one, what is your name?' It replied, 'Don't'!

In any case, all 'dos and don'ts' do not constitute moral injunctions. This raises the question of what is moral. The Introduction discusses such theoretical issues and tries to answer what is ethics, what is ethical, and why be ethical, as a background to the essays presented here. This book does not intend to be a comprehensive text on ethics. In the light of Gandhian perspectives, essays here explore ethical dimensions of issues related to economic development, environment, humanism, and religion. They also examine some philosophical aspects of ethics.

There are several approaches to ethics not necessarily exclusive to each other. A popular approach is to take ethics as what is ordained by God, as revealed through scriptures. Faith and a sense of duty play a more important role, than reasoning, in this approach. Invoking one's conscience, ('Inner Voice', as Gandhi called it), and a sense of duty guided by it is another way. The approach of *Dharma* in the sense of moral injunctions, doing one's duty, or following moral imperatives, may appear close to the above, but it is based more on reasoning. A modern version of this approach, called deontic or deontological in modern philosophy, is attributed to Immanuel Kant. One more approach is to go by what brings about the good or happiness of mankind and choosing to do what produces good consequences. This can be called the consequentialist or utilitarian approach. Although the two terms have been used by different philosophers in different ways, they can be clubbed together. The rights (*adhikaara*) approach covers not only human rights but also rights of animals and nature, in general. It assumes that human beings, animals, and nature are endowed with certain basic rights, which ought not to be violated by our actions. The virtue approach, which is as ancient as the Dharma approach, advocates building good character for its own sake, both as an individual and as a member of the society and polity. The feminist approach of care ethics insists on developing close and mutually satisfying relationships. It emphasizes feelings, empathy, kindness, affection, and emotional commitment more than rights, righteousness, justice, rationality, impartiality, or detachment. The Gandhian approach to ethics is not separate from, or independent of, the above approaches, but is inclusive of them as in a creative synthesis. Gandhi would not depend only on one of these exclusively, rather, reasoning with an open mind and drawing upon the 'Inner Voice', he would use them all. Evidently, Gandhian perspective is not confined to what he said or wrote. It means his approach, which can cover other thinkers with similar views.

The essays here are inspired by the Gandhian perspective or approach. Apart from a common concern with ethics in different contexts, it is this Gandhian perspective which integrates these essays together. Gandhi did not believe much in mere philosophical discussions, but practised what he believed was truth and said, 'My life is my message'. Apart from deriving lessons from his action-filled life, my book intends to use his perspective, which is holistic, open to reasoning, firmly committed to moral values of truth and non-violence, empathetic, compassionate, and partial to the weakest. Philosophy, particularly one which is rooted in the Gandhian approach, can have tremendous practical relevance in clarifying issues and facilitating decisions in situations of conflict. From the point of pursuing the Gandhian perspective further, this work can be considered as a sequel to my earlier book—*Hinduism* (2008). But the present book is not confined to Hindu ethics, and not even to Indian ethics. The essays here have an Indian ethos, but nevertheless, have a universal appeal, especially in the globalized world of today. Gandhian approach offers, perhaps, the only hope to overcome the torments of the present day. Globalization works mainly in the interest of the strong, but ethics is on the side of the weak. It is their only weapon and hope, which they have to recognize and use. The weak may be people within countries, or countries themselves. Often, ethical questions cannot be resolved until we see them in terms of a holistic-cum-philosophical analysis. A seemingly simple question of what is good may only be deceptively simple, until subjected to philosophical discussion.

The essays here are an outcome of my own struggle to understand ethics, rather than quench any desire of writing for others. But I am confident that many will find the essays useful, not necessarily for inducing sleep as my friend above said, but even in day-to-day life. Not only those interested in philosophy, but also book lovers in general, who like to read non-fiction, and others, who have to do with social sciences, law, social work, governance, and so on will find it interesting. That is why I dare to share the book with them.Though there are several books aimed at providing moral instructions and personality development, books on ethics as a discipline with an Indian ethos, are rarely written in India. This is a serious gap. In these perplexing modern times, we need to develop not merely ethical sensitivity but also ethical intelligence. This book is a modest attempt to fill this gap.

The essays here are presented in three separate but interrelated parts to facilitate easy reading. These are, 'Ethics for a Globalizing World'; 'Ethics: Some Philosophical Aspects'; and 'Ethical Foundations of Hinduism'. An overview of all the essays, for each part respectively, is presented in the last section of the Introduction.

The essays in this book are mostly based on invited lectures, some given at the Institute for Social Economic Change (ISEC), Bengaluru, where I am an Honorary Visiting Professor and some essays given outside. I am grateful to ISEC for providing the opportunities for giving these lectures. I have mentioned below only those lectures given outside of ISEC. Having benefited from the comments and questions raised at all these lectures, I heartily thank both their sponsors and audience.

The essay, 'Religion for Modern Times: Ethics-centred Gandhian Way', grew out of my talk at the Bhavan's Gandhi Centre of Science and Human Values, Bharatiya Vidya Bhavan, Bengaluru, in October 2007. Subsequently, I gave a public lecture on this in a more developed form at Dr V.K.R.V. Rao Birth Centenary Celebration Lecture Series at the Jnanajyoti Auditorium of Bangalore University in January 2008. The present essay is a further enlarged and revised version of this. I am grateful to L.C. Jain for chairing the lecture. 'Ethics and Development', is an outcome of my lecture under the auspices of Professor M. Madaiah Felicitation Endowment at the University of Mysore in March 2010.

The last three sections of the essay 'Ethics, Environment, and Culture: The Paradox of India' are based on my keynote address on 'Culture and Environment: Paradox of India' at a national seminar on Ecological Economics at ISEC, held jointly with the National Institute of Ecology from 30 September to 1 October 2009.

A shorter version of 'Interrogating the Idea of Justice', which grew out of a lecture at ISEC, has appeared in the *Indian Economic Journal*, 58 (1), April–June 2010. I am grateful to V.R. Panchamukhi, its Managing Editor, for valuable comments and for permission to publish the larger version here. 'Appearance and Reality' is a revised version of my Valedictory Address at the Eighth Monastic Dialogue Seminar on 'The Real Nature of Phenomenon and its Relation with Life: Ancient and Modern Perspectives', at Tashi Lhumpa Monastery, Tibetan Colony at Bylakuppe, Karnataka, in December 2008. This was under the auspices of Tibet House, New Delhi. I am immensely grateful to its Director, Most Venerable Lama Doboom Tulku, for giving me the honour of addressing the seminar in the august presence of venerable monks and philosophers, and also for permitting me to use the lecture in a revised form here. 'Holistic Approach to Knowledge: Contribution of the Bhagavadgita and its Relevance to Social Science Research and Ethics' grew out of lectures, one at ISEC, one at Indian Business Academy, Bengaluru, and another under the auspices of Academic Staff College at Karnatak University, Dharwad. Two shorter versions of this appeared in *Think India Quarterly*, 12 (2), April–June 2009, and the *Journal of Social and Economic Development*, 12 (1), January–June 2010, respectively. What appears here is a more comprehensive version. I am grateful to the editors of both the above journals for permission to use the articles here. The essay 'Humanism in Hinduism' is an enlarged and revised version of my Shri G.R. Bhatkal Memorial Lecture at the Indian Institute of World Culture, Bengaluru, in February 2009.

I had the benefit of discussions on several points covered in the essays here with V.M. Rao, C.T. Kurien, Sundar Sarukkai, P.R. Panchamukhi, R.S. Deshpande, N.S.S. Narayana, and M.V. Ramana. I am grateful to all of them. I should particularly mention V.M. Rao, who took the trouble of going through all the essays and providing very useful comments. In addition, he has obliged me by writing a Foreword to the book. The arrangement of chapters under three parts is following his suggestion. Gopal Kadekodi took a lot of interest in this book, for which I am thankful. My hearty thanks are due to the reviewers of Oxford University Press for their constructive comments. They helped in bringing greater clarity and cohesion to my presentation. I am also grateful to the editorial team of Oxford University Press for meticulous and prompt editing.

Dr V.K.R.V. Rao Library of ISEC has been very useful. K. Prakash and all his library staff were very kind and obliging. S. Arun Kumar typed most of the essays, diligently in his spare time. I thank all of them.

My daughter, Saraswati, my son-in-law, Chinmay, my sons, Anirudh and Makarand, and my daughters-in-law, Umeshwari and Amita, my brother, Kishore, and his wife, Sucheta, gave excellent support and encouragement. My dear departed wife, Ganga, though not physically present now, continues to inspire me ever as before.

I shall be grateful to my readers for conveying their reactions and comments on the essays here, by e-mail to mvnadkarni1968@gmail.com.

M.V. Nadkarni

Abbreviations

BJP	Bharatiya Janata Party
CEDAW	Convention on the Elimination of all Forms of Discrimination against Women
CPI	Corruption Perception Index
CSR	Corporate Social Responsibility
CWMG	*Collected Works of Mahatma Gandhi*
EAW	Employment at Will
EB	*Encyclopedia Britannica*
GDP	Gross Domestic Product
GNP	Gross National Product
HCN	Hydrogen Cyanide
HDI	Human Development Index
HDR	Human Development Report
ISEC	Institute for Social Economic Change
IUD	Intrauterine Device
MDG	Millennium Development Goal
MGNREGA	Mahatma Gandhi National Rural Employment Guarantee Act
MIC	Methyl Isocyanate
NGO	Non-governmental Organization

PCB	Pollution Control Board
PPP	Purchasing Power Parity
PT	Preferential Treatment
RCHP	Reproduction and Child Health Programme
RSS	Rashtriya Swayamsevak Sangh
RTIA	Right to Information Act
SC	Scheduled Caste
SEBI	Securities and Exchange Board of India
SEWA	Self-Employed Women's Association
UCC	Union Carbide Company
UCIL	Union Carbide India Limited
UNDP	United Nations Development Programme
UPA	United Progressive Alliance
WDI	World Development Indicators

Introduction

Good life is one inspired by love and guided by knowledge.

—Bertrand Russell
(Russell 2009b: 257)

A person who follows the path of dharma does not feel helpless.

—M.K. Gandhi
(*Harijanbandhu* 5 November 1933; *CWMG* 56: 183)

What is Ethics? What is Ethical?

Since the essays here are on ethics, we need to discuss what we mean by ethics and its nature. Another term for ethics is moral philosophy and the two are generally used as synonyms. The latter term is used more in Britain. While 'ethics' has a Greek origin, 'moral' has a Latin origin (Williams 2000: 546).[1] Ethics is not the same thing as morals, and is not even a set of morals. Russell says that 'the object of ethics, by its own account, is to discover true propositions about virtuous or vicious conduct' (Russell 2009a: 3). Morals or a set of morals can be derived from the propositions discovered by moral philosophy. That is how morals and moral philosophy, though conceptually different, are often taken together in common parlance. Morals may be taught out of intuition by good and wise persons without explicit philosophical analysis, but such intuitions themselves may be based on implicit reasoning. Philosophical analysis, explicit or implicit, is unavoidable in any discussion of what is moral and what is not, or what is good and what is not. Russell includes ethics among sciences (Russell 2009a: 4). Since ethics emerges in society and has much to do with social relations, it could very well be considered as a social science. But most writers on ethics are content with treating it as a branch of philosophy. Well, philosophy itself can be considered a science, that of logical investigation into abstract issues concerning all sciences, arts and experiences—an ultimate science. Not many philosophers, however, would agree that science, normally understood as an investigation into the natural world, could prove or disprove, or evaluate moral concepts. Although there can be an ethical evaluation of science and technology, yet it is for ethics to evaluate moral concepts and principles.

Ethics is not a mere matter of subjective opinion. Its propositions are not specific to particular individuals but apply equally to all. They have a degree of generalizability or universalizability, which can make it a systematic area of study, irrespective of whether one prefers to call it a science or a branch of philosophy. There is a noteworthy similarity between ethics and economics, though economics is considered to be more definitely a science. The similarity arises not so much because both deal with value/s, since the way they look at values is different. The similarity arises more, because both deal with problems of choice and also, development. Frank Knight observes, 'Ethics deals with the problem of choosing between different kinds of life, and assumes there is real choice between different kinds, or else there is no such thing as ethics' (Knight 1936: 71). Ethics deals with choice not only between what is good and what is bad but also between different moral principles or values or ends, because there can be several moral ends sometimes conflicting with each other. Freedom of choice is very crucial for moral decisions. Ethics becomes meaningful only in the context of choice. For instance, merely not stealing by itself does not make a person ethical. When, however, the person knows that under the circumstances faced there is no chance of being caught, and yet she does not steal, only then is she ethical. We may add that ethics is concerned not merely with choice, but also with survival in this mundane world and development of both individual and communities. It is particularly concerned with moral and social development, just as economics is concerned with economic survival and economic development. In the issues related to human development, both ethics and economics can overlap each other (though sometimes they may conflict with each other, when economic development is viewed narrowly in terms of growth of national income). Hence, both economic choices and economic development are subject to ethical evaluation too, and not just in terms of rates of growth and efficiency.

Russell observes that the first step in ethics is to be quite clear as to what we mean by good and bad (Russell 2009a: 5). It is also the most important question, the answers to which constitutes a major part of ethics. G.E. Moore also observed in his *Principia Ethica*, 'the main object of Ethics as a systematic science is to give correct *reasons* for thinking that this or that is good'. But he also added that unless the question of what is 'good' was answered such reasons could not be given (Moore, in Cahn and Markie [eds] 1998: 479). What is good is an age-old question. Plato's *Republic* mentions the argument of Thrasymachus, whose view may still be of interest. For him, what is just or good is determined from the interests of the strong and the ruling classes invented the concept to guard their power, prestige, and property. Thus, for Thrasymachus the question of what is good is inseparably linked with the question of good for whom. He even takes all ethics as 'doggy ethics', in the sense that we call a dog good when it is obedient and 'well behaved' (Richter 2008: 10–12; MacIntyre 2010: 33–4). Thrasymachus says that it is not in the interest of common people to follow such ethics, but they do it only under duress. All societies and states do have customs, laws, and moral codes to impart stability to themselves and security to its members. It cannot be denied that be denied that rigidities in customs, laws, and even in moral codes can produce injustice, which, for example, authenticated social evils like untouchability, slavery, and blasphemy laws. But to say that all ethics is of this type would be extreme cynicism. There is definitely much more to ethics than mere loyalty and obedience.

Quite in contrast with the view of Thrasymachus, Gandhi would think that justice is the main weapon of the exploited and the deprived. It is justice which gives them the motive, power, and moral courage to fight against injustice. Exploiters on the other hand would have to try hard for some rationalization of their wrong-doing. Erich Fromm has given expression to this essentially Gandhian stand: 'For everybody who is powerless, justice and truth are the most important weapon in the fight for his freedom and growth' (Fromm 1955: 247). The pertinent point here is that Gandhi would brush aside the question of 'good for whom', as he would regard morality is good for all, the rich and the poor, young and old, and it should be sought for its own sake as an end in itself. When it is so pursued, it results in happiness and well being of all. Without morality, society cannot just survive, including the weak. Morality involves mutual obligations and the necessity to ensure that it is conducive to the happiness of all sections of the society. Society would simply break down into disorder and chaos without a common or universal concept of what is good for all. Such a situation is dangerous particularly for the weak. Morality and ethics emerged because both the strong and the weak, individually and collectively, benefit out of it.

The concept of what is 'good', when used in a non-ethical sense, should not be confused with 'good' used in an ethical context. Aristotle raised the question, 'Good for what?' We can refer to a good knife, which cuts well, or a good farmer who knows and practices cultivation wisely (Scruton 1995: 278). Generally, though not always, in such non-ethical contexts, good is sought not for its own sake but as an instrument or means, while a significant feature of morality is that it is sought for its own sake though it may serve the function of enhancing the happiness and well being of the society. However, aesthetic contexts also may refer to 'good' as an end in itself, such as when we refer to Sachin Tendulkar as a very good batsman, since his batting is enjoyed for its own sake, like good music. Even morality can be an aesthetic experience sought for its own sake, both being spiritual experiences. It nevertheless leaves open the question of defining what is morally good.

Russell observes that 'we call something "good" when we desire it and "bad" when we have an aversion from it' (Russell 2009b: 255). But he hastens to add that our use of the term is more constant than our desires. Even if for the moment we may not desire a thing, we may call it 'good' if it is desirable otherwise. Moreover, not one or two persons but many should be able to agree about the desirability of what is good. 'Good' is thus not a mere personal view, but more a social or collective view. That is why, 'there can be more good in a world where the desires of different individuals harmonize than in one where they conflict. The supreme moral rule should, therefore, be: Act so as to produce harmonious rather than discordant desires' (Russell 2009b: 256). Russell adds significantly, 'if harmonious desires are what we should seek, love is better than hate'. Desire for knowledge is in harmony with similar desire by others, whereas a desire for, say, large landed estates can be satisfied by only a few, depriving many others. Desire for power over others is similarly a source of conflict. Desire for activities, which are creative rather than possessive, add to goodness in the world (Russell 2009b: 256–7).

The *Kathopanishad,* one of the early Upanishads, has a significant contribution to make to the discussion of what is good. Mere desire for a thing, even if many agree about the desirability of it, does not make it morally good. It distinguishes between *Shreyas* (what gives lasting or long-term happiness) and *Preyas* (what merely satisfies a momentary desire, or is pleasant, in the short term). It is shreyas which is morally good, and not preyas. The latter need not necessarily be immoral, unless one hankers after it all the time or seeks immoral means to satisfy it. seeking knowledge, capability to take care of self and others, cultivating character and culture, and spiritual pursuit (which is what the Upanishad mainly stresses), give us lasting happiness and therefore constitute shreyas. Sensual pleasures belong to the sphere of preyas.

Ethics is usually defined in terms of a normative way of looking, involving a comparison with some norm or ideal. But all norms may not be ethical in nature. A husband may tell his wife, 'Your cake is not as good as what my mom makes'. The wife may not take her mother-in-law's cake as a *moral* ideal, even if she is sporting enough to take it as a culinary ideal. Nor can others take it as a moral norm. The moral ideal or norm has to be something universally accepted as good in the sense of being beneficial to the society. We may often use the words 'good' and 'bad' in an amoral sense in other contexts too which have little to do with morality. For example, eating fruit and vegetables is good, and eating too much cake is bad. This statement may even be universally accepted. But why is this statement amoral? For two reasons. One is that a moral norm can be absolutized. Eating fruit within limits is good, but not beyond a limit. In contrast, we cannot, in principle, say that moral values should have a similar limit. We cannot, for example say that just as we should eat in moderation, we should also be moderately honest! In practice, people may observe some limits in being honest, but it is often done with bad conscience or when one moral value conflicts with another. Moral norms, at least in principle, are absolute. The second reason why the statement, 'eating fruit is good', is amoral, is because morality is in relation to others. Ethics is social. If instead of eating all fruits myself, I share them with others or offer to others, it becomes a moral act. In Hindu morality, the degree of morality is in inverse proportion to obsession with self-interest. According to Swami Vivekananda, self-abnegation is the basis of ethics (Vivekananda 2001: 23–4). It is the starting point of morality. As one transcends self-interest and becomes more and more concerned with larger circles—family, neighbourhood, village or town, country, and the world—the moral strength of the person goes on increasing, provided the concern is genuine and backed by suitable action. A householder who looks after his wife and children is certainly a good man even in a moral sense. But better still is a man who, after meeting his householder's obligations, finds time and resources to help others too. We can sum up by observing that an ethical norm is something considered as desirable or beneficial universally, and in an absolute sense, not just temporarily but in an enduring way, not just self-serving but showing concern or regard or love for others.

What is 'good' and what is 'right' may have a considerable overlap, but 'good' and 'right' are not exactly synonyms. The term 'right' is often used in the sense of what is proper and correct, both in moral and non-moral contexts. In moral contexts, it normally conveys the sense of what is just or fair. Justice is one of the principles of morality, but not an exclusive moral principle. The term 'right' may also be used when there are conflicting moral principles, raising a moral dilemma. When a choice is made for one of them as relevant to the situation faced, the chosen principle is taken as the right or correct one. The term 'right' has thus a comparatively relative flavour, while the term 'good' has an absolute sense. The good precedes the right, and the question of what is right cannot be decided in a moral vacuum without any notion of what is good.

The Enlightenment philosopher, Immanuel Kant (1724–1804) has made a very important contribution to the question of what is moral. He wrote a pathbreaking book, *Groundwork for the Metaphysics of Morals*, published first in 1785, which sets out his approach to ethics, apart from other books on philosophy. Very briefly and simply put, the morality of action, according to him, is not based on its consequences but on the motive, of doing one's duty, of doing what is right and for the right reason. Carrying out one's business honestly, for example, is certainly praiseworthy, but what makes it *moral* is if the motive in doing so is for the sake of honesty an end in itself, rather than merely because it is the best policy to attract and stay in business and make more profits in the long run. An action, if is to be considered as moral in Kant's view, is not something in response to our selfish desires or inclinations, but done as duty for its own sake. In following our desires or inclinations, we are not free persons, and only a free or autonomous person can be capable of moral action. But what is this duty? How is it made known to us? It is not something given by others, but is derived from our own free will. It is arrived at by our reasoning power, what Kant calls as Practical Reason, reasoning applied to moral questions. Since humans are capable of this reasoning as rational beings, all humanity is to be treated with due respect and dignity, according to Kant. No person is to be used as a mere object, a mere instrument to satisfy our own ends, but as an end in itself. Kant's emphasis on giving due respect to all humans, all humanity, subsequently gave rise to the concept of human rights.[2]

Coming back to the question of how Kant perceives our deriving what is our duty, he distinguishes between hypothetical and categorical imperatives. The former are conditional, as a means for doing something else. For example, if I want bread, I should go to a bakery. Such imperatives have no moral status. Only the categorical imperative has that. Kant gives several versions of the categorical imperative, but says they all amount to the same thing. His first version is: 'Act only on that maxim whereby you can at the same time will that it should become a universal law'. As Sandel observes,

the universalizing test points to a powerful moral claim: it's a way of checking to see if the action I am about to undertake puts my interests and personal circumstances ahead of everyone else's. ... We can't base the moral law on any particular interests, purposes or ends, because then it would be only relative to the person whose ends they serve. (Sandel 2009:121)

It is absolute value, which provides the basis for a categorical imperative. Humanity has such absolute value, and is an end in itself. Thus, Kant gives a second version of his categorical imperative: 'Act in such away that you always treat humanity, whether in your own person or in the person of any other, never simply as a means, but always at the same time as an end'. Self-respect and respect for others both flow from the same categorical imperative. It also follows from it that if I lie to someone, I am using her as a means, manipulating and degrading her, and is therefore immoral. Social hierarchy and discrimination, treating someone as a lower human being are similarly immoral. Thus from his basic imperative, several imperatives follow directly: speak truth, do not steal, do no harm to others, break no promise, help others, and so on. Respecting human dignity of others as well as one's own, is of utmost importance to Kant. Prostitution, even if voluntary, involves using one's own self as an object and hence degrading. Kant regards sex outside marriage as similarly degrading even if consensual, because it involves using each other as means, as objects. But he says, that 'marriage elevates sex by taking beyond physical gratification and connecting it with human dignity' (quoted in Sandel: 130). Kant says, 'only when two persons give each other the whole of themselves, not merely the use of their sexual capacities, can sex be other than objectifying' (quoted in Sandel: 131).

Kant's ethics, insisting as it does on duty irrespective of consequences, is quite demanding. Thinkers like Amartya Sen have been critical of such a duty-centred approach to ethics, which is discussed below in the chapter on 'Interrogating the Idea of Justice'. Moral dilemmas arise when exclusively following a single moral principle such as telling truth irrespective of consequences. Kant's own insistence on motive can be of help in resolving such dilemmas. Telling a lie, not out of a selfish inclination, but for a morally justifiable cause of saving a valuable life from attack or murder, is difficult to be dubbed as immoral. Kant himself faced a moral dilemma in his life, as reported by Sandel (2009: 134). King Friedrich Wilhelm II and his censors found Kant's writings on religion disparaging to Christianity and demanded a pledge from him to refrain from any further pronouncements on the topic. Kant responded cleverly with the pledge: 'As your Majesty's faithful subject, I shall in the future completely desist from all public lectures or papers concerning religion'. Kant was aware, Sandel says, that the king was not likely to live much longer, and when he died, Kant considered himself absolved of the promise, which bound him only as 'your Majesty's faithful subject'. A carefully worded evasion like this, Sandel says, is morally different from an outright lie because 'it pays homage to the duty of truth telling' (Sandel 2009: 137)! The evasion was justified also because in demanding a pledge of this kind, the king was restraining Kant from the duty of telling what the latter saw as truth, and had stood in the way of pursuing the noble cause of pursuit of truth.

Is the expectation of ethics, particularly avoiding selfishness, rather unrealistic? Self-interest, as Amartya Sen concedes, does 'play quite a major part in great many decisions, and indeed normal economic transactions could break down if self-interest played no substantial part at all in our choices'. But, he adds, 'the real issue is whether there is a plurality of motivations, or whether self-interest *alone* drives human beings' (Sen 1987: 19). Modern (neo-classical) economics has been faulted by Sen for assuming precisely that, and even worse, taking rationality as requiring it. Sen asserts, 'universal selfishness as a major requirement of *rationality* is particularly absurd' (Sen 1987: 16). Even in economic behaviour, the motivation of self-interest as the cause for success is not correct. Sen observes that behind the success story of Japanese industry and economy, there was evidence of 'systematic departure from self-interested behaviour in the direction of duty, loyalty, and goodwill' (Sen 1987: 17). Sen says, 'the mixture of selfish and self-less behaviour is one of the important characteristics of group loyalty, and this mixture can be seen in a wide variety of group associations varying from kinship relations and communities to trade unions and economic pressure groups' (Sen 1987: 20). That human beings have a lot of altruism in them in addition to self-interest is evidenced from the experience of even the common lot. It is not as rare as what some economists assume.

In deciding what is good or bad, Gandhi said that he relied greatly on listening to the 'Inner Voice' or conscience. Quite a few philosophers do not agree with this method, since they feel that conscience can vary from person to person, but ethics has consistency and universality, as observed above, and it is not a matter purely of personal view. For example, Hitler's conscience (assuming he had one) acted very differently from Gandhi's. Gandhi's reply to such criticism is that every person, whether a saint or a criminal, has an Inner Voice, but some suppress it and make it feeble. They let their egoism and selfishness overtake the Inner Voice. But even a criminal would know in his heart that what he is doing is immoral, and he may rationalize it somehow to soothe or stifle his conscience. However, an innate judgement of what is good or bad in a person's mind is a product of social acculturation. Even as a child, a person imbibes certain values taught by or observed from its parents or from social environment. This is at least one of the important reasons for the need to spread education widely, including moral education.

In judging what is good or bad, the Gandhian approach can be said to consist of three criteria: motive, means, and consequences. This approach is more comprehensive than that of Kant. This may not necessarily be an original idea of Gandhi, and he has himself acknowledged different sources of his inspiration and thought, but the approach has a typical Gandhian flavour. A person may find that his action has gone wrong and brought about unexpected and undesirable consequences. But if his motive was pure, and there was no carelessness or negligence on his part, his action may not be considered as immoral. Gandhi also insisted on the purity of means, as discussed in the next two essays here. Immoral means do not fail in bringing about undesirable consequences. That is the law of karma. Finally, the goodness of an act or decision is to be judged by consequences, especially on others, at least consequences as expected on the basis of rational, unbiased thinking, being cautious about wishful thinking. As discussed below in the essay on Ethics in Hinduism, dharma, truth, or morality are defined in terms of whether they are expected to contribute positively to the welfare of not only human beings, but also all beings.

Gandhi made it clear that morality is not guided merely by the motive of enlightened self-interest or prudence. In fact, he was critical of modern civilization on the ground that it reduces morality to enlightened self-interest. Morality, for him, was more positive and nobler, and was motivated by mutual consideration, compassion and love, and not by self-interest. Since morality is not merely calculated self-interest, it transcends dry reasoning and becomes spiritual in nature, in Gandhi's perspective. A moral person is more than rational; she or he is spiritual too. Not that Gandhi would push aside self-interest from the purview of morality altogether. But pursuing self-interest had to have a moral basis. For example, seeking independence for India from the British rule was not a question of mere self-interest for India, it was moral too. Colonialism violated the principle of equality of human beings, and deprived a large number of people of their dignity, freedom, and even economic well being. To rise against it was more than self-interest; it was a moral duty.

WHY ETHICS?

Taking a stand that morality is to be pursued for its own sake, as an end in itself rather than as means, is a lofty principle, which has the backing of great practioners of morality like Gandhi. But it may not enthuse or motivate all, particularly the 'practical' people, because following ethical principles may involve personal sacrifices. For example, it may be tempting and personally profitable for the powerful to take bribes. And they may be so powerful that they can easily cover their tracks and not be exposed. It is not good for the society if they behave so, but from their own point of view—why should they be ethical? It is quite tempting to be a 'free rider'. According to Scruton, the best answer was provided by Aristotle long ago. His answer is elaborate but briefly put: In considering why I should be ethical, I should take a long term view of myself, of what I should be, and seek the answer to the question of what I should do in that light (Scruton 1995: 293–5). Developing a habit of taking bribes, for example, will corrupt my very being and rob me of mental peace. 'In short, every rational being has a reason to cultivate virtues, regardless of his particular desires' (Scruton 1995: 295). This is how 'virtue ethics' developed after Aristotle. And this is the reason why all religions have emphasized the need to develop a strong moral character. Aristotle did not confine the scope of being virtuous to an individual in isolation. He urged people to be good citizens too, cultivating a healthy civic sense, participating actively in public or political affairs, and influencing decisions through active deliberations. He felt that it is by becoming a proactive member of the society and polity for achieving common good that one realizes one's moral potential. The contemporary relevance of this teaching for people, particularly in countries like India, can hardly be exaggerated.

The question of 'why be ethical' or 'why ethics' is closely related to the consideration of consequences of what is considered as good. Why should one feel bothered about consequences to others? This is because if I do not like a certain thing happening to me, I should also see that it does not happen to others. If I do not like other people telling me lies, I should not do so to others. Otherwise, the world cannot function. In a society of liars, nobody can believe another person, and nobody would like to be the member of such a society. It is truth alone which gives meaning to whatever we say. Imagine, for a moment, a society where, by custom or law, everybody is expected to speak lies and always so. In such a society, a couple in love cannot say to each other, 'I love you'. Instead, they will end up saying something like this: 'I love you. No, I don't. Oh, this is a lie! Oh, no this is the truth...' The matter is not solved by making a concession, say, by decreeing that one should generally speak the truth, but can speak lies sometimes. It would then be as credible as a person who says, 'I speak the truth, but sometimes not'!

Ethics is incredibly social and the very basis of human society. Man may be a basically self-centred brute by nature, but he sees many advantges of living in a society and even dreads loneliness, while enjoying the company of others for its own sake. This requires constant adjusting to others, without wiping out one's individuality. Man finds happiness neither in the absolute loneliness and freedom of a Robinson Crusoe nor in the absolute communism of a society of ants and honeybees. Acquisitiveness motivated by self-interest is not an absolute evil, as it does keep the society and the economy moving, after all. It needs only to be tamed, so that it is consistent with the best interests of all (including that of the environment, as we shall discuss later). Ethics has a vital role in achieving these mutual adjustments on a fair and equitable basis, making them mutually satisfying. Considering the consequences of how 'I' behave with others is at the heart of the matter. It is only when human beings pattern their behaviour towards each other based on this consideration that social relations are formed. It involves transcending our narrow egos. The Bhagavadgita has a very insightful verse in this context (Chapter 6, verse 32) that says, 'The one who judges others' pleasures and pain by the same standard which he applies to himself, such Yogi is the highest'. But the advice applies to common people as well, not Yogis alone. The Kural, an ancient Tamil classic on ethics by Tiruvalluvar, also says, 'Do not do to others what you know has hurt yourself' (Aphorism 310), and 'To avoid sorrow for yourself, eschew evil to others' (Aphorism 206) (in Sundaram [ed. and tr.] 1990: 50 and 39, respectively). The Bible says, 'Do unto others as you would have them to do unto you'. This approach, endorsed by the Gita, the Kural, and the Bible, is more popular even now, because it derives duties or imperatives from anticipated consequences based on practical reasoning. It calls upon each person to take into account other people's interests like one's own in one's actions, and implies that all are equal in moral worth. However, it does not mean that if I like boiled eggs for breakfast everyone should have the same, or imposing one's own personal preferences and views upon others. We have discussed above Kant's categorical imperative: 'Act only on that maxim whereby thou canst at the same time will that it should become a universal law' (in Cahn and Markie [eds] 1998: 293). His imperative can be very valuable 'as an instrument of negotiation and compromise between strangers, through which they can rise out of mutual enmity and confront each other as equals' (Scruton 1995: 290). The Kantian imperative, (as also similar imperatives from the Gita, the Kural, and the Bible), requires treating each other with respect and as ends in themselves, rather than as means or instruments (Scruton 1995: 285).

In substance, Kant's categorical imperative is very similar to the Golden Rule set out by the Gita, the Kural, and the Bible. But Kant felt that his approach is different in so far as it emphasizes duty more than consequences and also universalisability of moral imperatives more than the Golden Rule. The emphasis on duty could be crucial in situations like handing out justice. That I would like to be free does not mean that a criminal found guilty and sentenced to imprisonment also has to be similarly free. Everyone would like it to be a universal law that the guilty be brought to proper justice. Kant's imperative can, therefore, be said to have more precision and clarity.

The Kantian imperative and the imperative from the Gita and the Kural, to the same effect earlier, also help us to derive important principles of modern ethics—equality, liberty, and justice. If I feel that irrespective of my community, gender, colour, competence, and wealth, but as a human being, I should be treated with respect and concern and as invested with certain rights, I should equally extend the same to others. John Rawls in his celebrated book, *A Theory of Justice* (1971), conducts a thought experiment by constructing an 'original' position in which all people come under a 'veil of ignorance', forgetting their backgrounds in terms of race, gender, status, or other attributes that differentiate human beings from one another. They are all free and equal persons. They have no idea where they will end up, and have to take into account the possibility that one could end up being in an ethnic minority or be poor and helpless. But they are assumed to be both rational and self-interested. Every one can then judge others' pain and pleasure by the same standard as applies to one's own self, as per the Gita's words. Thus, they are in an ideal position and would derive two principles of justice. In Rawls's restated statement, these are: (a) Each person has the same indefeasible claim to a fully adequate scheme of equal basic liberties, which scheme is compatible with the same scheme of liberties for all; and (b) Social and economic inequalities are to satisfy two conditions: first, they are attached to offices and positions open to all, under conditions of fair equality of opportunity; scond, they are to the greatest benefit of the least-advantaged members of society (the difference principle) (Rawls 2001: 42–3).[3] In other words, the starting point or the base point is one of equality of all and equal opportunity for all where any inequality has to be socially justified. Inequality has to be functional, serving the social good. Rawls emphasized that it should be for the benefit of the least well-off, coming close to Gandhi's trusteeship principle. It is the duty of the better-off and the society at large to effectively act to eradicate hunger, illiteracy, ill-health, homelessness, and other signs of human deprivation from earth. The development of all—*sarvodaya*, as Gandhi put it—becomes a moral goal. It is not the utilitarian principle of 'greatest happiness of the greatest number', but the greatest happiness of all that Gandhi aimed at. Nobody is to be excluded from the gains of development.

The imperatives from the Gita, the Kural, and Kant [quoted above], as also the thought experiment by Rawls, explain why we should be good or ethical. Men in a state of nature may be moved mostly by self-interest. They must have soon discovered that 'clashes of self-interest are so damaging that it was more to their interest to forego doing injury to others than to continue in their natural way of life, so risking any injury that others might do to them' (MacIntyre 2010: 34). This applies not merely to physically injuring each other, but also to undesirable actions such as speaking lies, stealing, apathy to others' difficulties and the like. Paradoxical though it may seem, ethics owes its origin as well as practice to two opposite traits of human nature and their being in balance. One is that a human being is to a great extent autonomous and pulled by self-interest. Autonomy gives freedom of will and hence, moral responsibility.

The second trait is dependence of human beings not only on another but also on nature. Dependence on one another gives rise to social ethics, and dependence on nature to environmental ethics. As civilization makes progress, the roles of both types of ethics tend to become more dominant and siginificantly influence human action. It is in the very nature of ethics (of both types) to impose limits on human freedom, so as to promote the freedom and welfare of all.

The idea that ethics promotes the welfare of all has been basic since ancient times, both in India and the West. In the *Rigveda*, it was believed that *ritam* or moral order is behind the smooth functioning of the world, and of even the cosmos. Dharma is the subsequent and more popular term for ethics, (not at the cosmic, but at the individual and social level), used since the Vedic times, and its role was supposed to be similar as well. Dharma is often said to be that which promotes the welfare of all beings in the Mahabharata. The very derivation of the term, dharma, is from the verb, *dhri*, which means 'to uphold'. Dharma is that which upholds the world and the society. There was a similar thinking about ethics in ancient Greece too. 'The goal of life, Aristotle argued, is in achieving all of one's potential or the flourishing of one's capabilities' (Bilimoria *et al.* 2008: 6). This required ethical conduct. 'The question of human well-being [is] more a matter of how well a person carries out activities in life than how he is merely feeling as in happiness' (ibid.). It is not a matter merely of individual well-being in isolation. If all—or, at least most—people in a society behaved in an ethically acceptable way, it creates conditions where all human beings can realize their full potential, not otherwise.

Even a personal feeling of happiness is also an outcome of one's moral conduct. Being good boosts one's own moral courage, self respect, and mental well being. Gandhi insightfully observed, 'a person who follows the path of dharma does not feel helpless'. A just stand will win the support of others much more easily than an unjust stand, because a just stand is in the interest of the welfare of all. As the scriptures say '*dharmo rakshati rakshitah*' (dharma or ethics, taken care of, takes care of you in return). There is a related reason why religions, including Hinduism, have insisted on being good, namely that it helps spiritual progress. Morality and spirituality form a virtuous circle, each reinforcing the other. In *Brihadaaranyaka Upanishad* (IV.4.22–3), Sage Yaajnyavalkya tells King Janaka that 'one who knows Atman becomes full of peace, self-control, patient and self-composed, that evil does not consume him while he consumes [destroys] evil' (Mohanty 1999: 290). In other words,

Hindu scriptures believe that ethics cares for the soul and the soul cares for ethics. Interestingly, Wittgenstein also is reported to have conceived of ethics as the care of one's soul (Richter 2008: 205). The Upanishads and the Gita teach that when you care for your soul, you care for others too. Truth is at the very centre of Gandhian ethics, the ultimate moral value. His other important principle, non-violence (*ahimsa*) follows from truth, according to him. All religions and philosophers have emphasized the need to be truthful. What is truth? Bernard Williams explains two aspects of this virtue—sincerity and accuracy. Sincere persons tell what is in their mind. There is no inconsistency between what they say and what they believe. This makes them trustworthy and reliable. Accuracy ensures that one's beliefs are based on things as they really are (Williams 2002: 92–3). Hindu scriptures would agree with this, 'as in mind, so in speech; as in speech, so in action' (*yathaa chittam tathaa vaachah yathaa vaachastathaa kriyaah*), but they go a step further. They insist on the consequential aspect of speaking truth and say that if consequence is harmful, speaking truth is to be avoided. It is not the consequence merely in terms of personal interests but on general welfare, which is the criterion. The Mahabharata (Vanaparva 209.4) says: whatever is beneficial to the welfare of beings, that is to be regarded as truth (*Yad bhoota-hitam-atyantam tad satyam iti dhaaranaa*). The Kural says, 'Even a lie is truthful if it does unsullied good' (Sundaram 1990: 48). This principle is sometimes followed with good intention. A doctor may try to boost the morale of her patient by saying that he is improving, even if he is not quite well. If a child insists on eating more of something that may harm it, its mother may tell him/her that it is finished, even if in fact it is not. In certain exceptional times, what Hindu ethics calls *aapatkaal* (emergency), even a lie in personal interest may not be considered immoral. George Soros has observed that Nazis would have killed him when he was young, if his father had not arranged for him a false identity (Soros 2009: 227). Truth has to be tempered by discretion and love though deviations from it are not accepted as norm.[4] That is why Gandhi put ahimsa closely and inseparably with truth; the two have to go together. Ahimsa, for him, was not merely avoiding violence, but meant love and care.

IS ETHICS RELATIVE?

This leads to the question of so-called relativism in ethics. Is ethics absolute or relative? Was Tiruvalluvar in the Kural (quoted in the preceding para) advising relative truth? Is truth meant for following only when it is convenient to do so, merely for expediency? Sometimes it is held that morals are relative to each culture, and other cultures cannot make a judgement on it. But as Richter asks, 'Why should it be right for one society to oppress women, for instance, if this is not right for other cultures? Why should it be right for a society to enslave people or commit genocide?' (Richter 2008: 3). As Richter observes further, if ethics is all that relative, any statement like 'Nazis were wrong' could not possibly be true.

Relativism must be false, therefore, because it says that the United States in the days of slavery was right to accept it and right after the emancipation of the slaves *not* to accept it. It goes further than this in fact. It says that *whatever* the United States (or any other society) accepted any time must have been right. This surely cannot be true. (Richter 2008: 4)

If ethics were to be all that relative, it cuts the very basis of ethics from under, for everything and anything would be right, and there can be no distinction between right and wrong. Ultimately, ethics is the philosophy of how we can live and lead a meaningful life, and relativism is hardly a help in this.

All religions, including Hinduism, have rejected ethics of expediency or relativism in ethics. *Neeti-Shataka* of Bhartrihari says in verse 81: 'The learned may reproach or praise; wealth may come or go; death may come now or later; the (morally) courageous never deviate from the path of justice even by a step'. Nevertheless, absolute adherence to ethical norms may be extremely difficult, particularly if, in specific situations, there is a clash between different moral norms. The Hindu epics—Ramayana and Mahabharata—are rich in the discussions of such moral dilemmas, as discussed in the essay 'Ethics in Hinduism'. It does not mean that these epics or Hinduism believed in the relativism of ethics. It looks, absolutism in ethics is impossible to practice, and relativism is impossible to believe! Gandhian way for finding a solution to a moral dilemma is first to eschew self-interest, and then see what is in the interest of the weakest.

The presence of moral conflicts or dilemmas may be increasingly felt in the contemporary world, what with conflicting values like efficiency and social justice, or liberty and equality. They point in turn to an increasing need to sharpen what one may term as our ethical intelligence, ability to see through conveninet rationalisations clothed in highly moralistic terminology and arrive at just decisions. Daniel Goleman, author of two famous books, *Emotional Intelligence* (1995) and *Working with Emotional Intelligence* (1998), does not discuss *ethical* intelligence, but from his exposition of *emotional* intelligence, the two are expected to go together.

But they are not identical. Emotional intelligence underscores empathy, willingness to understand others' points of view, ability to stay calm, communication skill, ability to constructively manage interpersonal relations, initiative, and co-operation. An emotionally intelligent person knows that it *pays* to be good, helpful, and generous. Ethical intelligence includes all these, but underscores much more the values of honesty, commitment to truth, and aversion to any action that harms others. In addition, it includes the wisdom to differentiate between the right and the wrong *without being influenced by self-interest*, and the moral courage to act according to one's reasoned conviction without at the same time closing one's mind. While self-interest may not be eschewed in emotional intelligence, ethical intelligence is expected to be more unselfish. There is a complexity in ethical intelligence which may not affect usual intelligence tests. It is that any test of ethical intelligence may have to cope with multiple solutions each with its claim to be right! This only adds to the necessity of furthering one's capability for moral judgement through thoughtful discussion and openness to different points of view. Tests of ethical intelligence may be helpful, however, in revealing the type of personality involved, the values believed in by the person and the social class the person represents. But the challenge of ethical intelligence lies in going beyond one's self-interest and prejudices, even beyond one's class background, and arriving at a just solution.

There is an interesting perspective on this issue of moral dilemmas in the face of factual situations, expressed by Gerald A. Cohen. Its conceptual frame is borrowed from micro-economics. There is a trade-off between different moral principles, which can be conceived as fact-independent indifference curves, whose axes indicate 'packages of different extents to which competing principles are implemented'. Cohen says, 'the trade-off values, the rates of which we are willing to allow reduced implementation of one principle for the sake of increased implementation of another, are *a priori*: the facts determine only which implementation packages are feasible' (Cohen 2009: 38). A moral optimum so attained may still appear to be relative in the sense that it takes into account both moral principles and facts. Moral principles, *per se* or taken in isolation, are independent of facts or actual situations (though they may have been evolved in the context of society and actual world). But when it comes to their implementation in actual situations, conflicts between them arise and a trade-off becomes necessary. This does not make ethics relative, which would have been the case if the trade-off were between moral principles and expediency or self-interest. The trade-off, however, is between moral principles themselves, to decide which one is relevant and to what extent, without compromising one's moral integrity and honesty. Absolute morality, which is totally regardless of moral dilemmas actually faced, is inconceivable, because morality is for acting in this world. That is why Gandhi said he dealt with relative truth, which did not mean yielding to selfishness and dishonesty.

INDIVIDUALS TO INSTITUTIONS

Ethics is not meant only for individuals acting in isolation. On many aspects of crucial importance, such as fighting social evils like dowry, corruption, and environmental deterioration, we may have to act in concert. It needs coming out of our individual shells, co-ordinating with like-minded people, spreading awareness, and initiating group action. There are also important global issues requiring co-operation and co-ordination between countries. With increasing globalization, there is also an increase in the global responsibility in tackling mass poverty, illiteracy and ill-health, in averting environmental crisis, in implementing human rights, and in achieving durable peace. Countries not sensitive and responsible enough in this regard, have not only to be brought around but also assisted and supported by the global community. All this requires developing proper institutions and individuals' loyalty and support to them, without which neither individuals nor institutions can be effective.

To conceive of community ... is not to choose between a thoroughly instrumental vision within which everyone's sole concern is 'What's in it for me?' and a thoroughly constitutive vision within which everyone's constant preoccupation is 'doing what's best for the group'. There is a middle ground between these two visions, and it is likely to provide a more solid foundation for a healthy community than either a strictly instrumental or a strictly constitutive conception. (Dagger 2009: 313)

An individual can be a member of several institutions at the same time, and derive benefit from all of them, also contributing to their sustenance and development. The interests of the individuals on the one hand and of communities or institutions on the other can be reconciled if there is mutual appreciation of the value of each. This needs ethics of mutual respect, support, and care in the relationships between them. Problems can arise when individuals tend to derive their identities from institutions or communities on exclusive basis and get fanatical about them. They forget, what Amartya Sen pointed out, that we all have in fact multiple identities and that individuals derive their strength and support not from just one institution but many of them (Sen 2006). Fanatical attachment to one is not only blindness but also amounts an unethical attitude, as it has the potential of leading to violence.

Just as there are moral 'do's and 'don't's for individuals, they are there for groups, corporate enterprises, non-governmental organizations (NGOs), political parties, and governments too. Special problems could arise in institutional ethics such as about who is to be held morally accountable and how to ensure transparency in functioning. More important, an ethical issue is about what limits to put on the powers and functioning of institutions so that they do not affect the freedom and welfare of individuals, without making the institutions ineffective. There is a distinct possibility that business houses can even control the election process in a democracy through their funding and decide on matters of public policy purely for profiting themselves, in a way that may subvert democracy itself and harm public good. The evil potential of private financial institutions to upset the whole global financial system through their greed became evident during the world economic crisis of 2008.[5] Though ethics made a beginning by being addressed to individuals, both as individual persons and as members of groups, institutional ethics now will have to make headway due to the increasing dominance of instiutions in public life having a tremendous impact on individual freedom and welfare. But the basic ethical principles will be almost the same, except that values of liberty, equality, and justice, and issues like public welfare, transparency, and impact of institutional behaviour and policy on individual freedoms would receive greater attention at the level of the state and in institutional ethics. The issue of justice is dealt with in a chapter below separately, which overlaps with the values of liberty and equality to which we turn in the next section.

LIBERTY AND EQUALITY: RECONCILING THE TWO

Liberty and equality are among the most important values at the level of the state, in the sense that it is the responsibility of the state to ensure them and be on the watch out to see that they are not compromised. The state may not always do so on its own, and citizens' vigilance and pressure on the state would always be necessary to see that these values are respected and put into practice.

Though 'liberty' and 'freedom' can be used interchangeably, the latter is a broader idea. For example, 'liberty from hunger' would be an odd expression, while 'freedom from hunger' is not. 'Liberty' is the traditionally used word in political philosophy, while 'freedom' has been increasingly used more recently particularly since the close of World War II. 'Freedom' has been used in a way, which has incorporated egalitarian concerns (like 'freedom from poverty, hunger, and deprivation'), which the traditional usage of 'liberty' has not bothered about. Thus, while the values of liberty and equality seem to be ever in conflict, this is not the case between freedom and equality. The term freedom can be said to seek reconciliation between liberty and equality.

The arch advocate of liberty, Hayek describes liberty as 'that condition of men in which coercion of some by others is reduced as much as possible in society' (Hayek 1960: 11). He uses the concept of freedom to a collective rather than to individuals, such as when political freedom refers to the absence of coercion of a people as a whole from foreign yoke (Hayek 1960: 14). He does not favour the use of the concept of liberty (or freedom) in the sense of power or 'ability to do what I want' (subject to the condition that it does not harm others), because such a use can be employed to support the claim for redistribution of wealth (Hayek 1960: 17), and any forced redistribution would mean coercion for the enterprising who will be deprived of wealth and thus of incentive for enterprise. But it is precisely when liberty is interpreted as ability to do or achieve that it can be reconciled with equality, since such an ability cannot, in all fairness, be confined only to a few but has to be extended to all in a humane and just society. Restricting liberty to a merely negative connotation as absence of coercion does lead to conflict with equality. Equality is not so much about equal distribution of wealth or income, as giving an equal or fair starting point in life for all as far as possible. In a race, we cannot insist on equality of achievement, but should insist on equality or fairness in starting point. Once this equality is assured, liberty is necessary to allow each to achieve her or his maximum potential.

It is not enough to merely ensure equality before law, though it is the minimum necessary for ensuring a just society. It is not enough even to assure a formal equality of opportunities when some people suffer from serious disabilities and deprivations such as poverty, ill health and poor education or lack of any of it, in having access to opportunities. That is why Amartya Sen has been insisting on improving capabilities of the deprived, and minimizing differences in this respect. He does not advocate leveling down all capabilities to a low equal level, but on leveling up by paying attention to those who have been unfortunate enough in life to be unable use opportunities that economic growth provides.

All societies need incentives for their members to achieve their best. In this task it is necessary to assure that one gets what is due, which is the result of one's effort, skill, and talent. Otherwise nobody will give one's best to the society and no progress can take place. But unrestrained liberty to exploit people or nature can come in the way of achieving a humane and sustainable society. In a market economy, moreover, all disparities in income and wealth cannot be justified in the name of intrinsic talent. Much depends on how the market values different talents and capacities. Sandel gives a telling example of this: 'John Roberts, Chief Justice of the US Supreme Court, is paid $217,400 a year. Judge Judy, who has a reality television show, makes a $25 million a year' (Sandel 2009: 182). Such examples are not rare in India also. When market valuation is so erratic, taxing the rich to benefit the society as a whole and particularly the poor cannot be wrong. We cannot ignore the underdog, because if ignored, they can pull down those who sit smugly in ivory towers. That is why ethics of fair play and compassion is needed to moderate the ideology of efficiency to make the society and the economy more inclusive. That is where Gandhi comes in.

Gandhi steered clear of both libertarian market fundamentalism and totalitarianism, and showed his own third way. He recognized the role of the individual, but his individual was not the 'Economic Man' of the economists, maximizing utility and profits and thinking of nothing else. His individual was a Moral or Ethiclal Man, as Sudarshan Iyengar puts it, practising self-control in his wants and kindness and compassion towards others particularly the weak (Iyengar 2006). Freedom according to Gandhi could be said to be of two kinds—licentiousness (liberty to do whatever one wanted) and freedom to act according to one's conscience. The first is not freedom at all, while the second is real freedom according to Gandhi, which assumes a deeply ethical character (Datta 1986: 30). The Ethical Man strives to secure and use such freedom consistent with and promoting the interest of the society of which he is an active member. With such a person, there is no need for any overwhelming state control, even without which liberty and equality are reconciled with each other.

Unfortunately, however, all people may not behave up to the standards expected of an ideal Ethical Man, and it is necessary for the state and society to secure certain rights and protect them from infringement by others. These rights are of three kinds—liberty rights, rights to adequate welfare, and right to work and non-discrimination in employment. Liberty rights are rights to life, freedom, property, security, and resistance to oppression. These rights are fundamental to the survival and progress of every society. They are against all other persons and institutions, and made justiciable by law. The second type of rights consists of rights to food security and adequate health care, shelter, and education. These rights are necessary to achieve a humane and civilized society. There is no point in recognizing them without taking concrete steps to evolve necessary institutions and legislation to implement them so that they too are justiciable like liberty rights. By the very nature of these rights they are against state, which is responsible for implementing them. But in certain cases like family, they can be primarily against parents whose responsibility it is to see that their children receive adequate food, health care, and education. If the parents have no resources to provide them, it is for the state to do so. Once the state creates facilities to provide them such as education, it would be unlawful for parents to keep their children from schooling. Similarly, it would be unlawful for any husband to turn away his wife and children from his house and deprive them of their right to shelter and food, irrespective of whether the state can provide them. The third type of rights, namely right to work and non-discrimination in employment, goes a long way in assuring dignity to all citizens and helps in keeping adequate standard of living to all. These rights also need to be justiciable, through necessary legislation and creation of needed institutions. Liberty rights in the absence of rights to adequate welfare in the form of basic goods and services can lead to unacceptable levels of inequality. Inequality may not be eliminated by these rights, but can be brought down to at least tolerable levels. Right to employment and non-discrimination in it can further promote equality. Besides securing these rights, state will have to create conditions for equality of capabilities and provide equality of opportunities.

Concluding the essay, some may feel that in a world full of hypocrisy, falsehood, and violence, to speak of ethics may sound odd. Yet, the sad state of the world only further emphasizes the important role of ethics. The world would not have survived if the bulk of us had no respect for moral values. Ethics becomes particularly pertinent in mitigating the misery of the poor in a world of intense competition, with the Darwinian principle of survival of the fittest requiring significant modification. This is because even the fittest cannot survive unless others too survive and are cared for. The greater role played by mutual dependence and complementarity is not often seen, as competitive aspect is overstressed. What Gandhi did was to highlight mutual dependence and need for loving regard for each other (see Sethi 1991). J.C. Kumarappa's interpretation of Gandhian economic thought, particularly in pointing out the central tendency of development of the world towards less and less violence, or more and more non-violence, gives us new hope.[6] This is not an unrealistic assessment. We have only to compare the present state of the world (even if it is worse than what it ought to be), with what it used to be for common human beings as depicted in the novels of nineteenth century novelists like Charles Dickens, to see the truth in Kumarappa's interpretation. That is where ethics and humanity's commitment to moral values and social justice have helped, notwithstanding many failures. Relying not only on the innate goodness of humanity, but also on its instinct for survival and even betterment, we can reasonably look forward to a world where there will be more justice, compassion, freedom, peace, time and capability for creativity even for common people, and sustainability, than now. But such a world will not come about without our striving for it. Gandhi was emphatic on the role of individual responsibility of all of us in all aspects of life. 'Each of us must be the change we wish to see in this world', he advised (quoted in Rabbin 1994: 199). Further, 'the future depends on what we do in the present' (quoted in Singer 2007: 9). The present situation is not yet such as to make us feel complacent and smug. The powerful continue to capture most of the benefits of economic development. It is appeal to ethical principles and social justice, which serves as the most potent weapon of the weak. It is not merely economic development which would help achieving social justice, but politics too, with both economics and politics tempered by ethics.

An Overview
Ethics for a Globalizing World

Part I here, 'Ethics for a Globalizing World', consists of four essays, written against the background of the state of the present world. The world is undergoing globalization at a fast rate in manufacturing, transport and communications, services, religion, and culture. The process has gathered its own momentum, but there is a need to intervene in it to protect both human and environmental interests. On the one hand, we are in the process of the making of a Universal Man, *Vishwa Maanava*, an ideal dreamt by poets like Rabindranath Tagore and K.V. Puttappa, holding the prospects of a better mutual understanding and peace. On the other hand, severe tensions have erupted including even violence and terrorism, deprivation, exasperation of disparities, and risk of obliteration of cultural identities which is deeply resented. Fortunately for us, leaders like Mahatma Gandhi can show a way out of crisis.

Since the essays in this collection are mainly inspired by Gandhi and follow his perspective, the first essay is on: 'Gandhian Perspective: Essence and Some Applications'. Gandhian thought is meant mainly as a guide for action, and hence the application of his perspective to politics, economics, and environment are also discussed in the essay. There is also a brief discussion at the end of the essay about how far India has followed Gandhian ideals and principles. Gandhi may sound too puritanical to the taste of modern generations, but there is still a lot to learn from him and follow. The two essays directly on Gandhian thought bring out its relevance to the contemporary world. The other essays too bring out the relevance of his thought to contemporary issues in their respective contexts.

The essence of Gandhian perspective is formed by his firm faith in and commitment to truth and non-violence. For him, the substance of truth is morality, and non-violence is its vital part. Ahimsa or non-violence is a positive principle, which includes compassion and care. Truth finds expression through ahimsa; both are meant to be practised. He said, 'it is not enough for thought to be based on truth, the life must express it'. And that is what he did. After Jesus Christ, there are scarcely those like him who lived what they preached, and lived to such perfection, in spite of being immersed so much in politics. This is what lends credibility and respect for Gandhi and his principles. Though he saw in non-violence a powerful weapon for the empowerment of the weak and deprived, he refused to call it as a weapon of the weak. On the contrary, non-violence was the weapon of the morally strong and courageous, according to him. He strove to bring justice to the deprived and make them stand on their own feet with dignity. He did not believe in a centralized state and power. Power—both political and economic—had to be decentralized and distributed, to be meaningful to the people. His principle of self-restraint on wants is a key to environmental sustainability, and also integrated with his fight against inequality. The legacy of Gandhi is still alive. He has been an inspiration for several mass movements for social justice and environment protection.

Gandhi's contribution to religious thought is no less significant. The essay 'Religion for Modern Times: Ethics-centred Gandhian Way' brings out this aspect. Gandhi's contribution lies in providing a solution to a difficult modern predicament. On the one hand, in spite of a long history, religion has failed to make human beings humane enough. On the other hand, science and technological progress also failed in making human beings rational enough to raise all human beings to a position of dignity, happiness, and moral responsibility. However, he rejected neither, but put conditions on both. He accepted religion in so far as it left us with a common heritage of moral values, which need to be followed. He accepted science and technology only to the extent that they did not deprive human beings of their dignity and livelihood. For him, essence of religion is morality. His religiosity was unique, for he was a rationalist among believers and a believer among rationalists. He emphasized both reasoning and faith in one self and moral values in a creative unity. He eschewed all sectarianism in religion. 'Tolerance' is not what really captures Gandhi's approach to other religions. He not only advanced from tolerance to 'equal respect for all religions', but even beyond that by insisting on sharing the best from all religions. He honestly put this belief early in life to practice. He believed that no religion was perfect, and that one had to learn from all of them. His religion was simply one of truth and non-violence, without any necessity of rituals and priests.

This leads us to the next essay, 'Ethics and Development'. If development is for the welfare of human beings, taking care of environment too, as it should be, there has to be justice in development. The purpose of the essay is twofold: (a) to discuss how development as a goal, at the individual level and collective level, is meaningful and satisfying only when it has a significant ethical or humanist content; and (b) to argue that the means of development, especially economic development, should also be ethical or morally acceptable. The essay tries to show that integration between ethics and development promotes a reciprocal or mutually reinforcing impact. To be moral does not require being poor too. The significance of economic development at the collective level is that as result of this process, total income and wealth begin to increase, allowing greater absolute share of the national cake for different sections of the people. This theoretical expectation may not, however, be realized in practice without deliberate and planned human effort. The process of economic development has most often involved deprivation and exploitation. But it need not be so; it can be humane and ethical. In fact, taking a long historical view, Gandhi, as interpreted by his close disciple, J.C. Kumarappa, thought that the tenedency of development is towards non-violence. Gandhi is in the long line of saints of India who gave all emphasis on moral development and character building. These saints thought moral development is the basis of development on other dimensions too. A robust and sustainable process of even economic growth in the narrow sense of income growth of a country requires honesty, hard work, fairness, and willingness to share on the part of its people. Gandhi held the ideal of Sarvodaya — development benefiting all including the weakest, as also an ethically acceptable means to it. The weakest include not merely those within countries but also those between countries. A globalizing world has to accept moral responsibility for raising the levels of living particularly the poor in poor countries, and of course the poor everywhere, and for ensuring fair dealings between countries.

Modern economic development has created severe environmental problems. Ethics is at the very centre of environmental concerns. 'Ethics, Environment, and Culture: The Paradox of India' raises ethical issues of environmental concern. It also shows how cultural embeddedness of environmental concern can help, and discusses why India, in spite of having a traditional culture favourable to environmental protection, is witness to the paradox of its citizens being indifferent to it. The essay briefly reviews the contribution of some of the main thinkers and activists to environmental ethics. Had it not been for the environmental movements inspired by them, concern for environment would not have been reflected in public policy. India does show significant evidence of people's and intellectuals' movements on environmental issues, and they had some successes too. And yet, a new market-driven culture, countering traditional pro-environmental culture, also has emerged in the wake of modern economic development. The bulk of emerging middle class is more interested in lavish lifestyles, the demand for which is created by the market itself. With India poised for a significant rate of economic growth, environmemntal problems are bound to be exasperated unless a strong environmental ethic is built up in the culture of modern India and until it is reflected in public policy implementation. There is a need for environmental justice across the world too. It is the moral responsibility of advanced countries which have imposed huge environmental costs on the world, particularly the poor countries, to ensure greater equity in sharing the costs of cleaning up the world and in promoting sustainability.

Ethics: Some Philosophical Aspects

The second part contains three essays. Though they are focused on certain philosophical questions, they have a tremendous practical significance. The philosophical questions posed are: What is justice? What are the different approaches to it? How does our world view affect our ethics? Why is a holistic approach to knowledge needed in solving the problems of the world, including ethical issues?

The first essay in this part, 'Interrogating the Idea of Justice' is basically a review article on Amartya Sen's *The Idea of Justice* (2009). Sen examines in this book different approaches to the idea of justice, tells which he likes, and presents his own ideas. While my essay provides a critical appreciation of the same, it also goes beyond by taking into account a few other approaches and issues related to justice. Justice is a crucial and major aspect of ethics, though it may not constitute the whole of ethics. Some philosophers make a distinction between justice and benevolence. Justice demands strict implementation, violation of which calls for punishment. Justice can be codified, but benevolence cannot be. While implementation of justice is crucial to the survival of the society, benevolence improves its welfare and makes life worth living. Sen, however, takes a wider view of justice in the sense of equity or fairness. Drawing on the ancient Indian tradition, Sen distinguishes between *Niti* and *Nyaya*. Niti refers to behavioural correctness and propriety both with respect to individuals and institutions, while Nyaya refers to realized justice in a broader perspective. According to Sen, it is more crucial to go by Nyaya approach and prevent manifestly severe instances of injustice or human deprivation, such as hunger, poverty, ill health, and illiteracy. He dubs the Niti approach as 'transcendentally' or idealistically just, which may not necessarily yield unanimous solutions. But there can be much more agreement on problems of eradicating manifest injustice such as hunger and poverty. This does not mean that Sen is disillusioned with theories and would like to go only by 'common sense'. He has been an outstanding theoretician himself, applying theory imaginatively to empirical problems, and deriving theory from facts.

The way we see the world—our world view—has a significant implication for ethics. A world view which regards the phenomenal world as false or as illusion would logically have little to to say about how to live in the world. It may not also inspire economic development and concern for the weak and the poor, or for environment, because all this would be an illusion! The essay on 'Appearance and Reality' probes into this metaphysical stand, which is wrongly attributed to Advaita in Indian philosophy. It is a natural intellectual tendency of human beings to probe behind appearances into basic reality. Gandhi who declared that 'Truth alone is real; all else is illusion!' never regarded the world as unreal and never denied the role of human responsibility. The essay reviews different stands on the nature of reality, and argues that a probe into this need never come in the way of our duties to society and the world.

Man's eternal quest to know reality, raises the problem of how to approach knowledge. 'Holistic Approach to Knowledge: Contribution of the Bhagavadgita and its Relevance to Social Science Research and Ethics' deals with this issue. More than being an exposition of the Gita, this essay is an exercise in epistemology, drawing upon Indian intellectual tradition, particularly the Gita, without ignoring western traditions. Most of the training offered in social science research methodology, at least in India, is focused on quantitative techniques of inductive method. Such analytical techniques, while they have their use, suffer from serious inadequacy and are deprived of valuable insights which can come from holistic approach. The Gita calls a holistic approach to knowledge as *saatvik* and even defines it clearly, as distinguished from *raajasik* and *taamasik* approaches to knowledge. Apart from explaining the contribution of the Gita, the essay gives examples of insightful application of the holistic approach in social sciences, particularly economics, and in applied ethics. The examples of issues of ethical concern show that ethics is not merely a matter of merely philosophical interest, but of tremendous practical relevance.

Ethical Foundations of Hinduism

Part III of the book, 'Ethical Foundations of Hinduism', contains next two essays. Neeti and dharma are the two words used in India which convey the meaning of ethics. The former is relatively of more recent origin, but ancient enough. Neeti came to be used to convey the broad philosophy of ethics, as in *Vidura-neeti* in the Udyogaparva of Mahabharata. Dharma was more closely associated with the meaning of moral codes for day-to-day living, but was also often used in a broader sense indicating ethical ideals to be followed. Being more familiar with Hindu ethics, I have focused on it in this part. It is also because Hindu ethics was a main source of inspiration for Gandhi.[7]

The famous saying, 'one truth is spoken of variously by the wise' (*Ekam sat vipraah bahudhaa vadanti*) can be said to be the core of ethical foundation of Hinduism. It expresses its willingness to respect diversity of views and approaches. As Jawaharlal Nehru observed, 'Its essential spirit seems to be to live and let live' (Nehru 1994: 75). Following this spirit, Hinduism also indicates its strong inclination to reconcile on various fronts. Mahatma Gandhi simply defined Hinduism as 'Search after truth through non-violent means'. The essays also try to remove some misconceptions about Hinduism and Indian cultural attitudes. Nehru met one of the criticisms insightfully as follows:

In India we find during every period when her civilization bloomed an intense joy in life and nature, a pleasure in the act of living, the development of art and music and literature and song and dancing and painting and the theatre, and even a highly sophisticated inquiry into sex relations. It is highly inconceivable that a culture or view of life based on other-worldliness or world-worthlessness could have produced all these manifestations of vigorous and varied life. Indeed it should be obvious that any culture that was basically other-worldly could not have carried on for thousands of years. (Nehru 1994: 82)

The first of the two essays in Part III is on 'Humanism in Hinduism'. There is some difference in the usage of the word in common parlance, from the way it used in western philosophy. In the former, humanism is taken to be almost the same as humanitarianism, that is, concern for human welfare. Western philosophers use the word 'humanism', to connote a system of thought which believes in the rationality and intelligence of human beings, who can thereby lead their own life without guidance from religion. The essay here distances itself from the strong rejection of religion, which is associated with humanism in the west. In fact, religion is compatible with humanism, as the former insists both on concern for human beings (as objects) and responsibility of human beings (as subjects) to themselves as well as to nature. It is necessary to emphasize humanism in religion to discourage the strong tendency in religion towards inhuman and irrational fanaticism or fundamentalism. 'Humanism' is taken in the essay here as including moral responsibility of all human beings to themselves and to the world, and concern for human freedom, human rights, and well being. Humanism in this sense is not just charity. Gandhi was an all-round humanist, but could hardly have agreed to being called a 'secular humanist' in the western sense. Humanism was primarily an ethical concept for him, conveying responsibility to the weak and willingness to fight for justice. Since his religion meant truth and non-violence, his humanism was inspired by his religion. We can certainly talk of 'religious humanism' without fear of contradiction, provided the the word is accepted in the sense used in the essay. The essay shows that Hinduism, far from being inconsistent with humanism, shows concern both for human responsibility and human welfare, not merely in scriptures and other literature, but also in practice.

   The last essay here is 'Ethics in Hinduism'. Though Hinduism has shown a strong inclination to metaphysics and spiritualism, it has certainly not ignored ethics. On the contrary, among the four goals of human beings (*purushaarthas*), ethics as dharma comes first, and it is insisted that two other goals—*artha* (wealth and material welfare) and *kaama* (other desires, especially for sensual pleasures)—be pursued according to dharma. Moreover, dharma is also a prerequisite for the fourth and ultimate goal *moksha* (liberation or salvation). Though religion and ethics have a close relation (as discussed in the essay), it also shows that whatever is considered religious need not necessarily be moral, and whatever is moral need not necessarily be religious. It is possible to have ethics without religion, but no genuine religion can do without ethics. After clearing a few misunderstandings about ethics in Hinduism, the essay briefly presents the ethics of the Vedas, Upanishads, and the Gita. The foundation of universal ethics was laid in the Vedas and Upanishads. Though the Gita derives their essence into a lyrical presentation, it has quite a few significant contributions of its own to make, even if inspired by Upanishads. It is in the period of *Dharmasutras*, *Dharmashaastras*, and epics that intricacies of dharma were explored in depth, and moral dilemmas were presented through stories. The sants of medieval age not only brought moral teachings down to the masses in their own language, but also raised voices of strong protest against social evils, particularly caste discrimination. In the modern period, struggles for eradication of social evils were most intense ever, and reforms were initiated on a wide variety of fronts with state as well as popular support. Without belittling the importance of ethics, Hinduism, however, aimed at a fully meaningful human life, including aesthetic enjoyment as well as spiritual attainment.

Part IV of this book on 'Some Contemporary Concerns' has two essays— 'Ethics in Business' and 'Gender Justice'. Ethics in business is commonly known as applied ethics, which insists that the business world, even if guided by profit motive, cannot go out of the purview of ethics. Business ethics does not call upon the business world to give up the profit motive, but insists that profit cannot be its only motive and behavioural boundary. Business ethics need not be considered an oxymoron or impossibility. In fact, it can make abundant business sense to be committed to ethical dealings with all stakeholders—employees, customers, suppliers, shareholders, and the community at large (or the environment). The essay, 'Ethics in Business' shows why ethics is important in business, what moral issues and dilemmas arise, how they are resolved, and how success in business itself depends on ethics in business. It is not enough that persons acting in business as individuals are virtuous; the business enterprise itself, irrespective of whether it is individual proprietorship, partnership, private limited company, or public corporation, has to evolve a code of conduct for day-to-day behaviour and to resolve ethical issues as they arise, and create a moral environment of work within the enterprise. And, this code has to be seriously followed to inspire confidence among stakeholders.

The following essay in Part IV, 'Gender Justice', deals with an issue of grave concern in contemporary India as well as many other countries. The essay explains how gender justice is complicated, and how and in what forms and magnitudes it arises. In the process, different schools of feminist thought are discussed. Women cannot wait for their emancipation till capitalism and patriarchy are smashed, but they can work within the system, and begin to modify and improve it mainly by their own efforts, so that the system is just and fair to all. Apart from their individual participation, the respective roles of others including organizations and the state in the task of ending gender injustice are also discussed in the essay.

To solve the moral problems of the world, it is not enough that a few individuals lead moral lives. The supportive role of institutions, organizations, and the state also matters, to inspire and even compel ethical behaviour on the part of all, including institutions, making them accountable. There can be neither freedom nor well-being in moral anarchy.

Notes

1. Bernard Williams thinks that the two terms, 'moral' and 'ethical' have different resonances. 'Ethical' carries a broader conception, including a concern with the values of different kinds of life and activity; 'moral' ... tends to narrow its interest to rules and obligations, and to experiences and considerations most closely related to these' (Williams 2000: 546). In the essays here, no particular distinction between the two is suggested.

2. In summarizing Kant's ethics here, the chapter on Immanuel Kant in Sandel (2009: 103–39) was useful.

3. A few problems in Rawls's principles of justice, pointed out by Sen, are discussed in Chapter 5.

4. For an in-depth philosophical discussion on truth in Indian philosophy, see Chatterjee (1997).

5. Soros has summarized what happened and what produced the crisis: 'Credit standards collapsed, and mortgages were made widely available to people with low credit ratings (called subprime mortgages), many of whom were well-to-do. 'Alt-A' (or liar loans) with low or no documentation, were common, including, at the extreme, 'ninja' loans (no income, no job, no assets), frequently with the

active connivance of the mortgage brokers and mortgage lenders' (Soros 2009: xvi). This suggests a steep decline in the moral integrity of financial institutions handling public money, mostly out of personal greed, rather than any meaningful and deliberate attempt to help the non-creditworthy poor. The biggest defaulters on loans were the rich, who accounted for the bulk of the loans.

6. Chapter 3 has a more detailed discussion of this.

7. For a detailed treatment of not only Hindu ethics but also Buddhist and Jaina ethics, see Bilimoria *et al.* (eds) 2008, Crawford 1982, Dasgupta 1961, and Hindery 1978.

Part I

Ethics for a Globalizing World

1 Gandhian Perspective
Essence and Applications

Ahimsa is the means and Truth is the end.
...If we take care of the means, we are
bound to reach the end sooner or later. ...
We should not lose faith but should forever
repeat the mantra—'Truth exists, it alone
exists. It is the only God; there is but one way
of realizing it and that is ahimsa'.

—M.K. Gandhi
(*CWMG* 44: 59)

THE ESSENCE

The word 'essence', according to the Oxford English Dictionary, means 'the quality which determines the character of something'. It is a universal principle or philosophy which can be found in all its particular forms or applications. It is a unity which covers all its diversity. From this point of view, there is something essential about Gandhian thought which can be said to constitute a Gandhian perspective. We can use this perspective or approach to understand many facets of our individual as well as social or collective life, such as politics, economics, environmental issues, and education, and derive lessons or guidance for action. This is what Gandhi himself did. His thought was essentially a guide for action on a variety of fronts, in advancing the cause of justice, peace, and freedom.

To say that there is an essence in Gandhian thought which characterizes all his thinking and action in different situations and contexts does not mean, in any way, that he was a dogmatic, doctrinaire, or rigid sectarian. Far from it, it was an essential character of his approach to shun dogma and rigidity in thought. Gandhi denied that there is anything called Gandhism. He allowed enough flexibility in his approach to the point that he could even be seen as inconsistent, when narrowly viewed. His inconsistencies were at a superficial level, partly arising from the extreme complexities of the problem being dealt with. He always said that he learnt from mistakes. It was part of his constant search for truth, to which he was committed all his life, both in thought and action. He, therefore, permitted neither rigidity nor dogma.

Given this flexibility and freedom in courageously pursuing the path of truth, what is the essence of Gandhian perspective? There are few other personalities in world history who epitomize ethics through their life and thinking as much as Gandhi, who took up so many challenges on different fronts at the same time. Primacy of ethics dominated his entire life. He sought nothing short of moral development for all, and through it their spiritual development, while first following himself what he preached. Rather, his precepts followed from his practice and experience. This gave him great credibility all over the world, and allowed him to reform his society and polity. As Ganguli observed, 'Gandhi bridged the gulf between individual and social ethics' (Ganguli 1973: 99). His ethics were as much relevant to society and its institutions as to individuals. He subjected these institutions and even whole civilizations to stern evaluation, applying his principles of ethics. In chapter 13 of his *Hind Swaraj*, Gandhi defined civilization itself in moral terms, neither in terms of comforts created nor of technological advance. He said, 'Civilisation is that mode of conduct which points out to man the path of duty'. He also pointed out in Hind Swaraj that the Gujarati word for civilization is 'good conduct' (*sabhyataa*) (Mukherjee 1993: 35).

We do not have to labour hard for knowing what Gandhi's essential principles of ethics were, for he declared them often—truth and non-violence. He would reduce them again to one basic word, truth. Relentless pursuit of truth is the one principle in which were integrated all his strands of thought and applications to life's problems. He emphasise non-violence in his approach to all problems, but he asserted that it followed from truth, the basic principle. This does not mean that he gave secondary importance to non-violence. For him, both constituted a single principle basically—while truth was its abstract aspect, non-violence was its practical or applied aspect.

Truth for Gandhi was not a purely transcendental principle, unrelated to life. On the contrary, he looked upon life as a continuous experiment with truth, which was experiential and not just for mystics, but for all humanity. In this sense, truth was not esoteric, but was something with mass appeal. He even subtitled his autobiography as *The Story of My Experiments with Truth*. This experimentation was not confined only to his personal life, but was also extended to all his public actions, including his satyagraha (literally, truth-force; in substance, non-violent resistance to injustice) movements in South Africa and India. The inherent strength of truth lies 'latent until it is embodied in the actions as well as thoughts of a human being' (Iyer 2000: 152). Truth finds its expression in action.

According to Gandhi human destiny was a continuous search for truth, both in private or personal affairs and in collective or public actions. One may say that pursuit of happiness is the goal of every human being, and Gandhi does not disagree. He said, 'The key to happiness lies in the worship of Truth, which is the giver of all things' (*CWMG* 79: 426). There is greater security in truth than in falsehood, greater joy in helping others than in selfishness, and greater comfort and peace in justice than in injustice. The path to truth may not be easy. It could be the most challenging, but, nevertheless, is the most satisfying in Gandhi's views. Gandhi, however, emphasized that the pursuit of 'truth should be accompanied by firmness of purpose' (*CWMG* 83: 408), and humility. According to him, 'There is no scope for vanity in it and the only means of reaching it is through ahimsa' (*CWMG* 82: 39).

What is Truth? Gandhi said, 'truth is the sovereign principle, which includes numerous other principles' (Gandhi 1927: xi). Substance of truth is morality. He found the Sanskrit equivalent of truth, *satya*, as being more expressive and evocative. Satya, he explained, is derived from the verb '*sat*' (to exist). Therefore, satya alone exists and falsehood cannot survive. Truth can find acceptance by all and is universal. That is how pursuit of truth leads to knowledge. Gandhi's conception of truth, however, transcended ontological truth while being inclusive of it. One's statements corresponding to facts as they exist or to events as they actually took place are surely a fundamental aspect of truth, but the meaning of truth went beyond that for Gandhi and covered moral truth as well. In its moral aspects of non-violence, honesty, simplicity, self-control, righteousness, equity, and justice, it also leads to happiness of individuals, society, and even of the world at large. Truth is the very foundation of our lives, without which it would not be worth living. This is so, not only in the epistemological aspect of truth as in the acquisition of knowledge, but also in the moral aspects. Knowledge cannot be itself unless true or, at least, honestly believed to be true. Similarly life would have no meaning unless, at least, the large bulk of us follow some moral principles, like honesty, altruism, justice, and righteousness. They provide a basis for our very existence and survival and, therefore, constitute satya. In the Gandhian perspective, there is a unity in the epistemological and moral aspects of truth. Ethics is required in the pursuit of knowing what *is*; ethics is also the outcome of it. Herbert Marcuse echoes Gandhiji in observing, 'If a man has learned to see and know what really *is*, he will act in accordance with truth' (Marcuse 1964: 125). One could also reverse it and say that it is only truth and honesty which can lead a man to see what really *is*. Interpreting Gandhiji, Iyer says: 'It is not enough for thought to be based upon truth; the life of the thinker must express it, must represent it visibly in his actions' (Iyer 2000: 154).

Gandhi distinguished between absolute truth (or God) and relative truths. With regard to absolute values of truth and non-violence, Gandhi avoided both 'unlimited relativism of values' and 'narrow intolerant absolutism' (Allen 2008: 49). We have to constantly move closer to absolute truth as our relentless goal, but we live in a world of relative truths, where there could be conflicts and confusions between various principles and points of viewing truth. He said, 'If we had attained the full vision of Truth, we would no longer be mere seekers, but would become one with God, for Truth is God' (*CWMG* 44: 166). While we have to constantly strive to attain absolute perfection, it is not possible in practice. But this does not mean that absolute goals are of no meaning and relevance. Sometimes, Gandhi used to take the example of Euclid's line to illustrate his point. He said, 'Euclid's line is one without breadth, but no one so far has been able to draw it and never will. All the same it is only by keeping the ideal line in mind that we made progress in geometry. What is true here is true of every ideal' (Gandhi 1960: 261). It is the honest striving towards truth which he emphasized. The distinction between absolute truth and relative truths was not meant to defend expediency or convenience, but to emphasize our proneness to commit mistakes and go wrong, even while being honest of purpose and unselfish. This distinction served him to point to the need for humility both in thought and action, and that for dialogue and understanding. Respect for differences, in opinions and faiths, was a basic principle for Gandhi because no human being could lay claim to monopoly of truth. Truth emerges out of dialogue, discussion and accommodation of others' points of view. This was important both in the pursuit of knowledge and conflict resolution. A problem had to be seen in all its aspects and dimensions, taking into view different standpoints. Gandhi clarified that, 'tolerance obviously does not disturb the distinction between right and wrong, and good and evil' (*CWMG* 44: 167). A stand-point based purely on selfishness and dishonesty cannot stand scrutiny and cannot represent even a relative truth. Gandhi made it very clear, 'In the march towards truth, anger, selfishness, hatred etc., naturally give way, for otherwise truthwould be impossible to attain' (Gandhi 1927: 288). He put this into actual practice not only in politics but also in his legal profession (Gandhi 1927: 302). It is clear, therefore, that his distinction between absolute truth and relative truths was not for expediency or for being honest only '*as far as convenient*'. His insistence on the commitment to truth was absolute and total. He clearly said, 'To degrade or cheapen an ideal for our convenience is to practice untruth and lower ourselves' (*CWMG* 44: 80).

Gandhi was clear that truth was not necessarily the same as what the majority of people believed in, or what the law of the land provided. He could see that both criteria, while not irrelevant, do not necessarily point to either ontological or moral truth. He insisted on certain openness of our mind, in the sense of being receptive to new ideas and perceptions, to be subjected to reasoning and scrutiny, but not in the sense of being forever non-committal. Pursuit of truth was individual in the sense that one had to be receptive to the inner voice and to unprejudiced and unselfish reasoning. And when one finds that truth so arrived at differs from the truth as believed in by a majority, or as provided by law, it is the duty of such an individual to disseminate his/her own perception of truth, to be prepared for debate and even action to correct the law through nonviolent methods.

Satya led him to ahimsa as its practical or applied principle, not just because truth led to action and action had to be non-violent, but also because truth meant ahimsa. At times, he said that satya is basic and ahimsa followed from it, but often, he said that they are two sides of the same coin. He never doubled their inseparability, and more often felt that ahimsa was the means to attain satya (as seen from the opening quotation in this chapter). Ahimsa, for him, was not a mere negative concept of just avoiding violence, but a positive virtue of kindness, compassion, and care. Feminists regard abstract ethical virtues of truth, righteousness, honesty, and the likes as borne out of a male perspective, while kindness, care, and the likes are feminine virtues. Gandhi reconciled both 'male' and 'female' virtues into a composite and harmonious unity in his principle of satya-ahimsa. Since, he was an action-oriented person, ahimsa in practice could be said to have been more important, as guided by truth. His insistence on ahimsa was derived from his basic principle that the end is determined by the nature of the means used, and that the end cannot justify the means. There was an organic unity between the means and ends in his philosophy, and he believed that only ahimsa can bring about peace and justice ultimately, and not violence. He believed in non-violence, kindness, and love (even for his opponents), because it worked as well, apart from the innate goodness of the principle. The world cannot function without kindness and consideration. Family, a vital and primary unit of human sociality works because of it. A child cannot grow into a healthy and confident adult without the loving care of its mother. A person can be more effective only if she is kind and considerate, she be a teacher, a doctor, or even a shopkeeper. Kindness gives us peace of mind, wins friends, admiration, respect, and even success in career and life itself. Kindness and generosity cannot be of a patronizing type in order to be effective, but has to be combined with humility. Non-violence is the basis of all social and human relations. There was no doubt that he expected the principle of ahimsa to not only cover relations between human beings, but also between human beings on the one hand and animal life and nature-at-large on the other.

He explained the concept of ahimsa thus:

Ahimsa is not the crude thing it has been made to appear. Not to hurt any living being is no doubt a part of Ahimsa. But it is its least expression. The principle of Ahimsa is hurt by every evil thought, by undue haste, by lying, by hatred, by wishing ill of anybody. It is also violated by our holding on to what the world needs. (CWMG 44: 58)

Gandhi was probably the first to point out the relevance of non-violence in public and political life, to resist oppression and injustice. He insisted that non-violence is a weapon to change the heart, and believed in no enemy. In his satyagraha movements, there was no hatred. He asked, 'If God resides in every heart, then who dare hate whom?' (CWMG 81: 454). His approach was one of converting the other party through trusting, reasoning, and love. Non-violence is not a mere tactic, to be given up in preference to violence if the former fails. Non-violence is not only the more noble way, it is also more effective, swifter, and much less costly in terms of human lives and suffering. It is a weapon of the civilized and not of the brute. He emphasized the moral superiority of non-violence over violence, by stating that 'violence is the weapon of the weak; non-violence that of the strong' (*CWMG* 82: 447). Non-violence out of cowardice is not real non-violence; he would even prefer violence to cowardice. He asserted, 'That which looks for mercy from an opponent is not non-violence' (*CWMG* 82: 450). He instilled the courage to die among his followers participating in satyagraha movements. There was no question of fearing the opponent. He said, 'The root cause of most of our misunderstandings lies in distrust, and the root cause of this distrust lies most in fear' (*CWMG* 80: 436). It is violence which is rooted in fear not non-violence, in Gandhian view. The courage for non-violence as a weapon against injustice comes from satya or moral strength. Based on satya, a non-violent struggle believes in openness of mind, willingness to understand opponents' stand point, and in a spirit of accommodation and even compromise. Such compromises should not be out of fear, but based on the conviction that in certain respects the opponents' view may be right and has to be accommodated. This was the Gandhian approach to conflict resolution. But even non-violence is not to be used to achieve personal ends or for narrow selfish purposes. For example, Gandhi may not have approved of an indefinite fast on the part of a person as a protest over failure to get promotion in one's service or in getting selected for a particular post, even if there may have been injustice. Normal legal means have to be used for such purposes. Satyagraha comes in as a weapon where wider ends of social justice are involved. Non-violence basically meant commitment to humanism, peace, and universal brotherhood.

Gandhi's advocacy of non-violence was not absolute in the sense of being applicable under all circumstances. This was so both in case of an individual's private life and a country's public life. He conceded that there might arise conflicts within the practice of ahimsa, which can be settled only through viewing things in a larger perspective of truth, so as to avoid larger violence. There could be extreme or explosive situations where a non-violent approach may not be obviously effective, such as in cases of a rapist making a sexual assault, a suicide bomber about to kill innocent people, and mosquitoes causing disease. Gandhi conceded that in such extreme situations violence might have to be used to counter violence (Allen 2008: 46). Gandhi felt that absolute non-violence might not be possible, even in some normal situations. For example, though he liked to eat vegetarian food, he did not like to insist on it for others if they were accustomed to eating meat all their life, and particularly if enough vegetarian food was difficult to come by in the regions where such people lived. He clarified that his belief in the sacredness of subhuman life did not mean being kinder to this life in preference to human life (*CWMG* 84: 231). He nevertheless expected human beings to be kind and considerate both in principle and practice. A perusal of scattered writings of Gandhi on eating meat would suggest that he would approve it if it is for survival, but not if it is for mere fancy or pleasure when good vegetarian food is available and is less expensive.

Similarly in public life too, Gandhi could sense that non-violent sataygraha would not always work, as for example in countering or humanizing Hitler. He helped the British in their war efforts during the World War I. He approved the idea that free India would have armed forces as a deterrent to guard against aggression. He is reported to have agreed with the Government of India in deciding to send troops to Kashmir to repel invasion from Pakistan's side. But violence was to be resorted to under only exceptional or extreme situations, after honestly satisfying onself that non-violent strategies would not work at all in such situations. Even when resorted to, violence had to be under full control and should not be at the cost of innocent civil life and property. He bitterly resented the dropping of atomic bombs on Hiroshima and Nagasaki, during the World War II, by the Americans. According to Gandhi, even a war cannot eschew ethics both in motives and methods, and its predicted consequence had to be that it avoided larger violence. He would not approve of war as an instrument of domination or to settle disputes.

We may briefly summarize the Gandhian perspective as based on truth and non-violence, and hence compassionate, open to reasoning, yet emotionally committed, holistic, activist, and partial to the weakest.

APPLICATIONS: POLITICS

The scope for manifold applications of the Gandhian perspective emerges from the fact that he considered moral to be spiritual as well, and that spirituality should pervade all activities of life—individual and social. In *Young India*, he said, 'I do not believe that the spiritual law works on a field of its own. On the contrary, it expresses itself only through the ordinary activities of life. It thus affects the economic, social, and political fields' (Gandhi 1927). Practice of politics to Gandhi was a practice of ethics and spirituality in the public sphere.

Gandhi assigned an important role to politics and did not at all shy away from it. Not that he aspired for leadership or any personal glory through it. His interest in politics arose only because he could clearly see that it was necessary to mobilize people on different issues affecting them to bring about the desired change, and this involved politicizing them in the best sense of the term. For a man who firmly believed in the role of people in being active agents of change for their own benefit, politics was inevitable. But this mobilization of people, even for fighting injustice and oppression, had to be based only on non-violence.

By combining non-violence with truth, he could wield a powerful weapon for the empowerment of the weak and deprived—satyagraha. Gandhi asserted the right of the deprived and the victims of injustice to peacefully resist injustice and tyranny. Used for a just cause, such non-violent resistance proved to be formidable, first against racial injustice in South Africa and then against colonialism in India. The claim made by Gandhi in the following words was not in vain: 'Non-violence is the greatest force at the disposal of mankind. It is mightier than the mightiest weapon of destruction devised by the ingenuity of man' (quoted by Sonia Gandhi in Sharma 2007: 23). Explaining the concept and strategy of satyagraha, Bilimoria observes,

Gandhi, no longer content with simply 'turning the other cheek' or just withholding taxes, obligations, or advocating 'go slow', sought a method by which to bring the adversary to (a) confront the situation and, as it were, meet eye-to-eye on the issue in dispute, and (b) redress the evil or wrong without coercing or inflicting injury or violence on to the other party. (Bilimoria *et al.* [eds] 2008: 335)

Politics, thus, was the first field of the practical application of Gandhi's philosophy or perspective. His contribution to politics is unique, which consists in using a deeply spiritual and ethically charged approach of non-violence as a weapon by the victims of injustice, tyranny, and exploitation against their oppressors. As early as in 1920, in an article in *Young India*, he was very clear about such a role for non-violence:

Nonviolence in its dynamic condition means conscious suffering. It does not mean meek submission to the will of the evil-doer, but it means the putting of one's whole soul against the will of the tyrant. Working under this law of our being, it is possible for a single individual to defy the whole might of an unjust empire to save his honour, his religion, his soul and lay the foundation for that empires' fall ... And so I am not pleading for India topractice non-violence because it is weak. I want her to practice nonviolence being conscious of her strength and power. (Quoted in Iyer 1993: 238)

The uniqueness of the Gandhian approach to satyagraha, in fighting injustice or in conflict resolution, is the absence of any ill-will against the opponent. Injustice is separated from the perpetrator of injustice, who is looked upon as a human being and treated with compassion. As Narayan Desai observes, this principle or the method 'protects and enhances the dignity of both [sides]' (Desai 2009 vol. IV: 514). It makes the process of conflict resolution easier and leaves both sides better off. Among a few examples, Desai mentions how 'Nelson Mandela, after three decades of imprisonment, shared power with his white captors without a trace of bitterness'; and 'injustice was fought with justice, where tyranny was resisted with love' (ibid.). The futility and mutual destructiveness of many instances of violent strife stand in sharp contrast to successful and mutually ennobling examples set by Gandhi, Mandela, Martin Luther King, Jr, and several others following them.

His philosophy was used in other contexts of politics too, even for normal times or in non-adversarial circumstances. His emphasis on openness of mind, tolerance, readiness for discussion and dialogue, and spirit of accommodation are of immense value in running a democracy. Satyagraha was to be resorted to only when the opponent was too obstinate for dialogue. Even when satyagraha was resorted to, Gandhi insisted on willingness for dialogue with an open mind, and what is more, on loving and not hating the opponent.

Gandhi did not believe in centralized state power. Democracy or *Swaraj* (self-rule or people's own rule), according to Gandhi, can be effectively accomplished only when grass roots institutions at the village level are mobilized, empowered, and connected with each other and with individuals as the most basic units. In 1946 he wrote, 'Independence must begin at the bottom. Thus, every village will be a republic or panchayat having full powers ... every village has to be self-contained and capable of managing its affairs even to the extent of defending itself against the whole world' (quoted in Iyer 1993: 347). He never meant isolation of villages, on the contrary he emphasized interaction.

He wanted violence and coercion to be eschewed in matters of governance, and envisaged a non-violent police force of *satyagrahis*, who would use the moral force based on their own exemplary conduct and character to bring around rioters, or reform even criminals. In dealing with resistance to authority, the first task of authorities in charge of governance is to look into grievances, understand them, and act on them. As Vinoba Bhave, a very close disciple of Gandhi explains, Swaraj rests on rule by law and public opinion. He felt that respect for or fear of public opinion is more useful than coercion backed by violence. The most conspicuous feature of Gandhi's contribution, to both politics as practice and political theory, is that he tried his best to spiritualize politics. He taught as well as practised the principle that not only ethics should, but also could, play an important role in politics, in all its aspects. Truth and non-violence were the essence of this ethics. Non-violence for him was not just a strategy but a guiding philosophy.

ECONOMICS, SUSTAINABLE DEVELOPMENT, AND ENVIRONMENT

Gandhi applied his philosophy of truth and non-violence in the field of economics too. He wrote,

True economics never militates against the highest ethical standard, just as all true ethics to be worth its name must at the same time be also good economics. An economics that inculcates Mammon worship, and enables the strong to amass wealth at the expense of the weak, is a false and dismal science. It spells death. True economics, on the other hand, stands for social justice; it promotes the good of all equally including the weakest, and is indispensable to for decent life. (*Harijan* 9 October 1937; reproduced in Gandhi 1959: 31–2)

Gandhi made a powerful attack on modern civilization and industrialism, which in his perspective could well be applied to modern economic growth. This was done through a small book of about 30,000 words, titled *Hind Swaraj or Indian Home Rule*, published in 1909. Ramashray Roy has observed that Gandhi's critique was *total*, (at least it appeared so in this book), and not confined to some selected features of modern civilization (Roy 1984: 38). Gandhi announced some two decades later that he did not have to change his views on it.[1] His problem with modern civilization or economic growth was that it is propelled by continuous and unsatiable 'hunger for wealth and greedy pursuit of worldly pleasures'. This led inevitably to violence and inequalities, since the struggle for limited resources could not satisfy everybody and some were deprived and impoverished. Gandhi was not alone in criticizing modern technological civilization. Almost reiterating *Hind Swaraj*, Marcuse wrote half a century later that though scientific management and scientific division of labour vastly increased productivity, resulting in higher standards of living, this rational enterprise also 'produced a pattern of mind and behaviour which justified and absolved even the most destructive and oppressive features of the enterprise' (Marcuse 1964: 146). Interpreting Gandhi and summing up his views, Roy writes, 'Industrialism demolishes barriers between differing national economies, breaks their self-sufficiency, violates their internal coherence and by linking them up to a global economic process, sets in motion a process of homogenisation that tolerates no deviance and suffers no autonomy' (Roy 1984: 120). Gandhi felt that the whole process was selfish, immoral, and defeated the very purpose of human life, which is self-development and self-realization.

As an alternative to this kind of civilization and economic growth, Gandhi proposed an ethically acceptable and humane path. It would be geared to meeting needs rather than multiplying wants and meeting them in a ceaseless race. The humane economy would be addressed to developing human personality in a holistic way (instead of focusing on material possession), promoting human creativity, and helping the realization of human potential. In such an economy, or rather society, there will be no deprivation of some to the benefit of others, and equality would be promoted. For this purpose, he advocated production by the masses, in place of mass production, to the extent that some industries and services would have to be on large scale, they would be run on no-profit basis by the state or a philanthropic minded private enterprise (Roy 1984: 141).

Ajit Dasgupta raises an interesting question about Gandhian economics, firmly rooted as it is in ethics. Is it simply a dream of utopia, or meant to resolve problems of the real world? His answer is, clearly the latter (Dasgupta 1993: 132 and 134). The question above can be posed in a slightly different way. Can Gandhian ethics be practised under the prevalent economic system of capitalism, which functions on the basis of selfishness and unlimited multiplication of wants? Gandhi would have put this question on its head and asked, 'Can capitalism survive without moderating selfishness and curbing the unlimited multiplication of wants?'[2] The need for Gandhi's economic ethics arises precisely because there are real problems in our economic system. His ethics is practical and does not deny the role of basic economic instincts of self-interest. He said, 'no person in the world has found it possible to maintain something which is a source of constant economic loss. (CWMG 31: 276) But he did challenge the basic tenets of mainstream economics. As Dasgupta has observed Gandhi 'was one of the first writers to argue explicitly and in a systematic way that the non-economic aspects of welfare are important and that a single-minded pursuit of the maximum satisfaction of material wants might not lead to to the best of all possible worlds' (Dasgupta 1993: 140). Gandhi insisted that 'everyone must have a balanced diet, a decent house to live in, facilities for the education of one's children, and adequate medical relief' (CWMG 83: 27).

Economic development, including industrialization, is believed to be making it possible to generate enough surplus with which such minimum needs can be met. Gandhi, however, wanted to ensure that meeting such minimum needs is built into the very process of economic development and organization. He was not opposed to industrialization as such, as some mistakenly believe. How could he be when he used modern means of transport and communication? He only wanted industrialization, in particular, and economic development, in general, to have a human face, without reducing humans to robots or depriving them of their livelihood and employment or making some filthy rich and some abjectly poor. Gandhi said, 'I am not against machinery as such but I am firmly opposed to it when it masters us' (*CWMG* 64:118). Gandhi was one of those who were deeply aware of the social dimension of technology and of the fact that technological advance does not take place in a social vacuum. This awareness led him to develop an ethics of technology, technological advance, and industrialization. He wanted all these to be constantly subjected to ethical evaluation, monitoring, and correction. He accepted technology when it was emancipatory, relieving drudgery, improving skills and productivity, and raising human dignity, freedom, and creativity. He was sensitive to the fact that technology can lead to increase in inequity, when it favoured only a few at the cost of others. He used to often cite Singer's sewing machine as an example of desirable machinery, as it increased human comfort and productivity without depriving others of employment and livelihood. He similarly welcomed improvements in the technology of surgery and medical relief, as also in sanitation. Technological advance, for him, was not to be an end in itself and self-driven. It had to be driven by considerations of dignity and freedom for humanity at large, without harming any. Even if it harmed some initially, such people had to be adequately compensated and rehabilitated. An example of this is necessary rehabilitation of *bhangis* (manual cleaners of dry latrines), when dry latrines are replaced by sewage system and flush toilets. The emancipation of bhangis is not complete and effective unless they are rehabilitated in alternative and more paying and dignified occupations. The criterion was whether technology and industrialization, combined with necessary social or state action, improved human welfare of all. Such an ethic of technology was consistent with the alternative economic path he showed. What he wanted was *sarvodaya*, the development of all. His close disciple, Vinoba Bhave, renamed the ideal as *antyodaya*, the rise of the marginalized.

In Gandhian ethics, technological advance and economic development had no meaning unless they led to antyodaya. In Gandhian perspective, economic growth should not be at the cost of anybody's human dignity, but on the contrary should provide full employment to all and eliminate hunger, poverty, and deprivation. He certainly did not conceive economic development in narrow terms of Gross National Product (henceforth GNP) growth, but essentially in terms of human development.

To achieve this, he showed his own path of decentralized, grass roots based economic organization. In Gandhian perspective, the village is not only the basic unit of political self-rule but also of economy. He wanted decentralization of both governance and production system. Gandhi even asserted, 'Under my scheme nothing will be allowed to be produced by cities which can equally well be produced by the villages' (Datta 1986:13). Datta observes that this needs cautious interpretation because under the present disadvantageous position of the villages, especially with respect to access to infrastructure and markets, almost everything would be better produced in cities, except agricultural produce. Datta rightly says that before we decide as per Gandhi's advice, the disadvantageous position of villages in transport facilities and other infrastructure should be remedied (ibid.). Gandhi's economic strategy was well thought out to ensure the empowerment of the rural poor, particularly, and to end inequality, at the same time ensuring incentives for work and efficiency for the more capable. Gandhi pondered over the pros and cons of different models of political and economic systems and arrived at his own model. He rejected communism and centralized economic systems as coercive, violent, and not even ensuring the empowerment of the masses. But he agreed with the Communists in two important respects at least. For one, he accepted the Communist principle of 'From each according to ability and to each according to needs'; and two, in doing away with the state ultimately. At the same time, he saw the limitations of capitalist democracy, supposed to be run on the basis of one-man-one-vote, as promoting only the strength of the wealthy and greed for personal wealth, and not being able to tame the wealthy. Gandhi would hardly have been enthusiastic about modern welfare states, for he looked down upon patronizing welfare schemes based on the principle of charity. He wanted self-respect for all, both in consumption and production process.

Consequently, he envisaged a village or local community based economic democracy. Villages should not be mere producers of raw material and be at the receiving end of a price system and exploitative economy. He insisted on village self-reliance as essential to swaraj. Swaraj and *swadeshi* go together. As Dasgupta observes, Gandhi's emphasis on swadeshi was not for mere expediency, but was based on the ethical principle of first helping one's neighbour (Dasgupta 1993: 142). Gandhi felt that one must not serve one's distant neighbour at the expense of the nearest (*CWMG* 26: 278). It meant that production should first meet local needs, and local products should be preferred in satisfying one's wants. Swaraj and swadeshi did not mean that villages should not trade with other or with the larger economy, but it should be from a position of strength. Villages should also plan education, health care, water supply, sanitation, and other activities essential for the welfare of rural people, and should be self-sufficient in this regard. Here again, it does not mean isolation or that each village should have its own university or a multi-specialilty high-tech hospital. But all basic amenities should be provided at the village level. Gandhi did not rule out horizontal and vertical integration of villages. His following famous words sound relevant in this regard as well as in other respects, 'I do not want to stay in a house with all its windows and doors shut. I want a house with all its windows and doors open where the breezes of all lands and cultures blow through my house. But, I refuse to be blown off my feet by any'(quoted in Rolland 2004: 70–1).

He did not want the villages to be blown off their feet by the larger economy, even if they were open to it. This was the minimum he would insist on in his economic and political system.

There is no dearth of people who question the relevance of Gandhian approach to economics, along with its emphasis on local production meeting local wants and humane technology, in a globalizing world. Globalization is neither an unmixed evil, nor an unmixed blessing. Gandhi would have welcomed its advantages to the common man and the poor, and would have fought for a control by the poor over its processes so that its evils were avoided or mitigated. The world is globalizing not necessarily because it is in the interest of all. It is globalizing because in an unequal world like ours, it is the strong who run the show in their own interests. It involves serious risks that the weak may be further marginalized and deprived and that inequalities may increase. And that is where the relevance of Gandhi is most conspicuous. He is their hope and his methods and philosophy their weapon. Under Gandhi's inspiration, they can create some space for themselves and achieve a measure of dignity and equality which unbridled capitalism will never give them.

Any violent strife between the rich and the poor will be mutually destructive, and in the interest of neither.

It would be unfair to criticize Gandhi that he ignored the problem of social and economic inequality within the villages, or in the larger polity and economy, and the possibility that his village-based polity or economy could be hijacked by upper caste rural elite. He did feel greatly concerned about the plight of untouchables, whom he called *Harijans*, and tried his best to end discrimination against them and to improve their economic and social status. In his fight against untouchability, not only did he declare it as the gravest sin and openly assert that he would renounce Hinduism if he were convinced that it was a part of Hindu religion, he also took active steps to end untouchability. He actively supported the entry of untouchables into temples. He emphasized dignity of manual labour, and he not only participated in scavenging work in his ashram (hermitage), but he made it the duty of every ashram inmate to do it by turns. He adopted an untouchable girl as his daughter and made it a point to attend wedding ceremonies only if it was a wedding between an untouchable and an upper caste Hindu. He wanted all caste prejudices to be dropped from the village level upwards. In his ideal society, a scavenger would receive the same remuneration as a lawyer or a doctor, consistent with his principle of 'From each according to ability, and to each according to needs'.

As for steps to reduce economic inequality in practice, he advocated several strategies. One was through emphasizing the production of basic goods on priority like food, clothing, and shelter. He said, 'To a starving person, God will appear in the form of bread alone' (*CWMG* 82: 446). He evolved strategies to enable the poor to earn their own bread, rather than depend on charity, by ensuring employment in village level industries and other industries. He insisted that technology should not displace human labour but provide full employment, which was the basic goal and justification for economic development. Another strategy recommended by him was the adoption of the concept of trusteeship by the wealthy.

Gandhi's idea of trusteeship was an innovative way of reconciling the psychological need for incentive or reward for skills and entrepreneurship on the one hand and the social need to take care of the deprived on the other. The enterprising and better-skilled people need an incentive or reward for their work, which the society values higher, in the form of higher income and wealth. It gives them some sense of achievement and pride, but this does not mean that they need to keep all of their earnings to themselves. Gandhi felt that they should consider themselves as trustees for the income and wealth which is a surplus after meeting their basic needs, minimum comforts to maintain their skills, and reinvestment requirements, and spend it on the less fortunate in society who need these resources to end their deprivation. They can spend their surplus wealth directly for such purposes or give it to charitable trusts who can utilize this surplus wealth to meet the needs of the poor. Gandhi was against the government taking over the functions of entrepreneurs and owning all enterprises, and probably also against taxing the rich so highly that they there is no incentive for them for enterprise. He wanted to keep the role of the State to the minimum. Nevertheless, he was not unaware of the limits of private charity, at least as prevalent. The problem with relying only or even mainly on private charity is that there are not enough donors, resulting in utter inadequacy of it. Corporate enterprises may sometimes tend to create showpieces for own publicity, spending lavishly on a particular scheme or place and ignoring the rest. Gandhi, therefore, did not exclude legislative regulation of ownership and use of wealth, and high rates of taxes on wealth and inheritance, if voluntary effort was found inadequate. He did not mind the government stepping into give direction and filling the gap in this respect. He even thought favourably of a ceiling on income and wealth as a floor below which they would not fall, if the trusteeship principle did not work. On the whole, however, he wanted a production system and economy so organized that distribution takes care of itself on egalitarian lines, rather than having an economy that generates poverty and deprivation and then tackles them through welfare schemes of either private enterprise or the government.

Gandhi had another strategy too for reducing inequality and generating surplus for helping the poor and the deprived. This was by limiting consumption by the rich, eliminating lavish expenditure to display status and wealth, and limiting wants in general. It is unfair to criticize Gandhi on the ground of romanticizing poverty. While involuntary or imposed poverty had to be eliminated, he advocated voluntary poverty by the well-to-do. This was good for their soul, imparting moral strength to the persons limiting unnecessary wants, and also good for the society as it generated surplus wealth to help the poor. Gandhi may not have used the words 'sustainable development', but his following famous words point to the same: 'The Earth has enough to meet every one's needs, but not every man's greed'. He was appalled by the greed that provided the motive force for modern industrialization and its wastefulness. As early as in 1928, he expressed his anguish about this by saying, 'God forbid that India should ever take to industrialisation after the manner of the West. The economic imperialism of a single tiny island kingdom [England] is today keeping the world in chains. If an entire nation of 300 million took to similar economic exploitation, it would strip the world bare like locusts' (*CWMG* 38: 243). Not that he did not want economic development for India, but he wanted India to take its own harmless path, which in today's parlance may be called as sustainable development. Other aspects of his economic philosophy also point to the same—preferring to use manual energy to other forms of energy, and making the goods durable so that the culture of 'use once and throw away' can be avoided. Kumarappa's interpretation of Gandhian economic thought (to be discussed in Chapter 3) is strongly suggestive of sustainable development, and limiting reckless exploitation of nature and environment.

Gandhi's principle of social service is useful both in reducing economic inequality and helping environment. It is not enough to share one's wealth with the poor and for collective causes, it is equally necessary to give one's time and labour too. Voluntary service or *Shram-daan* is also useful for economic development in creative, rural, and economic assets and for protecting them—such as in constructing and renovating tanks, wells, canals, bunds, soil, and water conservation measures, afforestation, and regenerating *gomals* or village pastures. His idea of social service even extended towards *satyagrahis* supporting the victims of social or economic injustice when the latter wanted to resist oppression and exploitation. However, unlike some self-styled revolutionaries, Gandhi's emphasis on constructive activities on the part of satyagrahis was a conspicuous feature of his teaching, and was not confined to merely offering resistance.

Gandhi's constructive programmes, as Narayan Desai points out, took an integrated view of life (Desai 2009, vol. III: 218). He had a holistic view of economic development. Besides having livelihood concerns, particularly about the weak, the constructive programmes valued the principle of economic equality, and the governing principle of decentralization. They aimed at benefiting the producers and consumers most, in contrast to the ways of modern economy which allow and encourage a huge disparity between the producers' price and consumers' price. By catering to local needs as much as possible, the economic activities minimized unnecessary transport costs, thus saving on fuel too. The constructive programmes also had the moral aims of human development, including schooling and eradication of illiteracy, character building, promoting communal harmony, providing health services, teaching cleanliness, encouraging mutual co-operation, improving the status of women, avoiding alcohol, and so on.

Parekh has mentioned about how a group consisting of M.L. Dantwala and others, after a discussion with Gandhi, summed up his views on strategies to fight inequality, and that this draft had his approval after he made some changes. The final version cited by Parekh (2007: 144–5), published first in *Young India* (17 March 1931 and 16 April 1931), is as follows:

1. Trusteeship provides a means of transforming the present capitalist order of society into an egalitarian one. It gives no quarter to capitalism but gives the present owning class a chance of reforming itself. It is based on the faith that human nature is never beyond redemption.
2. It does not recognize any rights of private ownership of property except in so far as it may be permitted by society for its own welfare.
3. It does not exclude legislative regulation of the ownership and use of wealth.
4. Thus under State regulated trusteeship, an individual will not be free to hold or use wealth for selfish satisfaction or in disregard of the interests of society.
5. Just as it is proposed to fix a decent minimum living wage, even so a limit should be fixed for the maximum income that would be allowed to any person in society. The difference between such incomes should be reasonable and equitable and variable from time to time so much so that the tendency would be towards obliteration of the difference.
6. Under the Gandhian economic order, the character of production will be determined by social necessity and not by personal whim or greed.

Gandhi himself applied his basic perspective to several fields, not only to politics, including governance, and economics, which were his focus of interest, but also to others such as treatment of nature, including animal life, education, social relations, religion, science, technology, and culture. Only a few of the important applications of his philosophy are discussed in the essay here. In education, he stressed character building as its main aim; in social relations, love, empathy, and respect for the other; in religion, tolerance, openness, and freedom from dogma; in science and technology, humaneness; and, in culture openness combined with refusal to be blown off the feet. What is common to all his applications is the insistence on moral values, summarized in his concepts of truth and non-violence. A highly skilled technocrat or even a person with PhD would be considered as uneducated if such a person has no moral integrity. A most powerful political leader would be worthless if he does not have a faith in truth, non-violence, and organic unity between means and ends. A wealthy man's wealth would be useless if he does not lead a simple life and use his surplus wealth for the welfare of others.

Has India Followed Gandhi?

What kind of India (or, for that matter, the world) was Gandhi looking for in future? From his numerous writings and speeches, it appears to be one where everyone would have equal opportunities, and what is more, also capabilities to make use of equal opportunities. All would be decently employed, while there would be respect for manual work and regard for all irrespective of their station in life. It is one where everyone would be participating in the decision-making process actively, both in economic and political matters, and not just in the formal way of casting vote once in five years but in a more meaningful and substantive way. It would be a country where there would be no discrimination on the basis of caste, creed, or gender, and a fair measure of equality would prevail in income and wealth. It would have a society in which everybody is considerate to others and respectful to others' sensitivities, concerns, and rights. There would be respect for law, even while retaining the freedom to protest against injustice. There would be not only equal freedom of faith and expression, and freedom to make reasonable amount of private property, but also freedom from hunger and every form of deprivation, whether in respect of food, clothing, shelter, health, education, or access to basic amenities like safe drinking water and sanitation. And till such deprivation ends, there would be control on lavishness of consumption by the rich, their lifestyles and conspicuous symbols of personal wealth. It would be a country free from corruption and all similar attempts at immoral gratification and manipulation of one by another for selfish ends. There would be such transparency and accountability in public life, that citizens are satisfied with it. It would be free from violence and unlawful coercion, whether by the state, institutions, or individuals. It would be a country of civilized people, with due concern for avoiding dirt, squalour, and pollution in public space, and waste of precious natural resources. Its people would respect and nurture environment. They would, above all, be humane and compassionate to others, be they kith and kin, friends or even strangers. Unlimited wealth and income growth for its own sake was not on Gandhi's agenda, though he would welcome economic development to end poverty, meet basic needs, and to enable everyone to lead a life of dignity. In Gandhi's view, all these ideals were to be achieved not through the dominance of a centralized state, but through decentralized people's institutions and direct democracy as far as possible.

How far has India adopted this Gandhian perpective in its governance? How far does India's economic and social development reflect Gandhian principles? Most Indians now may be inclined to say, 'Not at all!'. I think, however, that it is a mixed picture, and the influence of Gandhi certainly goes somewhat beyond putting his pictures on the walls of government offices and currency notes, and formally acknowledging him as the father of our nation.

First, let me cite a few positive instances where we have followed Gandhi, implicitly if not explicitly. Then, of course, I try to point out where we have failed him. One of the first instances of at least partial application of Gandhian perspective was with regard to the Community Development Programme initiated during the early 1950s, intended to bring economic development down to the grass roots. This could not, however, succeed well in the absence of a proper empowerment of the villages. Though there were several attempts at this in different states, we had to wait till 1992 for a firm step in this direction in the form of the Constitution (Seventy-third Amendment) Act. This Act provided for a three-tier structure of governance—at the Union level, the state levels, and at the decentralized panchayat (village council) levels of village, taluk/ tehsil, and districts in every state. This is not a fully Gandhian model, as the Union remains the most powerful, followed by the state governments and then by the panchayat institutions. The panchayat institutions derive their power from and are dependent on the state governments in most respects, which was not how Gandhi envisaged. Nevertheless, steps like mandatory representation to women and scheduled castes have helped in broadbasing and democratizing the panchayat institutions. They have the potential to become stronger and more mature, and can demand more powers. Even as it is, they are entrusted with tasks of rural development and resources to perform them.

The second instance of our, at least, partially following Gandhi is guaranteeing some minimum employment in the rural sector under the Mahatma Gandhi National Rural Employment Guarantee Act (MGNREGA), in force since 2006. Employment under relief works especially during droughts was being offered since long, and a few states like Maharashtra and Karnataka had initiated rural employment assurance schemes after the famous drought of 1972. However, it was only in 2006 that the principle was adopted at the national level by the central government as its scheme, implemented by the states with financial support from the centre, though what Gandhi had envisaged was promotion and assurance of self-employment (also for which there are separate schemes), MGNREGA is still important to cover those who are unable to find full self-employment. It has thus become very useful in not only reducing rural poverty but also in empowering the poor. There is an urgent need to extend it to cover the urban poor as well, to cover more than hundred days of employment envisaged initially, and to cover all the districts of the country.

In the same year when MGNREGA came into force, another significant measure was taken which could be said to be in furtherance of Gandhian perspective—the Forest and Tribal Lands Act of 2006. Under this, each tribal family is given the right up to 2.5 hectares of land to own and cultivate, even if it is in a forest area, provided that the family had been cultivating the land for at least the specified number of years in the past. This has meant some security of livelihood and self-employment.

Other steps taken in the Gandhian direction are the Right to Information Act (RTIA) of 2005, which assured some transparency and accountability in the governance by public authorities, and the Food Security Act whereby the state undertakes the responsibility to ensure a minimum food security as a matter of fulfilling a right. More recently, the Right to Education Act 2009 has been passed to universalize education for children in the age-group of 6–14, and makes it mandatory for private schools to reserve 25 per cent of their total seats as government seats for poor children coming from the neighbourhood. This is expected to make up for the deficiency in government schools. This Act is hardly ambitious though it comes belatedly. Each of the above measures, well intentioned surely, have shown some weaknesses in implementation, which amounts to defeating Gandhian principles. It looks Gandhi is being followed grudgingly, and not with enthusiasm or even with sincerity. Yet, it is for the people to ensure that they are implemented well, as these Acts empower them to do so.

Gandhi's ideas are relevant for the private sector too, particularly his principle of trusteeship. This principle is not as impractical as it may sound to cynics. Consider the fact, for example, that 'two-thirds of Tata Sons is owned by charitable trusts which finance a wide range of philanthropic activities' (*The Economist,* 14 August 2010, p. 50). There are also several other philanthropic institutions promoted out of corporate profit earnings of business magnates in India, like the Infosys Foundation and Arghyam Foundation. Organizations like the Ramakrishna Mission, Chinmaya Mission, and All India Movement for Seva, the last promoted by Swami Dayanand Saraswati, have benefited mainly from donations from the social service oriented well-to-do persons. The scale of these private activities may at present be much smaller than what it should be, considering the social problems of the country, but there is still vast realizable potential for them, justifying the faith of Gandhi in the practicability of trusteeship principle.

In spite of these positive steps, there has been a negative legacy too, particularly in securing human welfare, which has not been in the direction of implementing Gandhian principles. Our greatest failure has been in respect of removing poverty and hunger, let alone homelessness. According to the UNDP's Human Development Human Development Report (HDR) 2013, the proportion of people below International Poverty Line of US$ 1.25 a day was 32.7 per cent and the same below National Poverty Line was 29.8 per cent. This is a very significant magnitude of poverty, especially taking note of the fact that a few other Asian countries, in similar positions as India around 1947, have practically wiped it out at least in terms of their respective National Poverty Lines. Prevalence of hunger and malnutrition, as indicated by the proportion of underweight children below the age of five according to the same report, was 42.5 per cent in India as compared to 3.8 per cent in China. The state of public health also leaves much to be desired. Under-five mortality rate per 1,000 was as high as 63 in India, compared to 18 in China and only 3 in Japan. Maternal mortality rate per 100,000 live births as in 2005 was as high as 200 in India, compared to 37 in China and only 3 in Japan. Access to improved sanitation facilities was enjoyed by only 34 per cent of population in India, as against 64 per cent in China and 100 per cent in Japan. Public expenditure on health as a proportion of Gross Domestic Product (GDP) declined in India from 1.3 to 1.2 per cent between 2000 and 2010, while it increased in China from 1.8 to 2.7 per cent during the same period.

The same sad state of affairs prevails in another social sector— adult literacy and education. Our adult literacy was 74.0 per cent in India in 2011, lower than in many other Asian and African countries. It was 94.3 per cent in China.[3] Female adult literacy rate was as low as 65.5 per cent in India, and 90 per cent in China. The proportion of population which has completed at least secondary education, aged 25 years and above, was one, 38.7 per cent in India in 2010, while it was 62.7 per cent in China. Primary education completion rate for boys has of course improved in India to 95 per cent from its earlier level of 75 per cent in 1991, and in the case of girls to 92 per cent from 51 per cent during the two decades, but China had attained the 100 per cent by 1991 itself both for boys and girls and almost maintained it since. As a result of our backwardness in human development, our ranking, as per the Human Development Report (HDR) 2013, in Human Development Index (HDI) is 136 out of 186 countries ranked, among the lowest one-third! Our HDI score itself (as against the rank) did show improvement, from 0.345 in 1980 to 0.554 in 2012, a gain of 0.209 points. Between the same years, China improved its HDI from 0.407 to 0.699—a gain of 0.292 points. We are both backward and slower in improving human development.

What would sadden Gandhi most is our failure in removing untouchability and in ending discrimination against the so-called untouchables—the Scheduled Castes (SCs) in our society. Any practice of untouchability and discrimination against SCs is a punishable offence under the Constitution of India. India has also a system of positive discrimination or reservations for SCs, Scheduled Tribes, and Other Backward Classes up to 50 per cent in educational institutions and government jobs, which is on a scale which is unparalleled in the world. As a result, a significantly higher proportion of these communities have entered the mainstream of our society and polity now than at the time of our independence (Nadkarni 1997). Nevertheless, atrocities against SCs continue to take place fairly frequently. Even as late as in 2009, SCs had to fight for right to entry in temples, some of which are still monopolized by the upper castes. Atrocities against women too have continued, and so has discrimination against women even if not consciously. In terms of gender equality, India ranked 132nd, slightly higher than its HDI rank of 136. In contrast, China's ranked 35th in gender equality, which is substantially higher than its HDI rank of 101.

Gandhi would not have liked vulgar consumerism by the rich in India, flaunting their wealth and status lavishly, instead of taking pride in using their wealth for social welfare. With rising growth rates, this consumerism too has increased, before economic growth showed adequate positive impact on human development indicators. Easy imports of luxury goods under liberalization and globalization have further encouraged this consumerism. This has siphoned off much needed resources from human development to elite pockets.[4]

Instead of a significant transfer of purchasing power from the elite to the poor, there is taking place the opposite process though miniscule purchasing power may trickle down to the poor under anti-poverty measures. Corruption defeats any attempt to help the poor. Governance by public authorities is plagued by widely prevalent corruption at all levels. This is a situation with which Gandhi would have felt disgusted. A Berlin-based organization, Transparency International, has been publishing a Corruption Perception Index (CPI) for different countries, and ranks them on that basis. Higher the rank, higher is the level of transparency. The Index takes the values from 0 to 100, with 0 indicating a highly corrupt and 100 indicating a 'squeaky clean' situation. A score of 50 in the index is a borderline figure, below which are countries with a serious corruption problem. In 2003, this Index was 28 for India and its rank was 83 out of 133 countries covered. According to the 2012 report, India improved its index to 36 (still below the borderline of 50), but its rank fell to 94 out of 176 countries.

Is there at least a long-term trend towards a Gandhian direction of a reduction in corruption in India? Several large-scale scams in both at the centre and the states, have rudely shaken this hope. An editorial in the *Economic and Political Weekly* dated 7 November 2009, entitled 'Marriage of Money and Politics', exposes an ugly reality of Indian politics at least at the state levels. It is not just corruption at the micro levels which is worrisome, but also the phenomenon of oligarchs and powerful industrialists becoming active participants in governance and policy making and even in shaping the government. They significantly finance elections, thus not only raising the cost of campaigning in elections, but also making it difficult to fight corruption. A common citizen without much money will in these circumstances find it almost impossible to effectively take part in elections, however competent s/he may otherwise be. This defeats the very definition of democracy given by Abraham Lincoln—a rule of the people, by the people, and for the people, and elections become a farce. It becomes a rule of the elite rich and for them.

There have been other failures too. We can only hope that with the significant positive steps taken during the last few years like the RTIA and the MGNREGA, we may still be able to move in the directions which Gandhi would have favoured and show to the world that the Gandhian legacy is not all lost and that we are a civilized people.

NOTES

1. As we will soon note below, this did not mean a total opposition to all modern technology and technological advance or even to industrialization.

2. Let us recall that capitalism is only of a recent origin, and cannot be assumed to be eternally fixed in its characteristics. It has already undergone several changes and adjustments since the last century.

3. According to 2011 Census of India, literary rates in India have climbed up appreciably during the last decade, from 75.3 per cent in 2001 to 82.1 for males, from 53.7 per cent in 2001 to 65.5 per cent for females, and from 64.8 per cent in 2001 to 74 per cent for both together. The gain in percentage has been higher for females, thus reducing the gender gap in literacy. (*The Hindu*, Editorial, 2 April 2011). There is some discrepancy between census figures and figures given in WDI.

4. Gini co-efficient for income distribution in India, according to HDR 2013, was 33.4 per cent, but even higher for China at 42.5. Sweden has the lowest Gini at 25.0 per cent.

2 Religion for Modern Times
Ethics-centred Gandhian Way*

A religion which takes no note of this world and
only harps on the one beyond, does not deserve the name.

—M.K. Gandhi
(*CWMG* 82: 447)

MODERN PREDICAMENT AND GANDHI'S SOLUTION

Within the course of one essay, it is difficult to do justice to this topic. Apart from Gandhi's own vast and wide-ranging writings and speeches on the theme, whole books have been written on Gandhi's approach to religion (for example, Chatterjee 1983 and 2005; Jordens 1998; Iyer 2000, Parel 2006, and Kamath 2007).[1] But, there is still a scope to do an overview of Gandhi's distinct contribution to religion, as it not only influenced all spheres of his actions, but also has a great relevance to our difficult times.

Gandhi was certainly no founder of a religion,[2] and is understandably not counted among Krishna, Buddha, Mahavira, Jesus, Mohammad, and other such religious leaders. He detested any appellations of 'saint', 'ascetic', or even 'Mahatma', though he became known as Mahatma throughout the world in his own life time. In spite of his possible protestations, he can be credited with making the most valuable contribution to religion in

* Based on lectures presented at Gandhi Centre of Science and Human Values, Bharatiya Vidya Bhavan, Bengaluru, October 2007 and Dr V.K.R.V. Rao Birth Centenary Celebration Lecture Series, Bangalore University, January 2008.

modern times by any leader in the world, for he interpreted religion in a new light suited to the modern times in a way which was relevant to all, irrespective of religious affiliations.

His contribution lies in providing a solution to a difficult modern predicament. The predicament consists in failure on two fronts. On the one hand, in spite of a long history of over three thousand years, religion failed to make human beings humane enough. Religion-based identities tended to be focused on breeding contempt and hatred for others' religions instead of humaneness. Inhuman practices including untouchability and gender discrimination prevailed, often invoking religion. Instead of liberating, religion enslaved, and the task of raising all human beings to a position of dignity and taking moral responsibility for it was almost off its agenda.

On the other hand, science and technological progress also failed in making human beings rational enough to raise human beings to a position of dignity, happiness, and moral responsibility. This provided the basis for Gandhi's critique of modern civilization, particularly as contained in *Hind Swaraj* (first published in 1910; reproduced in Mukherjee 1993: 1–66). It was hardly a systematic and scholarly critique, being more a collection of random thoughts. It would appear to be sentimental, romantic, impractical, and unconvincing to readers today, and it appeared to be so to many readers even at that time. But the gist of his criticism, which continues to be relevant, was that modern civilization was driven by the endless urge to multiply wants and by technology to satisfy them, while it sidelined moral values almost completely; it had no respect for dignity of human labour and even human happiness, though outwardly this civilization appeared to be making life more comfortable. By centralizing production and through uncontrolled and senseless urbanization, it deprived human beings of their humaneness and gave no time for rational and long-term thinking about human welfare, engaged as it was in a restless pursuit of material comforts.

For Gandhi, the essence of civilization consisted in directing human progress in a self-conscious way and with self-control, achieving the welfare of all (*sarvodaya*). For this, freedom—*Swaraj*—was essential so that each of us could exercise our moral responsibility. For him Hind Swaraj did not mean merely getting rid of the English rule and replacing it by a rule of Indians. It meant a civilizational change. As aptly observed by Jahanbegloo, 'by defining civilization in moral terms, Gandhi not only sets himself against the very basic ethos of the Modern West, deeply embedded, according to him, in the two principles of might is right and survival of the fittest, but also guides his readers towards a new definition and concept of swaraj' (2008: 31). The essence of swaraj above all was 'about individual autonomy, involving self-respect, self-restraint and maturity' (ibid.). The modern civilization and its values were no model for Gandhi in this task. Once asked what he thought of the western (modern) civilization, Gandhi wittily replied that it would be a good idea!

Gandhi recognized the failures of both religion and technological advance. But he did not reject either. He did not reject religion because he saw in it a rich potential for solving the modern predicament and overcoming the failure of modern civilization. He could not totally reject modern civilization and its technology, though he appeared to have done so in his *Hind Swaraj*. It would have been impractical to blindly stick to anti-modernity stance absolutely and uncritically; after all, modern technological advance did provide comforts which became indispensable for transport, communication (both of which Gandhi could not avoid using), and health care. He accepted technology, industry and machinery in so far as they are used only as a tool or means to further the happiness of every human (rather than only a few), keeping the focus on human welfare, but not when humans became mere tools for industrialization. There could be no confusion between ends and means here.

Similarly, he accepted religion and spirituality only in so far as religion left us with a common heritage of moral values, which need to be followed and nourished. He asserted that 'the essence of religion is morality' (Gandhi 1927: x), and that 'as soon as we lose the moral basis, we cease to be religious. There is no such thing as religion overriding morality' (*Young India*, 24 November 1921). He was convinced, however, that 'if morality has to sprout, it has to be watered by religion'. He did not consider atheism as immoral but only like a desert which is not likely to be very hospitable for moral values to sprout and flourish. He did ponder over the existence of God and need for religion, but by the time he wrote his autobiography, he felt he 'had already crossed the Sahara of atheism' (Gandhi 1927: 39). For him, however, the only justification for religion was as an inspirer and nourisher of morality and moral courage, and as a source of solace in situations of adversity and crisis. Scepticism about religion should not lead to rejection of ethics itself. He rejected religion when it became fanatical, oriented to hatred and superstition, and sectarian. Like the Buddha, he shunned theological and metaphysical questions and rituals which only divided humanity, while emphasis on ethics could unite and raise it.

He took the help of religion also in providing a solution to one of the gravest ills of modern civilization—its limitless multiplication of wants. He asserted that 'civilization in the real sense of the term consists not in the multiplication, but in the deliberate and voluntary restriction of wants ...' (Fischer 1998: 391). Fischer observes that 'Gandhi was a strong individual, and his strength lay in the richness of his personality, not in the multitude of his possessions. His goal was to be, not to have', (Fischer 1998: 486). This belief in limiting one's wants could be related to his faith in non-violence to nature too. Gandhi's philosophy has the potential of solving the earth's gravest crisis thus far—the environmental crisis.

His religion, understood in this essentially ethical and non-sectarian sense, rooted in Truth and Non-violence, was for him a guiding force not only in day-to-day living, but also in economics, politics, and technology. It could be applied also to environmental considerations to evolve an environmental ethic. It is a framework, perspective which could be applied to resolve any crisis or predicament. At the same time, it was a source of spiritual strength, as Gandhi knew that truth alone triumphs.

GANDHI—A RATIONALIST AMONG BELIEVERS AND A BELIEVER AMONG RATIONALISTS

Gandhi's religiosity was unique, for he was a rationalist among believers, and a believer among rationalists. His belief, his faith, did not exclude reasoning, nor did his reasoning exclude faith. Traditional religious leaders have always emphasized faith, and undermined reasoning. Rationalists, on the other hand, always upheld reasoning, and allowed little scope for faith. Gandhi did not belong to either tribe; or rather he tried to reconcile the two. He blended both reasoning and faith into a creative unity.

He was a rationalist among believers because he declined to accept religious scriptures as infallible, though he respected them. He shunned a literal application of everything they said, but he emphasized they should be subjected to the test of reasoning.[3] This is what the Buddha and the Bhagavad Gita too preached. The Buddha said: accept any preaching only if convinced after rigorous thinking. The Gita said, '*Vimarshyetad asheshena yathechchasi tatha kuru*' (XVIII.63), that is, critically and fully think over and then do what you want to do. Truth cannot be sacrificed at the altar of religion. He regarded even religion, not as an end in itself, but as a means for the pursuit of truth.

Gandhi was a believer among rationalists, because reason by itself is no complete path to truth. He once said, 'Rationalists are admirable beings, but rationalism can be a hideous monster when it claims omnipotence for itself'. Reasoning has to have a sense of noble purpose, and has to be enlightened by belief in certain universal moral values, principally by truth and non-violence. We have to have faith in these values, in ourselves and in our capacity to follow these values. Faith in moral values was a pivot, around which the whole human life revolved, and reasoning was like oil to lubricate the wheel of life in its smooth functioning.

GANDHI'S FUNDAMENTAL BELIEFS: TRUTH, NON-VIOLENCE, AND SERVICE

How could Gandhi reconcile both rationality and faith? Simply by holding truth as the highest value—as God. For him, truth was God, there was no other God. He considered this as a personal discovery, and an advance over his earlier belief that God was Truth. What he meant by this restatement was that Truth came prior to any concept of God and even the concept of God had to be consistent with Truth. Truth or God for him was the cosmic power which made the world move and also the moral order which ensured its own triumph over evil. God for him was not 'some person who defies all natural laws and performs miracles on fancy. My inner conscience which guides me to Truth is God. He is present in all, and is not external to us'. We live our life, searching for Truth, and the pursuit of Truth is our own. In this task, both reasoning and faith guide us, which in turn are guided by conscience, which is the voice of Truth. Truth thus leads to Truth. An advantage in this restatement that truth is God is that even an atheist who nevertheless pursues truth honestly can be considered as 'religious'. An even greater advantage in this restatement is that it enabled Gandhi to define religion in moral terms, since truth was meaningless without morality, and the essence of religion is pursuit of Truth. It is in this sense that he considered the role of religion all-pervasive.

Gandhi explained that 'the word satya [truth] comes from sat, which means 'to be', 'to exist'. According to him nothing exists in reality except Truth, and what is false cannot survive, cannot exist, as stated by the Gita (Naasato vidyate bhaavo naa bhaavo vidyate satah II.16). Satya is the basis of all existence, physical, moral, and spiritual. That is why he believed in the Upanishadic saying, 'satyameva jayate naanritam' (Truth alone triumphs, not falsehood). He believed in the moral inevitability in the triumph of truth. He clarified: 'It subsists by virtue of its own power; which is not supported by anything else but supports everything, that exists' (Jahanbegloo 2008: 38). It is the basis of human society and its survival as well. Thus Truth is not mere abstention from telling lies, but is the substance of morality, and the source of eternal and universal values, which could be applied to all fields of human activity (see Box 2.1). Non-violence is the expression of this morality. Gandhi believed that violence can never be moral, as it meant coercion and went against compassion and love. Just as truth is not a mere abstention from telling lies, non-violence or ahimsa was not just abstention from killing and hurting. It is a positive concept involving love, compassion, empathy, and *seva* (service). Basically, the universal values are the same satya for Gandhi, expressed as 'truth in the realm of knowledge, righteousness in the domain of conduct and justice in the sphere of social relations' (Iyer 2000:151).

Box 2.1 Eight deadly sins that the Mahatma frequently spoke about (according to Arun Gandhi, his grandson)

Wealth without work
Pleasure without conscience
Commerce without morality
Worship without sacrifice
Politics without principle
Rights without responsibility
Knowledge without character and
Science without humanity.
— As quoted in Jahanbegloo (2008:19)

There is a further significance to Gandhi's assertion that Truth is God. Since at the practical level of living our life and conducting the affairs of the world, truth is morality for him, it also means that morality is God, not vice versa. It implies that if there is a conflict between morality and religion or religious beliefs, Gandhi leaves us in no doubt that ethics prevails over religious beliefs, and not vice versa. Since he believed in the power of truth and the inevitability of its triumph, he invested Truth with spiritual significance. That is how Gandhi always felt that true religion did not have to conflict with ethics; both required mental purity. Religion imparts a sense of spiritual urgency to ethics, and an emotive flavour, which motivates ethical behaviour. So ethics and religion creatively and constructively complement each other in Gandhi's view.

It requires mental purity to lead a life of truth and righteousness. For Gandhi, 'goodness does not consist in abstention from wrong but in abstention from the wish to do wrong; evil is to avoided not from fear but from a sense of obligation' (Iyer 2000: 64). But the sense of moral obligation is to be based on an emotional commitment, putting our heart into the thing, and enjoying to do what ought to be done, according to Gandhi. Only then it would lead to effective action. This must result from free choice, not under a sense of duress. 'The crucial thing for Gandhi ... is not to teach people what is right ... but to get them to do what they know they ought to do' (Iyer 2000: 69). Action is important in Gandhi's scheme of things. Human beings have to rise to take up their moral responsibility, which included social responsibility. If one believes in seeking Truth, she or he cannot just remain passive looking at the misery of others. If there is injustice, poverty, or tyranny anywhere, it is the responsibility of humans everywhere to react and contribute to ending it. This was an important principle for Gandhi. Gandhi's spirituality, as M.V. Kamath puts it, consisted of identifying with the work of God's creation and expressing it through tireless service of humanity (Kamath 2007: ix).

How does one know what is Truth, and what is just? Though he conceded that ultimate Truth is Absolute, everyone's goal in life is to seek it, and one need not have sudden revelation from gods externally. He wrote in 1922 in a letter: 'As I proceed in my search for truth it grows upon me that Truth comprehends everything. ... what is perceived by pure heart and intellect is truth for that moment. Cling to it, and it enables one to reach pure Truth' (quoted in Iyer 2000: 157). He could see, however, that while one must have faith in Absolute Truth and absolute standards of ethics, it is inevitable that every man would follow Truth according to his inner lights. 'Indeed, it is his duty to do so' (Iyer 2000: 158). It means that each person should have the humility to see that one could go wrong and examine each step in the path to Truth. As Gandhi put it, in *Young India* (September 1925), 'a man of truth must ever be confident and diffident at the same time, confident in his devotion to truth but humble because of his consciousness of fallibility' (Iyer 2000: 161). Conflicts in differing perspectives of truth have to be resolved, therefore, through dialogue and not force. 'Truth requires dialogue, but at the same time the goal of dialogue is Truth' (Jahanbegloo 2008: 39).

For Gandhi, Ahimsa or Non-violence is deduced from *Satya* or Truth. First, since Satya is the essence of moral values and justice, our social relations have to be guided by Satya, which can give no scope for violence. Secondly, since humans are not perfect, all have to co-operate with each other in seeking Truth, which means we need tolerance, non-violence, understanding, and mutual help towards each other. Since Ahimsa thus becomes a means, a facilitator, in seeking Truth, it is subordinate to Truth. Yet, Gandhi saw so much significance attached to it that it had also supremacy of its own, even if subordinated to Truth. In a world full of violence, absolute non-violence may be impossible to achieve, in the sense that we cannot even live without violence to certain micro life forms, though such violence may not be intentional or consciously perpetrated. That is where search for Truth becomes the primary goal and purity of mind is necessary, according to Gandhi.

In the search for Truth and in wielding Satyagraha as a weapon or even in political career, a practitioner always may face a situation of moral conflict or dilemma. In such cases, Gandhi provides a practical solution, which also shows the orientation of his approach. In a Note of August 1947, he wrote:

I will give you a talisman. Whenever you are in doubt, or when the self becomes too much with you, apply the following test. Recall the face of the poorest and the weakest man whom you may have seen, and ask yourself if the step you contemplate is going to be of any use to him. Will he gain anything by it? Will it restore him to a control over his own life and destiny? In other words, will it lead to swaraj for the hungry and spiritually starving millions? Then you will find your doubts and your self melting away. (as quoted in Mukherjee 1993: 91)

His concept of God could be said to be that of a pure Vedantin, who found no use in idols or rituals. But he was a Vedantin of *Pravritti Marg*, and not *Nivritti Marg*! That is, a Vedantin who did not reject the phenomenal world or '*samsaara*', but accepted it as a field of action to realize God.[4] The practice of his religion was through service. *Seva* or service of humanity gave meaning and substance to his religion, his very life. He has summed up his philosophy thus:

I am here to serve no one else but myself, to find my own self-realization through the service of these village folk. Man's ultimate aim is the realization of God, and all his activities, political, social, religious, have to be guided by the ultimate aim of the vision of God. The immediate service of all human beings becomes a necessary part of the endeavour. (Gandhi 1961: 5)

'To a starving person', he said, 'God will appear in the form of bread alone' (*CWMG* 82: 446). For the poor, bread was God and their moment of Truth. Removing hunger, deprivation, and exploitation was for him his life's motto, more than winning swaraj. This was to be not through mere charity, but with identifying with the poor, helping them to resist exploitation and injustice, and enabling them to live a life of dignity. For Gandhi, being ethical was not just being 'goody goody', but readiness to fight injustice—non-violently, with all heart and energy at one's disposal. He put this conviction into practice through numerous struggles in which he identified himself with the exploited peasants, industrial labour and untouchables. He was emphatic that 'God could be realized only through service' (Gandhi 1927: 132), and also added:

Such service can have no meaning unless one takes pleasure in it. When it is done for show or for fear of public opinion, it stunts the man and crushes his spirit. Service which is rendered without joy helps neither the servant nor the served. But all other pleasures and possessions pale into nothingness before service which is rendered in a spirit of joy. (Gandhi 1927: 145)

Quite early in his spiritual journey-cum-political career, Gandhi believed in the sanctity and dignity of manual labour, not only in rendering seva or service to others, but in one's own day-to-day life. His insisted that all those who worked in his Ashram or community should value this principle in practice. They, including Gandhi, himself took turns in cleaning the latrines themselves. He used this insistence on the sanctity of manual labour to emphasize the fundamental equality of all human beings and in fighting caste hierarchy which devalued manual labour. Even his Ashram's common kitchens were used as a weapon to defy caste hierarchy and food rules. He declared that 'a barber's profession is just as good as the profession of medicine', and demanded equal respect. As Dalton observes, 'The extreme demands that he placed on political workers served not as an impediment but as an inspiration. In this new definition of politics as profession and creed, the performance of daily manual labour as a means to develop personal discipline, integrity, and identification with the peasantry became the litmus test for proof of nationalist citizenship' (Dalton 1998: xi).

Service or Seva was a way of integrating his basic principles of Truth and Non-violence into action. For Gandhi, it was not enough to merely intellectually know Truth, but express it in one's own life, represented by actions. It was thus an activist view of Truth and religion too. Prayers, meditations and so on are only to draw inner strength to perform actions in the service of Truth.

ENDS AND MEANS

No account of the fundamental beliefs and practice of Gandhi would be complete without at least a brief discussion of his stand on Ends and Means. Wily politicians have generally believed in a dichotomy between the two, and asserted that the end justified the means. That is, even if the means are crooked and immoral, they are justified so long as the end or the final outcome is good and desirable. Gandhi firmly rejected this doctrine, though he was a man of practice more than any other thinker.

Gandhi believed in an organic unity between means and ends, and rejected the traditionally assumed dichotomy. Satya represented to him, not an isolated and distant target, but an outcome, determined by the path taken. Unless the path taken is morally justifiable, a path of truth, it cannot lead to Truth. Evil means can never lead to a good end, he believed. As Iyer has insightfully observed, Gandhi derived this truth from the doctrine of Karma (Iyer 2000: 368). According to this doctrine, a bad act, a morally unjust act, inevitably results in bad karma or bad outcomes, while only good acts lead to good outcomes.[5] This is a moral law by which the world is governed, and politics cannot be an exception to this law. The content of Truth cannot be known in advance to the seeker, but she or he can be sure of one thing—the moral sanctity of the path taken determines the outcome, whether it is private life or politics. This was the major reason why he did not believe in violence as a solution to any problem, and relied on non-violence. This was also the major reason why he rejected communism as a doctrine or ideology, though he believed in social justice, the equality of human beings, and in the dignity and responsibility of each and every individual. That is also why he rejected prozelytization and propagation of religions through coercion, fraudulent means, and hatred towards other religions.

GANDHI IN THE FACE OF MULTIPLICITY OF RELIGIONS

It is this belief in reasoning as well as in Truth and Non-violence, which made him eschew any sectarianism in his religion. Mere 'tolerance' is not what really captures Gandhi's approach to other religions. He said, 'I have advanced from tolerance to equal respect for all religions' (*CWMG* 56: 155). In fact, he had advanced even further beyond 'equal respect' to 'sharing the best with one another, thus adding to the sum total of human effort to reach God' (quoted in Chatterjee 2005: 336). What if religions conflict? He thought that the criteria of non-violence and reason would suffice (ibid.). But he also stressed that in matters of moral principles, there is no conflict between religions.

He honestly put this precept into practice early in his life. As a result, he reflected a multi-religious character in himself. The difficulty of pinning down Gandhi's religions affiliation was described by Rev. J.J. Doke as early as 1909:

A few days ago I was told that 'he is a Buddhist'. Not long since, a Christian newspaper described him as 'Christian Mohammedan', an extra-ordinary mixture indeed. Others imagine that he worships idols. ... I question whether any system of religion can absolutely hold him. His views are too closely allied to Christianity to be entirely Hindu; and too deeply saturated with Hinduism to be called Christian, while his sympathies are so wide and catholic, that one would imagine that he has reached a point where the formulae of sects are meaningless. (Iyer 2000: 20)

Gandhi's religion was inclusive because as he believed, no single religion was perfect in itself to merit exclusive adherence and one has to learn from all. From Hinduism, he learnt relentless pursuit of Truth as the basic goal in life, and also giving respect to other religions as alternative paths to Truth. From Buddhism, Jainism, as well as Hinduism, he took the principles of Non-violence, self-restraint, and compassion to all living creatures. From Christianity, he imbibed the principles of suffering love and service to fellow human beings. From Islam, he must have taken the principle of equality. From Semitic religions, Vedantic Hinduism and Zoroastrianism, he accepted the principle of oneness of God. From Sikhism, he must have been inspired to resist tyrannical authority with moral courage. It is not that these religions did not have common features between them. They did have and they were not exclusive. Emphasis on ethics, for example was common to all religions, which formed the crux of his religiosity. Nevertheless, certain distinctive (not necessarily exclusive) features of each religion impressed and inspired him. His genius lay in combining these features within his philosophy of life to guide his action, in a seamless and creative blend. By setting his own example, he showed that learning from other religions and living an active life guided by them was perfectly possible. But this was only if one is willing to open one's mind, refusing to live in a narrow pigeonhole of parochialism.

In spite of the fact that Gandhi's vision of religion transcended individual specific religions, he had to encounter the real world situation which consisted of multiplicity of religions with separate followers. He not only accepted but valued multiplicity of faiths. He was once asked why if there is only one God, there should not be only one religion. He promptly replied, a tree has million leaves; there can be as many religions as humans, but all have the root in God (Fischer 1998: 584).

To appreciate Gandhi's stand in the face of this situation, we may imagine three alternative ways of encountering multiplicity of faiths, and see Gandhi's choice:

1. Only one of the religions, usually the religion of the majority, is recognized as official or state religion. Only this would have the right to propagate and convert others to this religion. Other religions would have the right of worship according to their faith, and even preach to its followers, but no right to propagate and convert others to their own religion. All religions other than the official are *tolerated*, but would have no equal rights.

2. All religions have equal rights to worship, preach, propagate and convert, each sticking to one's own faith fanatically, but allowing no interaction. There is keen awareness of the boundaries of and identities based on religion, and these boundaries are jealously guarded.

3. All have equal rights, but there is no fanatical observance of clear demarcation of boundaries. There is encouragement for interaction, for not only *respecting* each other, but also *learning* from each other, without any bar on imbibing values, traditions, and customs of others into one's own religion. There is no fanaticism, even if there is no syncretism.

The last one is Gandhi's path, which could be stated as inclusive, but without any intention of wiping out religious identities. He preached it, and also practised it.

The first milestone on this path was in convincing people of the repeated teaching of the sants of medieval age in India that God of all religions is one and the same. Whatever conceptual differences existed among different religions about God, melted into insignificance once we realize that God who created Christians could not have been different from the one who created Muslims or from the one who created Hindus. If that were not so, who created atheists? A Christian or Hindu God cannot be invoked to kill Muslims any more than Allah can be invoked to kill non-Muslims. To say that only the God of my religion is true and others are false gods hardly improves matters, when everyone can feel so. Gandhi declared that no religion has monopoly of God or Truth.

Though he frequently declared himself to be a Hindu, even a *Sanatani* Hindu, he also made it clear that his Hinduism was no narrow creed. By 'Sanatani Hinduism', he did not mean orthodox or conservative Hinduism, but a Hinduism which is based on everlasting universal moral values. He defined Hinduism as a constant search for Truth, which meant total rejection of dogma, and acceptance of faith in moral values as well as of reasoning. Even while asserting himself to be a Hindu, he could have the freedom to say that he would at the same time follow the lofty principles of all other religions too. He again and again reminded that Hinduism never regarded other religions as false. In his reply to a question by S. Radhakrishnan in 1935, he wrote, 'My religion is Hinduism which for me is the religion of humanity and includes the best of all the religions known to me' (Iyer 2007: 158). He explained, 'The Hinduism of my conception is no narrow creed. It is a grand evolutionary process as ancient as time, and embraces the teachings of Zoroaster, Moses, Christ, Mohammad, Nanak, and other Prophets that I could name' (*CWMG* 76: 375). Even in his early formative years, he had gone through not only the Gita, but also the Bible and the Quran. At his prayer meetings, recitations of all the three scriptures were a must. When communal riots broke out, he hardly sided with the Hindus, and spared no efforts to assuage the feelings of minorities and to douse the communal conflagration. For this he did not hesitate to undertake indefinite fasts risking his life. He had intimate friends and followers from all communities who trusted and respected him to no end.

By traditional criteria, Gandhi did not belong to any single religion exclusively. He did not exalt any religion including Hinduism as above all others. As Jordens says, 'What he did exalt above all religions ... was his own individual concept of the essence of religion: a religion of naked truth and non-violence, totally stripped of all cultural, historical and sociological, ritual and theological vestments' (Jordens 1998: 158). In this pure form, he could see the essence of all religions as well, having no scope for discord.

He played an important role in evolving India's own definition of secularism as equal respect for all religions and no discrimination against any, as against the western definition of keeping religion out of public sphere totally. Though he favoured politics being guided by religion, it was not in a sectarian sense of any particular religion, but religion in the sense of commitment to moral values and with equal regard for all religions. But if religion is viewed in the usual narrow sectarian perspective of individual or specific religions, he preferred separation of the state from religion. He certainly did not want the state to favour one particular religion and discriminate against others. He stoutly opposed any notion of making India a Hindu state, with all his heart.[6] That is why he consciously groomed Jawaharlal Nehru, a committed secularist, as the would-be Prime

Minister of India. He also kept a good distance from Hindu nationalist organizations such as the Rashtriya Swayamsevak Sangh (RSS) and the Hindu Mahasabha and their ideology. Yet he did not take a secular plank in the western sense, as he wanted to elevate the moral plane of the state and politics, and for this, sought the help of the common ethical heritage of humanity, derived from the wealth of diverse religions. As an astute politician who could feel the pulse of his country, he may also have felt that secularism in western sense could not take roots in the Indian soil, but secularism in the sense of equal regard for all religions had a much better chance and was a more positive concept. But this was not a mere matter of tactic. As has been perceptively observed, 'Mahatma Gandhi's mission was not to politicize religion, but to spiritualize politics' (Jahanbegloo 2008: 27). For this, his notion of secularism suited him very well.

GANDHI ON RELIGIOUS CONVERSIONS

Gandhi never had the intention of starting or founding a religion of his own freed from the defects of all religions. He could see that such an attempt would simply lead to yet one more religion, with its own limitations which would only increase over time as happened with all religions. Any idea of combining all religions into one artificial religion also was not his goal. He rejected the idea that it is possible to select the best religion among the available and convert to it if it is other than the one in which she or he is both. He could see that all religions had limitations, though all also had good things to offer to each and every one. Gandhi's idea was that whatever be one's religion, one has to adhere to it, but with complete freedom to reject any of its defects that objective reasoning guided by universal moral values points out, and to accept any good and appealing feeling of others' religions which again similar reasoning points out. When this is the aim, it was only logical and natural for him to oppose the idea of religions conversion as absolutely untenable. He believed that when assimilation from other religions and enriching one's own is possible, 'it cuts the ground from beneath the "need" for conversion, in that elements from other religions can be incorporated in one's own' (Chatterjee 2005: 319). Any competitive attempt at conversions and claims of superiority of one or the other would, he feared, was not only a sign of arrogance but would also vitiate mutual tolerance and understanding between religions. Religions conversions would only reinforce boundaries between religions and strengthen divisive characteristics of religions. He wanted a religious environment which would unite people, instead of dividing them as religions have done all along. He was contemptuous about the greed of missionaries to add to the numbers of their religion; as such greed only prevented religions from ushering in harmony and solace, but only increased strife and violence through divisive and destructive competition. The process of conversion was almost invariably preceded by calumny against one religion pitted against another, and followed by alienation and disruption of family. This violated both the principles of Truth and Non-violence. He was worried that 'proselytizing efforts demoralize society, create suspicions and bitterness, and retard the all round progress of society' (*CWMG* 65: 159). He went to the extent of saying: 'If I had the power and would legislate, should certainly stop all proselytizing. It is the cause of much avoidable conflict' (*CWMG* 61: 46).[7]

Even while he condemned the methods used by the missionaries, particularly the slander they used, Gandhi was also unsparing in his criticism of parochial tendencies within Hinduism and the enormous gap between its lofty principles and actual practice. More than winning political freedom for India, his priority was to reform the Hindu society, particularly to abolish untouchability, exploitation, and inequality, and to care for the poor and treat them with dignity, respect, and love.

Concluding the essay, we may observe that Gandhi's religion was not one of a relaxed and romantic poet-philosopher, inspired by gazing at the beauty of the dawn, or the mystery of distant stars deep in the night sky, or the ever moving waves of the ocean. It was a religion born of empathy with the hungry peasants, exploited labour and the victims of tyranny and oppression. Gandhi's religion or spirituality was extremely practical. It pervaded the personal and the public, individual, and the social and the political. In aiming to uplift the weakest of the weak, and in changing the heart of the brutest of the brute, an individual could always find fulfilment and realization of Truth—the God. Personal salvation was not something to be sought in private isolation, but in the arena of the world, struggling against poverty, hunger, tyranny, and injustice. It did not matter to him by what name such a religion was called—Hinduism, Buddhism, Christianity, or Islam—for it included them all. It was basically a religion for all humanity, a religion of humanism. He practised before he preached it. And thereby he showed that it was possible to live by it.

A great irony that haunts us is that we respect Gandhi with all formality, but do not care for his teachings. If respect for him means at least a little implicit intention to practise what he preached, then we are not living up to it. Yet, Gandhi will continue to influence us, or at least haunt us with all his soul-force. When he died to his assassin's bullets and was laid to rest, Sarojini Naidu, eminent poet and follower of Gandhi, did not pray as usual that his soul may rest in peace. Instead, she pleaded, 'O my father, do not rest! Do not rest in peace! Give us the strength to fulfil our promise!' (Payne 1997: 601).

NOTES

1. These books, especially Jordens 1998, have dealt with in detail how Gandhi's religious outlook took shape over the years, and the different influences on it. This task is not attempted in the essay here.

2. Gandhi observed in a letter of 1946 that 'Gandhism is a meaningless word for me. An ism follows the propounder of a system. I am not one ...' (Iyer 2007: 62).

3. Gandhi asserted, 'Every formula of every religion has, in this age of reason, to submit to the acid test of reason and universal justice if it is to ask for universal assent. Error can claim no exemption even if it can be supported by the scriptures of the world' (*Young India* 26 February 1929, p. 74).

4. Of the three main paths mentioned in the Gita—action (*karma*), knowledge (*jnana*), and devotion (*bhakti*), Gandhi favoured the path of action. Not that he ignored other paths, but he gave primacy to action, buttressed by knowledge and commitment or devotion. 'The more he studied the Gita, the more he realized that it supported a world-affirming spirituality' (Parel 2006: 190).

5. The doctrine of karma has been wrongly interpreted as a doctrine of fate or destiny. For a discussion, see Nadkarni (2008: 41–56).

6. The most poignant irony of the Indian subcontinent has been expressed by Louis Fischer, Gandhi's eminent biographer: 'The irreligious Jinnah wished to build a religious state. Gandhi, wholly religious, wanted a secular state' (Fischer 1998: 515).

7. For a more detailed discussion of Gandhi's stand on religious conversions, see Nadkarni (2003: 227–35).

3 Ethics and Development*

Economics which departs from or is opposed to ethics is no good and should be renounced.

—M.K. Gandhi
(*CWMG* 81: 436)

Whatever we take, we are snatching from the mouth of others. Therefore, whenever we acquire anything, let us see that it is really needed and that our wants are as few as possible.

—M.K. Gandhi
(*CWMG* 81: 436)

AT THE INDIVIDUAL LEVEL

Mahatma Gandhi firmly believed that ethics and economics should go together. If they do not, it is the economics opposed to ethics that has to be rejected, and not ethics. This does not mean that one should give up any goal of economic betterment altogether, but only that this goal has to be pursued in a morally justifiable way. What he decried was what he called as Mammon worship. Gandhi conceded the need for economic betterment even at the personal level, particularly for those left behind or deprived, but he stressed that it should never be forgotten that the basic purpose of human life is self-development—morally and spiritually. This required,

---

*Based on lecture given at Professor M. Madaiah Felicitation Endowment, University of Mysore, March 2010.

according to him, an outlook, which eschews a single-minded pursuit of economic betterment in isolation, to the exclusion of other aspects of development of human personality. It also required recognition that individual development can take place only in a harmonious relationship with others in a spirit of mutual concern and regard.

Traditional micro-economics which was the bedrock of welfare economics and dealt mainly with the behaviour of the consumer and the firm, had a narrow and static perspective. It focused only on the present, ignoring the issue of long term economic betterment of either the consumer or the firm. Krishna Bharadwaj, therefore, called traditional neoclassical micro-economics as shopping bag economics.[1] That is how it pushed aside ethics from its theory. But ethical issues can arise even in a static setting of micro-economics, and emerge more prominently in the issues of economic betterment of individuals and firms, and of economic development at the collective level.

The goal of economic betterment is relevant both at the individual or micro levels, and also at the collective levels—village, community, country, and even the world. At the collective level, it is generally called economic development. Development, however, is a broader term which is not confined to economic betterment, and includes human development, cultural development and—importantly, for our purpose —moral development too. Development at the collective level is more than a mere summation of economic betterment at the individual level. Collective issues like social justice, respect for human rights, inequality, public health, public amenities, and infrastructure emerge prominently in development, in addition to livelihood and economic betterment at the individual level. Individuals of course have to participate in collective development both as agents or drivers of it and also as its beneficiaries, as Gandhi perceived. People are not passive recipients from the top but have responsibilities, and without their being proactive, no meaningful development can take place. Gandhi saw the state playing mainly a facilitating role, though it can also be an initiator in due consultation with people. He was clear that this active role of people was both in economic and ethical aspects. Neither the state nor the people can set aside ethics in pursuing development.

My endeavour here is twofold: a) to discuss how development as a goal, whether at the individual or collective level, is meaningful and satisfying only when it has a significant ethical or humanist content; and b) to argue that the means of development, especially economic development, should also be ethical or morally acceptable. These two issues are highly inter-linked and are discussed together, but at the individual and collective levels separately. I shall also try to show that the integration between ethics and development promotes a reciprocal and mutually reinforcing impact. To be moral does not require being poor too.

Contrary to the view of certain western scholars like Max Weber, Indian religion did permit and even encouraged economic betterment at both personal and collective levels.[2] Economic betterment was called as pursuit of *Artha*, one of the main goals of human beings called *Purushaarthas*, the other three goals being *Dharma, Kaama,* and *Moksha.* Dharma in the sense of moral responsibility or moral development was not only a goal in itself, but was also a guiding criterion for the other three goals, including Artha. The pursuit of both economic betterment (Artha) and sensual enjoyment (Kaama) had to be according to dharma, that is, ethically acceptable.

The *Rigveda*, several millennia earlier, had made this quite clear. In its Tenth *Mandala* and Thirty-first *Sukta*, the second verse says:

> *Parichin marto dravinam mamanyaad*
> *Ritasya pathaa namasaa vivaaset /*
> *Uta svena kratunaa samvadeta*
> *Shreyaansam daksham manasaa jagrabhyaat //*

(Let a man or woman ponder well on wealth and earn it by the path of moral law or truth, and with humility. Let him/her take counsel with his/her own conscience and heartily gain justifiable prosperity).

In spite of being very ancient in origin, the verse is remarkable for its contemporary relevance. It does show that earning wealth is allowed, but it is subject to several qualifications or conditions. Wealth is not taken to be coming thoughtlessly. One has to consciously ponder (*parichin*) over in what form and how it is to be earned by the path of moral law or truth (*ritam*), and not by dishonest means. It has to be earned with humility (*namasaa*) and not arrogantly, since success depends on the Grace of God and owes it to the society of which one is a member, for making it possible. Consulting one's own conscience (*kratu*) also is important in deciding the ways in which it is earned. Once these qualifications are kept in mind, one can earn and enjoy wealth heartily (*manasaa*) and gain justifiable or upright (*daksham*) success or prosperity (*shreyaansam*). Though ritam in the *Rigveda* meant moral law, the *Dharmashaastra*s which came later, made it clear that wealth has to be earned according to the law of the land too, apart from being ethically correct.

Very interestingly, the Shantiparva (8.23) of Mahabharata points out a circular influence between Dharma and Artha. Artha has, of course to be earned according to Dharma, but even Dharma cannot be sustained in a situation of poverty. On the other hand, Dharma flows out of wealth and prosperity like a river out of a mountain (*dhanaaddhi dharmah sravati shailaadapi nadee tathaa*). Unless wealth is created, it cannot be distributed. You can hardly find poverty glorified in Hindu scriptures. Gandhi advocated voluntary self-control on wants, and simple living, but never glorified involuntary poverty. Neither Hindu scriptures nor Gandhi ever meant that a poor person becomes a sinner automatically, or that a wealthy person becomes automatically good irrespective of how his wealth was earned. The point is that even as ethics is necessary for the means employed for economic betterment, economic betterment in its own way tends to promote ethics. I will have more to say on this circular or reciprocal influence even with regard to development at the collective level.

Gandhi added a few more qualifications. A person earning wealth does so in a society consisting of other persons too and in interaction with them. This requires adjusting to others' needs, which is inconsistent with 'an economics that inculcates Mammon worship and enables the strong to amass wealth as the expense of the weak'. Such economics is 'a false and dismal science' (quoted in Ganguli 1973: 60). Gandhi's fear of ethics being separated from economics was hardly unjustified. Though all religions were emphatic on honest means of pursuing wealth and moderation of self-interest, the picture changed with the publication of Adam Smith's *The Wealth of Nations* in 1776. Henceforth, it is not ethics but self-interest which seemed to hold the society together, with self-interest promoting competition, competition promoting markets, and markets promoting provisioning of goods and services and creation of wealth. Markets in this theory are also believed to be providing automatic correctives to greed and other excesses. As history has shown there are serious problems in this theory. Competition and markets need not be fair and perfect, and can be vulnerable to manipulation in an unequal society. Markets also lead to periodic crises. But Smith's book did lead to an ideology that glorified self-interest and Mammon worship which has continued to hold its own sway. The scams during the recent recession in the world economy and India's own scams in 2010 bear a testimony to the sway of this ideology which separates ethics from economics. Gandhi does not reject all economics, but insists on its being tempered by ethics. He certainly frowns upon economic processes of one's betterment or even the nation's economic development that merely promotes concentration of wealth among the rich and marginalizing and immiserizing the poor. This amounts to violence, and the process of economic betterment has to be essentially non-violent. But even the process of preventing concentration of wealth has to be non-violent. He has a threefold solution for this: 'First, a man would reduce his wants to a minimum, bearing in mind the poverty of India. (Second), his earnings would be free of dishonesty. The desire for speculation would be renounced. ... (Thirdly), there should be trusteeship of the wealthy for superfluous wealth possessed by them'. (Ganguli 1973: 63).

Though earning and even accumulating wealth was allowed subject to the means being ethically acceptable, the enjoyment of this wealth only for personal use to satisfy endless personal wants was condemned. Gandhi often quoted the Gita describing a person doing so as a thief. One is supposed to share one's wealth for others' benefit selflessly and this altruism was also emphasized as dharma. That is why Shantiparva of Mahabharata says that Dharma flows from wealth, as a river springs forth from a mountain. Gandhi developed this idea as trusteeship: one holds wealth in excess of personal needs as a trust for the benefit of the society in which one lives, and the whole world can be one's society for this purpose. Thereby Gandhi reconciled the need to provide incentives for personal effort and enterprise with the social purpose of meeting society's needs. Thus, it is not enough for wealth to be created ethically. It is part of ethics to spend it also altruistically, unselfishly for social needs, or for the benefit of others who may be less fortunate.

If the rich did not act in the spirit of trusteeship as advised by Gandhi, he was not at all averse to taxing the rich to reduce inequality in income and wealth and use the proceeds for the uplift of the poor. However, he had his own reservations against a too dominant state which may tend to be violent, corrupt, and suppress individual initiatives and freedom. He preferred private individuals and institutions doing their best in social work, though the state may play a complementary role to address the gaps that remain. Though non-governmental organizations (NGOs) and private trusts in India have already proved their capacity to do exemplary work in social work focused on the poor and the deprived, our taxation policy is not yet attuned to encouraging them much. Though there is tax exemption on income donated to recognized charitable institutions, the exemption is only up to 50 per cent of income so donated, and not 100 per cent—the full exemption given only in the case of direct government sponsored funds like the Prime Minister's Relief Fund. The Income Tax Department can certainly keep a watchful eye on charitable institutions eligible for relief, and review their eligibility periodically as is being done. But having been so cautious, there is no case for a literally half-hearted tax-exemption. To make the donations more attractive to give, there is a case for giving full exemption for donations to approved charitable trusts and lifting the ceiling of 10 per cent of adjusted gross income. There is similarly a case for tax rates to be increased on non-donated and non-invested incomes beyond a certain limit, taking note of special needs of the persons involved.

Partnership between the state and private sector in social development is not only possible but also beneficial. In *The Power of Social Innovation,* Stephen Goldsmith mentions that society is on the threshold of the fourth stage of how it addresses problems like poverty, illiteracy, illness, providing employment and earning opportunities to the poor and other specific classes like ex-prisoners, helping youngsters to stay in school, and even helping them for a leap to higher education (see *The Economist,* 14 August 2010: 56–7). In the first stage, caring for people was left mainly to families and charities. In the second, the welfare state emerged, and private efforts were crowded out. In the third stage, a partnership between the state and also the private sector emerged mainly through outsourcing. But problems like the state becoming too prescriptive and focused on cost-cutting, and also corruption weakened the possible impact of meaures for social development in the third stage. In the fourth stage innovations in partnership between the state and private sector appeared. One of them, tried both in USA and Britain, was to invite the private sector to undertake projects in social development and give them an attractive return of certain percentage on the capital invested by them on these projects commensurate with the impact (ibid.). The advantage of such an arrangement is that instead of the government stretching out its scarce resources, resources of the private sector can be   mobilized for social development in desired channels, and more cost-effectively too than can be achieved by state machinery.

At the Collective Level

Recognition of the process of economic development at the collective level began to be registered in literature since the Industrial Revolution, particularly from the eighteenth century onwards. The significance of economic development at the collective level consists in the fact that as a result of this process total income and total wealth begin to increase, allowing greater share of the national cake among different sections of the people. When no such development takes place, the only way an enterprising individual can increase his wealth is at the expense of others. But an increase in the total income or wealth, allows such a person to create wealth without having to necessarily make other persons poorer. This is an ethical plus point in favour of economic development, even when seen narrowly in money or income terms.

In practice, however, the process of economic development was never so innocent, so innocuous. Industrialization which was the main form of economic development to begin with became a butt for criticism right from the beginning of nineteenth century. The criticism was on aesthetic, humanistic, environmental, and ethical grounds. Even in agriculture, there were adverse indirect effects on the third parties—what economists refer to as negative externalities. For example, though the Enclosure Movement in Britain increased productivity in agriculture, it also considerably reduced the access of cowherds and shepherds to grazing lands. The landlords became richer at the expense of the livelihoods of these graziers. In industry, the negative externalities became much more conspicuous. Ramachandra Guha has documented how nature loving romanticist English poets like William Wordsworth bemoaned the loss of beauty of the countryside (Guha 2000: 10–17). John Ruskin (1819–1900) in his celebrated book—*Unto the Last,* and also other works deplored the devastation caused to the countryside by industrialization and railroad expansion. Ruskin was also concerned about how artisans were being displaced by industry, and some were becoming richer making others poorer thorough their 'Mammon worship'. He was not just a writer but an activist too. He launched campaigns against rail road expansion, and set up a guild that ran farms and craft shops 'which stressed self-sufficiency and simplicity, producing food and weaving cloth for their own use' (Guha 2000: 15). One can find echoes of Ruskin's thought in Gandhi's first book, *Hind Swaraj* (1910, reproduced in Mukherjee 1993: 1–66), though Gandhi worried more about the human costs than aesthetic costs. Ruskin was not alone to criticize industrialization in the nineteenth century. Several English novelists made it their theme to depict the horrible living conditions of the poor, particularly the factory labour—work time going up to twelve hours or more, with little to eat, unsanitary habitats, lack of attention during illness, and no dignity and any charm left in their lives. This situation shocked Karl Marx (1818–1883) and

Friedrich Engels (1820–1895) which moved them to launch the most powerful attack so far on private profit oriented capitalist development. Theirs was essentially a humanist approach. Through their voluminous and most influential works, they pointed out how independent artisans were turned either into exploited proletariat or unemployed labour, how they were alienated, and how a few accumulated wealth at the expense of many whom they exploited and immiserized. They attributed environmental problems of industrialization also to the capitalist character of the economic development process, which was so obsessed with quick surplus generation and capital accumulation that human and environmental costs were ignored. Marx and Engels also showed a way out of these problems—through socialism and communism, which they believed that a united class of industrial proletariat was destined to achieve under its leadership with the co-operation of other exploited sections of the society like peasants and the unemployed.

The historical experience of the socialist countries—wrongly called in common parlance as communist, showed, however, that their process of economic development had even greater human and environmental costs than capitalist countries. Theoretically, the socialist state should have taken better care of issues like social justice, human rights, and environmental health than private enterprise dominated capitalist states, but in practice they proved to be worse. Gandhi had an insight into violence inherent in the so-called communist regimes and tried to chart out his own alternative. The actual human costs during the Cultural Revolution in China and the Pot Pol regime in Cambodia in terms of not only loss of democratic freedoms but in terms of basic rights to life and property proved to be even greater than what Gandhi ever imagined, though countries like Cuba have had much more humane and egalitarian states. The point is that the state dominated communist countries had the same economic compulsions in a highly competitive international capitalist order as the market dominated capitalist countries themselves, and they did not quite succeed in rejecting capitalist values, particularly, economism.

What is economism? At the individual level, it means a value perspective which regards earning income as the most supreme goal of one's life, disregarding others values like love and altruism. An executive devoting twelve or more hours of the day to business and unable to give even a little time for his family and for the care of others is an example of this economism. We have to distinguish between the economism of the rich from the economism of the poor. The poor may be compelled to concentrate very much on earning some livelihood and devote most of their time to it, because their productivity or remuneration for their work is extremely low. They have no choice. This is not the case with the economism of the rich. They may also believe that they too have no choice, but it is self-imposed. It is also necessary to clarify that having a profit motive in an economic enterprise by itself is not economism. After all, the very rationale of an economic enterprise or activity—be it production or trade, is to make a surplus over and above the costs. To that extent, economic efficiency is very important. But what transforms a legitimate profit motive to an obsessive economism is the tendency to earn excess profits, particularly through exploiting the weakness of the other party, through cheating, through hoarding and speculation, and such other unethical means.

Economism at the collective level includes economism at the individual level, but gains a deeper and wider ethical significance. It is the exploitation of the weak made possible by free unbridled economism at the individual levels that transforms itself into inequality and injustice at the collective level, with widening disparities. Even if in an overall growth process the poor do not become poorer than before, they certainly become much more poor compared with the rich. This is because economism operating in the economy ensures that the poor get a smaller share than the rich out of the incremental incomes or wealth creation.

Des Gasper lists a few features of economism, which are pertinent to the nature of economic development. They are summarized here:

- Primacy to the economic sphere;
- Separation of the economy and economic considerations from other spheres and other considerations (to ensure primacy for the former);
- Primacy to the value of economic efficiency, ignoring other values like social justice, human rights, and environmental sustainability;
- Most or even all of life is understood, valued, and managed in terms of economic calculation;
- Gross National Product (GNP) or a modification of it is accepted as the primacy, if not the only, indicator of the achievement and progress of the country;
- The expectation that 'the economy should be managed according to its own supposed inherent technical requirements and without political interference' (Gasper 2004: 80–1).

Most of the ills of modern economic development are the direct and indirect result of narrow and non-ethical character of economism and free reign to market forces. This has created serious inequalities both within and between countries. Vandana Shiva calls modern economic development as a 'continuation of the process of colonization; it became an extension of the project of wealth creation, which was based on the exploitation or exclusion of women (of the west and non-west), or the exploitation and degradation of nature, and on the exploitation and erosion of other cultures' (Shiva 2001: 285). She draws attention to R. Bahro's distinction between conditions of subsistence and condition of misery due to deprivation, and refuses to consider the former as a condition of poverty. 'Subsistence economies which satisfy basic needs through self-provisioning are not poor in the sense of being deprived. Yet the ideology of development declares them so because they do not participate overwhelmingly in the market economy and do not consume commodities produced for and distributed through the market even though they might be satisfying these needs through self-provisionig mechanisms' (Shiva 2001: 291–2). She quotes in this context Gustavo Esteva who said, 'My people are tired of development; they just want to live' (Shiva 2001: 294). Vandana Shiva feels terribly concerned at the way colonialism has taken new forms in the garb of development, by stealing the Third World's bio-diversity and even colonizing the seed, robbing its fertility and self-generating capacity, and self-reliance of the farmers in respect of the seed (Dumble 2001: 317). Shiva is not merely a thinker but also a staunch activist and is on the Gandhian path both in thought and deed. We will get back to her in the next chapter in the context of environmental ethics.

Gasper, however, believes that by using development as an intervention, state can counter destructive aspects of economism as well as market forces (Gasper 2004: 228), and make development ethically more acceptable. The question is what ethical principles can guide the state in pursuing development. Gandhi insisted on freedom as a necessary condition for development in a real sense, that is, self-development and and self-realization. He also stressed other values like equality, fraternity, and compassion, particularly for the deprived. A pursuit of economic development disregarding these principles would be demonic (Roy 1984: 123, 193). A problem even with ethical principles when applied to public policy is that they may not necessarily lead to a single unique solution in specific situations or cases. Different people, equally honest, may have different views. Public discussion, or in Amartya Sen's words 'public reasoning', helps in arriving at some consensus. This is one among several reasons why free democracy which makes it possible and honest leadership count very much in development issues and public policy (Sen 2009: xii, xiii).

Jeremy Bentham (1748–1832) formulated a principle called utilitarianism, which has influenced economics even now. This has been usually stated briefly as the criterion of 'greatest happiness of the greatest number'. Happiness (including avoidance of unhappiness) has been a natural goal of all creatures, but Bentham tried to measure happiness in terms of utility or use of commodities and that is how this approach came to be known as utilitarianism. Every person tries to maximize utilities or pleasure, and minimize pain or disutilities. For utilitarians, economics is the science of how this is done by individuals and at the collective level. But when we try to change *is* into *should be*, and use utilitarianism as a guiding ethical principle in development issues, some formidable problems emerge.

First is that utilitarianism makes no allowances for differences in the quality of pleasure or utilities, except insofar as they can be reflected in the market in terms of demand based on purchasing power, for example, it would not bother about which pleasure is higher between smoking and eating a fruit, or about which commodity needs to be given a higher weight—whether one is needed by a rich person or by a poor needy person. Hinduism makes a distinction between momentary pleasure (*preyas*) and lasting or durable happiness (*shreyas*). Utilitarianism makes no such distinction and claims to be value-neutral. A big problem arises when different people value (in terms of utilities) different sources of happiness, say, commodities, differently. The market solves this problem in terms of purchasing power. Those commodities will tend to be produced more which are demanded more, backed by more purchasing power. When there are distressing inequalities, this is not a satisfactory solution from the point of view of social justice. Structure of production then reflects wants more than needs. That is why we cannot leave everything to be decided by the market forces, so that needs as distinguished from wants get due attention.

Second, a great problem with the principle greatest happiness for the greatest number is that the two greatest may not agree! To illustrate this, let us assume that happiness is measured by income (as economists usually do), and there are two alternative economic policies—S and C, approximately (if not strictly) suggesting socialist and capitalist approaches, respectively. Assume again for the sake of illustration that S raises the income per person per day by Rs 10, for a thousand persons, the total income raised for all persons together being Rs 10,000. Policy C on the other hand raises the income per person per day by Rs 100, but only for 200 persons, the total income raised for all together being Rs 20,000. This is how a dichotomy can arise between the two greatest, and can pose a formidable dilemma to resolve. Policy S benefits the greatest number, but policy C produces the highest income. Though it is not a fully satisfactory solution to the dilemma, economists have generally preferred policy C, taking that it is more important to raise incomes to the maximum first and then take care of distribution. And that is how inequity in society gets aggravated.

Third, the greatest number need not cover all people. Even if a majority may be covered, a minority may be left behind. An important principle in ethics is that every individual is important and equal to others as a human being. If a minority is ignored by development, merely because it is a minority, it will amount to great injustice.

Economists like Amartya Sen have been countering narrow econ- omism of concentrating only on income maximization, and trying to add content and extra meaning to the process of economic development so that it is morally acceptable. For example, though he conceded that it is important to increase food production, he showed that hunger is often due to lack of entitlements to food, rather than shortage of food supply. The crux of the problem is to put adequate entitlements into the hands of the deprived. Sen looks upon development as expansion of Freedom—a variety of freedoms in fact, shifting the focus from income and production of commodities to human beings. Not that he ignores income or the markets, for he does acknowledge that income is necessary to realize certain freedoms, like freedom from hunger and deprivation, and that even the freedom to enter the market is itself an important freedom in its own right. Freedom gives choice, particularly choice of opportunities. It is not the formal freedom of equal opportunities that he stresses, but equalization of capabilities by maximizing the capabilities of those at the bottom, otherwise providing equal opportunities would have no meaning. He insists that income and markets are not ends, but have only instrumental values. He advocates attending to the objective of correcting conspicuous examples of injustice, such as hunger, ill health, illiteracy, poverty, and unemployment, rather than treating intervening instrumental values as ends (Sen 2000). Sen is critical of the tendency of philosophers to get lost on 'transcendental' conceptualizations or grand theories of justice; instead, he says, it is more fruitful to directly attend to such manifest injustices like hunger (Sen 2009).[3] For Sen, 'enhancement of human freedom is both the main object and the primary means of development (Sen 2000: 53). He adds, 'the instrumental roles of freedom include several distinct but interrelated components, such as economic facilities, political freedoms, social opportunities, transparency guarantees and protective security' (ibid.). To ensure these freedoms would require developing and supporting 'a plurality of institutions, including democratic systems, legal mechanisms and market structures, educational and health provisions, media and communication facilities and so on' (ibid.). In other words, economic development is not a one-dimensional growth of GNP, but development on a variety of dimensions all of which have a direct impact in terms of enhancing the freedom and capabilities of human beings. However, more than the mere plurality of dimensions of development, what counts is the shift from non-ethical economism to ethical humanism as the main ingredient of development goals as well as the strategies. Development processes as well as ends have to be guided and evaluated by values such as non-violence, freedom, fairness, justice, and democracy.

Economic development has not, however, worked towards ensuring social justice, environmental sustainability, and even transparency, both within and between countries. Thanks to the efforts of economists like Amartya Sen and Mahbub ul Haq, the world has now been moving from narrow economism to human development as its goal. The focus now is on comprehensive or holistic development, covering all aspects like education, health, social security, predictability in legal regimes, transparency, and democratic freedoms, which enrich the welfare and dignity of all human beings instead of only a few, rather than on the growth of only national income which tends to bypass many. This has brought ethics into not only evaluating but also planning proper development strategies (Gasper 2004).

The first concrete step in evaluating and even measuring development in this broader perspective was taken by the UNDP's publication of Human Development Reports (HDRs). The first report was prepared under the leadership of a Pakistani Economist, Mahbub ul Haq in 1990. The HDRs do not ignore national income per capita, but have also been taking into account three social indicators—life expectancy at birth, adult literacy rate, and enrolment ratio in education. Gross Domestic Product (GDP) is taken for national income and is adjusted for Purchasing Power Parity (PPP) differences. Together they are combined into Human Development Index (HDI). The methodology of construction of HDI has been undergoing changes over the years and when they occur, the HDI for earlier years is recalculated so as to provide comparison. Presently, instead of adult literacy rate (which is approaching 100 per cent in many countries), expected years of schooling, and mean years of schooling (both corrected for repetition rates) are taken in the HDR for 2010. HDRs and World Development Reports of the World Bank also give data on inequality in income distribution and poverty, infant mortality, material mortality, access to improved water sources and sanitation, and carbon dioxide emissions per capita. Women's development is also assessed separately by HDI indicators. We have thus a more balanced picture of our development achievements on several fronts, with an increase in per capita income being only one of them. This is set against reduction in poverty and other achievements in human development including women's status and empowerment. We have thus a better information base to evaluate our development processes and outcome now than ever before,[4] which should spur us to right action. The remaining tasks on the human development front are still huge especially in India, though we have been making a steady progress, as we noted in the last section of Chapter 2. An interesting aspect of the importance of improving human development is that in doing so, we also reduce inequality significantly, as the HDR for 2010 has shown.

Respect for human rights is an important dimension of ethical development, which is not reflected in HDI. Suppressing human rights in the name of fast economic development, defeats the very purpose of development. Means of development cannot afford to be inconsistent with the content and goals of development. Keeping people in prisons without charge sheet or trial for long periods, torturing them to extort confessions, and thus denying human rights is common in several developing countries including those with fairly high HDI otherwise. The problem arises not merely in the case of political issues, but also in the case of economic development projects. Unfortunately, a development process obsessed with economism tends to disregard human rights with disastrous consequences, resulting in displacement, deprivation, and worsening of poverty situation. Usually, it is due to the land needed for development projects and industrial enterprises. More people being expected to gain from a project than who would be deprived, provide no justification to go ahead with the project. The deprived have to be adequately compensated, rehabilitated, and resettled, and the cost of this has to be counted against the project concerned. The right to life, livelihood, and property of every individual is important and cannot be sacrificed without fair compensation and resettlement. Very often, deprivation may not be immediate or conspicuous, as in the case of air and water pollution, which may result in many hardships: for example, increased morbidity to both human beings and animals, which may at times be quite serious; decline in agricultural productivity in areas affected water and air pollution; and womenfolk forced to trudge for long distance to fetch drinking water which may cut into time available for remunerative work. Often common property resources like air, water; bio-diversity forests and grazing lands that are adversely affected causing significant loss of welfare both to present and future generations. Such a development is neither environmentally sustainable nor equitable. Unless development processes care for these adverse effects, it will amount to destructive development. If it is not possible for a development project to take adequate preventive or compensatory measures, it is better to drop such projects, even if the pace of increase in GNP thereby is adversely affected. Unfortunately environmental losses are not reckoned while estimating GNP. Human rights cannot be trampled for the sake of increasing such GNP. Economic development can never be inclusive so long as human rights are disregarded and negative externalities are not adequately taken into account.

Respect for the rule of law is also an important part of the ethics of development. In fact it is needed even for the survival of the society itself. Rule of expediency and free reign to personal discretion reduces predictability, but reasonable predictability is very necessary for not only economic development in narrow terms, but also for human development. Rule of law requires transparency in governance and also in business, as transparency helps in knowing if fair procedures have been followed. Even to the extent discretion is necessary, transparency helps in knowing if decisions have been above board. There is a strong and positive reciprocal relationship between transparency and both GDP per capita and HDI. They strengthen each other, creating a virtuous circle. On the other hand, there is also a vicious circle between corruption and development, the former driving down development, and low level of development promoting corruption levels. The coefficient of correlation for 174 observed countries in 2007 between transparency (measured by—Corruption Perception Index, CPI) and GDP per capita (PPP US$) was as high as +0.795, and between transparency and HDI it was + 0.701 which is a little lower but still statistically quite significant. These correlations based on the data during this very age of globalization, show that a positive and strong association between ethics and development need not be an idealist's dream but can be an empirical fact. Incidentally, the correlation coefficient between HDI and GDP per capita was also high at +0.728 in 2007.[5] Thus ethics is seen to be a very helpful value in development, both strengthening each other. As far as India is concerned, we have to both improve our image about transparency and attain higher levels of human development, as we noted in Chapter 2 above along with relevant data.

How far actual development is guided by ethics, depends upon the societal power structure or political economy of the state. In other words, it depends on the space given to the underprivileged to express and redress their grievances. If the elite continue to be power hungry and greedy and also dominate the state power structure, there would be bleak prospects for development proper or justice oriented development. Economic development with a narrow social base tends to have grave internal contradictions, resulting in restricted markets and unsold surplus production. As Marxists have since long been pointing out, this leads to recurrent economic crises affecting the very elite who produced these conditions. But if the above correlations are at least rough indicators, there is a tendency for more enlightened elite to emerge at higher levels of economic development and the underprivileged also tend to be more assertive and claim greater space for themselves in the long run. This holds good as much between countries as within. It would facilitate political and moral development in keeping pace with economic development.

While efforts are being made with some success to make economic development more humane and ethical, it is facing hurdles in a globalized economic order and unfair trade regime. That is why Acharya Vinoba Bhave called for *antyodaya* (raising those at the bottom) approach to development on Gandhian lines. Sen similarly pleads for focusing on enhancing the freedoms and capabilities of the weakest who are deprived of them. These precepts hold good across countries also in an unequal world. Stiglitz is emphatic on special attention to be paid to the needs and difficulties of the least developed countries. Fair trade is vital for developing countries in the very task of development. Otherwise they cannot equitably participate in the process of globalization of trade. Stiglitz points out how world trade is still very unfair in spite of several world trade agreements, as they are unbalanced: 'the advanced industrial countries were allowed to levy tariffs on goods produced by developing countries that were, on average, four times higher than on goods produced by other advanced countries' (Stiglitz 2007: 15–16). He further observes that agricultural goods of developed countries are heavily subsidized, while developing countries cannot afford to subsidize their agriculture so heavily because it would divert resources from development elsewhere. Developed countries feel that developing countries have the huge advantage of low wages, but as Stiglitz says, this advantage is more than offset by several disadvantages like high cost of capital, poor infrastructure, lower skill levels, and overall low productivity. He adds, 'it is not unfair to be poor and have low wages; it is unfortunate' (Stiglitz 2007: 71). Strictly speaking, world trade to be fair would require all subsidies and trade restrictions to be eliminated (Stiglitz 2007: 73). But this may be impossible in the present world order. So Stiglitz offers an agenda for reforms to make the world trade fair, by making it more pro-poor and pro-development, such as opening the markets of the developed countries to the less developed without insisting on reciprocity (Stiglitz 2007: 81–101). The details of this agenda need not detain us here, but this discussion is only to show how fair trade is important in a globalizing world.

CENTRAL TENDENCY IN DEVELOPMENT

We are accustomed to view development traditionally in terms of national income, which also reflects technological development. In this view national income is seen as the central tendency of development. It is only recently that we have been viewing development in terms of HDI, which does not ignore national income but also takes into account a few additional factors which reflect human development. The new approach thus takes a more comprehensive view. Quite a few eminent thinkers, however, have viewed development in terms of an ethical value as its central tendency continuing over long periods, though there may be short-term reversals. For example, Acton in his Lectures on Modern History (1906) sees the march of history as progress towards liberty. He says, 'It is by the combined efforts of the weak, made under compulsion, to resist the reign of force and constant wrong, that, in the rapid change but slow progress of four thousand years, liberty has been preserved and secured, and extended, and finally understood' (quoted by Carr 2008: 115).

Development need not be linear and continuous. There have been cyclical views of development, where the moving force is the moral health of people. The Hindu view of development was essentially cyclical. During Yugas (ages, epochs, or long-term eras), beginning with Satya, through Krita, Dvaapara, and Kali, the role of Truth tends to decline, reaching an abyss in Kali. The present Yuga is considered to be Kali. But this is not the end. Out of compassion for mankind, God is believed to 'descend' on the earth and lift the mankind back to the path of dharma or virtue. Arnold Toynbee had a similar cyclical view of the history of civilizations, though he does not bring in the descent of God on the earth for restoring moral order. According to him, reversals or disintegrations of civilizations are not inevitable, but occur where 'social schism' takes enormous scale and depth. Social schism in his perspective is only an outward sign of spiritual decay, as a result of which masses become estranged from their leaders who cling to their position and power and have no human concerns for others (Toynbee 1991: 211–54). Karl Marx's view of dialectics of development is well known—from primitive communism to feudalism, to capitalism to socialism, and finally to communism. Though the moving force behind the dialectics is the contradictions between the forces of production (technological) and relations of production (socio–economic–political) in his theory, at the very basis of all the dialectics, lie moral forces. What leads to a crisis of capitalism is not a mere technical factor, but a serious breakdown of social ethic, and what can save capitalism is also a strong emergence of this ethic and concern for the masses. Marxists, however, are quite sceptical about whether capitalism can accommodate such an ethic at all.

In his famous 1961 lecture on 'History as Progress' at the University of Cambridge, E.H. Carr says: 'Belief in progress means belief not in any automatic or inevitable progress, but in the progressive development of human potentialities' (Carr 2008:119). After noting that man has shown capacity for profiting by the experience of his predecessors both in terms of material possessions and mastery over environment, Carr raises a significant question: 'Has not the evolution of man as a social being lagged fatally behind the progress of technology?' (Carr 2008: 117–18). He concedes that the present times are difficult and trying. But he also says,

It appears to me simply untrue to say that our understanding of the problems of social organisation or goodwill to organize society in the light of that understanding have regressed. ... It is not that our capacities have diminished or moral qualities declined, But the period of conflict and upheaval, due to the shifting balance of power between continents, nations, and classes, through which we are living have enormously increased the strain on these capacities and qualities, and limited and frustrated their effectiveness for positive achievement. (Carr 2008: 118)

If Carr's view of development is to be reduced to a single idea or central tendency, it is in terms of human potentialities—both moral and material. Carr, however, observes that a class which leads today may be replaced by another leader group or class tomorrow.

Alexis de Tocqueville in his Preface to *Democracy in America* (1835) viewed history as a process of progressive realization of 'equality' (cited in Ganguli 1973:118). Whether what he observed in 1835 still holds good and where, may be a controversial point. While it is true that the innate tendency of capitalist development is to aggravate inequality in incomes, there is also evidence of the emergence of the masses with a powerful voice. The state has learnt at least to some extent how to reach the fruits of development to the underdog, though this may not be true of all countries. The advanced western countries seem to show some decline in inequality within them, though in the very process, disparities between them and developing countries have aggravated. But even here there are isolated signs of convergence, as between China and the West.

For Gandhi, the central tendency of development was ahimsa or non-violence. Though he was critical of modern civilization especially in his book *Hind Swaraj* (1910), he took an optimistic view of development in the long term. He said that

man has been steadily progressing towards ahimsa. Starting from the state of cannibalism and the life of nomadic hunters and pastoralists, man settled down to agriculture or civilized stable life, founded villages and towns and from a member of family he became a member of a community and nation. All these are signs of progress of ahimsa and diminishing himsa. Had it been otherwise, the human species should have been extinct by now. (cited in Ganguli 1973:116)

Interpreting Gandhi's economic ideas and proposals, his disciple Joseph Cornelius Kumarappa (J.C. Kumarappa in brief, 1892–1960), brought out two interesting books, among others, on *Economy of Permanence* in 1945 with a Foreword by Gandhi himself, and *Gandhian Economic Thought* in 1951. Kumarappa was Gandhi's economic researcher and carried out several economic surveys to study first hand economic conditions in Indian villages.[6] Like Gandhi, Kumarappa was an activist, not a mere thinker and writer. He developed an All-India Village Industries Association, trying to put into practice several Gandhian ideas on rural development, and creating employment opportunities for rural artisans, facilities for technical and marketing advice, and contributing to making village economy and village industries more viable. The focus was more on the human being, rather than on the economy or industry, making people not only happy but also free and creative. Having done his Masters in Economics at Columbia, Kumarappa gave a systematic and creative expression to Gandhian thought on economic and environmental issues. He envisaged a morally responsible role for human beings in harmony both among themselves and with nature. He is regarded by several as the father of 'green thought' in India for this reason.

Kumarappa has a model of economic development, with ethical criteria demarcating its different stages. The first stage is one of Parasitic Economy, where one grows only at the expense of another involving violence and ruthless exploitation, and is openly destructive. The second is a Predatory Economy, which involves cheating and stealing though in an innocuous garb, such as pick-pocketing, financial penetration of one country or social group or class by another and siphoning off the surplus, thus immiserizing the victim country or social group or class. The third is the Enterprise stage where the economy is self-sufficient and self-reliant. Even if interactions take place with others, they are not destructive or immiserizing. It is in this stage that economic growth could be said to have been started in a modern sense. The size of the cake is not given but increases, making it possible for all to become economically better off than before. A conspicuous example is that of man taking to agriculture. Thus even the third stage, which seems to characterize, the present state of economic development in some respects, could be said to have furthered the cause of reducing violence compared to the second. Trade relations can bridge ethnic and cultural divides and promote tolerance and reduce violence. The Fourth is a Gregarious Economy, which is, like a honey-bee colony, a collective economy, each working for a common good. Common good prevails over private profit here. Though such an economy may promote peace so long as there is equity in the relations between members, there is always a possibility that groups may emerge competing for resources, resulting in strife. If this can be amicably managed for the common good, it can mean not only further promotion of non-violence, but also greater care of the environment. The Fifth is a Service or Seva Economy,[7] which runs on the basis of altruism and service to others, and not selfish motives. This is the highest and the most civilized and ethical stage.

As the economy progresses from the Parasitic to the Altruistic, the amount of violence and hurt progressively decreases, mutual co-operation and trust increases, the harmony between the economy and nature advances promoting sustainability, and there is always a willingness to learn from past mistakes and to help others. The different stages in Kumarappa's model need not totally be separate from each other. For example, the Entreprise stage may have some pockets of collective economy (supposed to be characterizing the fourth stage) and even have several altruistic elements like charitable organizations and welfare schemes. But the final stage, the Seva Economy is altruistic, not just here and there in some pockets, but as a whole. It may look too idealistic at the present stage but not so in his vision of the future. It is an extension of the concept of family to the economy as a whole, when each one takes care of the others, and children and the weak receive special attention, everyone is looked after. It does not have to be based on selfishness to be functional.

Indiscriminate mechanization, catering to ever larger and larger markets through industries of gigantic size, and unscrupulous exploitation of people and natural resources will never achieve the type of progress, which Gandhi (and Kumarappa) envisaged. The focus instead is on the local—local production for local consumption and by local ownership. Village is the pivot of Kumarappa's development model, with an important role not only for agriculture and animal husbandry but also for village industries. He was for the diversification of the rural economy, enabling the village people to add to their sources of income and spread their risks. He was also for bringing modern science and technology for rural development, not to be adopted as it is, but after making modifications to suit Indian economic conditions. He did not support the concept of agriculture as an industry; it was instead to be nurtured and developed as an occupation under family farming. If not strictly, at least as much as possible on a priority basis, the principle is one of keeping the scale of production small, so that local control is not lost and the importance of the human agent is never ignored. These Gandhian ideas received a big boost from Schumacher, who wrote what is regarded in the West as a path-breaking book—*Small is Beautiful: A Study of Economics as if People Mattered* in 1973. It has by now gone into many reprints. It is essentially Gandhian in ideology.

In the present world harassed by terrorism, ethnic conflicts, wars, and weapons of mass destruction, Gandhi's perspective of the central tendency of development in terms of non-violence may sound unrealistic. Similarly in the present age of mega industries under multinationals, Gandhian ideas of small scale and decentralized production with local ownership also may seem very much out of place. Before we pronounce Gandhi as irrelevant in such times, let us think over the fact that status quo often gives the illusion of being a permanent state. But when contradictions and conflicts become intolerable, human ingenuity brings about a change. People will not helplessly accept violence and conflicts as inevitable. Even while mega industries and multinationals have become dominant, people's movements led by farmers, oustees, the unemployed, and other such unfortunate victims have been resisting them. They will initiate the needed change, and in such a resistance to injustice and deprivation, Gandhi becomes supremely relevant. His teachings help these people to create a space for themselves. Peace and non-violence as a long-term tendency may not come about as inevitable destiny, but only as a result of exercising the human will to fight greed, corruption, and injustice, and restore human goodness and rationality. Human ingenuity can so organize the polity and economy that there is always some space for creativity even for ordinary persons through small-scale production and handmade products. Even when large-scale production characterizes the main economy, if its tendency to cause human deprivation and alienation is duly offset by this creative space made for the ordinary men and women, safety valves would then have been created. The crux of the matter is whether violence in the economy and polity are eliminated or at least mitigated, and not the scale nor the technology of production. Gandhi was an optimistic person and had faith in the innate goodness of human nature. Had he been utterly wrong, humanity would not have survived to this day. There is an increasing awareness of our inter-dependence not only between individuals but also between communities and countries, in spite of aberrations. This could mean increasing sense of responsibility among people as citizens and as human beings, which will further improve with the spread of education. This has already shown some evidence of overcoming narrow economism and of serious attempts at achieving nobler goals.

NOTES

1. Krishna Bharadwaj used the phrase 'shopping bag economics' to describe neo-classical economics in a lecture she gave at ISEC around 1980, which I attended. In the three lectures she gave on the topic at Mysore University, Mysore, earlier in 1977, she did not use this expression, but used instead words like 'arith-momorphism' and 'methodological individualism' to describe the approach of neoclassical economics (see Bharadwaj 1980: 64).

2. For a detailed rebuttal of this Western view, see Nadkarni (2008: 28–32, 379–84).

3. These ideas have been expressed by Sen since the 1980s in different articles in books, culminating in his 2009 book *The Idea of Justice*.

4. Though there is a significant and high positive correlation between HDI and GDP per capita, being 0.728 for 2007 (for 174 countries observed), there are interesting deviations. For example, Philippines ranks 124 in terms of GDP per capita, but higher at 105 in terms of HDI (as in 2007). Respective ranks for Sri Lanka during the same year are 116 and 102, and for China 102 and 92. That is, there are examples of even countries with lower income showing higher rank in HDI. In the case of India, its rank in GDP per capita is 130 but still lower out of

134 in terms of HDI during 2007 (cf. UNDP 2009).

5. Thanks are due to Khalil Shaha of ISEC Data Bank for statistical help in obtaining these correlations.

6. For a more detailed exposition of the life, work and thoughts of J.C. Kumarappa, see Govindu and Malghan (2005).

7. This is not a service economy in the narrow sense of having service sector as the dominant part of the economy. The emphasis is on altruism.

4 Ethics, Environment, and Culture
The Paradox of India*

> The future is not some place we are going to but
> one we are creating. The paths to it are not found
> but made, and the activity of creating them changes
> both the creator and the destination.

—John Schaar[1]

> We cannot get the co-operation of nature purely
> on our own terms. Any attempt to do so will
> bring violent destruction in its wake.

—J.C. Kumarappa (1945: 16)

ETHICS AND ENVIRONMENT

Environmental problems like climate change, chemical pollution of air, soil and water, loss of bio-diversity, deforestation, extinction of species, desertification, and increasing shortage of water and energy sources, are no longer only what might happen in future. They are already under way. Not only is scientific evidence piling up in support, but even common people are feeling the changes themselves—erratic rains and seasons, scarcity

---

* The last three sections of this essay are based on a keynote lecture delivered by the author at the national seminar held at ISEC in collaboration with National Institute of Ecology, 30 September—1 October 2009, published as 'Culture and Environment: Paradox of India', in Sunil Nautiyal and Bibhu Prasad Nayak (eds) 2010. *Ecological Economics: An Approach Towards Socio-Economic and Environmental Sustainability.* Bengaluru: ISEC, pp. 65–74.

of water and energy, massive accumulation of urban waste, increasing incidence of cancer, and so on. And yet we don't seem quite ready to arrest the deterioration, taking place on several fronts, amidst seemingly increasing incomes and wealth. This is mainly because we are caught in the trap of modern economic growth. Its economics assumes that nature in situ is of no value and becomes valuable only when exploited and enters the market process. Vandana Shiva feelingly writes about this:

It is assumed that 'production' takes place only when mediated by technologies for commodity production even when such technologies destroy life. A stable and clean river is not a productive resource in this view; it needs to be 'developed' with dams in order to become so. ... Natural forests remain unproductive till they are 'developed' into mono-culture plantations of commercial species. (Shiva 2001: 287)

This attitude, Shiva complains, has devalued even women and women's work as most of it takes place outside the market process. She calls this attitude patriarchal, devaluing both nature and women, while the feminine principle is one of conservation and care, and is holistic. In any case, modern economic growth has been destroying environment both by depleting and using it as a waste-bin pushing effluents and emissions into it on a massive scale.

This is a conspicuous symptom of our massive moral failure. Ethics is at the very centre of environmental issues, for it determines our willingness to act. An ethically insensitive people are not likely to be duly concerned to tackle issues confronting humanity—poverty, hunger, illiteracy, and environmental deterioration. The basic reason for our failure on these fronts is not lack of economic resources, but simply our lack of ethical concern and seriousness. There is a lack of rationality also here, not in the narrow or short-term sense, but in the long-term perspective. It shows an irrational lack of concern for our own future. We prefer to drift in a current tendency, unable to think of our future, our children's future, and do not show enough evidence of having any urge and energy to face our responsibilities.

The basic nature of ethical concern can be seen as transcending narrow self interest from the centre, continuously on to caring for others in wider and wider circles. The least ethical is the most self-centred person, and as he transcends his self-interest from himself to the family, community, country, humanity, and then on to a even wider circle covering also non-human beings—living and non-living, his concern becomes wider and more and more ethical. This is what we learn from a verse in the Gita (ch. 6, verse 29), which Gandhi has translated as follows in his *Teaching of the Gita*:

The one whose self is disciplined by Yoga,
Sees the self abiding in everything
And sees every being in the self,
He sees the same in all beings.

(quoted in Whichner 1998: 23)

Self-interest transcends in an ethically sensitive person to cover not only the interests of all humans but also animals and nature, and from the present generation to cover the future generations too. The extent to which this is achieved determines the moral development of a person and people. Gandhi said: 'The greatness of a nation and its moral progress can be judged by the way its animals are treated' (Keene 2004: 118). The attitude to animals signified the attitude to the whole environment in terms of a wider and comprehensive scope of Self. J.C. Kumarappa's theory of ethical evolution as taking place through stages of development from a parasitic and predatory economy at lower stages rising finally to a morally most advanced stage of economy based on altruism (discussed in Chapter 3), can be applied at the level of the individual ethical development too. The self at the centre need not vanish; it only begins to accommodate wider and wider concerns, covering the whole earth at an advanced state. The reach of one's caring for others, in thought and action, thus becomes the measuring rod of one's moral standing.[2] This shows how ethics and environment are so closely related.

There are of course different approaches to environmental ethics, which are briefly reviewed here. The anthropocentric approach places human beings at the centre of ethical concern.[3] Because of their superior level of consciousness, human beings are taken as 'privileged entities, superior to other forms of life on the planet', as Sallie McFague suggests in her critique of Christian theology (2008). She suggests that it is just one step more in such biased ethics to regard a certain group of human beings with a certain racial and cultural background as more privileged than others (see FritzRoy and Papyrakis 2010: 99). When it is held that there is nothing sacred or divine about nature, the Divine being separate and above it, and that nature is for the free enjoyment of man, free exploitation of nature to meet endless human needs follows logically. McFague advocates an 'ecological church' which shows concern for God's creation, in addition to issues of poverty and human suffering which may also be related increasingly to environmental issues (ibid.). This is a very constructive suggestion because even an anthropocentric view need not go against environmental concern. A deterioration of environment cannot take place without seriously affecting the welfare of human beings.

The idea that man is just one of the members of a biotic community or land community was forcefully put forward by Aldo Leopold in a path-breaking collection of essays, *A Sand Country Almanac and Sketches from Here and There* (1949). It included his seminal essay on 'The Land Ethic'. Leopold wrote, 'All ethics so far evolved rest upon a single premise that the individual is a member of community of independent parts. His instincts prompt him to compete for his place in the community, but his ethics prompt him also to co-operate' (quoted in Callicott 2001: 178). According to him, ecology 'simply enlarges the boundaries of the community to include soils and water, plants and animals, or collectively: the land'. His land ethic 'changes the role of *homo sapiens* from conquerer of the land community to plain member or citizen of it. It implies respect for his fellow members and also respect for the community as such' (quoted in Callicott 2001: 179). Leopold was a staunch environmental activist, and pioneered wildlife management and conservation biology in America. In the 1920s, he argued passionately for a system of wilderness areas, and became a founder of the North American Wilderness Movement (quoted in Callicott 2001: 175).

Peter Singer (1975, 1985) and Tom Regan (1982) are the major proponents of animal liberation in the West. They have argued that the moral community, entitled for moral concerns, is not confined to the human species. According to Singer 'all sentient beings, those capable of feeling either pleasure or pain, are members of the moral community and possess rights to moral consideration' (as told by King 1991: 76). Singer calls the failure to take the moral standing of animals into consideration with that of human beings as 'speciesism' (ibid.). Regan, on the other hand, 'employs the criterion of consciousness, and in particular consciousness of oneself as a continuous subject, to demarcate the line between those who do possess rights and those who do not' (King 1991: 77).

King mentions that eco-feminists find the above criteria problematic. First because, they 'impose a value hierarchy separating those who do and those who do not count morally'. Second because, 'their conception of the moral community is defined through an emphasis on identity and sameness rather than uniqueness and difference' (ibid.). Their 'abstractness' and 'generality' obscures the 'importance of attending to the needs of those with whom we are in relation', according to Lauritzen (quoted in ibid.). For eco-feminists these relationships are very important, as they indicate interdependence and stress the need for caring. For them, the community of care extends beyond human beings to cover not only animals, but also trees and plants, places, and eco-systems (King 1991: 78). There is diversity and difference among the members of this community, but they nevertheless form a moral community.

'Deep ecologists' like Arne Naess (who introduced the term, 'deep ecology') consider all life as one, both human and non-human. They are also extremely critical of the anthropocentric ways of thinking and advocate 'ways of being that will recognize and respect the intrinsic, rather than merely the instrumental, value environment and its denizens' (King 1991: 79). But eco-feminists do not accept deep ecology as it seems 'to seek an erasure of differences among the individual members of the natural community, a kind of identity of each in the life of the whole' (ibid.). King says that according to the eco-feminist standpoint, 'what is needed is not the recovery of a sense of oneness but an understanding of the real differences in the way of fostering the growth of concrete, multi-faceted, caring relations among individuals, societies, and non-human beings and systems among whom they live' (ibid.). An abstract and vague concept of unity of human beings with nature, without regard for differences, does not make for a practical environmental ethic, according to eco-feminists.[4]

Women are closer to the natural environment than men, and it is, therefore, understandable that the eco-feminist approach reflects a caring concern for all forms of environment. When water sources dry up, it is village women who have to fetch water from longer distances. When sources of fuel wood vanish nearby, it is they again who have to trudge for miles to fetch it for cooking. In the process it is they who lose hours of remunerative work. When environment is polluted, it is their breast milk which shows traces of pollutants affecting infants' health. Since women are more vulnerable, they also become more caring.[5] It may be their own self-interest which inspires this care, and may be to that extent considered indirectly anthropocentric, but in instances like this, there is no real conflict between anthropocentrism and environmentalism. Some of the concerns in protecting bio-diversity are based on 'existence values', that is, on their use values rather than on use values in the case of things like the blue whale or coral reefs. But a caring concern, even if initially inspired by enlightened self-interest, can easily be extended beyond what is useful, to all creation.

But ethical dilemmas do arise between concern for human livelihoods and concern for nature. This became evident in India in the case of wildlife sanctuaries or reserves where tribal people also live. Wildlife conservation may be difficult if human habitats within reserve areas conflict with conservation. For example, forest-living people cultivating land and keeping domestic cattle may consider wildlife a nuisance and may even harm them to keep them at a distance. Evidently, conservation has to be sought without affecting human livelihoods, by either employing them in conservation work itself and diverting them from agriculture and animal husbandry, or by rehabilitating and resettling them outside forests, say, by giving them alternative land. It is thus necessary to find ways of resolving conflicts between man and nature conservation. It is evident, therefore, that in environmental ethics, we cannot do without human or social concerns.

Two important approaches in modern moral philosophy, though addressed primarily to human concerns, can very logically be extended to cover environmental concerns. One is the approach of John Rawls in his celebrated book, *A Theory of Justice*, whose two principles of justice were set out in the Introduction. In a situation of unequal access to environment, where the rich have more of the ecological space to exploit than the poor, Rawls's principles imply that the rich, be they rich countries or rich people within countries, have to restrain their consumption, and allow more access for the poor to ecological space so that they can improve their standard of living. Justice also requires that people dependent on natural resources including forests and bio-diversity for their livelihood have a stake in their conservation and share the benefits from doing so. Similarly justice requires that countries that have bio-diversity and natural resources in general have a right to them and to ensure their sustainable use. The preceding two requirements of justice imply clearly that when countries that have bio-diversity are compensated by world bodies for the direct and indirect cost of conservation (since the world too benefits from such conservation), the benefits of compensation should go to the local people who conserve it, instead of being appropriated mainly by state machinery. However, Amartya Sen observes in *The Idea of Justice* (2009) that people who are not part of Rawls's social contract may be left out. In the context of environment, plants, animals, nature in general, and future generations, may thus be left out. This is so if the social contract is narrowly interpreted, but not if the original parties to the contract are assumed to be environmentally aware and take wider responsibility.

The second is Amartya Sen's approach of improving the capabilities and freedoms of all, specially those of the worst off, and deal with manifest instances of injustice such as hunger, disease, illiteracy, homelessness, and other forms of poverty and deprivation. Martha Nussbaum has developed Sen's capability approach further and given a list of ten 'central human functional capabilities', many of which are closely related to the status of our natural environment (see FritzRoy and Papyrakis 2010: 90). Environmental disasters can significantly diminish our capabilities, most particularly of the poor. Similarly, exploiting resources beyond the rate of their regeneration and beyond the rate of finding economical substitutes for them, will directly and adversely affect the capabilities of future generations to meet their needs. Moreover, there is manifest injustice in the way the rich (countries/people) exploit nature, depriving the poor of their livelihoods and freedoms, which needs redressing in Sen's approach. Sen's approach can thus be easily extended to cover nature too.

Interestingly, the ethical approaches of both Rawls and Sen indicate the pressing need to address inequity in the use of ecological space. Though this inequity is present both within the countries and between them, we have data on inequity between countries which may be indicative of inequity within countries too between the rich and the poor. Per capita carbon dioxide (CO_2) emissions are a good indicator of the exploitation of ecological space and an important contributor to global warming. These emission rates are highly and positively correlated with per capita incomes. The shares of the rich countries in total carbon emissions are much higher than their shares in world population, while the shares of the poorer in these emissions are much lower than their shares in population as seen from Table 4.1. But even when we take into account population figures, India's contribution to carbon emissions, or for that matter, of low income countries, is not as high as that of developed countries, as Table 4.1 shows. The worry, however, is that developing countries, particularly China and

Table 4.1:   Share in World Population and World CO_2 Emissions

Country/Group	Share (%) in world population (2008)	Share (%) in CO_2 Emission (2005)	Share (%) in CO_2 Emission (2009)	Metric Tons of CO_2 per thousand $ of GDP (2005)	Metric Tons of CO_2 per thousand $ of GDP (2009)
(1)	(2)	(3)	(4)	(5)	(6)
USA	4.5	22.2	16.5	0.47	0.38
CHINA	19.8	19.1	24.0	0.96	1.51
INDIA	17.0	4.3	6.2	0.47	1.45
LOW INCOME	14.5	3.6*	6.1*	0.38	na
MIDDLE INCOME	69.5	47.6	54.1	0.61	na
HIGH INCOME	16.0	48.8	39.8	0.39	na
WORLD	100	100	100	0.47	na

Source: Calculated from World Bank, *World Development Report 2010, and World Development Indicators 2013.*

Note: India and China are included in the middle-income group.
Includes emission not allotted to specific countries, mostly poor.

India, are fast catching up with the advanced countries in respect of CO_2 emissions as seen from a comparison of their positions in 2009 with that in 2005 in the table. China has now replaced USA as the leading polluter. The inequity in appropriating ecological space across countries, as indicated by their per capita CO_2 emissions, is not the only ethical issue between developed and developing countries. The developed countries sometimes solve their environmental problems by inducing developing countries to import polluting industries from the former. The developing countries bite the bait because it creates employment opportunities, and in the process disregard huge health risks involved and safety standards required. In fact that is what makes such dirty industries 'paying' to transfer from the rich to the poor countries. The former sometimes even dump hazardous wastes in poorer countries by paying some money. What makes this most tragic and even barbaric is that such money often does not go to the actual victims as compensation or for their medical expenses, but to corrupt politicians and bureaucrats. All this goes in the name of economic growth, and those who oppose such barbarities are dubbed as environmental fundamentalists!

There are two ways to tackle the environmental crisis. One is to improve technological efficiency in a way that more income is produced in the process of generating one unit of pollution or emission, or, in other words, minimize pollution per unit of income produced. The second is the Gandhian way of reducing our wants, particularly of the type which involve a lot of energy use and pollution, and modify our lifestyles. The first is the main strategy being adopted by advanced countries, with the result that as the last two columns in the table above show, less CO_2 is produced in advanced countries per unit of Gross Domestic Product (GDP) than in the middle-income developing countries. The position has worsened in this regard both in China and in India between 2005 and 2009, while it has improved in the USA, as seen from the table. Interestingly, low-income countries, being at a low level of development are not carbon-intensive. It is when the development process is launched that carbon intensity increased, which can decrease again with technological efficiency. However, improving technological efficiency as the main or the only strategy gives the illusory impression that we can eat the cake and have it too. While we have to try our best to use cleaner technologies as much as possible—and it is the moral responsibility of advanced countries to help the developing coutries in this, technology alone cannot be *the* solution to environmental crisis. A cardiologist does not tell a heart patient: 'Eat what you like, and how much you like; sit before the TV as long as you want. I will prescribe you medicines and perform surgery if needed. I have the best technical expertise and equipment!' On the other hand, the cardiologist would advise the patient to change his lifestyle, avoid junk food, and exercise as much as possible. Yet, when it comes to environmental crisis, we harp mainly on technological improvement, and hardly talk of changing our consumerist, energy-intensive lifestyles which directly contribute to the crisis. Gandhi is regarded as *passé!*

Sen and others may have emphasized on freedom as an important value in right spirit. But it does not mean freedom to exploit our common environmental resources wantonly. It is precisely against 'the freedom of the commons' (commons as indicating all natural resources over which no property rights have been established), that Garett Hardin cautioned us in his famous paper on 'The Tragedy of Commons' (*Science*, Vol. 162:1243–8). Sen could not have meant this kind of freedom in which (in Hardin's words) 'all men rush, each pursuing his own best interest' to common ruin, each trying to grab before others do, so that the resource is destroyed quickly. Economists are generally in favour of establishing property rights over natural resources in some form or the other to prevent such competitive exhaustion of free and exhaustible resources. They do not necessarily mean private property rights. There could be collective or community or state property rights, so that the use of the resource is controlled and restrained. Since environment is a global resource, it has to be managed collectively by all countries in the best interest of all.

The ethical issue of equity very much crops up here, if in the process of establishing property rights the weaker sections are denied of access to the resource. Any arrangement of the management of the commons will have to be equitable. Moreover, merely establishing a property right may not necessarily ensure sustainable use of the resource. For example, a forest, even state owned but leased to a private contractor without effective restrictions to ensure sustainable use can quickly lead to deforestation of the area. In the Western Ghats, there was a massive depletion of bamboo, when the state itself allowed private paper mills to harvest bamboo at ridiculously low prices, while it charged a hefty price to poor basket makers (Gadgil and Guha 1995: 46). The state itself openly and consciously flouted both the principles of equity and sustainability of use.

A serious possibility in the use of the commons is what is known as the tendency to 'free-ride'. This is there, for example, in the case of common grazing lands analysed by Hardin referred above. Every herder thinks that he is one among many, and that his own contribution will hardly count. This thinking prompts him to unrestrained and exploitative use. When all think so and act accordingly, the common resource is depleted unsustainably. Free-riding is both irrational and immoral. It is irrational because everyone knows that others also can think and act alike irrespective of the collective ruin caused thereby. It is immoral because, the free-riders do not accept their moral responsibility.

The success of collective property right regime in the case of natural resources would depend on how effective and ethically sensitive the collective leadership is. Through intensive field work, scientists have shown that local communities have shown good evidence of conservation on a collective basis,[6] thereby justifying the faith in the innate wisdom, moral integrity, and competence of the rural and indigenous people. Whatever be the property rights, vigilance is needed by all concerned over the use of the resource taking into consideration both equity and sustainability. In any case, the property right would be exercised by a human agency, and whether this agency would also act in such a way as to ensure sustainable use of the resource, would depend on the state of law enforcement which in turn is determined by the sense of moral responsibility of the citizens of the state for nature.

John Passmore, an Australian philosopher, advocates a simple principle, 'Man's Responsibility for Nature', which is also the title of his well-known book first published in 1974 (revised and enlarged edition in 1980). He is pragmatic enough not to worry about whether the western tradition is anthropocentric or takes the whole world as sacred. He feels extreme principles can be a hindrance rather than a help. The anthropocentric view does not come in the way of human beings, as the most intelligent of all the species, taking over the responsibility for the protection of nature and solving environmental problems. Similarly, even if human beings do it for their own pleasure, it would mean that they would never endure slag heaps in towns and filthy rivers around them. Accepting nature as divine may not necessarily help, if it is taken to mean that nature 'would not be hurt whatever we do to it'.[7] We have, for example the river Ganga in India, regarded as so sacred that people seem to think that whatever we do to it, it remains sacred no matter how polluted it is. A hardly helpful thought for environmental protection! It is more important that man accepts his moral responsibility for nature. How it is justified is secondary.

But how do we make man undertake his moral responsibility for nature, including responsibility for the future? Economists more or less view environmental problems either in terms of a negative externality (costs such as on account of pollution or displacement imposed on a third party and not borne by the producer of the cost) or in terms of depletion (of renewable resources like water, forests, and exhaustible resources like minerals, fossil fuel). In both cases, wherever feasible, 'polluter pays principle' is accepted in law to enforce responsibility and restrain negative externality and depletion. It is the polluter's moral and legal responsibility to fully compensate the victim of negative externality and treat pollution generated according to standards prescribed, before releasing it back into the environment. Thereby, the negative externality is internalized and its producer bears its full cost. This makes him more cautious and restrained. Similarly, in the case of use of a resource that can lead to depletion, the user has to bear the full cost of the depletion including the cost on account of negative externality, and not just the market price of the resource. In the case of a renewable resource, the price of timber for example, should reflect not merely its market price but also the cost of regenerating the resource, apart from the externalized cost. Moreover, the use of the resource should be so managed that current use does not exceed the rate of regeneration. Such a rule is important to observe in cases like the use of water, forest resources, and fisheries. In the case of exhaustible resources, proper pricing would mean including not merely the cost of extraction and transport, but also the cost of negative externality[8] and the cost imposed on the future generations through increased scarcity of the resource imposed on them by making them go for costlier substitutes or, the increased research and development expenditure imposed on them to develop substitutes. In practice, pricing never satisfies these rigorous requirements, which is what makes it cheap to degrade environment. But, even if actual prices are raised to these levels, it may not necessarily restrain the consumption of the rich. Their incomes may be so high as to make them insensitive to the prices. It may even mean that the burden of environmental costs created by the rich is passed on to the poor! Nevertheless, the role of price, combined with subsidies only for the poor, may have an important role to play, though it does not obviate the role of other instruments like state regulation and voluntary restraint through ethical and environmental sensitivity.

Though Mahatma Gandhi did not develop any systematic body of environmental ethics or philosophy, his contribution to it may be considered tremendous. He inspired not only non-violent freedom movements and civil rights movements, but also environmental movements in several parts of the world. Among the latter may be mentioned particularly the movements led, respectively, by Sundarlal Bahuguna and Chandi Prasad Bhatt in the Himalayas and the ASTRA programme led by A.K.N. Reddy in India, and the movement led by Chico Mendes in Brazil. The environmental movement in America, though directly prompted by Rachel Carson's *Silent Spring* (1962), is also considerably influenced by Gandhian ideas. These ideas are listed below, not necessarily in Gandhji's own words, but certainly expressing his thoughts. Gandhian ethics flows out of basically his main principles of Truth and Non-violence. As applied to environment, this can be said to be leading to the following four ideas, which can be seen as the four pillars of his approach to environmental management: (a) concern for the weakest, including animals; equity not only among human beings but also between human beings and animals and plants; (b) restraint on greed and unnecessary consumption, and attention to meeting the needs of all, particularly the weakest; (c) putting people in charge of resource management through democratic decentralization and management by local communities, giving them a stake in the benefits of sustainable use of local resources and bio-diversity; (d) Appropriate Science and Technology for Rural Areas,[9] making technology to meet people's needs, without displacing or alienating labour from the product, but raising their skills, creativity, and productivity, and without being obsessed with large-scale production. Technology should be geared to meet local conditions and resource endowments as far as possible. Production should also be primarily to meet local needs, but excess could be marketed outside. Gandhian approach to environmental management is thus different from a centralized, bureaucratic, and elitist approach to it, and can even be considered as an alternative to it.

The alternative world view suggested by E.F. Schumacher in his popular book, *Small is Beautiful: A Study of Economics as if People Mattered* (1973) is essentially Gandhian in character. Schumacher puts the blame for many of the environmental and social problems squarely at the door of 'ideology of giantism'. His economics is holistic and spiritual, hence environment-friendly. He called it as Buddhist economics (an essay on this is in his book on *Small is Beautiful*). He was once asked what economics had to do with Buddhism. He replied that economics without Buddhism was like sex without love (Kumar 2006: 207)! He was aghast when he once saw a lorry full of biscuits being brought from Manchester to London, and minutes later another lorry full of biscuits taken from London to Manchester! He asked what the economic rationale of this transport activity could be, involving so much fuel consumption. Did the nutritional value of biscuits increase by this transportation? That is how he came to advocate small scale and local production as the main principle of his economics (Kumar 2006: 209). Schumacher was an activist too, not just a thinker. He founded the Intermediate Technology Development Group. 'It pursued economic development within people's cultural context, rather than looking at the non-industrialized world as "underdeveloped" Technology was envisioned to be environment-friendly, non-polluting, and non-exploitative of people or nature. Therefore, it also became known as appropriate technology' (Kumar 2006: 207–8).

ROLE OF CULTURE

There is thus a wide variety of ethical principles which can promote the cause of environment. Which of them would be actually accepted and followed depends on the cultural context of the people concerned. In fact, ethical concerns emerge as part of a cultural evolution of people, including environmental ethics. Paul R. Ehrlich says, 'our complex and flexible behavior is largely determined by our environment, and especially the extra-genetic information embodied in our cultures' (Ehrlich 2002: 32). Since culture influences our attitudes and behaviour, it can be used also as a resource to promote environmentally benign attitudes. Culture is not something hard and fixed set in concrete, but can evolve in response to new problems faced. Even if a culture is not initially benign towards environment, it can be influenced by leaders of thought and action who have insight into the future. By and large, all indigenous people have attitudes that favour sustainable use, limiting the use of resources such as forests, grazing lands, and fisheries within the limit of their regeneration. Economists generally presume that the poor discount the future heavily, that is, they have little concern for tomorrow. But anthropological studies show that traditional societies and tribal people have much more concern for future than is presumed. It is only the Industrial Revolution and the philosophy of private profit maximization coupled with freedom for the market, which broke these cultural traditions. Now that we know the problems caused by this philosophy, our culture and ethics can again be evolved to take up the new challenges on the environmental front.

If the cause of environment is left only to the state and market, we may hardly have satisfactory results, though we should not of course undermine their positive potential. We should, however, be aware of their grave limitations too. For example, if we merely pass a law banning spitting on the road, and do nothing else about its implementation, we can guess the results.

We can see a similar inadequacy of market signals in being a corrective to unsustainable behaviour. For example, the increasing prices of petroleum have hardly curbed its consumption. Though of course, high petrol prices have induced the manufacture of more fuel-efficient cars, that is, we get more mileage per litre of petrol now through each car, there has hardly been any effect on the number of cars produced and total consumption of petrol.

We should be open to other approaches as well, if not as alternatives, at least as complementary or additional measures. Traditional or pre-modern approach has been mainly cultural. Unless environmentalism is incorporated into the very culture or ethos of people, the modern approaches by themselves may not be successful when it comes to actual implementation. No law can succeed unless it has the backing of people, or at least of the majority if not all people. Such a backing can come through only a cultural orientation, education and awareness campaigns. The crisis of environment is now so serious that cultural resources available for the cause of environment need to be mobilized and strengthened. Cultural approach need not be an alternative to other approaches, but can effectively complement them so that the outcome is much better.

But what is 'culture'? How is it related to environment? Raymond Williams, a reputed cultural theorist, described it as a complicated word. In his first major work, *Culture and Society 1780-1950*, he drew attention to four important meanings attached to 'culture': - 'an individual habit of mind; the state of intellectual development of a whole society; the arts; and the whole way of life of a group or people' (as quoted in Milner and Browitt 2003: 2). Milner and Browitt offer their own 'non-definition' of 'culture' 'as referring to that entire range of institutions, artifacts and practices that make up our symbolic universe'. (Milner and Browitt 2003: 5). Even if we cannot accurately define the word because of the complexity of the concept, culture can be taken to refer among other things to mainly the set of values and beliefs held by the society, expressed in art, literature, religion, institutions, and to some extent in actual day-to-day life and behaviour.

Culture is a more holistic and inclusive concept than law, society, economy, politics and civics, all of which can be embedded in their own respective spaces within a culture. Thus we can speak of political culture, culture of governance, cultural values in law, business culture and civic culture. Even the kind of economic analysis we do may be a product of a particular culture. Culture can have a time dimension too, just as it has a spatial dimension. We can speak of culture in ancient India, medieval India and modern India (and 'post-modern' India, if you so prefer). Thus culture is not homogeneous and can vary across both time and space, and even at given time and place, across institutions and social groups. Applied to economy, it can also vary across rural economy vis-à-vis urban economy, business economy, and welfare economy. It would be naive to assume that only a business culture has a bearing on the economy as a whole.

In spite of this heterogeneity and complicated nature of culture it is still possible to speak broadly of Indian, Japanese, Chinese, Western, or Islamic cultures. There may be differences within, but they still have some common overall features. This is somewhat like the genus comprising species. But cultures, in spite of retaining their identities, appear to permit cross-cultural influences naturally and significantly to such an extent as to induce mutual modifications and adaptations, much more than between genera and perhaps, in a much shorter time. Thus, culture is not rigidly fixed and even in a country or region, where environmentalism has not been a strong tradition, it can still be incorporated into its culture. This need not necessarily be as a graft from outside but drawing from resources, within the same culture, which support environmentalism.

ENVIRONMENTALISM IN TRADITIONAL INDIAN CULTURE

Religion has played a dominant role in traditional Indian culture (as in most traditional societies), even influencing the day-to-day life. Indian religions did not believe that the world was created for the enjoyment of man. Veneration of nature has a rich tradition in India, which is several millennia old and has been a strong, almost unparalleled one. Hindu children were taught to recite a prayer, on getting up in the morning, which sought forgiveness from Mother Earth for stepping on her:

Samudravasane prithvi, parvatastanamandale/
Vishnupatni namastubhyam paadasparsham kshamasva me//
O Earth, clothed in oceans, with mountains for your breasts,
Consort of God, I bow to you; forgive me for stepping on you.

(Pandurangi 1999a: 61)

Indian religions respected animals and their right to live, and deplored violence on them. There was, of course, the practice of animal sacrifice during the Vedic period, but in the course of time the concept of sacrifice radically changed. The change was spearheaded by the Gita and also by Jainism and Buddhism. The latter two deplored animal sacrifice in no uncertain terms and emphasized non-violence. The Buddha called for care and compassion to all creation, especially to all the sentient creatures (Bilimoria 2001). Human beings may be more powerful than animals, but the Buddha argues in

Sutta Nipata that, 'we have responsibility to animals precisely because of the asymmetry between us, not because of the symmetry that that takes us to the need for co-operation. ... Buddha goes on to illustrate the point by an analogy with the responsibility of the mother towards her child' (Sen 2009: 205). Power gives us the responsibility to protect, not to exploit. Sen calls this as fiduciary responsibility (Bilimoria 2001: 251). This is Gandhi's idea of trusteeship, extended to nature. For Gandhi, non-violence or Ahimsa was an essential part of his religion as much as Satyam (Truth), which included compassion to the animal world. The benign attitude to non-human life and nature in general is evident in traditional Indian culture in many ways. According to the doctrine of rebirth, to which Hinduism as well as Jainism and Buddhism subscribe, a human being could have been an animal in the past birth and could become an animal in a future birth. This brings human and non-human beings much closer in Indian religions, and induces an attitude of empathy and respect to non-human life form.

Love and reverence for certain animals, of course, had an economic basis, which may have acquired a religious colour. For example, the veneration for cow and bull/ox was based on their tremendous economic importance in daily diet, in agriculture, and in transport. Even the veneration of snakes, particularly by farmers, may be due to their role in rodent control and consequent protection of crops.

This benign attitude to environment is also reflected in the conceptualization of God and related world view in Hinduism. This is expressed in two alternative views. In the first, God is both immanent and transcendental and She/He is not external to life and nature. God is in all of us—in animal life and all things—while also transcending the universe. The universe and everything in it is Her/His manifestation, hence divine, deserving respect, and reverence. In the second view, God, though different from nature, is its creator and nourisher, father and mother combined. Not only human beings, but all animal life and material things, like air and water, are Her/His creation or children. God did not create this for the enjoyment of human beings as such; creation emerged as the essential nature of God, as *Ananda* (extreme happiness) and *Karuna* (compassion). Human beings have no exclusive right to lord over nature as such a claim would amount to arrogance and defiance of God. Both views have a positive and caring attitude to environment. In both, God is not necessarily viewed as masculine. God can be worshipped in human form—as man or woman—or in animal form, or even as a combination of man and animal. God is essentially formless, and the love and veneration for God can be expressed in any way, left free to a devotee. God can be approached through veneration of nature or service to human kind and animals.

The concept of Gaia is not new to Indian culture. Hinduism considers earth as living mother—*Bhoomaataa*. The *Atharvaveda*, has a whole prayer in praise of Earth, called *Prithivi Sookta*—Hymn for the Mother Earth. Verse 11 in the Sookta is as follows:

Oh Mother Earth! Sacred are thy hills, snowy mountains and deep forests. Be kind to us and bestow upon us happiness. May you be fertile, arable and nourisher of all! May you continue supporting people of all races and nations! May you protect us from your anger (i.e. natural disasters)! And may no one exploit and subjugate your children.

(translated by Dwivedi 2000: 10)

Yajurveda, which is even older than *Atharvaveda*, commands explicitly, '*Prithiveem maa himseehi, antariksham maa himseehi, maapo maa aushadheehi himseehi*' 'Do not injure the Earth, do not injure the space, do not injure water and the plants' (*Yajurveda*, V.42, 43; and XIII.18).

It was also tried to put this teaching into practice in ancient India. Hermitages or ashrams of Vedic sages were out of bound for kings for the purpose of hunting. The concept and practice of protecting sacred groves (*pavitra van* in Sanskrit, *devara kaadu* in Kannada, *dev raan* in Marathi) has survived till today. Kautilya's *Arthashaastra* (around 300 BC) called upon rulers to protect forests and animals, particularly elephants. The *Arthashaastra* had already a concept of reserve forests for wild animals. Injuring wild life in these reserves was a punishable offence. Hunting in other forests was to be regulated by the State. Forests were also valued for their produce and revenue, but exploitation of forests had to be judicious and consistent with their protection, including that of animals. The reconciliation between different uses of forests was sought, in a way which appears quite modern, through classifying forests into three categories— forests for recreation and hunting, forests for economic exploitation of their produce, and reserve forests for wild animals. There were also special forest areas allocated to ashrams of ascetics and schools for teaching the Vedas. The *Arthashaastra* also gave instructions to make sustainable use of forests, even those in the category meant for economic exploitation, by replacing dead and cut-down trees and ensuring regeneration (Rangarajan 1992).

This attitude to forests in particular, and nature in general, did face painful dilemmas even in ancient times. As civilization began to expand, there was greater need for bringing more land under cultivation, both for cultivating crops and rearing cattle. So, stretches of forests had to be burned down. There is a description of the burning of the Khandava forests by Krishna and Arjuna in the Mahabharata. The principle of non-violence and reverence to nature had to be reconciled with a fact of life—'*jeevo jeevasya jeevanam*'— that is, life lives upon (other) life. Yet, the greatest lessons from the Mahabharata, both from its main story and explicit teaching, are non-violence and futility of war.

Another basic feature of Indian culture is its love of diversity, which is manifest in all fields—nature, culture, religion, art, architecture, languages, literature, and racial composition of people. The love of diversity follows not only from reverence of nature but also from conceptualizing God as revealed in many forms. Commitment to bio-diversity comes naturally to Indian culture, and is reflected even in the ritual worship of deities. The worshipping devotee is supposed to offer twenty-one varieties of flowers and leaves. This induced householders to grow varieties of flowering plants and herbs in their garden plots. It is also this love of diversity which made Indian farmers preserve many varieties of cereals, pulses, and vegetables, some of them suited to semi-arid and arid areas. This is a rich resource to drawn upon, and should not be squandered but protected.

The love of forests and bio-diversity among people was reflected conspicuously in the case of the movement against the Silent Valley Project in Kerala in the early 1980s. The project involved generation of hydel power and would have benefited people, both in terms of increased employment opportunities and availability of electricity. But, the project was to be in a forest area rich with bio-diversity, containing rare flora and fauna specific to the place, which would have been lost by the execution of the project. The people of Kerala opted for the preservation of this rich forest, rather than hydel power. Their agitation against the project was so intense and prolonged that it had to be given up.

Restraint on wants or self-control is a highly regarded value in all Indian religions, without which one cannot qualify for spiritual or moral progress. Wants have to be restricted to what is essential and legitimate, and consumerism for its own sake has to be curbed in terms of this value. The first verse of the *Ishopanishad*, which was Gandhi's favourite, is pertinent here. It says, 'Everything in the Universe belongs to the Supreme Lord; enjoy what is left for you as your legitimate share, and do not covet what is not yours'. It means, leading a simple life while avoiding greed and pomp. By emphasizing the value of self-control or austerity, traditional Indian culture could be said to have strongly supported sustainable development. We can seek enjoyment in life in several ways other than wasteful consumption, enhancing our capabilities, as Amartya Sen advocated, through increased leisure, devoting more time to art, literature, and eco-friendly sports.

Another feature of Indian religions, favourable to the environment, is the belief in free will. According to this, human beings are responsible for their own welfare and future. The doctrine of Karma presupposes free will and human responsibility. Karma, already performed, automatically yields fruit, but can be controlled, moderated, or averted by subsequent human actions itself. Thus, human beings are individually and collectively responsible for their own welfare (Nadkarni 2008: 41–56).

Gandhian preference for labour-intensive, rather than energy-intensive production, is very much a product of Indian ethos. Gandhi did not mind the use of machinery when it reduced drudgery and strain, but not when it caused unemployment. His main concern was to see that every person is fully employed, instead of keeping some over-occupied and some idle. But his approach was eco-friendly too, which, in fact, characterizes Gandhian thought as a whole. His emphasis on labour-intensive methods, self-reliance, the local or village economy (without necessarily isolating oneself from the world), decentralization, and his overriding philosophy of truth and non-violence constitute the essentials of an eco-friendly economy. He also picked up another value from Indian culture—durability—which is cherished in producing goods and infrastructure and is an essential feature of an eco-friendly economy, as it reduces entropy. Traditional Indian culture has looked down upon 'use once and throw away' habits.

We may now sum up the basic features of traditional Indian culture, which support the cause of the environment:

1. Reverence for nature—principle of non-violence extended beyond human beings, without excluding them;
2. Respect for diversity;
3. Self-control on want satisfaction;
4. Free will and acceptance of human responsibility;
5. Gandhian preference for labour-intensive production, not energy-intensive production;
6. Durability as a value—not 'use once and throw away' habit;
7. Self-reliance, decentralization, emphasis on village or local economy, without isolating from the world economy.

THE PARADOX OF INDIA

The reverence for nature did not remain at the level of preaching in the scriptures and texts, but percolated to people in traditional culture. Even in recent times, there have been agitations by local people against development projects which destroyed their livelihoods and habitat by harming the environment. The agitation against the Silent Valley Project in Kerala was not so much on livelihood issue, as it was on the purely selfless issue of preserving rich forests and bio-diversity, a natural heritage of the state. The institution of Sacred Groves has still continued, though their number and the area under them have declined during the last century, particularly in its second half.

We cannot, yet, say that there has been no dichotomy between traditional cultural values and the present practice with regard to environment in India. In the wake of modern economic development and unprecedented, uncontrolled urbanization, a counter culture has also developed. The new rich are more tuned to lavish lifestyles, promoted by market forces, than to traditional values. The signs of this are all too evident to be ignored. Per capita carbon emissions in India have increased significantly enough to make an impact on the total. In the business world, there is still a lot of hypocrisy and defiance of environmental law. Instances of effluent or emission treatment plants operating only when the Inspectors for Pollution Control Boards (PCBs) visited, and then shutting them down, became so rampant that now the PCBs are insisting on integrated processes whereby pollution treatment is in-built into the manufacturing process. Also, the people at large show hardly any respect for cleanliness in public areas and healthy sanitary habits. People spitting on the roads is a conspicuous phenomenon both in villages and cities. Urbanization has hardly improved matters. The litter on roads, consisting of plastic bags, plastic posters of political leaders, handouts and what not, provide an ugly sight in cities, villages, and even tourist spots. Even religious practices have become problematic to environment since the second half of the twentieth century. There is intolerable noise through loud speakers during major festivals. The immersion of painted idols during Ganesha festival and Durga Pooja releases toxic chemicals into the waters, apart from the tremendous amount of other waste which is also released at that time. Our rivers are highly venerated in traditional culture, but many now carry intolerable loads of pollutants. Clean Ganga Campaign, initiated during the Rajiv Gandhi era in the 1980s, has hardly shown any significant outcome.

This is indeed a big irony that a people having such a rich cultural heritage which is eco-friendly, should now turn out to be so shamelessly indifferent to the environment. It is not that all the people of India are indifferent, since there have been agitations against development projects that destroyed environment, particularly when such destruction was expected to adversely affect livelihoods. There also have been small scale initiatives by people in urban areas to induce urban households to dispose off household waste so as to permit composting of organic waste and recycling of other waste, in addition to the municipal corporations doing it. Bindeshwar Pathak almost single-handedly launched a movement for sanitation and a chain of public toilets both in urban and rural areas, which received good response.[10] People have shown willingness to accept pay-and-use toilets in urban areas. Yet, the overall situation is not satisfactory, and the paradox remains.

There are multiple factors behind this paradox and the relative indifference to environmental considerations among contemporary Indians. An important factor was the emergence of mass poverty and the country's economic backwardness, which tended to create indifference to environment. Around the middle of the eighteenth century, India was among the richest countries of the world. Within two hundred years, by the middle of the twentieth century, it became one of the poorest, thanks to colonialism. Endemic or mass poverty and even destitution on such a large scale, as was witnessed around 1950, was never felt before in its long history. Poverty, by itself, may not cause the environmental crisis, but it tends to sidetrack environmental considerations as struggle for survival becomes the main goal. A significant decline of handicrafts and domestic industry under the colonial rule, increased the pressure on agricultural land for livelihood and became an important factor in deforestation. The influence of this factor continued even after independence. Unprecedented population growth exaggerated the situation. Social and economic inequality may already have been there in India, but it aggravated greatly during the colonial period and thereafter. This created a grave cultural divide, and the masses were deprived of access to education and higher cultural values. Widespread habit of spitting on the roads is a reflection of this massive cultural deprivation. Neglect of universalizing primary and secondary education and the generally poor quality of this education, particularly in government schools, only worsened the situation.

The drive for modern economic growth took place in this situation of almost unmitigated economic, social, political, and cultural deprivation of the masses. The forces of growth unleashed the economic aspirations of all classes, which pushed environmental considerations to the background. This made the adjustment between growth and other considerations more difficult, producing lags which meant huge human costs. The drive for growth also helped in the emergence of an elite class and a rising middle class with elite aspirations, influenced by the demonstration effect of the consumption of the richer classes. Their real and substantive loyalty shifted to market values and consumerism of Western capitalism. The greed of the rich and the new-rich with their lavish lifestyles, unprecedented in the long history of India, has contributed more to the environmental crisis than the livelihood pressure on the environment from the poor.

Curiously, environmental awareness too increased significantly since the 1970s. Environmental legislation was in place and the institutions needed for its implementation, such as the PCBs, were also established at the Centre and the states during the 1970s. Reconciling economic growth with the goals of environmental policy was by no means easy, and it was tempting to resolve the conflict through hypocrisy in implementation. The emphasis on legislation, along with its lax implementation, meant widespread corruption and equally widespread hypocrisy. The crisis was as much moral as it was environmental. The cultural tendency to focus on symbols more than on substance is not unique to contemporary India. It was there earlier as well, to some extent, and also in the West, particularly in the wake of capitalism. A twelfth century social reformer and saint in Karnataka, Basavanna, had a sarcastic *vachana* (saying) on this tendency. He observed:

Kalla naagara kandare haalerevarayya,
ditadi naagara kandare kollirembarayya!
People pour milk on the cobra sculpted on stone.
But seeing a real one, they say 'kill it'!

Basavanna may have exaggerated a bit, because people even today are generally reluctant to kill cobras, especially around temples. But the tendency to pay lip sympathy for a cause and not minding to do exactly the opposite seems to be a fairly prominent feature of contemporary Indian culture. Though there has been a stricter implementation of environmental laws and policy during the last two or more decades, the environmental problems are by no means fully under control.

Indifference to environment is to be found most conspicuously on the roads and drains of urban areas, including even small towns. Capacity building of local urban institutions has lagged behind urbanization and economic growth. While municipal effluents are not treated adequately, urban waste collection and disposal have defied any control. Limitless consumerism has led to enormous waste creation. Organic waste and dry waste are not separated at the source, that is, at the household level, though some of it is separated later. In some cities, like Bangalore, some organic waste is turned into compost and sold, but not all of it is collected. Chemical waste is not separated from other dry waste, and collection of e-waste is also far from satisfactory. Hardly a fraction of urban waste is recycled, except in the case of newspaper as used newspaper gets a price and households sell it to *raddiwallah*s (scrap/paper dealers). Apart from the apathy and inefficiency of municipal administration, there are other reasons too for this pathetic state of affairs. Those who generate waste do not show much commitment to the cause of clean urban environment. It is difficult to enlist the co-operation of even clinics and hospitals to systematically and safely dispose off medical waste. They yield only under the threat of cancellation of licenses. If even the medical profession cannot be motivated to voluntarily co-operate in this regard in the absence of threats, then what do we expect from ordinary householders? There are many spoilers in the game of waste collection. Even when households dutifully put their waste together in a plastic bag and put it outside their gate for the municipal waste collector to pick up, animals on the roadsides, mainly cattle and dogs, tear open the bags looking for food and litter the waste all over the road.

An institutional arrangement for collection and disposal of urban waste is already in place in most of the cities and towns, if not all. It may, however, need more staff, a stronger motivation on their part to do a thorough and effective job with proper rewards for it, a little better design of the waste collection job even if it needs some more investment, and a widespread campaign to recreate a culture of eco-friendliness among people. Let me elaborate a bit. When roads as well as drains are littered with waste, it is too much of a task for municipal waste collectors to pick up all of it. Besides, the waste containers used by the municipal workers at the household end are not also big enough for the job. So they collect as much as they easily can, heap together plastic bags and leaves dropped by roadside trees and burn it. Wastes are sometimes burnt by householders themselves. Such unscientific burning creates a lot of smoke and carbon emission and even toxic emission from plastic bags. Not only should the waste collection staff be strengthened, giving them smaller areas for more intensive work, but their waste containers also need to be bigger, and the cart made easier to push. Additionally, each household or group of households in an apartment complex should be supplied with containers to put their waste bags outside their gate, which the animals cannot open.

There is an incentive now to put out waste for recycling only in the case of used newspaper. It is worth exploring the possibility to pay for other waste too handed over by households, such as used batteries, glass, plastic bags, other plastic materials and e-waste. *Raddiwallahs* constitute a chain already for used newspaper, and this institution can be used for collecting other waste too by paying some commission, who in turn may pay a nominal sum to households too. The expenses on this may be recovered partly through proceeds from recycling and partly through a cess on urban property related to property tax.

Private commercials have a lot of space on TV and other media. There should be more space in the media for documentaries and short bits to create environmental awareness. It should also be built into school education right from pre-primary level. Children should be continuously taught to avoid disgusting habits like spitting and littering in public places. Eventually, these measures will reduce the costs of urban waste collection and disposal, when people become more environment-conscious and co-operative. Legislation alone is not enough; nor are market instruments to solve the problems of environmental deterioration, without creating widespread awareness and stricter implementation. Recreating the cultural heritage of eco-friendliness and 'Earth-Spirituality',[11] can be an important way forward.

NOTES

1. http://www.organizeit.co.uk/2009/03/06/inspirational-quotes-alfred-souza-john-schaar-and-more, accessed on 18 March 2011.

2. How about a political leader who is in the profession of caring for others? Is he for this reason necessarily ethical? It depends on how genuine is his caring for others *vis-á-vis* his own self-interest. If he uses his profession merely to amass personal wealth by abusing his power, he is far away from ethics in practice. Similarly for a doctor who is in the profession of caring for others.

3. Lynn White in a path-breaking paper, 'Historical Roots of our Ecological Crisis' (1967) 'laid much of the blame of our current environmental predicament upon the door steps of Christianity', as it preached that 'we humans are uniquely created in the image of God, ... and that our role on this earth with regard to the rest of God' creation is to dominate and subdue' (Nelson 2001: 201–3).

4. For an authentic exposition of the eco-feminist view of environmental ethic, see Plumwood (1993).

5. Though some eco-feminists aim at separating woman from nature, others including prominent eco-feminists like Susan Griffin celebrate this close relationship (see Griffin 2000; Glotfelty 2001).

6. For example, Gadgil and Vartak (1974) showed the existence of 'sacred groves' in the Western Ghats, which were zealously protected by local communities. Gadgil and Malhotra (1982) showed how pastoralists in peninsular India minimized

competition among themselves and promoted sustainable use of resources. (Both cited in Guha 2006: 194–5.) Work by Jodha (1986) and Nobel Laureate Ostrom (1990) on common property resources also confirmed the capacity and willingness of local people to sustainably manage and use local natural resources.

7. For more details on Passmore, see Cooper (2001).

8. Mining, for example, can have several negative externalities like deforestation, loose earth leading to silting of tanks downstream, dust pollution, and dust deposits on agricultural fields thereby reducing yields.

9. About ASTRA, see Guha (2006: 194–5).

10. en.wikipedia.org/wiki/Bindeshwar_Pathak and www.sulabhinternational. org, accessed on 18 March 2011.

11. An expression used by Siddhartha of Fire Flies Ashram, Bengaluru, during a personal meeting.

Part II

Ethics: Some Philosophical Aspects

5 Interrogating the Idea of Justice*

To get an overall assessment of the ethical standing
of an activity it is necessary not only to look at its own
intrinsic value (if any), but also at its instrumental role
and its consequences on other things ... To ignore
consequences is to leave an ethical story half told.

—Amartya Sen (1987: 75)

We win justice quickest by rendering justice to the other party.

—M.K. Gandhi (1927: 151)

THE IDEA OF JUSTICE IN INDIAN TRADITION: *NITI AND NYAYA*

This is a review article as much on the idea of justice in general as it is on
Amartya Sen's book with same title (Sen 2009). The different principles
and approaches underlying the idea of justice are interrogated by Sen
himself, in addition to setting out his own approach. While this article
provides a critical appreciation of the same, it also goes a little beyond by
taking into account approaches and related issues to which Sen has given
limited attention.

Justice is a crucial and major aspect of ethics, though it does not
constitute the whole of ethics. There are other values too like compassion,
courtesy, generosity, tolerance, forgiveness, fortitude, and equanimity.

* A shorter version of this essay was published in *Indian Economic Journal*, 58
(1), April–June 2010, pp. 166–82.

But justice has received more attention of moral philosophers, because of its tremendous social significance, that is, relevance at collective level and in social relations, apart from individual virtue. Appeal to justice is of great value in correcting excesses of economism and achieving a just society, as discussed in Chapter 4. But what is justice? What are its criteria? How do we achieve it? Justice is normally understood in the sense of fairness or equity. By this, Aristotle meant giving to each what is due as deserved. This did not mean equality for him, but rewarding as per merit or virtue. But once we say justice is not equality but equity, it remains to be explained what after all is equity or fairness, and if it can really eschew equality. In fact, this is the burden of several philosophers on justice, including particularly John Rawls and Amartya Sen.

The idea of justice in Aristotle's sense was very much there in ancient Indian tradition too, as expressed by the *Dharmashaastras*. Though incidentally both Aristotle and some *Dharmashaastras* misapplied the concept by according a lower status to women and the labouring class, the idea of justice as the issue of giving one what is due had a large following both in the West and India. It was believed that justice or moral order held the world together and ensured the welfare of all beings, as far back as the *Rigveda*. A recent expression of this was given by Burke in the eighteenth century, who said that all societies are held together by 'laws, customs, and moral habits' (quoted in Das 2009: 411). The two traditions, Indian and Western, though independent of each other and having their own styles of thinking, did have some common ground, and the two could well be said to have found a confluence in the life and thought of Gandhi, and later also in Amartya Sen's *The Idea of Justice*. Sen has been brilliantly applying ethics to issues of social and economic concerns since long and this book can be said to be a culmination of it. The idea of justice has tremendous practical significance, since it can provide not only the basis for law but also for social action and economic and political policy.

Justice in a broad sense was subsumed under '*Dharma*' in India. Use of the word attained greater prominence during the age of epics (especially the Mahabharata) and *Dharmashaastras* (like *Arthashaastra* and *Manusmriti*). It is during this age that Dharma came to emphatically have the meaning of justice. The Mahabharata says clearly, 'Whatever has its beginning in justice ['*nyayayukta*'], that alone is called *dharma*; whatever is unjust and oppressive is *adharma* [against dharma]. This is the rule settled by those who can be respected' (Vanaparva 207.77; tr. Badrinath 2007: 86). Sen creatively uses of the distinction between two aspects of justice: *Niti* and *Nyaya*. Niti meant ethical or moral wisdom or justice in general, while nyaya meant applied or specific aspects of justice as administered or realized.[1] Sen makes use of this distinction almost as the foundation of his approach or entire book, discussing it at some length (Sen 2009: xv, 20–4). Niti refers to behavioural correctness and propriety both with respect to individuals and institutions, while Nyaya refers to 'comprehensive concept of realised justice'—comprehensive in the sense that it includes not merely the outcome but also the process (p. 20). Sen takes the example of *matsyanyaya* (justice in the world of fish) to make the point that avoiding this kind of 'justice' was considered essential in the world of human beings in Indian thought. Nyaya meant giving justice, while Niti was ethics *in general*. While however, Sen emphasizes the conflict between Niti and Nyaya, Indian texts as well as tradition saw harmony and logical connection between the two, since Nyaya is derived from Niti. *The Idea of Justice,* Sen's book, appears to have some penchant for emphasizing certain dichotomies, even where the harmony between the two opposed concepts or approaches is evident. Perceptions of dichotomy between Niti and Nyaya, between emphasis on duty and sensitivity to consequences, between Rawls's approach and his own approach (to be discussed below) are major examples of this penchant.

RATIONALITY AS THE BASIS OF JUSTICE

The dual use of Nyaya in Indian tradition to indicate logic or rationality and also justice, suggests close relation between the two. Plato thought there ought to be some consistency in our idea of justice or goodness. It cannot be relative to different times, people, or places (Janaway 2000: 379). It cannot be capricious, but should be rational. Plato classified the human soul into three parts—the rational, the spirited (lion-like or dog-like), and the monstrous. Interestingly, this comes close to the *Saankhya* classification of *gunas* (attributes or qualities) into *saatvik, raajasik,* and *taamasik*. Plato says that goodness and justice emerge when the rational part controls the other two (Richter 2008: 16, 25). A difficulty with Plato's proposition is that the rational and the moral are not necessarily identical, and leaves the question of what justice is unanswered (Richter 2008: 25). Rationality as the basis, if not the sole criterion, of justice cannot, however, be dismissed. What is conspicuously unjust or immoral cannot at the same time be rational. Amartya Sen devotes the first chapter of his book (after Introduction) to a discussion of the role of reason and objectivity. Nyaaya school of thought (one of the six *darshana*s) in India was very much based on reasoning. The Mahabharata says, 'Dharma and cultured conduct arise from intelligence [or rationality], and it is from intelligence that they are known' (Shantiparva 142.5; tr. Badrinath 2007: 96). As Sen points out Emperor Akbar also emphasized the rule of Intellect (*rahi aql*) as 'the basic determinant of good and just behaviour as well of an acceptable framework of legal duties and entitlements' (Sen 2009: 39). The age of Enlightenment in Europe later also eulogized the role of reason. A smart person may not necessarily be also a good person, but as Sen argues, 'being smarter can also give us the ability to think more clearly about our goals, objectives and values (Sen 2009: 32). But reasoning is mainly an instrument and requires an end, in terms of which, a policy or action can be rationally be viewed. If reasoning is done with a prejudiced instead of an open mind, it can lead to disastrous results. Where reasoning is applied to achieve an immoral end, such as a reasoned and foolproof strategy for a murder, the inadequacy of rationality as exclusive criterion for justice becomes very clear.

SOCIAL CONTRACT THEORIES AND RAWLS

The idea that a moral order is necessary to sustain society has been there in Western thought too since long, as in India. However, it requires a certain social consensus to decide what is good for the society and what is not. This led to social contract theories, first by Thomas Hobbes (1588–1679) and later by John Locke (1632–1704) and others. Hobbes felt that a state of nature as in the wild would make people constantly fight with each other, and their life will be brutish and short. That is why by a social consensus or contract, they permit a ruler to emerge, to whom they will pledge obedience and in return seek protection of life and property. Locke emphasized that the government is legitimate as long as it protects the rights given to individuals by the law of nature, particularly right to life and property. 'If it fails to protect these rights properly, then it is no longer a legitimate government and the people may rightfully overthrow it' (Richter 2008: 93). Justice requires of people to co-operate with and trust each other and the government, and of the government to protect them and their property and self-respect. Sen gives a long list of contributors to contractarian theories —from Hobbes and Locke to Rousseau and Kant and further in our times to John Rawls (1921–2002) and others (Sen 2009: 411).

Among them, it is with Rawls that Sen has a more serious engagement, though he does not ignore others. Sen starts by paying rich tributes to the leadership of Rawls in the development of ethics or moral philosophy, and particularly so in developing his concept of justice as fairness. Though Sen characterizes Rawls's book *A Theory of Justice* (first edition 1971; latest edition Rawls worked on 1999) as path-breaking, he also thinks that the main planks of Rawlsian theory of justice are seriously defective (Sen 2009: 53). His attention to Rawls is well-deserved because Rawlsian theory reigned supreme in the field.

Sen observes that Rawls's foundational idea of justice is to meet the demands of fairness. What is fairness? Impartiality. How to know what is impartial? Rawls resorts to the idea of 'original position', a situation of primordial equality, where parties involved have no idea of their own personal identities, not only in terms of wealth and status, but also in terms of race, ethnicity, religion, gender, and even education. They are covered by a 'veil of ignorance'. The parties involved here are not only equal but also free persons having the moral power to have a conception of what is good and make self-authenticating claims (Rawls 2001: 18–23). The situation may seem unrealistic, but is nevertheless useful in deriving principles acceptable to all impartially. It leads to a social agreement on the principles to guide justice, and evolve perfectly just social arrangements and institutions. To appreciate the need for the construction of an 'original position' by Rawls, let us recall the usual justification of distribution based only on merit. The principle does not favour distribution based on advantages of birth and similar fortuitous circumstances for which a person concerned has done nothing to achieve. But how far can we separate merit from from such fortuitous circumstances? Achievements supposed to be based on merit may depend largely on education received for which parents may be equally responsible, and to that extent are due to a fortuitous factor. To what extent then can such a person be rewarded *more* in life than others, keeping the necessity for incentive for education in mind? It is to answer such difficult questions that an artificial construct of an original position was felt necessary by Rawls. Two principles emerged from the 'original' position with unanimous agreement, as Rawls saw them (quoted in Introduction here). The first of these is about equal liberty compatible with similar liberties for all; and the second is that any inequality has to be justified by two conditions—it is attached to offices and positions open to all under conditions of equal opportunity, and it would be for the benefit of the least advantaged. While Rawls gives a high priority to individual liberty or freedom, he values socio-economic equality no less.

A major difficulty with Rawls's set of principles is that balancing the two principles and arriving at consensus is a grave problem. Sen argues that when there is a plurality of principles and perspectives, a unique solution which satisfies everybody is difficult to arrive. Sen points out that Rawls himself in the later formulations of his theory waters down his earlier claim to have arrived at a unique and unanimously agreement. But this climb-down hits at the very roots of Rawls's approach and theory (Sen 2009: 58). Different people may give different weights to the principles of liberty and equality, and agreement is not inevitable.

Different people have also different needs; for example, a disabled person, a child, a pregnant woman would need special kinds of attention, which others may not find necessary. Some are better capable of converting the same amount of income or an endowment of goods and services into capabilities much better than others who require special attention. Equating incomes need not necessarily mean equating welfare. That is why Sen strongly argues the case for moving from a focus on primary goods to an actual assessment of freedoms and capabilities. Sen feels that the focus of Rawls is on 'just institutions', rather than 'just societies'. Rawls's justice is 'decontextualized' and does not take it to account real lives and capabilities, which according to Sen are crucial for justice. There has to be a shift of emphasis from the ideal to the actual in Sen's approach. In the actual world, there exist several individuals such as the children and disabled who may be left out from the benefits of a social contract agreement. And this is the core of the problem of providing justice.

Sen terms Rawls's approach as 'transcendental' and 'totalist' and as not necessary for the actual issues of justice that call for action. 'The search for the transcendental justice can be an engaging intellectual exercise in itself, but ... it does not tell us much about the comparative merits of different societal arrangements' (Sen 2009: 101). 'The absoluteness of the transcendental 'right'... does not help at all ... in comparative assessment of justice and therefore in the choice between alternative policies' (Sen 2009: 100). Sen illustrates his point: the knowledge that Mount Everest is the tallest mountain the world may not help in comparing the peak heights of Mount Kilimanjaro with Mount McKinley. Similarly, Sen concludes, a transcendental approach to justice would have little to say about the concerns of the actual world—inequities of hunger, poverty, illiteracy, torture, racism, female subjugation, arbitrary incarceration, or medical exclusion—as social features that need remedying (Sen 2009:

96). But the 'ideal' is a standard, in terms of which an actual situation can be compared. To say that a principle or a standard does not help amounts to denying something in which humanity has believed all along. Knowing the height of Mt Everest, does not come in the way of measuring the heights of other peaks. It can help in knowing how far other peaks fall short of Mt Everest. Why do we rank countries in terms of Human Development Index after all?

Though contractarian approach of searching for the 'supreme alternative among all possible alternatives' is thus rejected as necessary by Sen, social contract as an approach has nevertheless one strength. It is that it brings out the role of social backing, necessary for any principle of justice. Without social backing, even the question of what is just, is difficult to resolve. For example, unless there is a social backing to the principles of protection to life and property, it will be difficult to implement these principles. There may not be a similar agreement on the respective weights to be given to the principles of liberty and equality, or about the precise content of these principles. But both are socially acceptable, and no effective implementation of either principle is possible without social backing, which may be brought about through public debate.

Approach of the Social Choice on the other hand, though difficult and sometimes impossible to arrive at, has relevance to the question of justice, according to Sen. It deals with actual choices; recognizes plurality of principles; concedes the need for re-examination; permits partial solution and alternative interpretations; emphasizes reasoned and precise articulation; and recognizes the role of public reasoning through debate (Sen 2009: 106–11). Sen finds the role of public reasoning central not only for making democracy more effective, but also for articulating the idea of social justice on the basis of demands of social choice and fairness (Sen 2009: 112–13).

RIGHTS APPROACH[2]

Social contract theories lead to the rights approach to justice. Recognition of individuals' rights are crucial to the implementation of social contract, as they are to liberty too. The principle of liberty is meaningless without rights. Various rights together ensure liberty—such as the right to life, right to freedom of expression, right to property, right to equal treatment, and so on. Rights which were not recognized earlier are now recognized as rights, such as rights to food, to housing, to employment, to a minimum education, which enable a human being to live a life of dignity. This is what social justice is about in minimalist terms. Rights, particularly right to liberty, are subject to respecting the rights of others too—that 'no one person should have any more right to liberty than any one else' (Sen 2009: 291).

Rights, however, need not be derived only from social contract, particularly if the rights of individuals who could not have been a part of the social contract, are not included, such as rights of children and rights of the mentally disabled. Nevertheless, the human society by an implicit consensus could be said to have conferred such rights even on such individuals. Animals and natural environment could not have been a part of a social contract, but now there is a broad agreement in society about the right of animals and of Nature for protection and kind treatment.

A one-sided concern with rights can be misleading, particularly with right to liberty. Such thinkers who did so did not worry about knowing what kind of social order, or distribution of goods, would emerge when justice is taken only as right to liberty (Scruton 1995: 298). It is only when the rights of others to security in terms of basic necessities like food, shelter, education, and health, and duties of all to each other are considered that we get a more balanced perspective on justice.

Rights invariably correspond to duties. If a child has a right to love, good upbringing, and protection, it is the duty of parents to provide it. Right to life not only means our duty not to kill anybody, but also to take care of say, a victim of an accident, on the part of those who pass by. Rights-centred approach thus can lead to a duty-centred approach, even if rights are not mentioned explicitly in the latter. According to Gandhi, rights and duties are two faces of the same coin. The same thing could both be a right and a duty. For example, every adult could be said to have a right to work as well as a duty to work. Interpreting Gandhi, Parekh says, 'one has a duty to exercise one's rights and a right to discharge one's duties' (Parekh 2010: 67). Rights have a moral status of their own, even if not codified. When codified, duties are also emphasized, at least implicitly. The rights approach is pertinent both to niti and nyaya, because rights are implicit in freedom and enhancing capabilities which Sen forcefully advocates. Besides, denial of nyaya does involve violation of rights and amounts to a case of manifest injustice.

While Sen gives due emphasis on human rights, animal rights, and rights of Nature get limited or summary attention. The concept of justice can be logically extended to animals too and to nature in general, as has been elaborated in the essay on 'Ethics and Environment'.

'MORAL SENTIMENTS'

Before we go to other candidates for the basis of justice, it is pertinent to take note of the contributions of David Hume (1711–1776) and Adam Smith (1723–1790), which overlap. Both argue there is something in human nature which feels what is moral and what is immoral, what is just and what is unjust. They call it as a 'moral sentiment'. But there is a variety of sentiments in us, some noble and some less so. Smith invokes the 'impartial spectator' in us to view our sentiments from a certain distance to rationally scrutinize them, and separate moral sentiments from vested interests (Sen 2009: 45).

Further, both Hume and Smith make a distinction between beneficence or 'benevolence' and justice. Justice demands strict implementation, violation of which calls for punishment. 'Beneficence is always free, it cannot be extorted by force', Smith says in *The Theory of Moral Sentiments*, his first book, published in 1759. 'We feel ourselves to be under stricter obligation to act according to justice than agreeably to friendship, charity, or generosity' (Smith 1976: 80). Justice, is therefore, codified, while beneficence is not. That is why Smith feels that beneficence deserves highest approbation and award. Justice is a negative virtue. 'We may fulfil all the rules of justice by sitting still and doing nothing' (Smith 1976: 82). The most sacred laws of justice, Smith observes, are those which 'guard the life and person of our neighbour; the next are those which guard his property and possessions; and last of all come those which guard what are called his personal rights, or what is due to him from the promise of others' (Smith 1976: 84). The idea of justice is no longer confined to guarding the rights to life and property but also cover now the rights to food and water, shelter, sanitation and health, employment, and even right to self-respect and dignity, and to equitable treatment. Rights are justiciable, while charity is not. Not that charity is unimportant, but a stricter implementation is possible only with justiciable rights. While implementation of justice is crucial to the very survival of society, beneficence improves the welfare of society and makes life worth living. Justice in this wider sense cannot, however, be met simply by 'sitting still and doing nothing' *a la* Smith.

IMPARTIALITY

Sen admires Adam Smith's device of an 'Impartial Spectator' to view our sentiments from 'a certain distance from us' for 'scrutinising not only the influence of vested interest, but also the impact of entrenched tradition and custom' (Sen 2009: 44–5). Justice requires some impartiality and objectivity. Rawls's device of 'original position' has the same purpose. But Sen prefers Smith's 'Impartial Spectator' because Smith's device can bring in 'judgement that would be made by disinterested people from other societies as well—far as well as near' (Sen 2009: 125). Sen feels that Rawls's device 'restricts the extent to which the perspectives of the "outsiders" can be accommodated' (ibid.). As an illustration of how a perspective from outside helps is given by Sen. It refers to how a culturally sequestered people in ancient times felt nothing of the practice of infanticide in the society. Only a view from outside could have made them aware of how horrible that practice was (Sen 2009: 175).

Sen's distinction between two kinds of impartiality: 'Closed' and 'Open' is relevant here. The former invokes the judgements of only the members of a given society, while the latter takes into consideration people outside too (Sen 2009: 123). He prefers the open concept, as it is inclusive and not parochial; and also because the impact of our actions can reach far and wide outside our own group or society. Openness to the views of others is helpful in overcoming the 'positional' prejudices and limitations by making us aware of other positions and perspectives.

Sen also refers to a famous maxim by Immanuel Kant as a criterion for impartiality: 'Act always on such a maxim as thou canst at the same time will to be a universal law' (Sen 2009: 117–18). Sen quotes Henry Sidgwicks's interpretation of the maxim as 'that whatever is right for me must be right for all persons in similar circumstances' (Sen 2009: 118). The Gita too has a verse to a similar effect, lauding the virtue of impartiality (ch. 6, verse 32, quoted in Introduction, p. 11). The Gita's teaching of detachment from selfish interest also is conducive to impartiality. Sen, however, does not refer to the Gita in this context.

Amartya Sen on the Deontology of the Gita

Sen makes a critical assessment of deontology—priority for doing one's duty as a candidate for the basis of justice (Sen 2009: 208–21). He takes the Gita as an instance of high deontology, duty centred and consequence-independent reasoning. Right on the battlefield two opposing armies are already facing each other, and 'Arjuna then expresses profound doubts whether fighting is the right thing for him to do. He does not doubt that theirs is the right cause, and that this is a just war, and also that his side will definitely win the battle' (Sen 2009: 209). But there would be so much death and carnage, for which, as he feels, he would be responsible. Arjuna is particularly sensitive about killing his kith and kin, and elders including his guru. Krishna rejects his arguments and stresses 'the priority of doing one's duty irrespective of consequences'. Krishna particularly appeals to Arjuna's duty as a soldier on the battlefield and a soldier has to fight with a sense of detachment, otherwise he would be misunderstood as a coward by his enemies. Sen feels that 'Krishna got away with an incomplete and unconvincing argument against Arjuna' (Sen 2009: Fn 212). Sen is uncomfortable about this duty argument being invoked repeatedly in Indian discussions on moral philosophy (Sen 2009: 209).

Doing one's duty regardless of consequences is not acceptable to Sen as a principle. He is, of course, aware that several other important issues too are raised in the Gita, and that the Gita is not about deontology only. He also concedes that 'there is nothing to prevent a general deontological approach from taking considerable note of consequences' (Sen 2009: 216). What bothers him, however, is that the *niti* of doing one's duty is raised in the Gita to a purist or absolute status. Sen has been advocating a concern for consequences of what we do, and the quotation at the top of this article taken from his book in 1987 shows that he has been consistent. Sen takes care to distance his emphasis on consequences from the old debate in the West between deontological and consequential approaches to justice. In this debate, consequential ethic was considered as relativist, with end justifying any means adopted. For Sen, 'processes' too are important (which Gandhi calls as 'means'). An outcome is 'comprehensive' if the processes or the means are fair and morally justifiable. This is distinguished from 'culmination outcome' where ethics of processes are disregarded.[3] Sen considers a comprehensive outcome as central to justice as *nyaya* (realized justice) (Sen 2009: 24).

Gandhi too faced the problem of interpreting Krishna's urging Arjuna to fight the war. He took the firm view that Gita preaches non-violence, because not only does the Gita mention Ahimsa as a virtue to be practised but also advocates several other virtues which are not consistent with violence. He saw the war in the Gita only as a metaphor for life's struggle that cannot be avoided. Secondly, even if it was an actual war, Krishna, it should be recalled, tried his best to avoid the war. He negotiated for at least one village where the Pandavas could live outside Duryodhana's vicious rule. But Duryodhana arrogantly refused and made the war inevitable. Respected and wise elders in his court also tried their best to make him see reason but failed. Thus, by the time the two armies faced each other for battle, all other strategies had been tried and limits crossed. The war was not Krishna's choosing. Thirdly, is it ethically alright for a soldier on the battle front to withdraw from war unilaterally? How should it be interpreted? Krishna warns Arjuna that he would be regarded as a coward if he withdraws at this stage. Is absolute non-violence practicable or even ethical? Were Russia and France wrong in resisting Hitler when he invaded them? Fourthly, the Gita does not advocate ignoring consequences. It condemns action taken without regard to consequences as *tamasik*, that is, morally of the lowest kind (ch. 18, verse 25). Sen misinterprets the Gita's advice to act or work without aspiring for the fruits of action as an exhortation to disregard consequences. The exhortation is only to act unselfishly. Sen is, however, right in considering the Gita's approach to justice as being alive to our sense of moral duty, but the Gita wants us to be duty-conscious in a detached way, that is, in an unselfish way. Moreover, Gita's concept of duty is not confined to a soldier's fighting in a battle, but goes beyond and covers among other things even the duty of serving people (*lokasangraha*). The human society runs smoothly only through all doing their duty honestly. Different kinds of duties evolved in society precisely because of their beneficial consequences. Affection and sentiments alone are not enough. It is the duty of parents to look after their children, get them educated and cultured, and keep them healthy. It is the duty of married couples to respect each other, be loyal to and help each other. If some one is hit by a vehicle and is lying on the road, it is the duty of passers by to help that person. It is the duty of government servants to serve people without seeking gratification. The consequences of ignoring duty will be far more disastrous than those of doing one's duty regardless of consequences. Action guided only by consequences, disregarding one's moral duty, could mean sliding down into a relativist and opportunist ethic of the end justifying its means. Moreover, outcomes may not always be under one's full control; they are determined by several variables all of which cannot be predicted. A sense of duty can be a more reliable guide for action than an assessment of expected consequences when they are uncertain, though such an assessment cannot also be ignored as part of one's duty even according to the Gita itself. Though Sen finds himself uncomfortable with duty-centredness of Indian ethics, emphasis on duty in Indian ethics is because duties are more directly enforceable than rights. Rights cannot become operative unless translated into corresponding duties.

It is not in the Indian tradition alone that a duty-centredness is emphasized. The very idea of justice can be defined in terms of duties that we owe to other persons, duties that state owes to citizens, and the duties that the global community owes to all humanity, though it may not be a complete definition. The Holy Bible asks us to love our neighbour and be a Good Samaritan in an hour of need. Kant, the most respected leader of the Enlightenment Age formulated his ethical doctrines in terms of duty to 'Categorical Imperatives' as he called. 'Kant's ethical theory is justly regarded as one of the best ever devised' (Richter 2008:139). For him, ethics requires responsibility, not just sentiment. We fulfil this responsibility through 'orders that we give ourselves' or 'imperatives'. He distinguishes 'hypothetical imperatives' from 'categorical imperatives'. An example of the former is: 'If (or whenever) you want a pie, then go to a bakery!' (Richter 2008: 125). This does not come under the ethical domain. Some things must be simply done, regardless of what you want, and these acts come under categorical imperatives or duties, under ethical domain. Kant distinguishes between imperfect duties and perfect duties. Imperfect duties are the ones which one may not do all the time, but as much as possible, like helping people. Perfect duties are the ones which one must do all the time. Kant gives the example of a perfect duty—never make a false promise; that is, we must never pretend to be promising to do something which in fact we have no intention of doing (Richter 2008: 127). Some duties may be pleasant, and some unpleasant. We may not even know the consequences of doing some duties, but duty remains a categorical imperative. Krishna and Kant seem to have a lot of common ground! However, Sen's basic difficulty in agreeing with Krishna or Kant is that he puts their ethic under niti (behavioural correctness, as a universal law) rather than under nyaya. But Sen's call to prevent manifest instances of injustice such as poverty, itself can be considered as deontological ethic, though of course he is more explicit on taking consequences into account.

HAPPINESS, UTILITY, WELFARE

A prominent claimant for the basis of justice is happiness. In common parlance, happiness, welfare and utility go together. Happiness as the basis for justice in particular and ethics in general has a long history. In the Indian tradition too Satya or Dharma is that which has the effect of producing welfare of people (lokahita). However, a distinction is made between what is merely pleasant or causes short term happiness (preyas) and what produces real welfare or long-term happiness (shreyas). It is because of its emphasis on the nature of the effect of an action, this approach is also closely linked with consequentialism. In a broad sense, the happiness approach is linked with rights approach too, since it is the enjoyment of rights that gives us happiness.

However, the approach came to be viewed in a narrow focus by the utilitarians, beginning with Jeremy Bentham (1748–1832) who remains influential even to this day in economics and economic philosophy. Bentham gave a rather crude version where pleasures alone counted which could be given a numerical score depending on the intensity and duration of pleasure, and all pleasures were of the same kind (Richter 2008:143). Neoclassical economics developed a theory of consumer behaviour based on utility maximization, seen as welfare maximization, as a goal. For the utilitarians, the criterion of the greatest happiness of the greatest number should guide even social action and policy to maximize welfare.

This kind of a narrow welfare approach, however, seemed more to pave the way for injustice than to justice. Sen presents a powerful critique of this (Sen 2009: 277–90), and he is not alone in this respect. There are several problems with this narrow welfare or utilitarian approach. First objection to utilitarianism could be that in pursuing the greatest happiness of the greatest number it would ignore the rights of an individual or a minority. This could happen even in democracies. Take for example, a development project like an irrigation dam that would help a great number of people down the stream, but could also displace many. Just because a greater number of people benefit from the project, could we justifiably sacrifice the livelihood and welfare of those whose lands and homes are going to be submerged? John Stuart Mill (1806–1873) who developed a more refined version of utilitarianism than that of Bentham emphasized the rights of individuals and liberty. This developed later into an important qualification for utilitarianism that interpersonal utility comparisons are not permissible. In the example of the dam above, we cannot then say that the sum total of utilities of the greatest number more than offset the loss of utilities of the displaced. Before a green signal is given to the project, necessary compensation and rehabilitation of the displaced has to be built into the project planning, such that nobody is worse off but is better off than before. But even this does not solve the problem of utilitarianism. Even if all development projects aim at maximizing happiness of the greatest number, duly incorporating compensatory provisions for the adversely affected, they may not necessarily do justice to people who tend to be bypassed by them. Some people may be persistently neglected with no opportunities to rise, and yet utilitarianism as a principle may be satisfied.

Sen observes another important difficulty. Those deprived may 'train themselves to take pleasure in small mercies' (Sen 2009: 283). They somehow adjust and survive. Sen, therefore, says, 'the terms of pleasure or desire fulfilment, the disadvantages of the hopeless underdog may thus appear to be much smaller than what would emerge on the basis of a more objective analysis' (ibid.). He takes the case of health measurement to illustrate this point. If the state of health is to be subjectively measured, even a person accustomed to periodic illness but adjusting to it may not report to a doctor about it. But a health conscious educated and a richer person may do so. This does not mean that the former is healthier than the latter (Sen 2009: 284–6). Utilitarianism, being a subjective approach, does not capture such problems.

A classic objection to utilitarianism has been that it assumes human beings to be nothing but selfish, and ignores other motives like altruism and love. Modern utilitarianism meets this objection by asserting that 'pleasure' need not necessarily be selfish, but can be derived by making someone else also happy. If I sponsor a child's education, I may feel very happy and the pleasure is mine. Williams observes that modern utilitarianism is more flexible and has a wider concept of pleasure and pain (Williams 2000: 552). If I am sensitive, I may feel pain at the deprivation and neglect of persons suffering from it, and may be compelled to act to end this pain. But this is a big 'if', and justice to the deprived may have to depend on the sense of charity of a few persons. Moreover, I may be sensitive to the suffering in my neighbourhood, and ignore others. Such 'charity' does not ensure justice. Those advocating the rights approach does not therefore find even modern utilitarianism useful!

The tendency on the part of the utilitarians to 'reduce all human values and objectives to something like preference satisfaction' has specially met with strong criticism. Such an approach 'seems notably false to certain aesthetic and (differently) environmental values to reduce them to matters of what people happen to like or prefer' (Williams 2000: 553). This may not ensure justice to works of art and to environment. Though happiness as a principle apparently sounds acceptable to common sense, it involves a lot of problems, especially if viewed in a narrow utilitarian or 'welfare' mould, and makes it the exclusive criterion for justice.

JUSTICE AS MUTUAL ADVANTAGE

There is an interesting episode in Udyogaparva of Mahabharata, which is pertinent. After their return from exile, the Pandavas send an emissary to Dhritarashtra, making their just claim to the Indraprastha part of the Kuru kingdom, and offering to avoid war. They wanted peace with justice. Dhritarashtra sends a classic reply to Yudhishthira, the eldest of the Pandava brothers, advising him that being a righteous person, he should practise self-abnegation, give up earthly desire for kingdom and wealth, and thus avoid war and destruction of his own cousins. Dhritarashtra admits that his son, Duryodhana, is greedy and obstinate, but Yudhishthira being a righteous understanding type, should give up his claims and take a path of spiritual pursuit, living in the company of Rishis. Dhritarashtra here is a proverbial case of a Devil quoting scriptures. He says—'ethics is for you because you are righteous, not for my son because by nature he is vicious'! In support he invokes the ethics of self-abnegation and non-violence, to be followed by only one party to the dispute and not the other. On behalf of Pandavas, Krishna sends a reply to the effect that Dhritarashtra has no right to advise thus so long as he or his son keeps Pandavas' share of the kingdom to himself, because there is no justice in it. A compromise without mutual advantage and justice, even to avoid a war, is no compromise and is not acceptable. A one-sided justice is no justice.[4]

'Justice as mutual advantage' as a principle of justice appears in bargaining games between two parties each with given endowments and preferences. John Nash's elegant mathematical formulation of the problem and solution in 1950 has made the approach well known, at least, among economic philosophers and mathematicians. Sen gives only a passing attention to Nash in a footnote (Sen 2009: 281), possibly because, though Sen does not say it, 'justice as mutual advantage' is regarded by some as no justice (Roemer 1996: 92).

The main difficulty with the bargaining approach is that the two parties may hardly be equal in terms of their endowments or preferences. Not only unequal resources, but unequal stature of preferences too could vitiate fair bargaining. For example, poverty of one party may make it accustomed to a miserable position, and it may not express a preference for some thing more. The parties may not also have equal bargaining skills. Traders duping farmers is a classic example of this. If there is an information gap, particularly for the weaker party, bargaining will be even more unequal and unfair. Thus, bargaining between unequal parties may hardly lead to justice. To make them equal, a 'laundering' of endowments and preferences would be needed, in which case it would no longer be a free bargaining game. If the game has to be 'impartial', the two parties would be required 'to put themselves in the shoes of others, that is, to

disregard aspects of their own situation (endowments and preferences)'
(Roemer 1996: 93). A Gandhian solution of each party aiming first to give
justice to the other party (see quotation at the top of this article) assumes
a degree of moral integrity and altruism, which may not always prevail.
Even where it prevails, it is no longer the bargaining game visualized by
those who advocated the approach. How then should a weaker party
secure justice vis-à-vis a stronger party?

Peace loving social and political workers and philosophers have always
preferred dialogue and negotiation to violence in settling differences
and securing justice. Negotiation need not necessarily or strictly be as
economists envisage, a game between two selfishly rational parties. The
principle of fairness to both parties has the best chance of achieving a
durable solution. Gandhi has been foremost in advocating fair negotiation
as a way of resolving disputes. He was always on the side of the weaker
party fighting against injustice by the stronger party, and used non-
violent agitation and preparedness for negotiation as his weapons. He
fought against almost every type of injustice—racism, colonialism, feudal
exploitation of peasants by landlords, and exploitation of industrial labour.
Yet he succeeded every time, though he sided with the weak, making
what seemed impossible, possible. The weak can still bargain with the
strong provided that the weak know their preferences clearly well, both
short term and long term. They should also overcome the information
gap, study the strong party and its interests and strengths and weaknesses
from all dimensions. They should try to overcome their relative lack of
endowments, through identifying their own strengths which the other
party does not have. And what is more, negotiations have to be in an
atmosphere of mutual trust and respect for each other, and not enmity.
This is the Gandhian way to bargaining for mutual advantage.

One more condition needs to be satisfied if mutual negotiation has to
be just. It is that it is not enough that the agreement arrived at between two
parties is fair only to the two. It should be morally acceptable in general
too and be consistent with universal principles of ethics. Two robbers
may reach a mutually fair arrangement for the distribution of their booty.
But the party from which the booty has been robbed will hardly be
impressed by this fairness between its robbers. This is an obvious case.
But this could well be the case also when two big corporate rivals reach
an agreement over the price to be charged by them to their customers, or
when developed countries reach a consensus among themselves to the
detriment of developing countries.

FREEDOM

Freedom as a basic idea of justice has been a prominent value in modern political philosophy, which has ignited struggles and revolutions over centuries almost all over the world. Even while it is admitted that an individual has no absolute freedom, his or her rights are restricted only by due process of law by the society to ensure that every person enjoys maximum possible freedom with due regard to others' freedom too. That is why Jean-Jacques Rousseau (1712–78) asserted that 'the individuals did not surrender their rights to any single sovereign but to the society as a whole, and this is their guarantee of freedom and equality' (EB, Vol.13, 1973: 155).

Why is freedom valued? Sen has something noteworthy to say on this. He says that 'freedom is valuable for at least two different reasons. First, more freedom gives more opportunity to pursue our objectives ... Second, we may attach importance to the process of choice itself ... to make sure that we are not being forced into some state because of constraints imposed by others' (Sen 2009: 228). Sen has an admirable knack for illustrating his points. To illustrate the distinction between the 'opportunity aspect' and the 'process aspect' of freedom, he constructs the case of a Kim (Sen 2009: 229–30). Kim decides one Sunday to stay home. If he manages to do what he wants, it is 'Scenario A'. Alternatively, in 'Scenario B', some strong armed thugs drag Kim out and dump him in a large gutter. In 'Scenario C', the thugs restrain Kim commanding that he should not go out of his house, with a threat of severe punishment if he goes out. In 'Scenario B', there are violations both to the opportunity aspect and process aspect of Kim's freedom. In Scenario C, he may be forced to do now what he had himself planned to do, but he does so under duress. The opportunity of Kim may not have suffered, but the process aspect does suffer in Scenario C. Freedom of choice is as important as freedom of opportunity. There is a difference, as Sen observes, between the opportunity to choose freely to stay at home rather than the opportunity just to stay at home (Sen 2009: 230). This is an important distinction in Sen's capability approach to justice, in which individual advantage is judged by 'a person's capability to do things he or she has reason to value' (Sen 2009: 231). For this freedom in both its aspects is necessary,

Kim's example may not appeal to economists. But suppose we have the following instances of inequality: (a) a woman gets lower income because of her gender; (b) a person gets lower income because he was denied of an opportunity to work in a better job though well suited for it; (c) a person gets lower income because of lack of application. Grand gives us the criterion of availability of free choice, to decide which instances involve inequity or injustice. If a person has a low income because of reasons which s/he could not help, then it involves inequity (Grand 1991:190). Gandhi's notion of freedom goes beyond mere availability of choices. Interpreting him, Parekh observes that for Gandhi, 'freedom consisted in being true to oneself, in living by one's own light and growing at one's own pace, and represented a form of wholeness or integrity' (Parekh 2010: 158). Needless to add that such freedom for one has to co-exist with similar freedom for others. Gandhi's idea of freedom was not meant only for individuals but also for whole communities. Denying this freedom meant violation of justice.

EQUALITY–CAPABILITY

Equality has been recurring as a prominent principle of justice again and again since ancient times. The Gita says that the learned are those who treat everyone with equal regard (ch. 5, verse 18; ch. 6, verse 29). It goes even further in saying that one should treat others with the same interest or manner as one treats oneself (ch. 6, verse 32). However, there is no elaboration of the concept of equality as applied to mundane social matters there. Aristotle (384–22 BC) has a concept of distributive justice, which is equal allocation among equals, and unequal allocation among unequals. This means equal reward for all those who are on equal footing, but a greater reward for a more meritorious person (*EB*, Vol. 13, 1973: 153). This principle is still in vogue. But once we accept this unequal allocation among unequals, it opens the door to inequality which, in course of time, may not be functional or socially useful. Moreover, how greater should the reward for the meritorious be compared with the ordinary persons? Ten times, a hundred times, or a million times? The 'meritorious' have a way of getting disproportionately higher rewards. There are also difficulties in defining a meritorious person. A skilled barber is a very ordinary person in society; but a clumsy surgeon is regarded as more meritorious and rewarded more than the former.

There may be no disagreement with a general statement that all should be treated equally. Once we start interrogating the concept, we land into controversies. But the questions are indeed necessary for clarity and for guiding action. For example, one important question is equality in what respect? What is it that we want to equalize? Should we try to equalize income or wealth? Or consumption? Taking into account different needs of different people (for example, the ill have to spend more on medical treatment), should we equalize utilities or welfare rather than resources or income? Given the need to give incentives to excel, should we instead equalize only opportunities—neither resources nor welfare?

Both Rawls and Sen have given intense thought to this issue, but apparently different solutions. Roemer regards their approaches as 'first cousins', considering the common ground between the two (Roemer 1996: 164). He points out that both Rawls and Sen 'have put forth theories which are best understood as responses on the one hand, to utilitarianism, and on the other, to the theories that view formal equality of opportunity as necessary and sufficient to distributive justice' (Roemer 1996: 163). By formal equality of opportunity is meant 'the condition that there is no legal bar to access to education, to all positions, and jobs and that all hiring is meritocratic' (ibid.).

Rawls advocates equalization in terms of what he calls 'primary goods' by maximizing their allocation among the least well-off group of citizens, so that the difference between them and others is minimized. His primary goods consist of '(a) basic liberties, including freedom of association, liberty and so on, (b) freedom of movement and choice of occupation, (c) powers and prerogatives of offices and positions of responsibility, (d) income and wealth, and (e) social bases of self-respect'. Rawls's focus thus is not on goods or commodities per se, which are only a part of his category of 'primary goods', namely, (d). (Roemer 1996: 165–6).

Sen on the other hand advocates equalization in terms of 'capabilities', and is critical of Rawls for a wrong 'equalisandum'. Sen's case for maximizing the capabilities of the least well-off and equalizing them over people and his critique of 'commodities' as the basis for this are by now well known, as he wrote a whole monograph on this earlier (Sen 1985), and followed it up by forcefully arguing his case further (Sen 2000). It may appear that Rawls's 'primary goods' in his broad perspective are translatable into Sen's capabilities. For Sen, however, 'primary goods are merely means to other things, in particular freedom. ... [and] the motivation behind Rawlsian reasoning, in particular his focus on advancing human freedom, is quite compatible with, and may be better served by, a direct concentration on the assessment of freedom, rather than counting the means towards achieving it' (Sen 2009: 234). Sen's approach directly takes into account 'a person's capability to do things he or she has reason to value... . The focus is on the freedom that a person actually has to do this or be that—things that he or she may value doing or being' (Sen 2009: 231–2). Sen is emphatic on this freedom, while Rawls is not.

The capability approach of Sen 'does not demand that we sign up to social policies aimed entirely at equating everyone's capabilities, no matter what the other consequences of such policies might be' (ibid.). Sen, for example, does not demand that every person be made as capable as Albert Einstein. His approach only draws 'attention to the huge significance of the expansion of human capabilities of all members of the society' (ibid.), including particularly the weaker members who are less capable of looking after their needs in food, education, health, housing, and opportunities to progress along with others. As he asserts, the focus is 'on human life, and not just on some detached objects of convenience such as incomes or commodities that a person may possess' (Sen 2009: 233). His approach proposes a 'a serious departure from concentrating on the means of living to the actual opportunities of living' (ibid.). A great merit of thinking in terms of equalizing capabilities is that the approach goes beyond providing formal equality of opportunity, but proposes to compensate persons for disabilities or disadvantages imposed on them by differences in birth, handicaps and lack of access to education and health. The approach aims at enabling them to overcome these disabilities and come even. That is how this approach amounts to 'reducing manifest injustices that so severely plague the world', instead of concentrating on building some 'transcendentally just' set of institutions' as other philosophers do (Sen 2009: 263). In fact, this is the main point or sum and substance of his entire book.

Interpreting Gandhi's notion of equality, Parekh observes that equality for him 'did not mean that I should get what others get, but rather that I should get what I need for my development' (Parekh 2010: 160). Equality did not mean uniform treatment. It was basically a 'relationship of mutuality and fellowship', since it is in the interest of all that no body should be degraded and demeaned as doing so would degrade and demean all (ibid.). None should be constrained in developing his or her capability to the full.

MANY APPROACHES

A major reason for Sen's lack of enthusiasm for 'transcendentally just' solutions, is that there could be many approaches to it, and no single best solution may be possible. He interrogates several candidate principles for the basis of justice, criticizes most, and agrees with some, as this review here has shown. But no single candidate could be chosen as the most satisfying and free from limitations and controversies.

Sen illustrates this problem in the Introduction itself with a puzzle of three children and a flute (Sen 2009: 12–15). The problem posed by the puzzle is who among three children—Anne, Bob and Carla—should get a flute, which is the only one available. Anne claims it because she is the only one who knows how to play it. Bob claims it because he is so poor that he cannot buy one on his own. Carla claims it because it is she who made it diligently and with skill. 'Theorists of different persuasions, such as utilitarians, economic egalitarians, or no-nonsense libertarians, may each take the view that there is a straight forward just solution staring us here....But almost certainly they would respectively see totally different resolutions as being obviously right' (Sen 2009: 13). Sen does not provide his own solution, because his whole point is to show that no single solution is possible because of the multiplicity of approaches. This is where his nyaya approach has an advantage over the niti, since with the latter we may be lost in searching for theoretically perfect solutions, while with the former we begin treating the manifest ills of the society right away. However, the different principles of niti will still be useful not only in sharpening our reasoning but in identifying what may constitute as an instance of injustice justifying social action.

E.H. Carr refers to the reciprocal relation between principles and facts or 'materials' (Carr 2008: 127–8). Though his observations were made about history, they seem to be equally applicable to the question of justice. We may go by grand theories about what is just. When our conscience revolts against instances of 'manifest injustice', which do not fit into received theory, we modify it or look for new theory. Better equipped theoretically, we better understand and identify 'manifest injustice'. Take the example of treating ill-health. A doctor will certainly take note of manifest symptoms like fever, pain, and weakness, but will also examine the patient in the light of his received theory about the case in point. She will also advise the patient on steps that lead to good health—eating wisely, exercising regularly, and so on which appear 'transcendental', going beyond symptoms. Coming to the case of poverty, we may treat it through poverty alleviation measures, but unless the causes that reproduce and perpetuate poverty and other forms of injustice in society are also simultaneously addressed, poverty will continue to persist. There is therefore need for caution in jumping to a conclusion from Sen's book, to treat only manifest cases or symptoms disregarding grand theory. He has been an outstanding theoretician himself all along, applying theory imaginatively to empirical problems, and deriving theory from facts. Through his theoretical work, welfare economics became more deeply humane. He had seen no conflict between theory and practical matters of policy, and demonstrated the reciprocal influence and relation between the two. Even in this book, he does prefer some theoretical approaches to others. We cannot therefore interpret this book as disillusionment with theories on the whole.

Inadequacy of a purely practical approach as one of tackling manifest or conspicuous instances of injustice such as poverty becomes evident once we begin to raise questions like whether only absolute poverty is to be tackled or relative poverty too. Confining the scope of anti-poverty measures to only absolute poverty or only conspicuous instances of injustice may be seen as viable in the first instance, but this would amount to ignoring the goal of an egalitarian society. Can we just throw some food in the plates of the poor to pacify our conscience and forget about equality? But this is certainly not what Sen has in mind, because he also speaks of equalizing capabilities of all by removing deprivations and disabilities—both absolute and relative. Besides, the extent of 'conspicuous' poverty is not fixed but will vary with levels of economic development. As Gross National Product (GNP) increases and with it the general level of development, the poverty line, which was earlier fixed in minimalist terms, would have to be raised from time to time. After all, the niti of egalitarianism is closely connected with nyaya. It guides the nyaya of redressing conspicuous instances of injustice.

Nevertheless, Sen's insistence on attending to manifest cases of injustice indicates his emphasis on the practical relevance of the idea of justice. This is not an issue of mere philosophizing but solving the problems of the world with fairness. In fact, the idea of justice, equity, or fairness constitutes the very heart of economics. As Sen observed long before, 'distancing economics from ethics has impoverished welfare economics and also weakened the very basis of a good deal of descriptive and predictive economics' (Sen 1987: 78). And ethics is taking action, as Gandhi emphasized, not just an idea or theory. At the very heart of the major debates in economics today like development, globalization and world trade, there is this question of fairness in practice. That the existing world economic (and political) order is inequitable, with so much poverty other manifest instances of injustice. Sen's valuable contribution through his latest book (2009) lies in arousing public conscience on these issues of justice. Philosophy can be a powerful force behind action, both at the individual and collective levels.

An important lesson which Sen conveys is the value of public reasoning to settle disputes, especially regarding approach to justice and mitigating injustice.[5] He has tremendous faith in the efficacy of both public reasoning or discussion and democracy in securing justice. He points to intimate connection between democracy and justice (Sen 2009: 326). He adds significantly that 'we do not have to be born in a country with a long democratic history to choose that path today' (Sen 2009: 332). But 'an unrestrained and healthy media is important', not only because it can nurture democracy, but also because of its more immediate and practical contributions to freedom of speech and press, informational role, protective function in giving a voice to the poor and disadvantaged, formation of values relevant to securing justice, and facilitating public reasoning (Sen 2009: 335–7).

Sen has been coming out with one outstanding book after another. What is more, each improves our theoretical understanding, and more importantly, can stimulate and guide social action and policy. This thought-provoking and inspiring book not only summarizes his earlier contributions to the subject in a single volume, but also fills several gaps in our understanding and can spur public action.

NOTES

1. In other contexts, nyaya has been used in the sense of logic or rationality.

2. Three kinds of rights are discussed in the Introduction, under the section on 'Liberty and Equality—Reconciling the Two'.

3. Emphasis on the morality of means and purity of processes should, however, be understood in the sense and context which Gandhi and Sen had in mind. By processes, they certainly did not mean creating a maze of lengthy bureaucratic procedures and monitoring mechanisms which defeat the very purpose they were supposed to achieve. Blind obsession with mindless means or processes that become counterproductive, is called as instrumentalism, where instruments become ends in themselves (see Damodaran 2010: 225).

4. See chapters 5 and 6 under Udyogaparva, in Kamala Subramaniam (2001: 386–99).

5. Incidentally, Rawls also strongly emphasizes the importance of public reasoning and public justification in this regard (Rawls 2001: 89–92).

6 Appearance and Reality*

Absolute Truth, God... alone is real and all else is unreal

—M.K. Gandhi (1927: xi)

Those who wish to sit, shut their eyes,
and meditate to know if the world is true or lies,
may do so. It is their choice. But I meanwhile
with hungry eyes that can't be satisfied
shall take a look at the world in broad daylight.

—Rabindranath Tagore[1]

QUEST FOR THE REAL BEYOND APPEARANCES

A standpoint on appearance and reality determines our world view—the way we see the world. Our world view in turn has an equally significant implication for ethics, especially the guidance given (or not given) for moral action. A world view which regards the world as it appears, phenomenal world, as false, a pure illusion or as unreal, will logically have little to say about how to live in this world. But apart from the ethical point of view, the theme of appearance vis-à-vis reality is of larger philosophical interest—that is, with our quest for knowledge about what

*This is a revised version of the valedictory address at the Eighth Monastic Dialogue Seminar on 'The Real Nature of Phenomenon and its Relation with Life: Ancient and Modern Perspectives', Tashi Lhumpa Monastery, Tibetan Colony, Karnataka, December 2008.

exists as the real behind the appearance. The theme is explored here from both viewpoints. While briefly reviewing a few important but differing perspectives of reality behind the appearance, the main issue is, whether our quest for the real behind phenomenon, necessarily means ignoring our concern for life and the world we live in. I argue that the two can, and do, go together. I discuss this mainly in the context of Indian religions, particularly, Vedanta philosophy.

Why do we have this urge to probe into the 'Real' nature of phenomenon? First, as human beings we are in a perpetual state of a predicament, which we always try to overcome, and hope that knowledge of the 'Real' helps. The predicament consists in the fact that there are many things outside human control, and we are confronted with a lot of uncertainty, frustration, and sorrow as we go through our life. Even while man aspires to do many things, he is also made aware of the limits to his power. There is too much change and perishability around us which we cannot comprehend. We thus get a feeling that what is perishable or changing cannot be real. Second, said to have evolved from monkeys, we are also insatiably curious to know more and more. Our more evolved brains have only further sharpened this simian urge. Both these reasons contributed towards probing into the 'real' behind the appearance. The fact that what appears to our sense perception may not always be real was known quite early in human history. We knew that what appeared in mirage as water was an illusion. Oars appeared bent when immersed in water, but the boatmen knew it to be straight. Two parallel sides of a straight road appeared to meet at a point at a distance, which again was an illusion. These experiences perplexed us and made us think over what is appearance and what is real. Science later explained most of such experiences, but even after science entered the scene as the most important source of knowledge about the phenomenal world, the urge to know the beyond has not vanished. Science may have made our life easier, controlled diseases, and extended our longevity, but the basic elements of the human predicament have continued as before, and so has our quest for the real behind the phenomena.

This quest has continued in two different ways—metaphysics and physics, or religion and science. While the probe by religions—at least Indian religions—has been inward towards consciousness, the probe by science has been outward towards matter and what lies even beyond matter. For example, quantum physics has shown that what outwardly appears as inert matter, say a table, is full of ever moving and restless energy particles in energy packets called quanta. In this case, the table is an appearance while the quanta behind it constitute basic reality. Science does not normally use the word 'ultimate reality' because it is ever being probed and we—with our human limitations—cannot assert that some particular thing is an ultimate reality. Interestingly, whatever the basic reality as known so far, whether it be quanta in the case of inert matter or DNA in the case of human beings and animals, science does not call the appearances in the form of matter or living beings as unreal. But in the case of religion, if not religion per se, at least certain mystics wondered if the appearances are real at all. Though mystics generally emphasize personal experience more than logic, the logic used in explaining their stand is one of analogy, that the phenomenal world is like dream; and that as long as we are in a dream, we do not realize it is not real but only a dream. Similarly, according to this logic, as long as our consciousness is focused on the phenomenal world and immersed in it, we do not realize its dream-like character.

But even dreams cannot exist without a real world causing them. Dreams are derived from the real world in the sense that they represent reactions of the unconscious mind to happenings in the real world. There are also fundamental differences between a dream and what we consider as the real, even if mundane, world. One is that a dream has no coherence, no logic, and no pattern or order. Though there is some uncertainty and randomness in the world, there is also some order, some pattern, and some predictability. Otherwise, no science or no knowledge as such would have been possible. Even our day-to-day life as we lead it would not have been possible. Secondly, dreams just happen, and we have no control on them whatsoever. We have no responsibility to shoulder in a dream, we just drift. Everything is determined for us. Though in the phenomenal world, there are many things outside our control, still we have some scope to exercise our free will. We are not mere robots. We have some responsibilities in the world which we solemnly accept and carry out. The world is not, therefore, just a dream. Even if the world is an appearance of an ultimate reality beyond or within us, the world is not unreal.

Jawaharlal Nehru has made an insightful observation which is pertinent here:

As a man grows to maturity he is not entirely engrossed in, or satisfied with, the external objective world. He seeks also some inner meaning, some psychological and physical satisfactions. So also with peoples and civilizations as they mature and grow adult. Every civilization and every people exhibit these parallel streams of an external life and an internal life. Where they meet or keep close to each other, there is an equilibrium and stability. When they diverge conflict arises and the crises that torture the mind and the spirit. (Nehru 1994: 81)

Fortunately, the bulk of religions, even Hinduism, do not regard the phenomenal world as false or as an illusion. As shown below, even Shankara's Advaita philosophy, alleged to be world-denying and the source of much misunderstanding, does not do so. How else could Swami Vivekananda, who professed to follow Advaita, call upon us in a lion-like roar to 'Arise, awake and stop not till the goal is reached!', if he believed that the world is false? How else could Swami Chinmayananda, also a believer in Advaita, advise, 'Be a master of all situations. Don't be slave to every uncertain happening. Be strong! Be bold! Refuse to be unhappy!' Religion is more addressed to overcoming the human predicament than to showing that the world is unreal, just as science is addressed to make our external life easier as much as to satisfy our insatiable curiosity to go beyond appearances. Religion, in its own way, also tries to see what lies beyond the world, but in doing so it does not have to reject the world. Although different, these two approaches—religion and science—are still complementary. There can be no internal peace and equanimity, without making our external life at least tolerable.

ROLE OF ETHICS

All religions have shown their concern towards the human predicament. Both, ancient and modern, thinkers and philosophers have reflected over the human situation. The Buddha was one of the earliest to think systematically on this. He recognized that *dukkha* (sorrow) is a universal condition of this world, but out of compassion and love for all, he also proposed a practical solution to overcome this human condition. It consisted of controlling desire and following an ethics-centred way of life.

The Hindu tradition has conceptualized the phenomenal world of births and deaths as an ocean—*bhavasaagara* or *samsaara*—which offers temporary happiness as well as misery, alternatingly. The ultimate goal of a human being is said to be overcoming the duality of samsaara. In doing this, however, a human being has to first get rid of ego or *ahamkaara*, along with the attendant evils of greed and ignorance. The human weaknesses which come as obstacles are listed by the Bhagvadgita (or the Gita 16.12) as:

Aashaapaasha shatairbaddhaah
Kaamakrodha paraayanaah l

Eehante kaama bhogaartham
Anyaayenaartha sanchayan ll
Bound by a hundred ties of desire, prone to lust and rage, they strive to secure by even unjust means hoards of wealth for sensual enjoyment.

(Tr. by Swarupananda 1982: 343)

The Gita, thus, describes human weaknesses in several verses, but only one verse is quoted here. It does not say that these weaknesses are universal or essential to humans. It also lists the *daivee* (divine) qualities which humans can be endowed with. But the pertinent point here is that human weaknesses are ascribed to over-attachment to the phenomenal world and greed, which act as obstacles to spiritual progress. Treating the world with a certain sense of detachment and unselfishness is different from rejecting the world.

According to Jainism, the material world is all real, but there is no creator God. But our life in the world is full of temptations against which we have to guard, and we have to follow the path of moral and spiritual purity so that we can attain godhood, for which every human being has the potential. This ultimate destiny (*kaivalya*) is not inevitable but comes as a result of our striving for it. Like Buddhism and Hinduism, Jainism too underlines the need for curbing our ego and over-attachment to momentary pleasures.

The 'absurdity' of human condition has engaged the attention of modern Western philosophers too. This absurdity has very much to do with man's relationship to the phenomenal world. Jean-Paul Sartre, a leading twentieth century philosopher from France, observed,

Primary absurdity manifests itself as schism: the schism between man's aspirations for unity and the insurmountable dualism of mind and nature; between man's desire to obtain the eternal and the *finite* nature of his existence, between the 'concern' that constitutes his very essence and the vanity of his efforts. Death, the irreducible pluralism of truths and of beings, the unintelligibility of reality, chance– these are the components of the absurd.[2]

Sartre also perceptively observed that man is free but has to find his freedom; he is human but has to humanize himself.

How to overcome what the Buddha called dukkha, the Hindus called samsara and ahaamkara, and what Sartre called the 'absurdity of the human condition'? The Buddha took a very pragmatic view and recommended a practical solution in terms of the eightfold path. This, in brief, consists of curbing the ego and sticking to righteousness in all aspects of human behaviour—thought, speech, action, and livelihood. He did not feel it necessary to invoke an ultimate reality or to raise metaphysical questions which cannot be answered. He taught that if man has moral integrity, compassion, a balanced state of mind, and right conduct, he can face the challenges of the mundane world and overcome dukkha.

The Hindu tradition also emphasized detachment (while being actively, sincerely, and enthusiastically engaged in the world), curbing obsessive desire, and the need for right conduct, without which one cannot cross the ocean of this world (the bhavasaagara) or samsara. But this crossing is to reach the shore of ultimate reality, the source of everything and what lies behind the phenomenal world. This never meant that one could ignore one's role and duties in this world or the need to be righteous. The Upanishadic seers were certainly emphatic on ethical conduct but as a qualification to realize the ultimate reality which alone could impart everlasting happiness. They had an irrepressible urge to go in search of truth and seek to know what lies behind the phenomenal world, irrespective of whether such knowledge solved the problems of life.

As will be discussed below, there was no unanimity about the nature of ultimate reality behind the phenomenon. Depending on the perceptions of the ultimate, each school of thought offered its own solution to overcome the human predicament. Despite theological or metaphysical differences about the ultimate reality, there was an agreement on the ethical issues and the need for moral integrity. The Gita offers three paths, which are not separate but could be integrated—the paths of knowledge, devotion, and selfless work or service—and which are possible to take only in this world, where only a commitment to moral integrity can yield success on these paths. The central message of Krishna in the Gita is, 'Don't escape from your moral responsibilities and duties; perform them selflessly, equipped with knowledge and devotion'. Such a message would have been inconsistent with any stand on regarding the world as unreal.

Gandhi saw the whole issue of reality vis-à-vis appearance essentially in an ethical framework. He asserted that the moral strength of Truth or *Satya*, is derived from the fact that, the root is *sat* (to exist or be) as he often pointed out, 'nothing exists in reality except Truth, everything else is illusion' (quoted in Iyer 2000:150). This reminds us of a significant line in the Gita— '*naasato vidyate bhaavo naa bhaavo vidyate satah*' (ch. 2.16). It literally means, 'the unreal never is; the real never is not'. But its interpretation lies in Gandhi's quotation above. It does not mean that the world is false. He viewed truth philosophically as the only thing that exists, but also essentially in moral terms. He knew, of course, that there is a separate category of scientific or empirical truths, different from moral truths. While empirical truths are fallible in the light of new evidence or fresh inference, moral truths are infallible. To give a unity to the concept of truth, empirical truths could more strictly be called as existing knowledge, rather than truths. Though moral truths are infallible, man is fallible due to wrong or incorrect interpretation of moral truths. It is man's destiny to continuously strive to attain truth, whether it be on empirical or moral plane. Gandhi insisted that a moral commitment to truth is necessary even in the investigation of empirical truths. But he had no doubt that ultimately truth alone survives. Falsehood cannot survive, whether intentional or not, and the illusions created by falsehood are bound to collapse. There is close connection between moral truths and actions, for actions have to follow moral truths, otherwise they are bound to fail sooner or later. Moral integrity has a strength which can shake empires, which Gandhi not only believed but actually demonstrated. The world is the stage where truth plays its role.

WESTERN MISCONCEPTIONS: WHAT ARE THE FACTS?

The quest for reality beyond appearance in India has, however, created a lot of misunderstanding among a few Western scholars, particularly in terms of its relation to day-to-day life. Their criticism left even some educated but uncritical Indians in a state of confusion. It is, therefore, necessary to clarify Indian perspectives on reality vis-à-vis the phenomenal world.

In his well-known book, *The Protestant Ethic and the Spirit of Capitalism*, published in 1905, and his later book *The Religion of India: The Sociology of Hindusim and Buddhism*, Max Weber took the stand that eastern religions are other-worldly, having a negative view of life, and as such could not produce capitalist development and the Industrial Revolution as in the West. Schweitzer (1936) and Kapp (1963) also held similar views taking Indian religions as world-and-life-negating. Let alone economic progress, such an attitude to life was held to be inimical to develop even a robust ethics that could guide day-to-day life, because life as such is considered to be meaningless. Weber's followers attributed the problem of widely prevalent poverty and economic backwardness in the Indian subcontinent to indifference to poverty, which in turn was allegedly due to indifference to economic development. The low rate of growth of the Indian economy, since independence up to the mid 1970s, was termed as the 'Hindu Rate of Growth' by Raj Krishna.[3]

What are the facts? First let me briefly examine whether indeed the alleged attitude of world-and-life denial had an impact on day-to-day life of Indians, and then briefly examine whether indeed such an attitude characterized Indian religions, at least Hinduism, with which I am more familiar.[4] Both Vedic religion and day-to-day life then were highly materialistic. They were very earthy people, praying not for liberation, but very much for success in this very life, for prosperity, for children, and happiness thereafter too in heaven. Their motto was 'Nandaama sharadah shatam' (let us enjoy a hundred autumns). They enjoyed life, cultivated wheat and barley, and raised cattle. They also enjoyed drinking soma-rasa to elevate their spirits and for health and longevity. Their rapturous wonder at the beauty of nature found expression in many hymns.

The later Indians, in spite of the Upanishadic quest for ultimate truth, also were very earthy people. They originated the concept of zero and the decimal system of numbers, they were the first to assert that the earth was round, to point out its diurnal motion around the sun, and to suggest even the force of gravity (Sen 2005: 78–9). They developed a system of astronomy, which was sophisticated by the standards of that time. They also developed Yoga and Ayurveda for physical fitness combined with spiritual happiness, and also surgery and metallurgy. These achievements of Indians, even when the influence of religion was strong, hardly support the view of the Western scholars referred to above.

Have the Indian religions shown any social concern for poverty, exploitation, human rights, and so on? Definitely yes, but I will not dilate on this issue now, because I have dealt with it at length elsewhere, particularly with regard to Hinduism (Nadkarni 2007; Nadkarni 2008: 384–403, also see the essay on 'Humanism in Hinduism' in this volume). The reason for poverty and economic backwardness has to be sought elsewhere, especially in the expropriating nature of British colonialism. At the end of eighteenth century, India was no less economically advanced than the West and had comparable standards of living. British colonialism turned one of the world's most prosperous countries into one of the poorest (Katju 2009).

The so-called Hindu Rate of Growth at 3 per cent per annum, was still better than what was experienced during the British regime, when it was zero or near zero. It was after India's independence that the country started an era of positive and significant rate of economic growth. Indian religions did not come in the way of this, or in its registering a jump in these growth rates after 1980 and rising to over 7 or 8 per cent.

Now about the alleged world negating doctrines and theology. The main basis for misunderstanding was Shankara's statement—'Brahma satyam *jagan-mithyaa'* (*Brahman* alone is real, the phenomenal world is false). This misunderstanding was further reinforced by Shankara's concept of *maya* (illusion), which again was misinterpreted. What Shankara meant by mithyaa, is not false in absolute terms but only relatively to the ultimate reality of Brahman, in the sense that appearance is not the ultimate reality which Brahman is. Maya does not mean illusion, though it is usually so translated. It only connotes the creative capacity of Brahman to manifest itself in myriad forms, both of life and matter. Depending on the context, maya is also taken as the tendency to take the form itself as the essence, as happens usually when the body is mistaken as Atman or the real self, resulting in a false ego. There is an excellent treatise on Advaita world view by Rambachan (2006) which clears misunderstandings about it. (see also Dayananda 1985).

What advaita says is that there is only Brahman, which is ultimate or essential reality, and the phenomenal world is one of name and form—*naama* and *roopa* of the same reality. In the words of *Chandogya Upanishad* (III.14.1), 'verily, this whole world is Brahman' (*Sarvam khalvidam brahma*). The Upanishad makes it further clear in the words of Uddalaka to his son, where he takes the examples of clay and its different forms, gold and its different forms, and iron and its different forms (VI.1.4–6). The forms are also real, but the basic realities behind the forms in these examples are clay, gold, and iron (Radhakrishnan 1994: 391, 446–7). The examples are used in the Upanishad to only convey that similarly the world is a form of Brahman. According to Rambachan, 'what Shankara emphatically denies is that the world has a reality and existence independent of Brahman. The world derives its reality from Brahman, whereas the reality of Brahman is independent and original' (Rambachan 2006: 77). The names and forms are neither false nor an illusion, but they do not constitute the essence. Swami Dayanand (2007) also gives other examples of the ocean, its waves, and water to explain the Advaita view. Water, though one entity, takes three distinct forms—ice, liquid water, and water vapour. All the three are real, but they are only forms of water. Similarly, Advaitins argue that Brahman, the universal awareness/ consciousness, is one entity and reality, but takes myriad forms. Atman (the Self) is the same reality or consciousness at the individual level. To distinguish naama and roopa from the basic reality of Brahman, the word maya is used to denote the former. Liberation consists in realizing one's divine nature, which is also the nature of others. This comes very close to the Buddhist view of regarding every individual person as having the Buddha nature, basically one of compassion and innate happiness.[5] Condition of sorrow is neither innate nor permanent but can be overcome. Though, post-Einstein modern physics regards matter as basically energy, it does not mean forms of matter such as a table are unreal or that it is meaningless to use them. Similarly Vedanta regards Atman (the Self) as Sat, *Chit* (conscious or sentient), and *Ananda* (happy), but it does not necessarily mean that the body is unreal. The body has its own reality, even if the Atman is regarded as the ultimate reality. When the famous mystic, Ramana Maharshi, was down with cancer in his last days, doctors and his attendants were 'amazed at Sri Bhagavan's [as the Maharshi was also called by his followers] indifference to pain and complete unconcern, even during an operation' (Osborne 1992: 181). Osborne also quotes what he said to his devotees: 'If the hand of a Gnani [Knower] were cut...there would be pain as with anyone else, but because his mind is in bliss, he does not feel the pain as others would' (ibid.). The Maharshi symbolized the Vedantic separation between the Atman [Self] and the body, acknowledging both, but transcending the latter.

A major philosophical problem which arises here is that if everything is Brahman, the ultimate reality, how is it that there is pain, evil, dirt, and squalour? How could Brahman take such undesired forms, which are not consistent with its description in terms of *Satyam, Shivam*, and *Sundaram* (truth, auspiciousness, and beauty)? The answer probably lies in the nature of creation. Creation occurs when Brahman appears or expresses itself in different forms of the universe. What is *nirguna* (attributeless) becomes *saguna* (with attributes) in the process of creation. It is in the inherent nature of creation that there are opposites in it—happiness and pain, cleanliness and dirt, beautiful and ugly, good and evil. Happiness has a meaning only in relation to its opposite of pain. And similarly is the case with cleanliness *vis-à-vis* dirt, beauty vis-à-vis ugliness, good vis-à-vis evil. The opposites remain so long as creation remains. The human beings are a unique form, invested with free will and moral responsibility, and it is for them to overcome undesirable opposites and realize their ultimate nature. It is their challenge as well as destiny. Without this challenge and destiny, life would have no meaning, no charm, and no interest.

The charge against Indian religions, Hinduism in particular, of life-denial and world negation is due to being obsessed with one particular interpretation of the Advaita view. But Indian faiths, including Hinduism, also produced a whole lot of other literature like the great epics Ramayana and Mahabharata, not only in Sanskrit but also in other regional languages, which could hardly by any stretch of imagination be considered as world-negating. How can a culture that produced Vatsayana's *Kamasutra*, Jayadeva's *Gitagovinda*, and Vidyapati's *Love Songs*,[6] be ever dubbed as ascetical and life-denying? Hindery approvingly quotes historian A.K. Warder's conclusion about Indian religion and culture: 'Fundamentally Indian religion is not ascetical and hostile to the world' (Hindery 1978: 161).

A philosophy of world negation emerged in the West too.[7] Such a view creates serious problems for day-to-day life. If the world is false, an illusion, then life has no meaning, our activities would have no meaning, and there would be no basis for any moral code of conduct and duties and rights of man. Why should a mother raise her child if everything is illusion? Why should we have any concern for environment and society? When his teacher lectured in his class about space and time being, mere concepts having no reality of their own, a student who became a philosopher in his own right later, George Edward Moore (1873–1958), simply asked, 'If space is not real, does it mean that the wall just behind me is not nearer than the library building over there? If time is not real, does it mean that this class will not end by noon?' (Donald Palmer 2001: 309). When confronted with a similar view about the phenomenal world being just an idea and unreal, Samuel Johnson said, 'I refute the view thus', and kicked a boulder nearby. He hurt his toe thereby, but showed that the boulder is real and the pain too.

Both Advaita and modern physics, according to both of which there is ultimate or basic reality beyond appearances as discussed above (also see Capra 1992), give rise to the question of whether appearance has no significance or meaning of its own and if it is different from ultimate or basic reality. If energy particles are the basic reality in physics, does it mean that what we see for example, as a table, an animal, or a human being are all unreal, or that they have no meaning and significance of their own? Quanta may be ultimate reality in physics, or DNA may be ultimate in biology, but the names and forms they take, say, as a table, an animal, or a human being, have definitely more significance in day-to-day life, and this is what matters. Appearance has its own significance of being at least our first exposure to reality. As Weiss observed, 'We confront appearances. These are outcomes because realities have made an appearance. Appearances are because realities are surfaced' (Weiss 1974: 64). Brahman may be the ultimate reality in Advaita, but the phenomenal world still has significance for life in which we not only live but also use it to realize the ultimate reality whatever it may be. Where else but in this world and through this world, can we realize the Purushaarthas, life's basic multiple purposes—*Dharma, Artha, Kaama,* and *Moksha*?

PLURALITY OF PERCEPTIONS

Advaita is not the only perception of reality in India or even in Hinduism. There is a plurality of perceptions and Advaita is only one of them. The overwhelmingly large majority of perceptions about the world are positive and even about our life in the world. As seen above, the Vedas are full of the zest for life. Though they did recognize that there are problems and difficulties in the world, they did not deviate from their motto of enjoying life fully, of course subject to *Ritam* or truth or moral law. They accepted and venerated the world full of diversity and beauty.

The Upanishadic sages indulged in mystical and metaphysical thought, and lived in forests in pursuit of the knowledge of the ultimate. Nevertheless, nowhere did they declare the world as unreal. There is a signicant passage in *Brihadaaranyaka Upanishad* in chapter 2, section 3, as follows:

Dve vaava Brihmano roope, moortam cha, amoortam cha,
martyam cha, amartyam cha, sthitam cha, yat cha,
sat cha, tyat cha.

S. Radhakrishnan translates it as follows: 'Verily, there are two forms of Brahman, the formed and formless, the mortal and immortal, unmoving and moving, the actual or existent and true being' (Radhakrishnan 1994: 192–3). The significance of the passage lies in the fact that it speaks of two forms of Brahman or reality, and accepts the world also as a form of Brahman itself. There is no question of treating it as unreal or even as a secondary, less important reality.

The six *Darshana*s, that is, philosophical schools of thought in Hinduism had their own individual perspectives. Vedanta, also called *Uttara Meemaamsaa*, is only one of them and its views expressed in the Upanishads and Brahmasootras are already discussed above. The ancient Saankhya school of thought saw reality as consisting of two principles— *Purusha* and *Prikriti*. The former is the male principle, representing consciousness. By itself it does not act, but it observes. All action and movement takes place in the female principle of Prikriti—in the nature, the phenomenal world. Both are real and exist together. Mind comes under Prikriti. There are as many purushas as sentient beings, and prikriti also takes myriad forms. The Nyaya-vaisheshika schools of thought believed that atoms (*anu*) constitute the basic reality of the world behind numerous appearances. Both Nyaya-vaisheshika and Saankhya schools are pluralist in approach as also realist. An ancient but unorthodox school of thought in India, *Lokaayata* of Charvaaka, emphatically denies any supernatural reality beyond the phenomenal. For them the nature is the whole and the only reality, and there is nothing like a soul or consciousness without or independent of the body, hence there was no question of rebirth. The Buddhists thought of basic reality as one of continuous flux, for them nothing is fixed or permanent or stable. The cosmic order is like a wheel and goes on moving. Everything is momentary *(kshanika)*. There is constant becoming, neither being nor non-being. The world is real but fleeting. That is how the Buddha considered over attachment to the world as improper leading to dukkha (Tiwari 1983: 51–2). Like Buddhism, Jainism also does not believe in a creator God as ultimate reality. Its world view is realistic as well as pluralistic *(anekaantavaada)*. There is principle of motion (dharma) as well as of rest *(adharma)* in the world (Tiwari 1983: 72). Jainism, incidentally, uses the terms dharma and adharma, in its own unique way, which should not be confused with their use in Hinduism and Buddhism. While for Buddhism everything is in a state of flux or motion, for Jainism things are moving as also at rest.

There is a strong and well sophisticated tradition of Dvaita philosophy in Hinduism which also believes that reality is plural and diverse and not a single entity. God is of course One, but His creation is different from Him. It is also immensely plural, myriad, and diverse. All the diverse creation may be ultimately dependent on God, but it is also real. While the relation between God and his creation can be compared with gold and its ornaments or the ocean and its waves in Advaita, it can be compared with potter and his diverse pottery in Dvaita. This is also a pluralist view of reality. The bulk of Indian philosophical thought believes in a pluralist world view, which is most explicitly world and life affirming. Even Advaita does not negate plurality; it only takes plurality as myriad manifestations of the same Brahman, who is both immanent and transcendental. Even when all manifestations in all forms are dissolved into Brahman, Brahman remains.

Another great tradition, which chronologically comes between Shankara and Madhva, is Vishishthaadvaita of Ramanuja. According to this philosophy also, the world is real. All matter, living beings and souls form the body of Brahman. 'It admits plurality, since the supreme spirit subsists in a plurality of forms as souls and matter' (Radhakrishnan 2000: 661). Though the three Vedanta philosophies appear very different from each other, there is some harmony between them. If Advaita of Shankara can be treated as seeing all reality as unity, Vishishthaadvaita of Ramanuja sees it as unity in diversity, and Dvaita of Madhva sees it as only as diversity. Reality thus depends upon one's perspective. We cannot say one is correct and another is wrong, all perspectives are correct in terms of their respective perspectives. But none of them deny our moral responsibilities to the world.

If his advaita had prevented him from undertaking moral responsibilities in this world, Shankara would not have travelled the length and breadth of the country to establish four or five *matha*s (Hindu monasteries). Out of his regard and love for his mother, he rushed to her at her last hour and performed her last rites as a responsible son, in spite of being a *sanyaasi* (renunciate monk). Advaita did not prevent him from composing many mellifluous hymns in loving praise of several deities of Hinduism in Sanskrit. He was not just a dry philosopher but a poet too.

Indian religions, including Hinduism, have not prevented us from seeing the world 'with hungry eyes' and 'in broad daylight' as Rabindranath Tagore expressed in the quotation appearing at the top of this essay, and enjoying it. Sanskrit literature as well as the literature in other Indian languages is full of verses in praise of all aspects of the diverse beauty of the world, including the beauty of man and woman. Vedic sages exhorted— '*Jeevema sharadah shatam, nandaama sharadah shatam*' (we should live for a hundred autumns, and enjoy a hundred autumns).

An important issue about reality is whether it is stable or in a state of flux. Buddhism regards reality as one of perpetual restless change, while Vedanta tends to view ultimate reality as stable or changeless, but its manifestations as ever changing. There was a debate about this in ancient Greece too. A pre-Socrates philosopher, Heraclitus, was of the view that everything flows and nothing abides. For him 'the only thing that does not change is change itself' (Palmer 2001: 26). This has raised a question in Vedanta if whatever is changing or transient is real or not real. A fresh natural flower may not last long, but does it make it less real than a plastic flower which may be enduring? Though there is a view that whatever is *nashwara* (perishable) cannot be real, there is also a strong Indian tradition which believes that truth is essentially dynamic, and what lasts in terms of value and significance is what is dynamic, and not what is static. This view found a beautiful expression in a famous *vachana* (saying) by Basavanna, an eminent religious reformer in Karnataka in the twelfth century. He said, '*Sthaavarakkalivuntu jangamakkalivilla*, that is, what is standing (*sthaavara*), fixed or static perishes, but what is moving or dynamic (*jangama*) does not'.[8] Basavanna wanted to convey a definite humanist world view through his philosophy. What he suggested is that it is the human beings who are more valued and sacred than the static temples (even if humans are mortal).

The Vedantic view that while the ultimate reality, absolute truth, is unmoving (*achala, sthaanu*), its manifestation in name and form is ever moving, may seem rather dichotomous. Vedantins also assert that Brahman can have no attributes and is too great and magnificent to be understood by human senses or intellect. Immanuel Kant, the eighteenth century Enlightenment philosopher comes close to Vedanta in distinguishing between appearance or phenomenon (see Blackburn 2008: 274) and the ultimate reality behind it, the Noumenon or 'Thing-in-Itself'(see Blackburn 2008: 255). He said the analytical categories such as time and space, though useful in understanding the phenomenon, could not be applied to Noumenon, and as such we had no means of knowing it. However, according to Vedantins, Brahman is amenable to experience in consciousness. For Vedantins, the Self or atman is itself consciousness or awareness. Is consciousness static or dynamic? When it is turned inward and has no object, when the seeker himself or herself is sought then what is experienced is *shoonya* (nothingness), it is beyond attributes, and at that point, consciousness could be considered as changeless or *achala*. But when consciousness has an object in name and form, it is moving and dynamic. While Buddhism considers consciousness as dynamic, saankhya philosophy takes it (*purusha*) as changeless non-doer. Awareness may shift from one object to another, but awareness itself is the same. Purusha can be compared to the sun, and *prakriti* nature to the earth. Earth moves around itself and also the sun, with the sunlight falling on its different parts alternately, but the sun remains stationary (at least relatively to the earth). It is thus prakriti which moves or changes but not purusha in saankhya, though purusha like the sun plays a very important role.

The Upanishads have characterized reality as '*dhruvam adhruveshu*', or the changeless amidst the changing. To understand this, we need to distinguish between change according to some pattern and order, that is, discernible and predictable change on the one hand, and change which is totally random and unpredictable. There is a lot of dynamism and change in the universe, but it also follows some laws which are enduring and can be considered as constants. If the phenomenal world is so very changing with absolutely no predictability, there can be no science, for no generalizations can be drawn. There is indeed a vast amount of randomness, uncertainty, and flux even in the phenomenal world, including at the ultimate level of quanta in physics, but still there is some order in the universe and some scope to derive more enduring laws and generalizations, which constitute the findings of science (like the law of gravity), and which is Upanishadic *dhruvam* (changeless, sure or definite). Even random change can be tried to be understood in terms of laws of probability. Thus, dhruvam is not to be understood as something absolutely unchanging or rigid, but as something amenable to certain enduring laws which hold for all time. In another context, it refers to the ultimate reality or Brahman who is eternal and stable amidst its changing manifestations, and remains even when all its manifestations are dissolved into it.

Faced with a dichotomous nature of reality, Indian philosophers—both Buddhist and Hindu, distinguished between two types of truth or satya. The ultimate reality, the 'Ground of Being', was called by Hindus as '*Paaramaarthika satya*', and the phenomenal, the secondary or dependent reality as '*loukika satya*'. The eminent Buddhist scholar, Nagarjuna, called them almost in similar terms, respectively as '*satyam paramaarthatah*' and '*loka samvriti satyam*'. The latter was not an illusion or false entity, but only a dependent or derived reality, compared to the primary reality which was the former. This distinction has a great practical and humanist significance. Whatever be the nature of basic or ultimate reality, philosophically or in metaphysics, we as human beings have no alternative but to encounter the day-to-day reality we face. Sartre said, existence precedes essence (Sartre 2007: 22–3). A human being is born first and has to develop and find her or his own essence, own role, own significance. This is not very different from the law of karma which is common to Indian religions. Karma is not fate or destiny; it is made by human beings themselves through their own action. In terms of this law, human beings have the freedom and responsibility to make themselves and their future. Even if the world is a large drama of God or a Supreme Reality, we have got to play our role, and cannot afford to escape from it. And we have to play it in such a way that we contribute to human happiness rather than be a nuisance disrupting the system in which we have to operate.

In terms of Advaita view, the ultimate reality is not a personal God. But it does recognize the need for a personal god as manifestation of the same Brahman, as it helps in self-realization and liberation. When we pray to a personal god, we mobilize our inner spiritual resources, draw strength and moral courage. Meditation also has the same effect. As observed above, Shankara himself composed many beautiful poems in praise of several personal gods of Hindus, as manifestations of the same Brahman. Even Acharyas who did not subscribe to the Advaita philosophy invoked personal forms of God as the one and the same Brahman who is common to all. The important point, however, is that neither prayer nor meditation can allow human responsibility to society to be given up. Any religion that is not socially and humanely engaged is a misfit in the present times.

There are bound to be different world views and different religions have different world views. Within Hinduism itself, there are many—each aiming at finding a meaning in our lives and in this world, in which we are thrown without our consent, as a philosopher put it. Any fanaticism about one world view alone being correct and the others being incorrect can lead to inhuman behaviour. That is why Gandhi emphasized tolerance, openness, and humility. But he never denied the reality of the world and the role of human responsibility. Whatever be one's world view, it has to be consistent with the need to be compassionate and concerned about others' welfare. It cannot afford to make us escape from this responsibility. While metaphysics may divide us, ethics and humanism can unite us. Ultimately, as Sartre believed, human beings have to rise to take full responsibility of their human condition and for its improvement, irrespective of whether there is God or there is no God or the nature of God. It is we the human beings who make or mar our own future and our condition, though many things are not in our control including the outcome of our action. Grace of God may help us, but it does not absolve us from our responsibility to this world. As the Dalai Lama rightly observed, the purpose of our existence is to seek happiness (Lama and Cutler 1998: 3). He has also emphasized that one cannot be happy without being compassionate and loving, which is also innate human nature. Our task is to realize this innate nature. The advaitic view that the Self is basically divine gives us the hope that we are not powerless in realizing our ultimate potential. There is equally good hope in other theistic views which believe in the grace of God helping us in playing our role.

NOTES

1. From 'I Won't Let You Go—Selected Poems' by Rabindranath Tagore, Translated by Ketaki Kushari Dyson (2003; first edn 1992). New Delhi: UBS Publishers and Distributors, p.107.

2. As stated in 'A Commentry on *The Stranger*' in (Sartre 2007: 74–5).

3. This expression by Raj Krishna is often quoted. See, for example, Ahluwalia (1995: 1).

4. For more detailed discussion, See Nadkarni 2008, esp. chs 1 and 7.

5. In his personal communication to me commenting on the earlier draft of this paper, M.V. Ramana observed that the idea of innate human nature is problematic. This is because, apart from the debate over nature *vs* nurture, the question arises about how or from where then evil comes to humans. He feels that the argument for being compassionate is strong by itself, and does not require any assumption about innate nature. The existence of evil is one of the most difficult problems in the philosophy of religion, which is yet to be resolved to the satisfaction of all. Vedantins try to resolve this by saying that evil comes from false ego and ignorance about one's real nature. But this begs the question of why false ego and ignorance emerge in the first instance. Is this due to *Maayaa*? Brahman

being essentially free, his forms, particularly human beings, are also free, having free will. Even when God is taken as Creator separate from his creation, he is believed to have given free will to humans, imparting freedom to choose between the good and the evil, or change from being evil to being good.

6. See *Love Songs of Vidyapati*, Tr. by Deben Bhattacharya, with an Introduction by G.W. Archer, Delhi: Orient Paperbacks. The *Love Songs,* composed in Maithili, are dated by Archer between AD 1380 and 1406. Hindery observes, 'the primary significance of Vidyapati's songs is the simple persistent, dramatic, and commonplace testimony ... that this life and world are not to be scorned in the name of religion' (Hindery 1978: 170).

7. F.H. Bradley, for example, tried to show that our common sense world was a world of 'mere appearance', in his book, *Appearance and Reality* (1893). See Scruton's article on 'Appearance and Reality', in Scruton (1995) pp. 112–20.

8. The full *vachana* as translated by Ramanujan (1973: 19) is as follows:

> The rich will make temples for Shiva,
> What shall I a poor man do?
> My legs are pillars,
> My body the shrine,
> The head a cupola of gold.
> Listen, O Lord of meeting rivers,
> Things standing shall fall,
> But the moving ever shall stay.

7 Holistic Approach to Knowledge
Contribution of the Bhagavadgita and
Its Relevance to Social Science
Research and Ethics*

> When we see the wholeness of a thing from afar that is the true seeing;
> in the near view trivial details engage the mind and prevent us from seeing
> the whole, for our powers are limited.

—Rabindranath Tagore (1989: x)

There is a story of a PhD student newly enrolled in a university, who took
her parents from a village to show her new educational institution. After
seeing one by one all the buildings, her department, hostel, library, and so
on, her father asked the daughter, 'you have shown us so many buildings,
but where is the University'? This typical error in thinking is known by
the phrase, 'missing the forest for the trees', and is also illustrated by the
Panchatantra fable of the elephant and the nine blind men. We tend to
miss the whole, while being obsessed too much with the parts.

Unfortunately, an approach which compartmentalizes a problem,
splitting it into several separate parts and studying each in isolation, is too
common with academics to be ignored. This also goes under the name of
rigorous analysis. This is in contrast with a holistic approach which looks
at the problem as a whole, with all its aspects and parts and their cross
connections.

* This is based on shorter versions of this essay which were published in *Think
India Quarterly*, 12 (2), April–June 2009, pp. 32–45 and *Journal of Social and
Economic Development*, 12 (1), January–June 2010, pp. 26–42.

This is less a question of the nature of reality, but more one of understanding or approaching it. Yet, both questions are linked with each other. Approach to knowing reality is tailored to the theory of reality, and a theory of reality may well be the outcome of the approach. The issue has been debated both in modern western philosophy and in Indian philosophy. In the west there has been a bitter dispute between 'methodological holism' and 'methodological individualism', while in India it has been between holism and pluralism. In both cases, approach is related to the conception of reality taken as actually existing. While the dispute in the West took place mainly in the context of social explanation or social science as such, in India it was in a much more general context. But as shown below, the Indian contribution of approach to knowledge, particularly as found in the Bhagavadgita (the Gita, henceforth), has astoundingly direct and significant relevance to research methodology in social sciences too. We have something to learn from it even now. Before taking up the Gita's contribution, it would be useful to briefly review holism vis-à-vis individualism standpoints in Modern Western thought, and holism vis-à-vis pluralism standpoints in classical (post-Upanishadic) Indian thought.

Individualists like Mill, Weber, Schumpeter, and Popper argue that social facts must be explained only in terms of the actions, beliefs, and desires of individuals. Holists like Durkheim and Marx, on the other hand, tend to bypass individual action and focus attention on the society or groups or the economic system as a whole (Bhargava 2000: 359). Holists argue that intentions of individuals are embedded in social practices and that identification of such intentions is meaningful only in a social context. There is a social ingredient in all individual intentions and actions. However, the argument of some holists like Durkheim that a reference to individual actions is not even necessary has been hotly contested (Bhargava 2000: 359). Such an attitude of these holists provoked an equally extreme condemnation by K.R. Popper, a staunch individualist. 'For Popper, the great wickedness of holism is that it goes along with a Fascist or Communist belief in group destiny, a belief which enables self-styled beneficiaries of this destiny to trample on the rights of the weak with an easier conscience' (Ryan 1970: 177). The dichotomy between holism and individualism, however, is not as irreconcilable as it appears from such mutual attacks. Even while holism takes note of the wholes, it cannot ignore the parts, any more than a car mechanic while test driving a car can afford to ignore the working of individual parts of the car. Similarly, as Ryan points out, individualists are not concerned with specific individuals named X or Y, but with 'typical' individuals in a particular logic of situation in a social or economic context of general significance (Ryan 1970: 178). This would suggest that we can consider holism and individualism as complementary, rather than as opposed to each other in social analysis.

In classical Indian thought, the Nyaya–Vaisheshika School of Hindu Philosophy believed in the whole or wholes being a distinctive reality, which is different from its parts taken together (Matilal 2002: 5). However, it has also a pluralist view of reality. According to the Buddhist schools of philosophy, the whole is not distinct from its parts taken together. Even if conceptually different, the whole has no separate existence apart from its parts taken together (Matilal 2002: 6). Bhartrihari (fifth century AD) contributed to an absolute holistic view, corresponding to the absolute monism of Shankara. According to Bhartrihari, reality was an undifferentiated unity, but language sliced the whole into parts resulting in concepts (Matilal 2002: 359). According to Shankara, there is only one absolute reality, and everything is Brahman, though its appearances or manifestations may be many. Later Hindu philosophy developed two further schools of thought on reality (among others)—Vishishthaadvaita of Ramanuja and Dvaita of Madhva. While the Vishishthaadvaita school is both holistic and pluralistic, Dvaita school is purely pluralistic. The former could be said to be a theory of unity in diversity, where diversity is not conceptual but real. Two other prominent schools of Indian philosophy—Saankhya and Jaina are also pluralistic in their view of reality. The foregoing debate about holism vis-à-vis pluralism in India was more about the nature of reality than about the approach to knowledge. All the schools of Indian philosophy have developed their own approaches to knowledge, but they were not necessarily couched in terms of methodological holism vis-à-vis individualism or pluralism. It is only in the Gita that there is a direct and explicit discussion of it. The interesting point, however, is that when contemplating or probing into the nature of reality, the approach adopted has been holistic, irrespective of whether the perceived ultimate reality allowed for diversity or not. Whenever questions of the type—'what does it all mean?' or 'what does it all add up to?'—were raised, a holistic approach was found indispensable. It does not mean that holistic approach is relevant only when such philosophical or metaphysical questions are raised. In the Gita, there is not only a direct and explicit reference to a holistic approach to knowledge, a culmination of the Upanishadic thought, but relevance of the approach to even mundane issues of knowledge becomes very clear.

THE BHAGAVADGITA AND THE CRITERION OF THREE GUNAS

The Bhagavadgita (the Gita) is an important sacred scripture of Hinduism, which, in addition to being a moral guide to day-to-day living, is also recognized as a source of teaching on the nature of ultimate reality and of knowing and realizing it. However, its teaching can be interpreted, not in one unique way, but in a way as to derive support for all the three views of reality referred above—Advaita, Vishishthaadvaita, and Dvaita. The three eminent acharyas associated with these three schools respectively have all drawn support from it. Even when apparently the same methods of knowledge are used by two persons, their perceptions may differ resulting in different views of reality. According to the Gita, there is a unity or consistency between knowledge (*jnaanam*), object of knowledge (*jneyam*), and of the knower (*parijnaataa*), just as there is such a coherence between the instrument or the means of action (*karanam*), action (*karma*), and actor or agent of action (*kartaa*) (ch. 18.18). They influence each other. This can give rise to genuine differences in perception and conclusions, even if all the seekers of knowledge adopt apparently impeccable approaches to knowledge, and the moral integrity of all seekers is also equally impeccable. However, there could also arise differences due to faulty approaches and due to prejudices and self-interest of the seekers. There is thus a need for some guidance in assessing relative merits of different perceptions. In this task, the teaching of the Gita elaborated in this article can be of some help. A very interesting aspect of the teaching of the Gita is that it can be applied to pursuits of knowledge, which are mundane, and not necessarily to only spiritual knowledge or knowledge of the ultimate mystical reality. The Gita's teaching can be relevant to methodology of social science and to resolving ethical dilemmas too.

The key to the understanding of the Gita's approach to either knowledge or action is its teaching that they are to be assessed according to three levels of quality—*trigunas*. This need for assessment applies not only to the approach to knowledge or means of action but also to the knower and the actor. There is a fairly lengthy discussion of trigunas in the Gita, especially in the chapters 14, 17, and 18.[1] Three levels of qualities or gunas are *saatvik, raajasik,* and *taamasik. Saatvik* is morally at the highest level; it means virtuous, free from sin, good, gentle, affectionate or loving, detached (unselfish), sage-like, wise, and is associated with happiness (*sukha-sangena badhnaati*, ch. 14.6). Raajasik means emotional, passionate (*raagaatmakam*), born of desire and attachment (*trishnaasangena samudbhavam*, ch. 14.7), prone to anger and aggression, clever (more in the sense of cunning rather than wise), active, energetic, dynamic, and outgoing. Taamasik means dismal, indolent, dull, born of ignorance (*ajnaanajam*), depressing, illusory, clumsy, prone to committing mistakes (ch. 14.8). While the outcome of saatvik is happiness and enlightenment, raajasik provokes action, and taamasik masks knowledge and leads to mistakes or wrong-doing (ch. 14.9). The Gita is emphatic that the quality which leads to knowledge is saatvik (*satvaat sanjaayate jnaanam*, ch.14.17). That is why both the knower and actor also have to be saatvik, equipped with detachment and free from selfishness, prejudices, and from likes and dislikes (ch. 18.23). Though detached, they have also to be at the same time courageous and enthusiastic (*dhrityutsaaha samanvitah*, ch. 18.26).

According to the Gita, it is not that one person is always saatvik, or another always taamasik. Persons are mixtures of all the three gunas, with one guna emerging as dominant over the other two depending on circumstances and natural inclinations. The Gita tends to apply the criteria of these three gunas more to things like work, charity, food, and approach to knowledge than to persons. However, the teaching is that every person should try consciously to be saatvik and avoid being taamasik. A person gets the attribute based on what or how s/he does. For example, saatvik work is done without a selfish motive and with skill and commitment, and the doer of such works thus also becomes saatvik. Similarly, raajasik work is that which is done with a selfish motive or with arrogance, and taamasik work is that which is done with a malicious intention of harming others or work done unmindful of its consequences (ch. 18.23–5). An act of charity is termed saatvik, if done selflessly and with humility, giving respect to the recipients and if it is not done merely in return for a benefit received. It is raajasik, if done with self-interest, expecting something in return, or in return for a benefit received. It is taamasik, if done grudgingly or with arrogance and or contempt towards recipients (chs. 17. 20–2).

THE GITA'S EVALUATION OF WAYS TO KNOWLEDGE

Interestingly, this threefold criterion is applied not only to work, but also to the way of gaining knowledge and understanding. Three verses—20th to 22nd—in chapter 18 of the Gita provide a key to this. Besides these three verses which are directly addressed to the approach to knowledge, there are also other relevant sayings in the Gita which also are taken into account here. The first of these verses is as follows:

Sarvabhooteshu yenaikam bhaavamavyayam eekshate /
Avibhaktam vibhakteshu tatjnaanam viddhi saatvikam //(18.20)

Understand that to be the highest or *saatvik* knowledge which sees the enduring unity in different things or the common (universal) in diversity.

(Tr. by author)

Knowledge that synthesizes, which views the object of knowledge holistically, and finds what is unifying, common, or universal from the diversity of particulars, and sees how different parts relate to each other or affect each other, thus constituting the whole, such knowledge is highest, according to the Gita. In other words, saatvik is a totalizing or philosophical knowledge, which finds the meaning that lies behind everything observed. Seeking universals from the particulars is a part of the holistic approach, but it is also much more as can be seen from the following discussion. It looks at the whole, as more than a sum of its parts. It is not necessary that the whole should exist as or should be seen as an organic unity in an undifferentiated way. It does not deny diversity. Nor does it have to declare diversity as false. In fact, the Gita declares elsewhere that Truth can be approached both as one and as of separate or manifold parts (*ekatvena prathaktvena bahudhaa vishvato mukham*, ch. 9.15). There are several other verses in the Gita which emphasize the diverse and pluralistic nature of Truth (chs.11. 5 and 13; chs.13.3, 27 and 30). But truth is fully perceived and knowledge emerges only when the unity in diversity is grasped, which is what the saatvik approach is about. The approach can even look at parts as wholes within a whole, each part having its own diversity and yet bound together either conceptually or ontologically in a unity.

Swami Vivekananda goes so far as to assert that knowledge results only when a particular is related to the universal, and there can of course be several universals. He asks, 'What is meant by knowledge?' and answers in his simple and yet profound way: 'Destruction of peculiarity. Suppose a boy goes into a street or a menagerie and sees a peculiarly shaped animal. He does not know what it is. Then he goes to a country where there are hundreds like that one, and he is satisfied; he knows what the species is. Our knowledge is knowing the principle. Our non-knowledge is finding the particular without reference to the principle' (quoted in Vidyatmananda 2006: 12).

Social Science research or most research in fact, is essentially holistic in the sense that it seeks to get a larger picture or the meaning that lies behind particulars. It is totalizing in essence. Explaining what real research is and how it is different from mere data gathering, Kurien gives the example of a crime scene to illustrate his point. A police constable may record all particulars of the scene of the crime, which may be necessary for investigation (research), but it does not constitute research itself. Research is when a senior police officer has a look at the overall scene, studies all the particulars, forms hypotheses and tests them, seeing the larger picture and taking a holistic view of the crime (Kurien 1973). This may not be the end of the process, and has to be validated in a court of law by a detached judge, who also has to take a holistic view. In such a view, particulars are not ignored, but are related and totalized. This leads us to an important feature of holistic explanations or theories. It is that 'the structure of holistic theories is concatenated (linked together) rather than hierarchical, as in formal theories. A concatenated theory with its several independent sections and subsections provides a many-sided, complex picture of the subject matter'.[2]

There are thus two distinct ways to holistic knowledge: one, conceptualizing the whole comprising several parts, yet finding the special features of the whole transcending its parts, without ignoring the parts, as in the case of studying a forest or an economy as a whole; second, deriving the general from the diverse particulars, finding what is common or universal among them, as in the case of studying a set of individuals making up a distinct society. Both are valid ways to holistic knowledge, in fact to any meaningful knowledge. An approach which stops at the particulars, without transcending them to get at the whole is considered by the Gita as a lower level of knowledge, which it calls raajasik.

The next verse (that is, 21st) in the same chapter of the Gita deals with what it calls the raajasik knowledge. In this context, raajasik does not mean emotional or selfish, but simply a stage lower than the highest. If the highest knowledge is totalizing, or holistic, the lower stage is disaggregating or disjointing knowledge, which the Gita calls as raajasik. While saatvik transcends particulars even while grasping them, the raajasik is focused on the particulars, and on the diversity, without seeking the connectivity between them. The concerned verse is:

Prathaktvena tu tatjnaanam naanaa bhaavaan prathak vidhaan /
Vetti sarveshu bhooteshu tat jnaanam viddhi raajasam //(18.21)

It means: 'Understand that knowledge to be raajasik, which looks at different entities separately, treating each as different and separate'. There is no note of condemnation of this approach to knowledge here, and the concern for particulars may be necessary both in any plan of action and also in ascending to the higher approach of saatvik. But the method has limitations, as can be seen from concrete examples given below. Its major limitation is that it stops short of full, holistic knowledge, which may provide new insights, which may not come from being focused on the particulars. What makes an approach to knowledge raajasik is not that it includes analytical techniques, but that it excludes a holistic vision or misses the larger picture. If it includes the larger picture, it becomes saatvik. In other words, saatvik may well include analytical categories or techniques, but by itself an analysis without a holistic vision or perspective, is narrow and may not be productive of new insights; on the other hand it may even be misleading. Saatvik may not only include, but actually may need analytical techniques. Intuition plays an important role in a holistic or saatvik approach, but intuition unsupported by analytical corroboration may not carry conviction.

The 22nd verse in the same chapter describes lack of knowledge or knowledge which is misleading and leads only to darkness or ignorance, and is called as taamasik. The verse is:

Yattu kritsnavad ekasmin kaarye saktam ahaitukam /
Atatvaarthavat alpam cha tat tamasamudaahritam //(18.22)

It means: 'That is said to be taamasik which is confined to a small single unit but treats it as if it is the whole, in a way which is purposeless or without understanding the objectives (*ahaitukam*) and without grasping the essence, and thus sheds little or no light'.

The verse needs some further explanation. Taking a small sample and examining it as representing the whole is not taamasik by itself. What makes it taamasik is if it is done without proper awareness of the objectives of investigation (*ahaitukam*), and without any theoretical framework or backup (*atatvaarthavat*), and if the sample is too small (*alpam*) to be representative. Under such conditions, the investigation would be misleading and hence taamasik. This one verse thus captures the essence of sampling theory and cautions against pitfalls of sample survey. What makes an approach to knowledge taamasik is narrowmindedness out of conscious or unconscious prejudice, which leads to ignoring some parts or aspects of the whole, and even the objective of our search, resulting in misleading knowledge.

Some Clarifications

Why is a holistic or totalizing approach considered by the Gita as on a higher plane than a disaggregating approach? Does a disaggregating approach have no value or utility at all? And, why is this teaching of the Gita considered here as relevant to social science research? These are interrelated questions and can be taken together. The disaggregating method can be interpreted either as a formal deductive process of reasoning, taking a premise separately and drawing inference, or in its literal meaning of concentrating on individual parts and missing (or keeping aside) the larger picture.

The debate between sense perception and inference seems to have been settled in the Indian intellectual tradition much earlier than in the west. The Nyaaya-Vaisheshika school of thought accepted four *pramaana*s or valid means of knowledge—sense perception, inference, comparison, and verbal or textual testimony. On the other hand, the Buddhist scholars— Dinnaaga and Dharmakirti—rejected the last two and felt that ultimately only sense perception and inference were basic (Williams 1998: 813). That is, even comparison and verbal or textual testimony had to be subjected to the rigourous scrutiny of experience and reasoning. There was no dispute, however, between sense perception and inference, both taken together in a synthesis were considered necessary.

Immanuel Kant, eminent philosopher of the eighteenth century, drew attention to the limits of human reason or analytical faculty perhaps more than any one else in his celebrated work, *Critique of Pure Reason* (see Kant 1998). At the same time he was equally emphatic on its merit and even indispensability, particularly if it were to be superseded by human passion, blind beliefs, and authority of others. He called upon people to have the courage to think for themselves (*Sapere Aude!*). However, he rejected the purely empiricist school as well as the purely rationalist school. Empiricists like Bacon believed that 'all knowledge is derived from and justified by sensory experience', while the rationalists held that 'knowledge is obtained only through rational thought'. Kant argued that 'knowledge involves a synthesis, in which the faculty of sensation and thought come together' (Scruton 2000: 442). Kant's approach goes well with the Gita's. Its holistic approach would include a synthesis of both the inductive and deductive methods, but conceived in terms of a larger picture of all possible facets and variables. It does not rule out a rigorous systematic analysis, but at the same time insists on a larger perspective.

The necessity of taking into account the larger picture and using a holistic method becomes very clear when we become aware that by its very nature, analytical reasoning concentrates on a particular point to the exclusion of others. Faced with the problem of predicting what a rational choice would be among alternatives presented, analytical reasoning need not point to one unique choice. In spite of upholding the importance of reasoning and rational analysis, Amartya Sen points out that there could be competing reasons and there could be 'more than one alternative that could count as rational'. He observes, 'Even if every actual choice happens to be invariably rational in the sense of being sustainable by critical scrutiny, the plurality of rational choice makes it hard to obtain a unique prediction about a person's actual choice from the idea of rationality alone' (Sen 2009: 183).

Holistic method is not just mystical monism and can be applied to the study or understanding of physical and social realities too. While monism tends to disregard diversities and disjunctions as either unreal or secondary, a holistic method takes full note of them as important parts or aspects of the whole and probes into the interconnectedness and the functioning of the system as a whole. When Gandhi said that he 'endeavoured always to look at all the sides of a question' (*CWMG* 53, 1972: 441), he was describing a basic requirement of the holistic approach. He may not have used the word 'holistic' to characterize his approach, but it was essentially 'Gandhi's way of looking at social, economic, political and educational institutions not only as interacting with each other but also as parts of a larger single reality' (Pandit 1990: 136). Holism does not deny that reality can be multifaceted; on the contrary, essentially it assumes that reality is complex, multifaceted and evolves over time, involving dynamic interaction between its parts.[3] Apart from being multifaceted, social reality—or for that matter, physical reality as well, is interrelated, uncertain to some extent, and subject to change in many respects. Social reality is better understood as communitarian, involving communities, rather than as a machine which can be dismantled piece by piece in different parts for separate study. Even for a machine, its functioning is better understood holistically than when analysed part by part. A holistic view allows us to understand interconnectedness, apart from overall functioning. In the case of social issues, a holistic approach is even more important than in the case of a machine like a car. Social reality is evolutionary rather than static, and a community is much more than a collection of individuals. That is why in understanding conflicts, managing and resolving them, the holistic approach has been found particularly suitable (Pandit 1990:136). This is what characterized the Gandhian way to conflict resolution. He integrated his approach with ethical principles too, as they were an essential part of it.

While a holistic view integrates human welfare considerations both in the type of questions probed and in the method of inquiry, and is experiential in character, a formal analytical model, particularly of the deductive kind may not at all be so. The latter may not even be helpful in knowing the truth. The truth behind the premises and the way the questions are posed are no less important than the rigour of formal analysis. Take for example the following syllogism: 'All men are compassionate. Hitler was a man. Therefore, Hitler was compassionate!' The formal deduction may be correct, but it can still be far from the truth.

A holistic view, apart from carefully assessing its assumptions, examines its object of study from multiple perspectives, and sees how they can be reconciled. Specifically, ethical, environmental, and equity issues are vital in social, economic, and political issues, and not just the efficiency issue alone. A holistic understanding includes all these considerations. On the contrary, the analytical or formal method tends to get narrowed down to single issues, often in isolation, which can be a serious handicap if studies are used as a guide for policymaking. Therefore, the type of questions asked may qualitatively and quantitatively differ between a holistic and a purely analytical approach. For instance, when it comes to agriculture, the analyst will ask how to increase crop yields and may recommend an increased dose of fertilizers, pesticides, weedicides, and irrigation. A holist, on the other hand will ask how to increase the productivity of the eco-system and ensure its sustainable use, and increasing crop yields becomes only a part of his probe. It is because of the need to take into account all the factors that have a bearing on the object of knowledge (which the Gita calls as *jneyam* or *kshetram*), that Pani terms it as 'Inclusive Method' and attributes it to Mahatma Gandhi (Pani 2001: 2004). Pani is, of course, aware that in evolving this method, Gandhi was inspired by the Gita.

But this does not eschew the use of an analytical method of disaggregating and focusing on the particulars or units that constitute the whole. The analytical method is after all crucial for science, including social sciences, as it verifies or falsifies individual propositions and leads us to truth. Analytical tools can be useful even in a holistic approach. For example, Karl Marx used the concept of class and class conflicts as analytical tools to understand the capitalistic system as a whole. Without a holistic view, an approach can tend to be blind like the nine men studying parts of the elephant and missing the elephant as a whole. But without analytical tools, a holistic approach may not have the limbs or instruments to work the approach.

Moreover, a holistic approach can be regarded as having gone astray if it is divorced from parts or particulars. A doctor is welcome to treat a human being as a whole instead of going by symptoms alone, but when some thing is wrong with the patient, the doctor ought to find out from where the problem originates. In the name of holistic treatment, the diseased part or limb can hardly be ignored. A focus only on the whole ignoring its parts, or on the general without relating to particulars, may not be enlightening, and may be even misleading. An example will clarify this point. In India, almost till 1971, poverty was considered only at the aggregate level of the country as a whole in terms of the country's general economic backwardness. It was only when Dandekar and Rath came out with their famous study on *Poverty in India* in 1971, that poverty began to be seen in its particularities, which was more meaningful to evolve policies for poverty alleviation. It was not enough to project the economic backwardness of the country as a whole, it was equally or even more necessary to know who the poor were, how many they were, and to what extent they were poor. It is possible that a country as a whole may not be poor in terms of its per capita income, and yet it may have a significant number of the poor. Similarly, policies aiming at boosting the economic growth of the country as a whole may not significantly impact on poverty. Just as a narrow analytical method has its limits, narrow holism too has them. That is why the seeker of knowledge has to be very clear about what she wants.

Holistic method does not consist of merely increasing the number of variables in the model adopted for analysis. Much depends on the whether the results singly and as a whole stand up to rational intuition or sound common sense, and if all relevant variables are included and if the hypotheses made about them are sensible. There is not much difference between intuition and sound commonsense or wisdom. Sometimes, intuition may be misleading. For example, 'the Sun's apparent motion through the sky is intuitively best explained by the hypothesis that it does move relative to a stable Earth' (Hales 2000: 135). What is intuited need not necessarily be true. Yet, it is not only a source of testable hypotheses, but can even serve as a source of enlightenment when results of analysis are amenable to conflicting conclusions and are not by themselves definitive.

We may recall the Gita's observation about the coherence between knowledge (including methodology), the object of knowledge, and the knower, noted above. The Gita is thus aware of the risk of subjectivity of knowledge, but this is not an insurmountable risk. Pani takes note of this problem (Pani 2001: 47–50) and observes that the problem is overcome both through the insistence on the inclusiveness of the method (so that some factors bearing on the object of knowledge are not subjectively and selectively ignored), and also through insistence on non-selfishness and freedom from narrow considerations on the part of the knower. Though Pani is mainly concerned with the method as applied to action or policy, it is equally applicable to knowledge. The point is that a holistic method overcomes the risk of subjectivity in knowledge, which can be an important limitation of the analytical method when applied narrowly. This becomes obvious when we recall that a murder or even mass murders may be planned most analytically in a cold calculating way, working out all possible details of benefits and costs, and devising escape routes to avoid risks. Analytical rationality can be only an 'instrumental rationality' (Nandy 2006: 111) as Ashis Nandy calls it. This narrow rationality neither questions the goals nor considers the various consequences, unlike the holistic method which goes into all these questions and insists on the moral purity of both the knower and the actor. The intellectual tradition of the analytical method in modern science, including social science, tends to separate normative and ethical questions and even the moral status of the knower from its methodology. On the other hand, the Gita's insistence on the purity of the intentions of the knower, her selflessness, honesty, benevolence, and moral status in general makes its approach unique and even superior both to a narrowly holistic approach and a purely formal analytical approach. One could say that even a holistic method by itself cannot be called as saatvik, according to the Gita, unless the moral status of the knower is known and ethical dimension of the object of knowledge is explicitly included.

In spite of such advantages of the holistic approach, it is not necessary that it leads to unanimity. Two persons both using a holistic approach to a particular field of knowledge may arrive at totally different conclusions, simply because either their perceptions or their situational contexts may differ. It may be misleading to adopt the criterion of unanimity for objectivity. As observed above, a more helpful criterion of objectivity is to see if the knower has her/his own axe to grind or is on the contrary unselfish and detached in the pursuit of knowledge. Even if holism need not lead to unanimity, it is expected to lead to greater understanding, and what is more, tolerance and respect for differences in views. It is possible that all views may not stand the scrutiny of inquiry, but the inquiry should be honest and detached. That is why the Gita emphasizes the moral purity of the knower and her purpose.

The holistic approach should not be construed as applicable to only the absolutely largest level of reality. One can conceptualize large wholes and small wholes, and wholes within wholes. Basically, a holistic approach can be applied at any ontological level, right from the cosmos to a single individual. The essence of this approach is not the level of aggregation, but whether, to the maximum extent possible, all facets, all components, all connections and all the factors bearing on an object of the study are being considered. That is why the distinction between a holistic approach and a purely analytical approach does not correspond to the difference between macro-economics and micro-economics. Caution, however, is necessary against mechanically applying the conclusion from the analysis of an individual firm to the economy as a whole.

Similarly, the holistic approach need not be the same thing as systems analysis. The latter is certainly concerned with interconnections between the components of a system and its functioning or dynamics as a whole. It may or may not include finding the philosophical significance of the system and its evaluation on the basis of multiple criteria including particularly a moral assessment of its working. A holistic approach, on the other hand, does not have to put up a show of value-neutrality. It may consciously include a comprehensive moral evaluation and bring out the philosophical significance of the thing studied. If a system analysis also does it, it may amount to a holistic approach.

Knowledge may not always be pursued by a single person, but by a team. Team research has now become a prominent mode in most fields of knowledge. Different members of the team may be assigned different tasks, all of which form parts of the research of the team as a whole. While it is absolutely necessary that a team leader at least has a holistic grasp of the purpose and approach of the research project as whole, it is very desirable that all members of the team also share this holistic vision. Otherwise, the individual members doing segregated tasks may develop a sense of alienation, which may suppress their creativity. Their work may simply become joyless and mechanical. If on the other hand, they are involved in sharing the holistic vision of the project as a whole, they will be in a position to better contribute to the team effort. Holism need not be the exclusive prerogative of team leaders.

Most of the research methodology courses in social sciences hardly mention, let alone include, the holistic method. These courses provide partial training for another reason too. While the research methods consists both of deductive and inductive methods, courses normally teach only the inductive method covering data collection and analysis. This is in spite of the fact that even economics, a discipline known for using quantitative methods more than other social sciences, evolved mainly by using the deductive method. This is so with regard to both classical and neoclassical economics. Ignoring the deductive method probably follows from the fact that it is based on deducing from postulates, but postulates are derived in turn from a holistic understanding. Without a holistic outlook, we may not be able to even formulate postulates needed for the deductive method. Students trained in such truncated research methodology would hardly be equipped well to handle social issues and cannot be competent to guide policy-making. Interestingly, this preference for data collection and analysis, to the exclusion of theoretical and philosophizing approaches, gets rationalized. The quantitative methods are considered as painstaking, and, theoretical and philosophical writings as arm-chair research. That is how, though intuition is so important in research, particularly in arriving at a larger or holistic picture, there are hardly any attempts to train researchers in developing their intuitive capabilities. The point is that even pragmatic research, fieldwork, and quantitative analysis require an overall perspective in terms of which we have to do our study, without which research may be hardly inspiring or productive of insights useful for policy. But, let alone developing any formal training for this, even the need for this is not emphasized in the courses and books on research methodology. The result is suppression of creativity in research.

SOME EXAMPLES FROM SOCIAL SCIENCES

The need for holistic research and the limits of exclusive reliance on narrow analytical work, become clear in the light of concrete examples given below. A classic example of failure to take a holistic view is the narrow outlook of public policy during the Great Depression that started in the world economy in 1929. When employment levels and prices started crashing, wage cuts were ordered, with the hope that enterprises will not cut back on jobs, even if they do not increase employment following wage cuts, as is normally expected in a micro-economic setting. In an economic environment dominated by pessimism, a wage cut may not increase employment even at the micro-level. But this apart, the wage cut policy was based on the confused reasoning that what applies at the micro-level of individual enterprises applies at the aggregate or macro-level too in a holistic setting. This was an example of treating an individual unit or a part as the whole itself, termed by the Gita as a 'taamasik' approach. As a result of wage cuts, depression only deepened and widened. As John

Maynard Keynes, who took a holistic view, showed later that wage cuts only made aggregate demand decline and increased unemployment. He recommended deficit budgets and increased public spending to boost aggregate demand and fight the Depression. Thanks to this lesson learnt, the recession during 2008–9 did not reach the same magnitude as the Great Depression of the 1930s.

Another classic example of the superiority of the holistic method is the Marxian theory. Karl Marx took a grand view of economic systems as a whole and could derive great insights about how the capitalist system worked and why poverty emerged. In spite of his focus on the capitalist system as whole, Marx did take into account the issue of the dignity of the individual and the alienation of the individual worker under the system. Social science has never been the same after Marx and Keynes.

Taking economic development purely or mainly in terms of growth rates of Gross National Product (GNP), could also be considered as an example of *taamasik* approach. Development has to be considered much more broadly in terms of the extent of poverty, health, literacy and education status, gender equality, overall distribution of wealth and income, public hygiene, civic sense and responsibility among citizens, freedoms enjoyed and environmental status. Such a holistic view of development could be considered as saatvik. According to Sharma, holistic development should balance market values (efficiency, generation of wealth, accumulation, want satisfaction), with not only social values (distribution, equity, full employment, social security, ecological soundness), but also with moral and spiritual values (honesty or truthfulness, compassion or concern for others, civic sense) (Sharma 2006: 85–7).

The holistic method works at smaller or lower levels too, and need not be confined to understanding grand systems alone. Take the case of vehicular pollution in cities. The problem is being tried to be tackled mainly by legally putting a mandatory ceiling on the extent of pollution generated by each vehicle. But even if all vehicles obey the norm, it may not bring down the total level of pollution generated. A policy of reducing road congestion by widening the roads and constructing flyovers for faster traffic may solve the problem only marginally. A holistic policy on the other hand would recognize that neither of these above policies would solve the problem fully if there is no control or restriction on the total number of vehicles, discouraging private cars, and encouraging public transport and bicycles.

Take another common problem in India. Say, some farmers in an irrigation command area have complained about inadequate and irregular availability of irrigation water. If the focus is exclusively on the farmers suffering from shortage of water as the whole problem, then it would be an example of a 'taamasik' approach. If instead the whole command area is studied, including the farmers in the upper reach, it may then be found that these more fortunately placed farmers abuse their easy physical access to water, and illegally cultivate water-intensive crops or use other wasteful methods of over-irrigation, thus depriving the farmers in the lower reaches. A holistic approach to command area management of an irrigation project will not be confined merely to distributing water equitably, but will consider doing it in a sustainable way too. It has to decide how much water can be distributed without killing the river, restricting the flow to environmentally viable volumes, without also increasing salinity in the soils irrigated.

The relevance of the holistic approach both in governance and policy-making at large and in corporate management is now being appreciated increasingly.[5] For example, Personnel Management or Human Resources Management in a factory or corporate enterprise would be 'taamasik' if the human resources are treated as only employees, focusing attention only on what they do in their work place. A saatvik way would be to treat them as human beings, taking note that they may have other aspects to their life apart from working in a factory, such as family, and caring for all their concerns. Workers would then get a feeling that they belong to an extended family which cares for them, and their loyalty and commitment would improve enormously.

The Gita's threefold criterion can be applied to the study of Comparative Religion too. A saatvik approach here would be to seek common ground between religions and identify the scope for reconciliation, improving mutual understanding and tolerance. A *raajasik* approach would focus on the differences between religions. A taamasik way would be to use the study of comparative religion mainly to project one's own religion in better light, asserting one's own religion as the only true religion, and one's own concept of god as the only true God.

A great advantage of the holistic approach is that it enables the emergence of new paradigms, which may be needed to solve a fresh set of problems. It gives rise to fresh thinking and more effective policies, leading to greater happiness and welfare as the Gita says (sukha-sangena badhnaati). More than training in a fixed set of techniques, one awakens to such an approach by an open mind and wide reading, very necessary for researchers.

RELEVANCE TO ETHICS: PRACTICAL INSTANCES

Holistic approach to knowledge becomes relevant to ethics in two ways at least. One is that our research processes in any field have to be honest and ethically acceptable. A research is ethically acceptable when it is not doctored by some vested interest, and is open-minded in the sense that the researcher is open to any research outcome provided it is rigourously tested on the basis of scientific observation or experiment. A holistic perspective is necessary here to study the problem from all possible angles, so that no aspect is left out either by negligence or by wilful prejudice. That is why honesty of the researcher (*parijnaata* in the Gita's terminology) is an absolute necessity.

Another way the holistic approach becomes relevant is in arriving at a decision or judgment on delicate ethical issues or moral dilemmas of practical significance. An important criterion of what is good or ethically acceptable (dharma, or satya) is that it leads to the welfare of all beings, as the Hindu scriptures say repeatedly. What is stressed here is long-term happiness (*shreyas*), and not short-term pleasure (*preyas*). Quite a few western philosophers have also the same view. For example, in his 1958 book, *The Moral Point of View*, Kurt Baier suggested that the moral rules are by definition, '*for the good of everyone alike*' (quoted by Rachels 1998: 472). It should be good for everyone alike to be ethically acceptable or just, and not good for some only and harmful to others. And that is where dilemmas arise.

There is story in the Mahabharata about an ascetic being asked by a robber which way a traveller went. The ascetic knew the consequences of telling the truth to the robber, but to avoid telling a lie, he told the robber which way the traveller went, resulting in the latter being robbed and killed. If he had said he did not know, that would have been a lie. The Mahabharata says that in the process of avoiding the sin of telling a lie, the ascetic incurred the more serious sin of helping the robber in robbing and killing an innocent traveller. The ascetic did not take a holistic but a narrow view of truth and ethics. A holistic view is necessary because there could be more than one ethical value involved in a given situation, and there could be conflict of values. For example, in the story above, apart from the principle of telling the truth, there are more important principles of compassion and considering the effect of an action on persons involved. The person deciding on an ethical issue, has to consider all ethical principles involved and arrange them in a hierarchical order of priority by giving them weights. In deciding on the weights to be given, care has to be taken to avoid personal vested interests and to take an honest view. In the story above, the ascetic may have been honest but did not take into account other principles involved. Consequence of his decision was not alike for the two persons involved. It was bad for the traveller but good for the robber. Was the ascetic morally right from this point of view? Since the robber's motive and profession were immoral and the traveller was innocent, there was no moral dilemma on this account. But a moral problem could arise in other cases with conflicting consequences.

Take, for example, a hydroelectric or irrigation project. It is estimated to benefit a large number, say, a hundred thousand households, and promote the economic development of a large area. But it is also estimated that it would submerge some lands and displace, say, a thousand households, depriving them of their livelihood. Just because the project benefits a larger number of people than it harms, is it ethical to ignore the latter? No, because both have rights to livelihood which cannot be sacrificed. In ethics, every person has a value, everyone has *atman* (soul). Justice to everyone alike would require that either the project (government) or the beneficiaries together or both take the responsibility of adequately compensating and rehabilitating the losers—the displaced households. If it is estimated that welfare gain of beneficiaries is not large enough to meet this requirement, it would be both uneconomical and unethical to go ahead with the project. What helps the decision here is a holistic approach.

The example above would be ethically more dilemmatic if the land which is going to be submerged by the project consists of forests very rich with flora and fauna and a significant loss of bio-diversity is feared. Here is the question of rendering equal justice to environment and future generations who too have equal right to the natural heritage like us. Merely valuing the environmental loss and comparing it with the welfare gain of the project would involve arbitrariness and be misleading. Those with a vested interest in the project can get the valuation doctored and underestimate the environmental loss. If the forests along with their flora and fauna can be replicated elsewhere effectively, and if such replacement costs are less than the welfare gains from the project, then the project can go ahead. But this is a big IF. In case the forests going to be submerged are a bio-diversity hotspot, and the loss to bio-diversity is irremediable and unestimably large, the project may have to be dropped. What decides the issue is a holistic consideration of honestly weighing the environmental loss against the welfare gain of the project, instead of taking only the direct costs and gains from the project.

There are several other delicate ethical issues in our contemporary society which have raised a lot of debate. In their excellent collection of articles on ethics, Cahn and Markie (1998), have presented two or even three articles on each of these issues arguing for and against: abortion, euthanasia, sacrificing luxuries by some to prevent starvation of others, and ethics of using animals in medical research, of death penalty, and of positive discrimination or affirmative action. I briefly review below only some of these issues, offering my own conclusion. Brief reviews have the limitation of a summary, and readers interested in more details may go to the originals (Cahn and Markie 1998: 733–887). The complex nature of these ethical issues is such that only a holistic approach of taking into account all aspects of the issue can allow a fair and reasoned conclusion.

Taking the issue of abortion, it is necessary to distinguish it from the issue of the use of contraceptives. Gandhi clubbed them together and opposed all forms of artificial birth control, extolling the virtue of self-control. Such an extreme view today is impractical for the bulk of people. Besides Gandhi himself called for a due role for rationality and reasoning, and not to go by his opinions in every case. The case for contraception is straightforward and strong in a world with high population pressure. Even if we regard lifestyles of the affluent as the main cause for environmental degradation at present rather than population pressure, resources required to bring an enormously large and growing number of people to a comfortable standard of living will mean huge costs to the environment. Population pressure apart, the spread of sexually transmitted diseases also makes the use of condoms indispensable.

The issue of abortion, however, is more complex. Opposition to abortion is most often made on the ground that the foetus (fetus) is a person, a human being, from the moment of conception. Michael Tooley (in Cahn and Markie 1998: 749–66) argues, however, that a right to life can be conceded only to 'persons', and a foetus is not a person because it has no concept of self as a continuous subject of experience. He applies this to just-born infants too. Judith Thompson argues in the same volume that even if they are persons, their right to life is subject to certain constraints. In cases where there is medical evidence that the foetus concerned will not grow into a normal healthy human being and an impossible burden may be imposed by multiple disabilities both on the person to be born and on the mother, abortion may be considered permissible. Similar is the case where the mother's life is itself threatened by the continued growth of the foetus in her body. What about conception resulting from rape? The mother may like to forget the indignity, humiliation, and violence imposed on her by ending the evidence of it. It is mother's body which has to host the foetus. Feminists therefore argue that it is up to her to decide about it, without harming her own life. While prevention of conception through contraception has to be the preferred alternative, there is no case for a blanket ban on abortions. At the same time one cannot deny the violence involved in abortion. And there is no case also for wanton liberalism about it. India has strict laws against prenatal sex determination so as to avoid abortion of female fetuses. Judith Thomson takes the stand that 'while I argue that abortion is not impermissible, I do not argue that it is always permissible' (in Cahn and Markie 1998: 747). This seems to be a balanced view taking note of all aspects of the issue.

Coming to the issue of death penalty or capital punishment, Gandhi was quite opposed to it. He said, 'An eye for an eye may make the whole world blind' (*CWMG* vol. 45: 359). Many have questioned the ethics of capital punishment and the 'eye for an eye' principle. Death penalty is regarded as cruel since rehabilitation is ruled out once for all. Its usefulness as a deterrent is also alleged as not yet proved. In case, the convict were to be found later to be innocent in view of some new evidence, the case would be beyond review if execution has already taken place. Apart from these traditional objections to death penalty, a new objection was added by Stephen Nathanson (in Cahn and Markie 1998: 849–60). It is on account of the fact that death penalty is imposed in an arbitrary manner. As he says, 'current laws do not embody the judgment that all people guilty of homicide deserve to die' (in Cahn and Markie 1998: 851). Only some get the death penalty. What is worse, it was even found that decisions are not random, but reflect a possible bias. For example, in USA, 'blacks who killed whites were among those most likely to be executed, while whites who killed blacks were least likely to be sentenced to die' (in Cahn and Markie 1998: 852). A similar prejudice prevails elsewhere too. If the victim is a Very Important Person (VIP) and the convict is an ordinary man, death penalty is more likely, but in the reverse case it is least likely. When an attempt was made to remove arbitrariness in some states in USA by making death penalty mandatory for certain types of crimes, the Supreme Court declared it as unconstitutional since such attempts 'failed to permit considerations of individual differences among defendants' (in Cahn and Markie 1998: 853). Another strategy was then tried in USA, namely, issuing guidelines to juries specifying what kinds of reasons may be used in a judgement involving death penalty vis-à-vis life imprisonment. This attempt at guided discretion was accepted as constitutional by the Supreme Court, as eliminating arbitrariness, allowing discretion at the same time. Nathanson, however, argues that some arbitrariness can continue still, and that it is an important and relevant argument against death penalty.

Intellectual opinion is still divided on the issue, and there are some like Ernst van den Haag who have been staunch defenders of death penalty. Den Haag says that polls indicate most people in favour of retaining death penalty (in Cahn and Markie 1998: 838). He also disputes the claim that death penalty has no deterrent effect. He quotes an outcome of 'new and sophisticated studies' which showed that 'an additional execution per year ... may have resulted (on the average) in 7 or 8 fewer murders' (in Cahn and Markie 1998: 841). He therefore says, 'It seems immoral to let convicted murderers survive at the probable—or even at the merely possible— expense of the lives of innocent victims who might have been spared had the murderers been executed' (in Cahn and Markie 1998: 842). He concedes that the deterrence is effective on people as yet not committed to a criminal occupation, but slight on those who are already committed, and that 'crime can only be reduced, but not eliminated' by punishment (in Cahn and Markie 1998: 845). But 'punishment', he asserts, 'must be proportional to the gravity of the crime, if only to denounce it and to vindicate the importance of the norm violated' (in Cahn and Markie 1998: 847). Den Haag disputes the claim of arbitrariness of death penalty as an objection to it. He observes:

Justice requires punishing the guilty—as many guilty as possible—even if only some can be punished and sparing the innocent—as many of the innocent as possible, even if not all are spared. Morally, justice must always be preferred to equality. ... Justice cannot even permit sparing some guilty persons, or punishing some innocent ones, for the sake of equality—because others have been unjustly spared or punished.

(in Cahn and Markie 1998: 840).

To illustrate the point, take the case of a thief who is caught red-handed. Can he ask, 'You have not caught all the thieves; I am only one of the many. Why punish me alone?' Taking all the arguments and aspects of the issue into account, it would appear that while it would be advisable to retain capital punishment to assert the society's norm, it should be awarded in the 'rarest of rare' cases regarded as instances of extreme and deliberate cruelty, irrespective of the status of persons involved. This principle seems to have been adopted in India.

A policy of preferential treatment (PT) to members of historically disadvantaged social groups in admissions to colleges and universities and in recruitment to government and other public institutions (including universities) has been adopted both in India and the USA. In India, it is known as reservations under a quota system, and in the USA as affirmative action. The term, 'affirmative action', is preferred to 'positive discrimination' or 'reverse discrimination', both of the latter being pejoratives. While in USA, the affirmative action is taken in the case of 'minorities' (mainly blacks) and women, reservations in India are for Scheduled Castes (former untouchables) and Scheduled Tribes and for Other Backward Classes, but not for women though women are also a historically disadvantaged group. Women have been denied a PT due to the fear that upper castes which have educated women in much larger proportion, would walk away with the bulk of benefits. Yet, perhaps no other country in the world has adopted a policy of PT on such a vast scale as India, since reservations go up to 50 per cent, which is a ceiling imposed by the Supreme Court so as to minimize injustice to the merited, or to balance considerations of social justice with merit justice. PT on such a large scale is justified because it is known that even a larger than 50 per cent of population belong to socially disadvantaged groups. In spite of the adoption of PT in both countries, there is raging debate about it in USA, and even in India, there are many who feel strongly against it resulting sometimes in outbursts of public protest, and sometimes in resentment against the beneficiaries of PT in spite of strict laws against humiliating anyone on caste basis.

It needs to be appreciated that 'equating equality with equal treatment ignores deep material differences in social position, division of labour, socialized capacities, normalizing standards, and ways of living that continue to disadvantage members of historically excluded groups (Young 2009: 362). These differences produce and reproduce 'durable inequality' in access to resources, power, and capabilities. A difference-blind approach to equality then cannot achieve equality. As Iris Young says, 'to remove unjust inequality it is necessary to explicitly recognize group differences and either compensate for disadvantage, revalue some attributes, positions, or actions, or take special steps to meet the needs of and empower members of disadvantaged groups. ... These people's deficiencies are not their fault of course. So a decent society will support their needs ...' (Young 2009: 364).

Cahn and Markie (1998) present two articles on this issue in their collection on ethics, one by Thomas Hill Jr in favour, and another by John Kekes against. Though written in the context of USA, they have much relevance for India too. I review them together and come to my own conclusion. The arguments for PT rest on several principles. The most important and popular among them is what is known as backward looking in the sense that it takes into account its historical background. Since historically certain social groups were targeted for oppressive, exploitative, and humiliating treatment in the past, they are now relatively backward educationally and in economic stature, which needs to be remedied. The remedy is through PT. In any competition based on open merit, these social groups would have an unfair disadvantage, requiring a level playing field. PT is employed only in the case of admissions to educational institutions receiving government aid and in jobs in government and universities receiving state funding. It applies only to a part of the society or economy, since the private sector is left out where merit can play a full role.[5] Even where PT is employed, the minimum essential qualifications are not relaxed for anybody, but a concession is given only in desirable qualifications. Besides being a compensation for a disadvantage on which they have no control, PT is also a buffer against any prejudice that may lurk unconsciously as a habit of thought against the disadvantaged groups. PT is also a redistributive measure in an unequal society as it tends to divert some benefits at least to disadvantaged groups.

Kekes objects to such arguments by saying that 'preferential treatment does not mandate or even recommend finding out whether the individuals in question [selected through PT] have actually suffered any injustice that would warrant compensation or redistribution' (in Cahn and Markie 1998: 883). Making matters more unjust, Kekes points out, the individuals selected are least likely to have been selected from families who have been really backward like impoverished slum dwellers. The assumption that they are backward just because they are members of a social group involves as much prejudice as the prejudice which actually PT attempts to check, though the prejudice now is against innocent individuals who belong to what is presumed to be a socially forward group. Kekes further says that even among the forward groups, there may be poor and disadvantaged and there can be at least as much a good reason for PT for them as for members of backward social groups. The approach which does not look into the socio-economic status of individuals to be selected for PT, and is only concerned with birth in a social group, is both flawed and unjust, and reproduces the same injustice which it claims to remedy. A principle of retaliation is unjust because neither the persons who exploited nor those who were exploited are present now, and the present generations cannot be held responsible for injustices in the past.

Kekes argues further that impact of this flawed approach of PT on beneficiaries is not likely to be altogether good. 'It seems likely that their attitude would be a mixture composed of resentment, shame, guilt, embarrassment, pride, self-doubt, and a desire to prove themselves. ... But whatever happens, their position would not be that of a traditional academic and the obstacles in the way of achieving normalcy would be formidable' (in Cahn and Markie 1998: 885). In sum, Kekes and other similar thinkers are not against PT *per se,* particularly if applied to individuals taking their personal disadvantages beyond their control into account, but are opposed to it in principle if applied to individuals merely as members of a particular social group by birth irrespective of their personal or family background determining their advantage or disadvantage.

Hill concedes the weaknesses of traditional arguments taken separately, advanced in favour of PT. But he advocates seeing the whole problem in a fresh holistic perspective. Suppose you are born in a village to which you return after a gap of a few decades. Say, the village had a history of two segregated social groups, the well-heeled and barefooted. The former used to ruthlessly exploit, oppress, and humiliate the latter, and the latter felt deep resentment at this treatment. During the gap, the older generations of oppressors and the oppressed have both gone, and people from outside not belonging to either group have also come. The kind and extent of oppression and segregation which used to prevail earlier has come down drastically though not disappeared. But the memories of the injury and insult still remain fresh particularly in the minds of the latter group, now no longer called as barefooted but as cross-towners, which has not ended their resentment. To worsen the situation, sporadic instances of atrocities against the cross-towners, vitiate mutual trust and bonhomie, thanks to increased sensitivity. The economic divide between the rich and the poor in the village fairly, if not perfectly, overlaps the social divide between the two groups. All this makes the mental divide even more intense. Hill asks, how would you remedy the situation, given the need for mutual trust and harmony? Not just by preaching 'forget and forgive'. Forgetting the past may be easy for the forward group, but not for the other. The 'village' here is a replica of the state of the national society as a whole, both in India and USA. To remedy the situation what appears most proper at the village as also at the national level would be accepting and regretting the past, resolving to make a new beginning of mutual trust and respect, stopping all atrocities by sternly and promptly punishing the guilty, and as a token of the regret and new resolve, agree to a policy of PT which would work towards gradually eliminating the social divide. This is what Hill sees as the logical necessity of the situation, and this is what is followed in both the countries.

But PT alone would not be enough. To help the really poor and backward, quality of education particularly at the primary and secondary levels has to substantially improve in India. The access to education at these levels should also be universalized by subsidizing it heavily and making it free for the poor. Giving merely PT without these educational reforms would defeat its very purpose. Secondly, any atrocities against the historically disadvantaged group including humiliating them on caste basis should be promptly and sternly dealt with, giving a clear message that they will never be tolerated, taking care to see that allegations made are genuine. Thirdly, anti-poverty programmes should be strengthened and extended, making their implementation more honest and effective, so that conspicuous poverty is eliminated and basic needs of all are met within a reasonable time frame. Fourthly, as and when more and more persons from the historically disadvantaged group rise in stature and get into the economic mainstream as a result of PT, which after all is the very rationale of PT, they should be taken out of the scope of PT. There has been a demand since long in India to keep the creamy layers among the historically disadvantaged out of the scope of the PT, since they do not at present have to face such disadvantages. For example, the children of highly placed government officials, successful professionals, and political leaders cannot be said to face the traditional social disadvantages even if their ancestors may have faced them. This will bring greater pride and self-confidence among them, and remove the undesirable effects of PT on the beneficiaries which Kekes feared. This will also induce greater support from the forward group to PT for the remaining among backward social group. Since the very purpose of PT is to gradually improve the representation of the backward group into the economic and social mainstream, it is only logical to expect such an outcome of the policy, because otherwise there would be no case for it. And to the extent such is the gradual effect of this policy, it is only logical to make it temporary rather than permanent and to introduce a self-destruct clause in it of the kind advocated above, instead of imposing arbitrary time limits. It will then be viable to have a policy of PT only for the economically backward persons irrespective of their birth in a social group. To the extent there are a larger number of poor among a certain social group, it will automatically be the major beneficiary of PT even if reformulated on the basis of personal background rather than birth. A bitter fact of the Indian society is that even the social groups broadly characterized as Scheduled Caste or backward are hierarchical, and within them there are even more backward sub-castes. As long as long these lower sub-castes have to compete with higher sub-castes, they will be subject to the same injustice and disadvantage which prevailed between broader groups of upper castes and lower castes in the absence of PT. Having benefited from PT, now it would be the turn of elites among these social groups to renounce further such benefits for their children and leave the field open to the less fortunate sub-castes. However, subject to the desirable exclusion of the 'creamy layer', the policy of PT based on disadvantaged social group approach may have to continue, as long as the proportion of their representation in higher education and jobs continues to be significantly lower than the proportion of their population in the overall economy or society.

These examples of issues of ethical concern would show that ethics is not a matter for philosophical discussion for its own sake, but also one of tremendous practical relevance. But a philosophical discussion of arguments involved particularly from a holistic viewpoint is helpful in arriving at clear and balanced decisions.

NOTES

1. The concept of the three gunas (trigunas) originated from the *Saankhya* school of Hindu philosophy, which preceded the Gita. For a fuller presentation of the concept of trigunas along with application in various fields as taught by the Gita, see (Nadkarni 2008: 179–83).

2. See 'Holistic Method' on http://www.nd.edu/~cwiber/pub'recent/edupehol. html.

3. Ibid.

4. See for example Pani (2001) and Sharma (2007). They do not however discuss the holistic method in the context of Gita's evaluation in terms of the three gunas. Pani's term for the holistic method is 'Inclusive method'.

5. There has been a demand in India to extend PT to the private sector too, with a provision for denying loans from scheduled banks to those not obeying. These banks come under the control of the Reserve Bank of India, apart from the fact that most of the important banks are owned by the government.

Part III

Ethical Foundations of Hinduism

8 Humanism in Hinduism*

WHAT IS HUMANISM?

There is some difference between the usage of the word 'humanism' in common parlance and in Western philosophy. In popular and commonsense usage, humanism is considered almost the same as humanitarianism, that is, being kind and considerate to fellow human beings, forgiving and helpful, and having concern for human welfare in general. However in Western thought, the word is used to connote a system of thought which believes in the rationality and intelligence of all human beings, who can thereby lead their own life without guidance from religion. The essay here distances itself from strong rejection of religion, associated with humanism as understood in the West. Secular humanism, as a system of ethics devoid of any religious impulse, runs the risk of being as exciting as a plastic flower. At the same time, humanism here is taken to include moral responsibility of all human beings to themselves and the world, concern for human freedom and human rights. Humanism in this sense is not just charity.

William Murry defines humanism as 'affirmation of the worth and dignity of every person, a commitment to human betterment, and the necessity for human beings to take responsibility for themselves and the world' (Murry 2007: 1). Humanism means that 'every human being is potentially rational, and therefore, the potential locus of freedom and

*This is an enlarged and revised version of Shri G.R. Bhatkal Memorial Lecture, Indian Institute of World Culture, Bengaluru, February 2008.

dignity' (Miri 2003:120). From this arises the notion of human rights. 'Human rights are rights which belong to human beings, qua human beings, as beings who can exercise freedom through reason' and such rights 'apply universally to all human beings' (Miri 2003: 129). Humanism believes that while some economic differences among human beings may be inevitable, everyone—low or mighty—has the right to dignified treatment. Humanism also includes commitment to reduce these economic differences.

While I would like to subscribe to this concept, I do not take rejection of religion as a necessary requirement of humanism, though I understand why it was thought to be so in the West. The rise of humanist values and of humanism as an ideology in the West was associated with resisting the authoritarianism of religion. Religion in the West, particularly under the Roman Church, had a tradition of being opposed to scientific advance and freedom of thought. Many were burnt alive at stake for alleged blaspheme, and one of them was a renowned scientist, Bruno. Even now the theory of evolution is opposed by creationists as being opposed to the Bible and Christianity. It was, therefore, natural that free thinkers, who put human beings in focus rather than God, associated their movement with secularism. For them, humanism meant secularism plus ethics. Secularism in the West meant finding meaning in life here and now, without bothering about anything like a supernatural power controlling human destiny. Secular humanism puts human beings in the centre and makes them responsible for their own destiny. But we can extend the concept of humanism from being only an object to being a subject too. That is, as human beings we need to treat even nature and animals with concern and dignity as a part of human responsibility. Religion can be compatible with humanism, since it insists both on concern for human beings (as objects) and on moral responsibility of human beings (as subjects) for themselves as well as other creatures and nature. In fact, it is necessary to emphasize humanism in religion to discourage an undesirable tendency in religion towards inhuman and irrational fanaticism or fundamentalism.

GANDHI AS A HUMANIST

In this context, Gandhi could surely be considered as all-rounded humanist. He could hardly be called as a secular humanist, since his humanism would make no sense if religion is kept out of it. But even in his religious outlook, human beings were the focus of his faith, and not some God above and outside humanity. Humanism was primarily ethics for him, and his ethics was action-oriented. Enriching human freedom and dignity, contributing to human welfare, and fighting injustice of every kind were the basic goals of his activism, which gave meaning to his life and humanist philosophy. Mutual regard and love for each other, service and generosity, courage of conviction, and ever-preparedness to even die for a cause constituted the core of his ethical humanism.

He accepted even science and technology, and industrialization going with it, only on the condition and only to the extent that they were humane and advanced human welfare, and not if they dislodged human beings from a position of dignity and freedom. As Ganguli observed, 'Gandhi worked for a social order which would remove the tragic isolation and powerlessness of the individual in a society based on mass production and mass consumption' (Ganguli 1973: 12). Gandhi felt as much concerned as Karl Marx about the problem of alienation in the wake of industrialization. There are several similarities between Marx and Gandhi in their outlook, particularly in their attitude to the dignity and primacy of labour and their concern for inequity created by private property and mindless profit motive (Ganguli 1973: 130–1).

Gandhi's humanism had a broad vision, and included not only right to adequate means of living and employment, but also right to freedom of expression and right to one's own culture and religion. His religious outlook meant commitment to truth and non-violence, and not to any ritualism and subordination of reason to scriptures. Thus it came naturally to his teachings to emphasize human freedom, reason, and responsibility. But this responsibility was not confined to the sphere of human beings alone, but extended to environment and animals too. Religion basically meant an absolute commitment to moral values, and to serve God residing among the poor (*Daridra-narayana*). Gandhi prided in calling himself a Hindu, which he would not have done, had he found Hinduism devoid of humanism. His Hinduism, as he himself often clarified, was no narrow creed.

HOW IS HINDUISM HUMANISTIC?

Hinduism is quite supportive of humanist values, faith in reasoning, freedom of thought, and even in emphasizing the need for human beings to take up their responsibility to society and world. In Hinduism, one may not believe in a personal God, but none may avoid dharma, the path of virtue and duty. One may not even believe in *moksha* or liberation, but none can take the liberty of rejecting the moral path or the license to refuse to take one's responsibilities to humanity and to environment around us.

This applies even to a monk, who can free himself from the obligations to his family but not to humanity. Not only Hinduism, all eastern religions go very well with humanism, free as they are from authoritarianism, but imbued with respect for difference in viewpoints and for diversity, even while emphasizing unity of ultimate reality. But I concentrate more on Hinduism, with which I am familiar.

Let me also concede right at the start that Western religions like Semitic religions, Zoroastrianism, and Bahaiism also have shown tremendous social concern, which is central to humanism. Without concern for the poor, the exploited, and the deprived, no religion can lay claim to being supportive of humanism. Any religion that is not socially and humanely engaged is a misfit in the present times. How does Hinduism fare in this regard?

I am answering this question here on three fronts. First, I will meet the criticisms about Hinduism as providing a weak foundation for humanism, and show that these criticisms are misplaced and irrelevant. Second, I shall go beyond this defensive way and show positive features and evidence in Hinduism that are strongly supportive of humanism, both by taking into account dynamics of development of Hinduism and scriptural support for humanism. Third, I shall argue that not only in theory but in practice too, Hinduism has shown good evidence of social concern and humanism. At the end, I shall also point out where reforms are still due at least in practice, so that Hinduism becomes even more strongly humanist.

CRITICISMS OF HINDUISM FROM A HUMANIST ANGLE

Let me discuss important criticisms levelled against Hinduism from a humanist point of view. The first charge is that Indian religions, inclusive of Hinduism, are other worldly, world-and-life negating, and hence cannot provide any robust scope for humanist ethics, let alone economic development. It breeds indifference to poverty and human suffering, on the ground that all this is illusion! This criticism has already been dealt with above in Chapter 6 under the section 'Western Misconceptions: What Are the Facts?' and need not detain us long. Even Advaita philosophy, which caused the misunderstanding, does not mean that world is to be ignored. Moreover, Advaita is only one of the several philosophies in Hinduism, and all these philosophies take the world as real.

Let alone doctrine, have Hindus ever shown an attitude of world denial or life negation in practice? Vedic people were very earthy, praying for progeny and prosperity, cultivating wheat and barley, and enjoying a drink of soma-rasa for health and longevity. It is with the Upanishads that we find a quest for the beyond, but they also did not reject life as false. Indians are credited with developing the concept of zero and decimal numerals; Aryabhatta, much earlier than the West, pointed to the diurnal motion of the Earth around the Sun; and Hindus had since long developed surgery, Ayurveda, and metallurgy. How could they have done it when the hold of religion was strong, if they believed that world to be an illusion? Poverty in India was the result of British colonialism, not of Hinduism. India was one of the most prosperous countries in the world in the middle of the eighteenth century when British entered, and became one of the poorest when the British left. Hinduism did not come in the way of India's economic development after Independence, and faster rates of growth now.

The second criticism is about the Law of Karma, which is interpreted as fatalistic. A human being under this law is alleged to be taken as a puppet in the hands of destiny, which hardly provides any foundation for humanism, as humanism believes in responsibility and an active role for human beings. But, to interpret the Law of Karma as destiny or fatalism is a gross misunderstanding. On the other hand, it says a human being makes his or her own future. What we are today is the result of what we did in the past, and what we will be will be the result of what we do today. There is thus a great responsibility assigned to human beings. But how do we look at the suffering or poverty of others? Do we simply say, it is their karma, their problem, and we have nothing to do with it? Hinduism on the other hand lays great emphasis on compassion and help to others. If I am indifferent to the suffering of others or poverty of others on the ground that it is their karma, I fail in my duty, in my responsibility, to help others, and hence incur a bad karma or a sin. The Law of Karma is thus very supportive of humanism and human responsibility.

The third main criticism is about the caste system in Hindu Society, its inequity, its hierarchy, and its inhuman custom of untouchability. In the second chapter of my earlier book (Nadkarni 2008), I have shown with documented proof that caste is not, and never was, an intrinsic or organic part of Hinduism, and that caste developed because of factors which had nothing to do with Hinduism. Moreover, caste even in its hierarchical significance, was not a feature of Hindu society alone, but of all religious societies in the Indian subcontinent, including followers of those religions that came later into India like Islam and Christianity. It should not be ignored that there has been a strong tradition within Hinduism which has opposed caste right since the Upanishadic times. Moreover, several communities like Ezhavas and Nadars have come up into mainstream within the framework of Hinduism, without having to convert to other religions. Caste survives today, but not its ritual hierarchy and its inferior-superior notion. We can't deny, however, that in practice, caste system meant indignity and injustice to a majority of population, and orthodox Hindu religious leaders, out of tune both with the *shruti* texts of Hinduism and the needs of the times, supported caste system, which injured Hinduism grievously. The sooner we repair this damage to Hinduism, the better it will be for all concerned.

Support for Humanism in Hinduism

Going beyond defence against critics of Hinduism, let us note positive features within Hindu philosophy, which show evidence for social concern and strong support for humanism. Human values constitute the very definition of *Sanaatan Dharma*, which is the traditional or Indian name for Hinduism. *Sanaatan* does not mean orthodox as commonly interpreted, it means eternal or everlasting. *Brahmanda Purana* (II. 33. 37–8) explains what this Dharma is:

Adrohaschyaapyalobhashcha tapo bhootadayaa damah /
Brahmacharyam tathaa satyam anukroshah kshamaa dhritih /
Sanaatanasya dharmasya moolametad udaahritam //
The roots or basic principles of Sanatana Dharma are said to be in being free from malice and greediness, in austerity, compassion, self-control, chastity, truth, tenderness, forgiveness and fortitude.

(Tr. by author from Kane 1990, vol. V, part II, p. 1629, fn. 2612)

These qualities are essential for individuals as well as communities, as they help in moving along in life peacefully, reconciling with different people with different interests and faiths, in a spirit of live and let live. Both Jawaharlal Nehru and Arnold Toynbee observed that this spirit characterizes Hinduism and India in general. A religion is expected to help its followers by creating the right kind of attitude favourable to reconciliation with others, extending the sphere of co-operation and controlling competition within humane limits.

Belief in the law of karma is very conducive to moral action or as Chapple puts it, 'action oriented morality' (Chapple 2008: 351–2). This morality is not confined to negative virtues like avoiding telling lies and violence, but is a more activist one of doing good deeds by helping others. The law of karma thus logically leads to *karma-marga* of Bhagavadgita.

The Gita can be well interpreted as a humanist document. Its central message can be summed up as: Don't escape from your duties or responsibilities; perform them selflessly, but enthusiastically, equipped with knowledge and devotion. We find here an emphasis on the role of human beings and need for them to take up their responsibilities. *Karma Yoga* is unselfish action. The Gita recommends *loka sangraha* in chapter 3 (verses 20 to 26) which means securing welfare and maintenance of people. Karma yoga can be pursued through being engaged in loka sangraha. The Gita also teaches a great humanist virtue and lays down a basic principle for ethical conduct:

Aatmoupamyena sarvatra samam pashayati yoarjuna /
Sukham vaa yadivaa dukkham sa yogi paramo matah // (6.32)
He who judges pleasure and pain everywhere by the same standard as he applies to himself, that yogi, OArjuna, is the highest.

(Tr. by Swarupananda 1982: 154)

If I do not like to be harassed or exploited, I should know that others also do not like it. If I do not like to be discriminated against, I should know that others too would not like it. A medieval saint-poet from Gujarat, Narsi Mehta (1500–1580) has a beautiful song, which became Gandhi's favourite, *Vaishnava janato tene kahiye* .... Only the first stanza of this song is given below as it echoes a whole philosophy of Hinduism.

Call that one a true Vaishnava [devotee of God]
Who feels the suffering of others,
Who seeks to relieve other's pain
And has no pride in his soul.

(Tr. by Vauderville 1987: 39)

One of the most inspiring verses in the Gita from the point of boosting self-confidence and stress on freedom of will, which are essential to humanism, is:

Uddharet aatmanaatmaanam naatmaanam avasaadayet/
Aatmaiva hyaatmano bandhuh aatmaiva ripuraatmanah // (6.5)
A man should uplift himself by his own will, and never allow one self to be corrupted. Self is a friend of oneself, but it can also be an enemy.

Freedom of will is an important ingredient of humanism. The Gita leaves no doubt that human beings are given free will. Krishna tells Arjuna in the last chapter, 'You have listened to all this from me. Now reflect over it critically and fully, and then do what you want to do' (*Vimarshyetad asheshena yathechchasi tathaa kuru.* 18.63).

Another philosophical justification for humanism and social concern of Hinduism lies in its concept of God. God in Hinduism is both immanent (*sarvaantaryami*) and transcendental (*ateet*). This makes all life and environment sacred. Particularly, humanity is a manifestation of consciousness or *chit*. Even animals are attributed with chit in Hindu epics and Puranas. The human body particularly is considered the abode of God. *Deho devaalayah proktah dehee devo Niranjanah* (the body is a temple and its dweller is God himself who is free from blemish). Basavanna (twelfth century AD) has articulated this in his beautiful Vachana. A.K. Ramanujam's translation of the Vachana is as follows:

The rich will make temples for Shiva,
What can I a poor man do?
My legs are pillars,
My body the Shrine,
The head a cupola of gold,
Listen, O Lord of the meeting rivers
Things standing shall fall
But the moving ever shall stay.

(A.K. Ramanujan 1973: 19)

Basavanna suggested here that the moving temples of Shiva, in the forms of human beings, have more long lasting significance than static temples of stone, and that they are more valued and sacred than temples. Basavanna was a humanist par excellence. He was also a great leader of the Bhakti movement. This movement had a great humanizing and democratizing impact on Hinduism. It started first in Tamil Nadu in around sixth century AD, and then spread to the whole of India. The origin of Bhakti can be traced to the Gita itself. Narada in his Bhakti sutras defined Bhakti as *saa tu parama prema svaroopa* (bhakti is nothing but supreme love). The main feature of Bhakti movements is that their leaders came from all castes and corners of the country and from all classes. They denounced caste distinctions, asserted equality of all humans including gender equality, and emphasized that nothing else is necessary for God realization, no rituals, no intermediaries, not even temples, but what is needed is only intense love for God, which all humans are capable of, irrespective of caste or class. This love for God also meant love for human beings and all of God's creation. Bhakti saints emphasized not only man's love for God, but what is more, Gods' love for humanity. God rushes to help his/her devotees like a mother, *Maauli*, to her child.[1]

All scriptures of Hinduism emphasize charity. They also tell, in what spirit or attitude, charity is to be given. *Taittiriya Upanishad* (1.11.3) says: *Shraddhayaa deyam. Ashraddhayaa adeyam. Shriyaa deyam. Hriyaa deyam. Bhiyaa deyam. Samvidaa deyam*'. (Give with commitment. Do not give without commitment. Give generously. Give with humility. Give with respect. Give with understanding) (translated by author.) What is giving with commitment? It means not half-heartedly, not for namesake. The Gita says that charity has to be given without any selfishness and without any contempt for recipients, and without any arrogance. In the seventeenth chapter in verses 20 to 22, the Gita distinguishes between three types of charity:

Saatvik—unselfish, given without expecting anything back.
Raajasik—given, expecting something in return.
Taamasik—given with contempt to the recipients.

In ch. 16, verse 15, Gita condemns arrogance on the part of the giver. Veerashaivas give so much importance to humility and self-effacement in charity, that they call it as *daasoha*, derived from *daasah aham* (I am only a servant of God, and God is the giver).

We have all heard the English proverb, 'A friend in need is friend indeed'. We have an equivalent of this as far back as in *Rigveda* (x. 117. 4):

Na sakhaa yo na dadaati sakhye
Sa chaa bhuve sacha maanaaya pitvah

It means: A friend is no friend if he does not help a friend, but the one who helps is a real friend.

But humanism is not just charity. It goes beyond and strives for social justice, empowerment of the poor and the deprived, and end to discrimination and exploitation. Is this concept foreign to Hinduism? No. Take this beautiful *subhashita*, bringing out the humanism in Hinduism:

Taaditaah peeditaah ye syuhu taan mama iti abhyudeerayet /
Sa saadhuriti mantavyah tatra drastavya Eeshwarah //[2]

It means: One who declares those who are oppressed and harassed as his own and helps them, he is to be regarded as the real saint. It is here that God has to be seen or realized.

Humanism as Practised in Hinduism

One may say—well, Hinduism may have preached it, but has it practised this teaching? Yes, indeed! If a tradition like fighting against social evils like inequality, ill-treatment of women, dominance of orthodoxy and mindless ritualism, is an indication of humanism in practice, Hinduism has witnessed it conspicuously for centuries, particularly since the rise of Bhakti movements. This tradition of resistance to injustice has continued to modern times too. Christian Theology of Liberation emerged to oppose exploitation in the context of Latin America in the 1960s. We have something corresponding to this, developed by Hindu *sanyaasi*s (monk). Swami Vidyananda took a lead in mobilizing peasants in Bihar around 1915 and 1920s. Swami Sahajananda Saraswati continued to lead peasant resistance in Bihar in 1930s and 1940s. He co-founded Bihar Pranth Kisan Sabha first, and then started the All India Kisan Sabha in 1936 along with the socialist veteran N.G. Ranga. He saw no contradiction between being a sanyaasi and being a peasant leader. When landlords accosted and questioned him about this, he quoted a shloka from Mahabharata:

Naaham kaamaye raajyam na swargam na chaa punarbhavam /
Praninaam dukkha- taptaanaam kaamaye dukkha-naashanam //
I desire no kingdom, no heaven, not even Moksha. I desire only that beings afflicted of sorrow be relieved of it.

(Tr. by author)

He explained, it is the selfish who seek individual liberation to the neglect of others. He could not do this. For him, liberation or moksha meant liberating the poor from exploitation and suffering.[3] Swami Sahajananda has written a commentary on the Gita in Hindi, entitled, *Gita Hriday*, in which he has observed that the Gita is supportive of humanism of Marx (Agrawal 2006: 29).

What greater example do we need than that of Mahatma Gandhi who not only preached the principles of *Satya* (truth) and *Ahimsa* (non-violence), but also practised them to the last minute. What is more he showed by example that following these principles, one could fight even the mighty British Empire. He practised it in other important cases also, resisting the inhumanity of racism in South Africa, and in calming down communal frenzy in India. He also tried his best to root out untouchability and declared that caste has nothing to do with religion. He gave a prominent place for women in his freedom struggle. He fought with peasants in their struggle for justice in Champaran in Bihar and Kheda in Gujarat.

Gandhi believed not only in fighting injustice, but also in inspiring self-development, and through self-development social transformation. He and Vinoba Bhave led the movement of Sarvodaya mainly on the basis of his philosophy. His philosophy in doing social service and rural development came vividly in the following statement: 'I am here to serve no one else but myself, to find my own self-realization through the service of these village folks' (Gandhi 1961: 5). He imparted spirituality to rural development and to economic development in general. Later the same philosophy was adopted effectively by Pandurang Shastri Athavale in Gujarat, through his well-known *Swadhyaya* Movement. A detailed and inspiring account of this is given by Anantha Kumar Giri in his book on *Swadhyaya* (Giri 2008). The movement spread to the Middle East, the UK, and the USA too. As Giri says, *Swadhyaya* draws inspiration from the *Bhagavadgita* that God resides in everybody's heart. There is universal connectedness in every heart as locus of God'. (Giri 2008: 2). Athavale, the founder of the movement, observed in his Templeton Prize Acceptance Speech: 'I see Bhakti as an understanding of God's profound love for us. We respond to that in the form of active concern for this creation' (Giri 2008: 4). His mantra was: 'Social transformation and economic development through self-development'. Swadhyaya was a movement, essentially within the Hindu tradition, observes Giri. But it was not a fundamentalist movement, and involved no antipathy to other religions (Giri 2008: 21). In the villages which came under the influence of Swadhyaya, there was significant improvement in the education of women and children, in intra-family relations, and in the inter-community relations, cleanliness in public place, and enthusiasm for *shramdaan* (donating one's labour) or *kriyabhakti* for common good, such as construction of wells and tanks and community halls. There were instances when there was change of heart among people living on dacoity, who gave up violence. It opened new mental horizons for people, as it encouraged the habit of reading among the youth. Social change through self-development is a holistic change, a genuine change.

Mahatma Gandhi, Swami Sahajananda, Swami Vivekananda, all of them tried social change through moral development. Athavale had only to follow these great humanists. What about day-to-day life of ordinary Hindus? Did it, does it show evidence of humanism? Did Hindu institutions show humanism? In other words, Hinduism does not lack social concern and humanism. But how about Hindus? Prevalence of social evils among Hindus, such as untouchability, discrimination, and even violence against women, practice of dowry, make it difficult to say that humanism is practised by ordinary Hindus in a day-to-day life, and show that there is still scope to improvement. Indeed, no society is free from social evils, but Hindu society seems to have more than a fair share of them. Yet, the picture is not too dismal.

Hindu institutions engaged in social work, however, are emerging more and more. We have such noble organizations like the Ramakrishna Mission, Chinmaya Mission, Arya Samaj, Brahmakumaris, Radha Soamis, Swami Narayan, ISKCON, AIM for Seva, Art of Living, and Isha Foundation, who are doing exemplary work. They are known as much for social work, humanist work as for providing spiritual guidance. Modern age gurus like Shri Satya Sai Baba, Mata Amrutaanandamayee, Sri Sri Ravi Shankar, Swami Dayananda Saraswati, Sadhguru Jaggi Vasudev, and others are without exception engaged significantly in humanist work. Our temples and mathas too have been engaged in humanist work since long. The famed temple of Tirupati was in the field of social service right since the sixteenth century by developing irrigation and drinking water facilities in drought prone areas. Mathas are increasingly engaged in providing education, and health care. New caste associations also sprang up to take care of social, educational, and health needs of their members, besides making arrangements for spiritual guidance.

Yes, several shastras of Hindus were more concerned with safeguarding caste purity than with promoting humanism. But we do find humanist elements and concerns in them too, strangely co-existing with expressions of inhumanity too. In any case, Independent India has rejected shastras as the basis for constructing their legal and constitutional framework, and had no hesitation in adopting modern, secular, humanist laws and constitution. But to some extent the legacy of shastras in matters of caste prejudice and discrimination against women have continued. We have to get rid of the negative elements of this legacy. Even earlier, there was consensus over the fact that where Shruti scriptures like the Vedas and Upanishads and humanist values like compassion conflicted with shastras, the former would prevail and not the shastras. Gandhi had no hesitation in declaring that even scriptures be considered under the light of reason.

Hindu society is at the crossroads now. For bringing about moral change and self-development, we have, on the one hand, the path shown by Gandhi, Sri Sri Ravi Shankar, Athavale, and the likes. On the other hand there is also the path of intolerance shown by some fundamentalist outfits which though advocated in the name of moral development and reviving Indian culture, has only shown the promise of alienating the youth and being anti-women and counter-productive. Even morality cannot be justified if imposed in inhuman, arrogant, and stupid ways. Moral arrogance is also arrogance and cannot be human because it can be more dangerous and violent. A lot of inhumanity has been perpetrated in the past in the name of morality and religion. We have to learn from this history.

NOTES

1. For a detailed presentation of the philosophy and leaders of Bhakti movements, see Nadkarni (2008), chapter 5.

2. http://www.sculmrthi/2010/04

3. For details on Swami Vidyanand and Swami Sahajanand, see Das 1982: 48–82.

9 Ethics in Hinduism

Ete satpurushaah paraartha-ghatakaah
Svaartham parityajya ye
Saamaanyaa tu paraartham-udyata-bhritah
Svaartha-avirodhena ye /
Temee maanava-rakshsaah parahitam
Svaarthaaya nighnanti ye
Ye tu ghnanti nirararthakam parahitam
Te ke na jaaneemahe //

—Bhatrihari's *Neeti-shataka* (verse 74)

Those are the noblest persons who, giving up self-interest, bring about the good of others. Those that undertake a business for the sake of others, not inconsistent with their own good, are the common lot. Those who harm the welfare of others for their own selfish interest, are demons in human form. We know not what to call those who harm others' welfare for no purpose at all.[1]

Bhatrihari is an eminent poet in Sanskrit who belonged to the first century before Christ. He is famous for composing three *shataka*s (sets of hundred—actually 108—verses) each on *neeti* (ethics), *shringaara* (romance), and *vairaagya* (renunciation). In Hinduism, each has its own place. The verse quoted above is from his *Neeti-shataka*. Interestingly, the composition begins with a religious prayer to the infinite, the pure consciousness or awareness (*chinmaatra-moorthi*). *Tirukkural* (The Kural), an ancient Tamil text of aphorisms on ethics by Tiruvalluvar (dated anywhere between second century BC to eighth century AD) also begins with the praise of God, pure intelligence or pure awareness (*vaalarivan*).

Religion has always inspired ethics in Hinduism right from the Vedic times. Hinduism may have shown a strong inclination to metaphysics and to some extent even to rituals, but its ethical concern has never been diluted. For medieval sants and certainly for Gandhi in modern times, ethics was the essence of religion, neither metaphysics nor rituals. Even in the ancient times and during the classical period of Hinduism, preceding the medieval, almost every religious leader and scripture has shown due concern for moral values. Bhartrihari's *Neeti-shataka* and the ancient Tamil classic, *The Kural,* by Tiruvalluvar were entirely didactic, but such texts on moral instruction alone were rare. Apart from directly imparting moral instructions in didactic passages or verses, Hinduism also widely adopted the method of combining narratives with the didactic, as Matilal points out. In the epics like the Ramayana and the Mahabharata and in the Puraanas, it is not easy to separate the didactic from the narrative (Matilal 2002: 42). Even the Upanishads have quite a few stories to tell with ethical and spiritual implications. Collections of stories, like the Panchatantra and the *Hitopadesha* had the main purpose of giving moral instructions and hints on how to make one's life meaningful and successful, but they did it through stories. The latter two are not regarded as religious texts, but the epics have always had a religious flavour. Even in *Tirukkural,* there are several religious aphorisms, though the bulk of them is on ethics as such. Religious texts served as a very useful vehicle to convey moral values. Between religion and ethics, it is difficult to tell which serves as a means and which as an end. Just as ethics was advocated as requisite for taking religious or spiritual path, religion also served as the means and occasion for moral instruction. Hinduism is not unique in this respect, since other religions also have shown the same feature.

Every religion has the following components: (a) metaphysics and concept of God, (b) ways to salvation or liberation, (c) mythology, (d) rules or customs governing social institutions and rituals, (e) basic ethics. Religions may differ from each other significantly in the first four components. But they more or less agree on the basic ethical principles like commitment to truth, compassion for the weak, and self-control. Since each religion tries to relate different components with each other, ethics may have a distinct flavour in each religion. But their substance is really the same across religions. While the other components of religion divide people on religion, ethics has the powerful potential to unite them on a common footing. Within Hinduism, the different philosophical systems like Advaita, Vishishthaadvaita, and Dvaita differ from each other in respect of the first two components, but they share other components, especially ethics on a common footing. Since all Hindus, irrespective of their philosophical affiliations, also have a common veneration for epics, which also in turn preach ethics, it is certainly possible to speak of a common ethics in Hinduism, overlapping with ethics in other religions, particularly Indian religions including Sikhism.

The closeness between religion and ethics is so intense and deep, that it is easy to mistake one for the other. Yet, it is useful to draw a distinction between the two. Though by and large, the genuinely religious may also be ethical, in quite a few cases they may fall apart. In a public garden, I saw an elderly lady plucking flowers without any feeling of guilt, not minding others watching her. On being asked why she did so in spite of a notice there asking people not to pluck flowers, she replied it was for God's *pooja* (worship) and asked in turn what was wrong. She felt she may have been breaking a rule of the park, but hers was not an immoral act as it was religious. What was religious was automatically moral for her. This of course is a relatively harmless case. But there could be more serious deviations of the religious from the moral. For example, *Dharmashaastras* not only authenticated the caste system but prescribed stringent, unjust and inequitable punishments for infringement of caste rules and customs. Brahmin widows on the death of their husbands, till about 70 years ago, had to shave their heads, wear very simple and unattractive dress, shun ornaments and flowers, and eat simple non-stimulating food. All in the name of religion and custom. In the case of Christianity and Islam, laws against heresy, blasphemy, and apostasy were so strict as to even invite punishment by death. Cases of religious dictats going against morality arise because they are not cases of genuine religion.

Just as what is religious need not necessarily be moral, what is moral need not necessarily be religious, particularly if religion is interpreted narrowly. For example, if one's acts of benevolence are in a secular rather than a religious sphere, they may not be regarded as religious, however good and beneficial they otherwise are. V.K.R.V. Rao, for example, wanted to improve the quality of economics teaching and research in India on par with the West. He established and brought up, therefore, three institutions of teaching and research in economics and other social sciences, two in Delhi and one in Bangalore. He gave opportunities to many youngsters to make a good career in social sciences (I being one of them). These activities were certainly of high moral value, but may not be regarded as religious. The point is that morality is not confined to the religious sphere. It has to extend to other spheres as well, professions, media, business, research, politics, civic life, entertainment and sports and social relations. By its very nature, ethics are intended to cover all activities of life. That is how the spokesmen of ethics from ancient sages to modern exemplars like Mahatma Gandhi envisaged the role of ethics. When Gandhi took up the cause of mill workers and peasants against their exploiters, he was doing a deeply moral duty, even if in common parlance, it was not a religious activity.

In fact, it is possible to have ethics without religion, but religion without ethics is not worth its name. One can be very ethical without being religious, but cannot be religious without being ethical. In spite of this, a combination of ethics with religion can be useful. Religion lends a fervour, a resoluteness of purpose, and a sense of compulsion, which makes following ethics easier for common people. Gandhi saw no conflict between the two, as his religion was pure and genuine, shorn of narrowness, and truth was his God. When religion is taken in its essence and is deeply spiritual, difference between religion and ethics is significantly reduced because spirituality without ethics is just not possible. Similarly, a deeply moral person cannot escape being religious. This is because such a person sees morality not just as an instrument of keeping peace and order, but as a responsibility to the whole world community including its plants and animals, soils, and water. As the Gita (6.29) says, he sees himself in all, and all in himself. This amounts to nothing less than spirituality.

MISUNDERSTANDINGS ABOUT ETHICS IN HINDUISM

Lord Curzon, the then Viceroy of India, in his Convocation Address at the University of Calcutta in 1905, called Hindus compulsive liars, having no sense of truth (Chatterjee 2005: 75). He was only an administrator, not a scholar, though as Viceroy, he should have known better. But quite a few Western scholars also, among them Max Weber (1930, 1958), Albert Schweitzer (1936) and W.J. Kapp (1963), though not as damaging and devastating as Curzon, did create a lot of misunderstanding about ethics in Hinduism and the Hindu world view. An attempt is made here to clear these misunderstandings, not author by author, but point by point.

Chapter 6 in this volume, 'Appearance and Reality', has already refuted one of the main criticisms that Indian religions are world-negating or life-denying and could not therefore develop a proper ethic, which is possible only if one accepts moral responsibility in this world. For the same reason the criticism further alleged that Indian religions remained indifferent to solving the problem of poverty and the need for economic development. It was pointed out in the essay above that even Advaita school of philosophy, which was just one of the many developed in India, duly emphasized our responsibilities to the world, and that there was no question of any philosophy in India, including Advaita, being indifferent to, or inconsistent with the importance of ethical living.

The second criticism is that ethics in Hinduism is mainly deontological, focused on duties, and expressed in terms of do's and don'ts. This preoccupation with duties allegedly came in the way of emergence of any analytical ethics, or meta-ethics, or moral philosophy as such. The neglect of developing moral philosophy, it is pointed out, becomes obvious in the six Darshanas—philosophical systems of thought: Saankhya, Nyaaya, Vaisheshika, Vedaanta, Meemaamsa, and Yoga. These systems gave scant attention to ethics.

In Chapter 5 in this volume, 'Interrogating the Idea of Justice', Amartya Sen's criticism of the Gita as being highly deontological to the point of ignoring consequences, has been referred and also refuted. Main points of my reply to the criticism are summed up here. Call for duty does not mean ignoring consequences. Duties are evolved by taking into account consequences and for the long-term good of the society as a whole, not ignoring long-term interests of individuals. Hinduism, therefore, does not see any general conflict between duty-centred and consequentialist approaches. When in specific situations conflicts arise between the two, Hinduism has even tended to favour consequentialist approach, without diluting the emphasis on duty as a general principle. The language of moral instruction in terms of do's and don'ts is not unique to Hinduism. The famous Ten Commandments in the Bible are in this language only. Contemporary thought emphasizes rights more than duties. Gandhi on the other hand emphasized duties more than rights. Duties involve moral responsibility, which is the basis of ethics. Rights and duties could be considered as two faces of the same coin. Rights cannot be implemented unless corresponding duties of someone are also identified. One may enact a law giving people the right to education, but it cannot be implemented unless duties of the state and of parents/guardians as well are specified in the same Act.

It is not true that there was no attempt in Hinduism or in Indian religions to develop moral philosophy. Only their method was not the same as in western philosophy. As Matilal has observed (in Ganeri

2002: 42), the didactic and the narrative were fused together, so that the moral lesson is well received and remembered by people. The epics like the Ramayana and the Mahabharata, the Puraanas, story books like the Panchatantra, *Jaataka*, and *Hitopadesha* were all meant to present moral lessons, and show how ethics was put into practice and how moral conflicts were resolved. They were not meant only for the intellectual elite but for the mass of people who could remember moral lessons through stories. It is not enough if ethics were confined to intellectuals. What these texts aimed at was to elevate both the moral and intellectual level of ordinary people including even the illiterate. About the alleged neglect of ethics in the Darshanas, Hindery observes:

… applied Hindu morality was already so capably administered by law codes (Dharmashastras), epics, and other popular classics and oral traditions that philosophical systems could simply bypass the ethical task entirely. … The Indian philosophers need not have feared either de-emphasis or downright detraction of moral law and order, because morals were already adequately secured in the Shastras, rituals, dramas and hearts of the people. (Hindery 1978: 188)

Hindery's justification does not mean, however, that deeper philosophical questions like what is truth and why we should be truthful or moral, were ignored in Hindu ethical thought, as will be clear during the course of this essay. Ethical analysis, such as we get in the epics, Darshanas, Sutras, and Shaastras, may be scattered and not systematic, but is nevertheless very much present.

The third criticism of Hindu ethics is that it is not absolute and universal, but relativist. Shankara's distinction between two levels of truth—*paaramaarthika* (transcendental) and *vyaavahaarika* (practical) is alleged to have created such confusion that people believe that truth can be bent for our convenience for being practical, resulting in relativist ethic or ethic of expediency. This, in fact, is a more serious criticism than the above two, and the reply to this has to be more elaborate, extending beyond this section in the essay.

First of all, we have to remember that Shankara was only one of the many philosophers in India, and that philosophers in other traditions did not make any such distinction between transcendental and practical truths. Even for Shankara, there were no two systems of ethics as such. All religious thinkers and philosophers in India, including Shankara, accepted ethics as absolutely essential, not only in day-to-day activities of our practical life, but also as a preparation for taking the path of self—or God realization. There was no concession either in the former or in the latter. Honesty was always commended and hypocrisy condemned. One of the popular *Subhaashitas* (selected 'well-said' verses compiled from different sources) is as follows:

yathaa chittam tathaa vaachah yathaa vaachaasththa kriyaah/
chitte vaachi kriyaayaancha saadhoonaam ekaroopataa//
As in the mind so in the speech, as in the speech, so in the deeds; good persons are the same in mind, speech and action.

(Herur 2001: 75).

The moral path (dharma) was never to be abandoned. *Chaarucharya* says clearly—'*na tyajet dharma-maryaadam api klesha-dashaam shritah*' (never transgress the limits of dharma even if in difficulty) (Herur 2001: 244). The Mahabharata also says the same thing: 'One should not abandon *dharma* under the influence of sensual desire, fear or greed. *Dharma* is eternal, our pains and pleasures are only passing'.[2] For the sake of passing pleasures or pain, lasting values of dharma should not be ignored, according to the Mahabharata. Do any of these quotations—and there are many such, suggest that ethics is only for expediency, accepted when convenient and rejected when not?

The criticism of ethics in Hinduism as relativist or as expediency-oriented must have been occasioned by the penchant in Hindu epics for projecting moral conflicts and dilemmas for special attention through stories. The Gita itself originated from one such moral dilemma (see Chapter 6 above). The Ramayana and the Mahabharata raise these dilemmas one after another and the question of how to decide about what is dharma in such situations. The situation is such that in following one moral duty, another has to be sacrificed. This is not a simple question of moral duty conflicting with self-interest, and yielding to self-interest ultimately. That would have been simple expediency. Moral dilemmas are more complex. In the sections below, some of them would be discussed.

One more criticism is that the doctrine of karma is fatalistic, giving no scope for moral responsibility. This criticism has been refuted in detail in my previous book (Nadkarni 2008: 41–5), and also briefly above in the essay on 'Humanism in Hinduism'. The main point of this refutation is that actually the doctrine of karma gives full moral responsibility to the individuals because present karma determines one's future. The doctrine of karma is meaningless if freedom of will is denied. A puppet cannot be subjected to the law of karma. The law of karma also does not reduce moral responsibility for social evils and suffering of others. If I ignore a poor man on the ground that it is his karma, I incur the sin of ignoring my moral responsibility and if I come into any difficulty, others may also think so about me. The Gita teaches us how to reduce the burden of karma through detachment. It emphasizes that inaction does not save us, but detachment and discrimination can. Role of grace of God is also stressed, which can come after genuine repentance (*paschaattaapa*) to a sincere devotee.

ETHICS IN THE VEDAS AND UPANISHADS

The Foundation of Indian ethics, not Hindu ethics alone, lies in the Vedas. Vedic ethics has its own distinct flavour. The *Rigveda*, composed some 2,500 years before Christ, had a concept of *ritam*, or cosmic order, by which both the physical and the social worlds were sustained. When a sceptic asked who has seen god Indra, he was told to see him in the working of this world itself, and in the beauty and order resulting from the working of the moral law—ritam. Ritam was ordinarily understood in the sense of righteouness. Ritam quickly developed into the concept of *satyam* or truth, with strong ethical implications. Sometimes, both words are used simultaneously, as in the following:

Ritam cha satyam cha abheeddhaat /
Tapascha adhi ajaayata // (Rigveda X.190. 1).
Righteousness and truth upsurged,
kindled from self-discipline.

(Tr. by Hattangdi 2002: 127).

The word, *satyam*, occurs often in the *Rigveda* itself.[3] An aphorism declares: 'God is the source of Truth' (*satya-savam savitaaram—Rigveda* V.82.7) (ibid.:183). *Rigveda* exhorts people—'speak truthfully, and act truthfully' (*satyam vadan satya karman*, X.113.4, ibid.: 134). It assures, 'God escorts us on to the path of righteouness' (VI.44.8; ibid.: 169). There is ardent prayer to God to lead us along the path of righteouness (X.133.6).

Sins were regarded as something which apart from displeasing gods, adversely determined the future of individuals as well as that of the society. That is how the doctrine of karma developed later, but its seed was already there in the Vedas. Cheating others, arrogance, cruelty, and indolence were regarded as sins, while the acts of charity, helping others, hospitality, truthfulness, self control, chastity, courage, and humility were considered as virtues, which led us on the path of ritam (Dasgupta 1961: 9; Crawford 1982: 3–16). Though sins were feared as making gods angry, virtues were praised and followed for their own sake too, and for the good of the society or also for heaven. Vedic people do not appear to have developed the concept of *moksha* or liberation. They were content with heaven, and surely before that, happy with realization of worldly aspirations like prosperity, children, and peace—both social and mental, to be achieved through the path of righteousness. In this sense, Vedas could be said to be 'this-worldly' and life-loving. For this, certain ethical values were considered essential, which they identified and developed.

The word dharma, originated from the *Rigveda*. It occurs there not once or twice but many times, as Kane has observed (1990, vol. I: 1). But it is used with different meanings in different contexts—moral ordinances, as synonym for satyam, duties, and ritual obligations. The word is derived from the verb *dhri,* that is, uphold, support, or sustain. World is believed to sustained by dharma (*prithiveem dharmanaa dhritam*—*Atharvaveda* 12.1.17). The word is used in Jainism and Buddhism as well, with ethical implications—not ritual. In spite of its ambiguity—or rather, multiple meanings, dharma became the most popular word in all Indian religions, forming the main vehicle for expression of ethical thought. The word was never used in the Western sense of religion in the traditional texts or even in popular usage. Since Indian languages did not have an equivalent word for religion, the use of the word dharma in this sense came into vogue only with modern times.

An interesting feature of the Vedas is the evidence of congregational prayers, conveying a strong sense of fraternity and even equality and bonding. The following prayer from *Rigveda* (X.191.3) is still in vogue:

May our prayer be one and the same;
May we belong to one fraternity;
May our minds move in accord;
May our hearts work in unison
For our supreme goal;
Let us be inspired by a common ideal;
Let us sing Thy praises in congregation.

(Tr. by Vidyalankar: 218).

The Vedic religion is considered generally to be polytheistic. There are many gods, with Varuna and Mitra and even Indra keeping the moral order, ritam. Crawford observes that 'on the whole, the gods are approached through love rather than fear' (1982: 6). There was no image worship during the Vedic and Upanishadic period, and no temples. There is simultaneously the concept of One God (*Ekam*) also in the Vedas. The oft-quoted saying', *Ekam sadvipraah bahudhaa vadanti'* (One Truth is spoken variously by the wise) is from *Rigveda* (I.164.46). The plurality of gods is taken to represent different aspects of the One. Various gods take the fight on behalf of goodness, while *raakshsa*s or *asura*s (demons) represent evil. They are always in conflict with each other. But the fight often seems to take place through humans! Humans seem to be caught in the proxy war between the good and the evil. 'Because ultimate reality is *Sat* (Truth), it follows that in a world structured by Truth, men should live by the principle of Truth' (Crawford 1982: 9).

Crawford observes that women in the Vedic and Upanishadic period were treated with regard, enjoying both educational and religious rights. The wife invariably joined the husband in religious rites. She had also the right to select her husband. Boys and girls had the freedom and opportunity to meet each other in the Vedic society. Women participated in public lfe and debated in public assemblies. Monogamy was the generally prevalent form of marriage (Crawford 1982: 13).

When we come to the Upanishads, we find that not only the basic moral values of the Vedic period were retained, there was also a further development of ethical thought. Though Upanishads were more concerned with metaphysics, they always thought that a moral life is a prerequsite for taking the path of spirituality and that they go together. The highest good was in attaining self-knowledge, but without controlling selfishness and anger, and without equipping one self with self-control, compassion for others, and generosity, no self-knowledge can come, however intense one's efforts at meditations and reflection may be. Good news here is that, meditation and right reflections help one in leading a moral life. They can form a virtuous circle.

However, the Upanishads gave greater priority to attaining spiritual and long-term happiness, *Shreyas*, than to worldly or sensual pleasures which gave only a momentary happiness, *Preyas*. The distinction between the two may already have been conceived in a dormant form, but it became conspicuously clear in the Upanishads. They declared that the wise are those who know this distinction, and those who do not are ignorant. Ignorance and delusion (*avidyaa*) are very much looked down upon in the Upanishads. They gave a higher priority also to study, meditation, reflection, and debate, than to religious rituals. Ethics received more weightage than rites. The famous Convocation Address exhorts pupils who have completed their studies with their Guru to pursue a path of truth and righteousness,or virtue and not to deviate from studies:

Satyam vada, dharmam chara,
Svadhyaayaanmaa pramadah,...
Satyaat na pramaditavyam,
Dharmaat na pramaditavyam,...

Deva-pitrakaryaabhyaam na pramaditavyam /

(Taittireeya Upanishad I.11.1)

Speak the truth. Practise virtue. Do not deviate from study. Do not deviate from truth. Do not deviate from virtue. Do not deviate from your duty to gods and parents. (Tr. by author)

The Upanishads emphasize ahimsa (non-violence) for the first time, which was to become a major virtue in Indian religions later. The *Chaandogya Upanishad* (VIII.15) exhorts pupils to practise ahimsa with all living beings (*ahimsa sarva-bhootaani*). The same Upanishad emphasizes austerity, charity, and uprightness along with Ahimsa (III.17.4). These virtues are stated to be more potent than animal sacrifices. The Bhagavadgita (Gita) takes up this clue to change the very meaning of Yajna (sacrifice) as we see below.

THE GITA'S CONTRIBUTION TO HINDU ETHICS

Though the Gita is a part of the Mahabharata (forming chapters 23 to 40 in Bheeshmaparva), it is considered to be the essence of the Upanishads, bringing out their moral philosophy, and is venerated as a scripture along with the Vedas and the Upanishads. Because of its small size and simple language, many more Hindus know about the Gita than about the Vedas and the Upanishads. A hymn on the greatness of the Gita says that all the Upanishads are cows, their milk is the Gita, and Krishna is the milkman who has squeezed the milk out of the cows. But the Gita has also its own contribution to make to ethics. Its message is mainly for those engaged with the world. D.V. Gundappa calls his Kannada commentary on the Gita as *Jeevana-dharma-Yoga*. It is dharma for living day-to-day life actively, and leading one's life by its teaching is Yoga itself. That is why the background of war in the Gita, is considered by Gandhi to be only a metaphor for life's struggles.

The contribution of the Gita is on several counts. First it establishes Hinduism (Sanaatana Dharma) firmly on the basis of ethics more than on rituals. It repeatedly enumerates virtues to be cultivated and vices to be avoided. For example, Chapter 16 begins with stating qualities which make a human being divine (in verses 1 to 3):—fearlessness, purity of heart, steadfastness in knowledge, studiousness, charity, self-control, uprightness, austerity, non-violence, truthfulness, tranquility, compassion for all living beings, uncovetouness, gentleness, forgiveness, cleanliness, humility, and absence of anger, hatred, and fickleness.

The chapter also mentions (in verse 4) qualities that make a man demon-like: arrogance, anger, harshness, cruelty, and ignorance. These qualities are mentioned in the Vedas and Upanishads too, but the Gita's speciality lies in its greater emphasis on ethics than on outward religiosity or even mere learning and contemplation. Gita expects us to make ethics a way of life, doing one's duty dispassionately, and facing life not only with equanimity but with active enthusiasm. The Gita also gives a valuable criterion in terms of three gunas—*satva, rajas,* and *tamas*—by which to judge the morality of different things we face not only on the path of spirituality but also day-to-day life.: work, knowledge, perception, prayer, charity, happiness, and even food (see chapter 8 above). For example, prayer is *saatvik,* if it is for pure love of God or for the welfare of the world; *raajasik* if it is to meet one's own desire; and *taamasik* if it seeks to harm others. It is significant that the Gita does not apply this criterion of gunas to *varnas,* nor even to individuals. The Gita says that we have all the three gunas in varying proportions, varying in the same person from time to time.

The Gita is also quite emphatic on justice and equality of all beings. Its chapter 6 elaborates the concept in a few verses (29–32). The key verse (6.32) has been quoted in original along with translation in the previous chapter here (p. 205), which briefly put, asks us to feel the pleasure and pain in others as our own. The significance of these verses is not for metaphysics alone, as some have mistakenly interpretetd. It has social relevance too. For example, it follows from them that the caste system has no ethical or spiritual validity. Krishna declares in the Gita, *Chaturvarnyam mayaa srishtam guna-karma vibhaagashah* (4.13), which means, 'I created the four varnas on the basis of qualities and occupations'. Krishna removes any possible ambiguity about this in *Uttara-gita* in his reply to a question by Arjuna:

Na jaatih kaaranam taata gunaah kalyaanakaarakaah/
Vritastham api chaandaalam tam devaah braahmanam viduh//
Birth is not the cause, my friend, it is virues which are the cause of welfare. Even a *chaandaala* [a low caste] observing the vow is considered a Brahmin by the gods.[4]

Consistent with this stand, the Gita opened the door to all castes and classes, particularly the lower, which had been closed to them by narrow-minded priests. This was by showing a new path for spiritual upliftment through bhakti, simply love of God, without the necessity of rituals or even contemplation, which was mostly beyond the lowest varna of Shudras. Bhakti on the other hand, was open to all including even the illiterate. The Gita took this step several centuries before the bhakti movements in

India, which also did the same job. In the same spirit, the Gita changed the meaning of *yajna* (which meant Vedic sacrifice earlier). The word was stripped of its rigid ritualism, and taken in the sense of offering, which anybody without wealth or high varna status could do. Such an offering to God could be in the form of help to others (*lokahita*) by way of giving food, clothing, shelter, vessels, knowledge, or service.

The Gita pioneered the concept of karma-yoga or karma-maarga—undertaking all work with a sense of detachment, selflessly. Even if is work intended for one's own benefit, it is to be done unattached, in the sense of doing one's duty well and leaving the fruit of its action in God's hands, without unduly worrying about it. But the Gita's emphasis is more on altruistic work, which is morally of a higher level. Doing one's work with detachment does not mean doing it without interest. On the other hand, work has to be done with fortitude *and* enthusiasm (*dhrityutsaaha-samanvitah*) and with due regard to consequences (18:23 and 26). The Gita's advice to do loka-sangraha, that is, doing good to people, is in chapter 3 (verses 20–5). Elsewhere too it exhorts people to do loka-hita, which is also the same. Thus, the Gita teaches us both how to do work and what type of work to do.

The Gita also authenticates the pluralism of sanaatan dharma. It advocates different approaches to God realization as suited to the aptitudes of people—*Jnaana-maarga* (path of knowledge), *karma-maarga* (path of detached and altruistic work), and *bhakti-maarga* (path of love or devotion), or a path integrating all the three. Krishna gives a firm assurance:

Ye yathaa maam prapadyante taan tathaiva bhajaamyaham/
Mama vartmaanuvartante manushyaah Paartha sarvashah// (Ch. 4:11).
In whatever way people approach me, I reward them in the same way. O Paartha [Arjuna], people can follow my path in all [different] ways.

(Tr. by author)

This is not just pluralism alone, but liberalism too. It is this spirit which marked the respect of Hinduism to other religions. *Naarada Bhakti Sutras* say clearly, 'It is not proper to enter into a controversy about God, or spiritual truths, or about comparative merits of different devotees. For there is room for diversity in views; no one view based upon mere reason is conclusive in itself'. (Sutras 74 and 75; translated by Tyagisananda 2000: 20).

An important contribution of the Gita to Hindu ethics consists in its reconciling the different human goals known as *purushaarthas*—Dharma, *artha, kaama,* and *moksha*. While the pursuit of wealth (artha) and satisfying desires (kaama) had since long been considered as legitimate goals, the Gita insisted that it be in accordance with dharma, that is, by just means. The Gita is clearly world-affirming in doing so—emphasis on ethical means being part of this. We can enjoy life in this world, but without coming in the way of similar enjoyment by others and without cheating and deceit. Just as artha and kaama are legitimate only if in accordance with dharma, dharma would be empty in the absence of artha and kaama. After all, why do we need ethics unless meant to be used as a guide in worldly pursuits? But the Gita also suggests that true happiness does not lie in selfish enjoyment, but in transcending it. And that is where the idea of moksha becomes relevant. Moksha consists in transcending the narrow cage of personal ego, and identifying with the wider Self (Atman) which is in all. That is the culmination of ethical life, the most supreme human goal. The Gita shows that even this goal can be achieved while being engaged in this world according to dharma. The Gita thus removes the tension among purushaarthas, which otherwise can be bothersome.

The Gita's God is accessible to all directly, without any medium of priests. The Gita co-opted all people left out by the Vedas and Upanishads into the mainstream of sanaatan dharma, and imbibed into them a strong sense of ethics. Its philosophy is activistic and inspired people to resist injustice and evil. Aravind Nadakarni, a noted poet and author in Kannada, observes that in resisting foreign invasions from the North-west, Buddhism in India succumbed to them, while activist teachings of the Gita and also epics enabled Hindus to successfully survive their onslaughts (Nadakarni 1998: 22–4). Buddhism in India proved to too pacifist to face such invasions, while Hinduism could rise to the occasion and survive. But this would not have been possible if vast masses of people had been left out of Hinduism. The Gita, epics, Puraanas and the latter Bhakti movements corrected the elitism of Vedas and Upanishads to a great extent.

INTRICACIES OF DHARMA

The exposition of 'dharma', continued during the post-Vedic/Upanishadic literature of Hinduism, namely, the phase of *Dharmasutras* and subsequent *Dharmashaastras*, including Smritis. The age of the composition of major epics—Ramayana and Mahabharata is uncertain and could be the same as that of *Dharmasutras* (sixth to second century BC) or even earlier. The epics expound the tenets of dharma through stories and dialogues. Puraanas including the *Bhaagvata* came subsequently. Their main purpose was to reach ethics and religion to the mass of people. Dharma is the most common topic of discussion in all these texts.

The Mahabharata defines dharma in terms of its purpose and consequences:

Dhaaranaat dharma ityaahuh dharmo dhaarayate prajaah /
Yat syaat dhaarana samyuktam sa dharma iti nischayah //

Karnaparva ch. 69, verse. 58.

It means: 'Dharma sustains the society. Dharma maintains social order. Dharma ensures the well being and progress of humanity. Dharma is surely that which fulfils these objectives' (tr. by Jois 1997: 2). Dharma is said to be crucial even in promoting individual welfare. In reply to a question from Yudhishthira, Bheeshma observes that dharma in the sense of righteousness is the truest and most dependable friend of human beings. He says, friends and relatives part company after death, but dharma clings and protects them even after one's death.

Depending on the context, dharma connotes rules of moral conduct or virtue, religious duties including obligatory rites, and also duties to society, both in the *Dharmashaastra*s and epics. It was never used in the sense of 'religion' in the texts. In the Shaastras, dharma meant both *varnaashrama dharma* (specific to each varna and aashrama) and *saamaanya dharma* (universal or common dharma). In the post-Vedic age, caste system had developed as a major feature of the Hindu society. Though originally, there was only a system of four varnas (*brahmana*, *kshatriya*, *vaishya*, and *shudra*) based on division of labour or occupation, it consolidated itself into a birth-based caste system. There was opposition in scriptures to this deterioration of the original concept and repeated clarifications that it is not to be based on birth.[5] Simultaneously with varnas, there was also the system of *aashrama*s, consisting of four stages of life: student (*brahmachari*), householder (*grihastha*), forest-dweller (*vaanaprastha*), and recluse or monk (*sannyaasi*). However, it was not necessary for a man to go through all the four stages. A venerated ancient Tamil text, *Tirukkural* by Tiruvalluvar, says for example that 'if a man goes through the householder's life along the way of dharma, nothing is left for him to attain by becoming a recluse or staying in the forest' (tr. by Rajagopalachari 1999).

Saamaanya-dharma means moral obligations common to all, irrespective of one's occupation or aashrama. This dharma is absolute and universal. *Manusmriti* (X.63) explains what common dharma is:

Ahimsa satyamasteyam shoucham indriya-nigrahah /
Etam saamaasikam dharmam chaaturvarne abraveet Manuh //

It means: 'Nonviolence, truthfulness, not acquiring illegimate wealth, purity, and control of senses, are, in brief, the common dharma for all the four *varnas*' (tr. by Jois 1997:26). Among specific dharmas, *Raaja-dharma* was taught to princes, nobles and to administrators in general. It was derived from several sources, especially, from Kautilya's *Arthashaastra*.[6] It was not meant exclusively for kings, but mainly for governance and government, and included moral principles. *Arthashaastra*, for example, says: 'In the happiness of his subjects lies the king's happiness; in his welfare, his welfare; He shall not consider as good only that which pleases him but treat as beneficial to him whatever pleases his subjects' (1.19.34; translated by Rangarajan 1992: x). Specific dharmas are thus derived from a sense of fairness and justice, that is, from Saamaanya-dharma. In spite of differences between specific dharmas, it was made clear by teachers and in scriptures that Saamaanya-dharma was mandatory for all without exception. Dharma is both social and individual. Values of individual morality are common and mandatory, but duties to society could differ. But relative or specific dharma is subordinated to the universal or basic dharma, and if there is a conflict between the two, the universal dharma would prevail. It would be unfair to call this as relativism.

In judging the righteousness of an act, according to the principles of dharma, three criteria are useful. They are: the motive, the means adopted, and the consequences. This was Gandhi's approach too, as explained in Chapter 1 above. Purity is insisted upon both with regard to motive and the means. For example, a man can choose his wife only through wooing and by her consent, and not by force. A forced marriage is considered as *raakshasi* (devilish, demonical). Consequences of an act, both intended and realized, constitute the third criterion. In fact, dharma or satya is defined as that which achieves the welfare of all. An assertion to this effect occurs in several places in Mahabharata and also other texts. Take for example, the following verse from Shantiparva of Mahabharata (329.13):

Satyasya vachanam shreyah, satyaadapi hitam vadet /
Yadbhootahitam atyantam etat satyam matam mama //

It means: 'It is good to speak the truth; to speak what does good is still better. What is ultimately good for the welfare of all beings is what I consider as truth'.

Even then, how to decide what is good, what is dharma? Often, there may be conflicts even among texts and no clear path may be in sight.

In such situations of conflicts between texts themselves, the *Smritis* (*Dharma sutras, Dharmashaastras*, epics, and so on) have themselves have clearly said that the opinion in the *Shrutis* (Vedas and Upanishads) should prevail. But even the *Shrutis* may not be clear for specific cases. The texts advise two ways to resolve this problem. One is to rationally think over from all sides of the problem. When even this is not helpful, go by the advice of the wise and good persons.

Dharma is sometimes taken as unsentimental in the same sense as justice is taken as blind. But it does not preclude rationality and humanism. In the Gita, Krishna asks Arjuna at the end of his sermon to critically think over what all he has said and then act as per his will (*vimarshyetad asheshena yathechchasi tathaa kuru*—18.63). In the considered opinion of philosopher, Matilal, 'dharma tradition developed through an attempt at rational criticism of itself' (in Ganeri (ed.) 2002: 51). Reasoning does not take place in an intellectual vacuum. Even while reasoning out what is right or wrong in specific situations, we need some values given by Saamaanya-dharma. The Gita gives a valuable hint as help in this (ch. 6, verse 32. It calls upon us to judge happiness and sorrow in others by the same standard as we apply to ourselves. The Kural also says 'do not do to others what you know has hurt yourself' (tr. by Sundaram 1990: 50). The Panchatantra says the same thing; '*atmanah pratikoolaani pareshaam na samaacharet* (*Kakolaleeya* 10–2), That is, whatever is harmful to oneself, should not be done to others.

In spite of this insistence on rational judgment in the light of moral principles, there are quite a few who have emphasized that decisions on dharma have to be tempered by compassion. Basavanna (Basaveshwara), an eminent social reformer and leader of Bhakti movement in Karnataka in the twelfth century, asked: '*dayeyillada dharma-vaavudayyaa*' (what kind of dharma would it be if it is without compassion?). To discourage irrational sentimentalism, D.V. Gundappa, an eminent poet-philosopher of twentieth century Karnataka, responded to this with a counter question: *dharma-villada daye enthadayya?* (What kind of compassion is it if it is without dharma?) As Gundappa explains, a mother cannot go on giving whatever the child asks, for it can only spoil the child—both its health and conduct. A wicked person bent upon harming others and found guilty, cannot be let off free, as compassion to him this way would mean harm to his potential victims (Gundappa 2001: 70). Dharma requires love and compassion to be combined with rationality, justice, and responsibility.

There could be situations when even rational reflection on the instructions in the shruti may not yield a solution. Yudhishthira observes in the Mahabharata:

> The scriptures are many and are divided; the Dharma-shaastras are many and different. Nobody is called a sage until and unless he holds a different view. The truth of dharma lies concealed in a dark cave (of the human heart?). Therefore, the way to dharma is the one that is taken by mahaajanas (great persons or a great number of persons)
> (Tr. by Matilal in Ganeri [ed.] 2002: 41).

The advice to go to the wise and the good for counsel on dharma is in *Manusmriti* also (2:1):

Vidvatbhih sevitah sadbhirnityam advesharaagibhih/
Hridayenabhyanujnaato yo dharmastvam nibodhata//

It means: 'Know that to be true dharma which the wise and the good and those who are free from passion and hatred follow, and which appeals to to the heart (or conscience)'. (Tr. by M.K. Gandhi) (*CWMG* Vol. 75: 375)

A difficulty with the advice of taking counsel from even the wise who are also good, is that there may be no unanimity among them in specific cases involving moral conflict. That is, ultimately, one follows what appeals to his heart or conscience. This again could expose such a decision to a criticism that it amounts to relativism or ethics of expediency. This would be unfair because that is not the spirit in which this approach to dharma was developed. There are many verses in religious texts and texts of moral instruction to be strict follower of ethics, come what may.[7] Moral dilemmas or conflicts may arise such that they defy an easy solution, because in following one moral duty, another may have to be violated. There are several instances of them in the epics, which are briefly reviewed in the following section. We may only note here that the awareness of differences in points of view regarding dharma promoted a degree of tolerance in Hinduism which is almost unparalleled.

'ETHICS AND EPICS'

'Ethics and Epics' is the title of the collected essays of philosopher, B.K. Matilal (Ganeri 2002). The main theme of the essays in the book is to discuss moral dilemmas faced in the epics—Ramayana and Mahabharata. There is another book of essays edited by Matilal himself, *Moral Dilemmas in the Mahabharata* (1989) which also deals with the same issue. A recent book by Gurcharan Das, *The Difficulty of Being Good* (2009) is also on moral dilemmas or conflicts. A few other books on Hindu ethics, such as that by Crawford (1982) have also attended to this. Though moral dilemmas in the epics have thus received considerable attention, they still haunt Hindu thinking minds. We may, therefore, take up this issue here though briefly, and the interested readers may go further into this with the help of above books.

In the Ramayana, there are at least three incidents which morally question the decision taken by Rama, who is otherwise venerated as *Maryada-Purushottam*, a paragon of virtues. For the sake of honouring his father's word of promise to Rama's stepmother, Rama gives up his throne and goes to the forest. Even as the king later, after his return to Ayodhya, his rule is considered as exemplary from the point of his commitment to the welfare of his people. But even such a person had to face serious moral conflicts. The first is his killing of Vaali by shooting an arrow from behind. It was for the sake of Rama's friend, Sugriva, whose wife Vaali had taken away by force. In ancient India, there were certain ethical rules of warfare or battle, one of them being to fight face-to-face, and not by cheating. The mortally wounded Vaali questions Rama about the morality of his action and Rama's replies are not convincing (Matilal in Ganeri 2002: 45–6). But Ramayana explains this conduct by saying that Vaali was blessed by God that he would be invincible in any face-to-face combat, which made him arrogant and reckless. Matilal does not refer to this explanation. Matilal says that embarrassed by Vaali's admonition, Rama offers to bring him back to life, but Vaali, a devotee of Rama, did not agree and preferred to die seeing his Lord face-to-face. Matilal observes that 'the theology of bhakti absolved Rama here of any immorality in the act' (Matilal in Ganeri 2002: 46). But karma is said to have pursued Rama in his next birth as Krishna, who was killed by an unseen hunter's arrow.

The next incident is Rama's killing of Shambuka, a shudra by caste, for doing penance which was forbidden to shudras as per varna-dharma. This was when Rama returned to Ayodhya and took over as king after 14 years of forest dwelling. When there was a drought in a part of Rama's kingdom, his subjects there said that there must have been a transgression of dharma and asked Rama to find out. His spies reported about a shudra doing penance, transgressing his caste duty. Rama actually did not seem to have believed in such caste rules himself, for in his forest dwelling days, he visited sage Maatanga and paid his respects, and Maatanga belonged to an untouchable caste. When Shabari, a tribal woman, out of her devotion to Rama, offered berries to him when visited her, he ate with relish. She had offered them after biting each one of them to see if they were good. But in Shambuka case, Rama had to bend to the will of his people, who believed that the drought occurred because of violation of varna-dharma. The third incident was also for a similar reason. This time, Rama had to abandon his own pregnant wife and leave her in the hermitage of Vaalmiki, because some of his subjects believed that her chastity was violated by Raavan when she was in his custody. People believed that when the king's wife was not chaste, the kingdom would be in peril. Rama deeply loved his wife, he himself had no doubt that she was pure, but still he felt that he had to bend to the will of his unreasonable subjects. It was as if his subjects ruled Rama, more than he ruled them.

If Rama appears like a tragic hero, Krishna of Mahabharata appears more like a cunning politician with the difference that he is staunchly committed to the cause of his friends, the Pandavas, and not his own personal interests. In the war, he defends his friends against all odds even if it meant adopting some low tricks, not regarded as morally acceptable. Krishna, in human form at least, is hardly the omnipotent God he claims to be in the Gita, for he failed to avert the war and secure justice to the Pandavas without war, though he tried his best for it. Or, it could be that once human beings are granted free will, God puts limits on his own intervention in human affairs. On his way back to Dwaaraka after the conclusion of the war, Krishna happens to meet his devotee Uttanka. The latter is surprised that being God, Krishna could not prevent so much bloodshed and death. Krishna replies that there was so much hate and hostility on both sides, the war became inevitable, that he tried to negotiate peace but Kauravas did not listen. 'All he could do was to try to see that justice was done in the end, and the kingdom returned to Pandavas' (Das 2009: 208).

The situation was becoming more and more grim for Pandavas with the progress of Kurukshetra war. Their army was much smaller and had less number of great warriors than on the Kaurava side. One after another, Bheeshma, Drona, Karna, and Duryodhana were showing signs of invincibility on the Kaurava side. If Krishna had not intervened with his tricks almost at each stage, Pandavas would have lost the war. Krishna did not want Paandavas to lose, because justice was on their side. Kauravas had 'tried to burn Pandavas in the house made of lacquer, usurp Pandavas' kingdom through a crooked game of dice, and tried shamefully to disrobe Draupadi [in public]' (Das 2009: 190). How do you tackle an unscrupulous evil-doer who is also very strong? Can you allow the doctrine of 'might is right' to succeed? Is it moral? This was the moral dilemma which Krishna faced.

On the eve of the war, both Kauravas and Pandavas agreed to a code of just war (*dharma-yuddha*) on humanitarian grounds. For example, nobody should fight and kill a person who is running away from the battlefield, also one who is unarmed and defenceless; it should be through one-to-one combat and ambush was to be avoided; in a fight with maces, no one should hit below the waist; all fighting should cease after the sunset and resumed only after sunrise, and so on (Matilal in Ganeri 2002: 94–5; Das 2009: 207). Yet both sides broke the code. Drona led the ambush of Abhimanyu, a teenage son of Arjuna, and killed him surrounded by seven warriors. Drona also started killing fleeing soldiers of Pandavas (Matilal in Ganeri 2002: 95–6). Of course, Bheeshma and Karna were honourable men and played no tricks. But they were on the side of Kauravas, for no other reason than that they were under Kaurava patronage. Bheeshma had a sympathy and respect for the just cause of Pandavas, and yet when he faced the moral choice of either staying neutral or fighting on the side of his patrons, he decided on the latter, knowing well that they had committed heinous crimes against Pandavas, including the attempt to disrobe Draupadi in public.

Gurcharan Das draws a parallel between the World War II and the Mahabharata war. World War II was a 'just war'. 'A world dominated by a victorious Nazi Germany would have been even more intolerable than the one ruled by Duryodhana. In that war the victorious Allies did some nasty things. In the five months of of World War II in the Pacific theatre, American "fire bombing" raids killed more than 90,000 Japanese civilians—and this happened before they dropped the atomic bomb on Hiroshima and Nagasaki. In the European theatre, the British killed more civilians with their bombing of German cities than were killed by Germany's blitz on Britain. The Pandava's acts seem like indiscretions by comparison' (Das 2009: 203–4).

If that is the case, why are we so bothered by Krishna's tricks by which Bheeshma, Drona, Karna, and Duryodhana, the most invincible warriors on the Kaurava side, were killed one after another, without Krishna's shooting a single arrow? That is because Krishna is supposed to be God's incarnation, who preached high morality to Arjuna in the Gita. How could God resort to tricks? Just as he prevented disrobing of Draupadi by a miracle, when she remembered and prayed to him though he was not present on the scene, similarly he could have through some miracle solved the problem! That was Uttanka's question too, referred above.

But by so doing, Mahabharata would have lost much of its interest and excitement. It continues to be read and retold in stories by millions of Hindus and even others, made into numerous dramas and films all over the world with undiminished interest for over two thousand years. The intention of Mahabharata appears to be to raise these moral dilemmas, tickle our brains and keep our moral quest alive.

But Mahabharata does not absolve Krishna or try to defend him. It speaks through Duryodhana, when he lay morally wounded, by enumerating Krishna's guiles one after another. Through grieving Gaandhaari (mother of Kauravas), the epic pronounces a curse on Krishna that his ethnic group would perish through infighting, and makes it come true. The Mahabharata does not leave us with an impression that the end morally justifies the means. It leaves us in no doubt that the means too have to be morally acceptable. But the dilemma remains to tickle our brains. How do you tackle a clever, strong, and unscrupulous evil-doer, to ensure justice in the world? How does morality work in a situation of conflict between an oppressive and arrogant but a strong party on one side, and a weaker party deprived of its rights by the strong? Whatever the answer may be, the adoration for Krishna has only increased over the centuries, not excluding the modern times. He is looked upon by his devotees as the One who will take them through all the difficulties and evils in life, just by taking refuge in Him with full faith, and He will in addition ensure lasting happiness hereafter too.

Ethics raises also an important question of how to treat a person who deviates from dharma, but sincerely regrets it. Hinduism concedes that man may sin and go astray from dharma. But, as in Christianity, there is liberation from sin (paapa) through genuine repentance, with a resolve to desist from further sin, and seeking forgiveness from God. There are several legends in Hindu epics to illustrate this point. Two of them are well known. One is from Ramayana—the legend of Ahalyaa. She is the beautiful wife of a sage called Gautama. Indra, King of celestial beings, develops a strong urge for her. Taking the disguise of Gautama, he enters the sage's hut in his absence. Ahalyaa sees through the disguise but is tempted and allows herself to be seduced by Indra. Gautama returns and finds what has happened. He curses his wife to turn into a stone. Indra does not escape from the holy rage of the sage. As a result of his curse, Indra loses not only the respect of all human beings, but his testicles too. When God takes the incarnation of Rama, Ahalyaa is redeemed by an act of his grace and reunited with her husband to the joy of both. While this is a story of a momentary temptation of sin, Ajaamila's story from the *Bhaagavatam* is an illustration of lifelong of sin. With advancing age he repents from his heart and seeks the forgiveness of God, and he is liberated through an act of Grace. Such liberation, however, does not come to persons who wilfully indulge in sin without any repentance. Duryodhana, the villain of the Mahabharata, says:

I know what is dharma,
but have no inclination to it.
I know what is against dharma,
but cannot desist from it

(quoted in Pandurangi 1999b: 27)

There is no liberation for such a person, who has to go through the cycle of death and birth, unless, through grace of God, he gets the wisdom to take a path of virtue. There is no eternal damnation in Hinduism. It is the destiny of all beings to attain union with God.

ETHICS OF SANTS AND SOCIAL REFORMERS

Though there is no dearth of condemnation of the caste system in the scriptures of Hinduism and also in anti-caste legends, the system continued, and the opposition to it also continued. But this time the opposition came from the lower castes themselves, joined sometimes by Brahmins too. The sants in bhakti movements came mainly from the victimized castes, even from the the outcastes—the untouchables. The notion that human beings were equal and that service of other human beings was like service of God, came to the fore as never before. Such a philosophy, expressed earlier in the scriptures, was now reemphasized and felt to be necessary to humanize religion, more than in the past. Some of the most trenchant critics of the caste system were the Siddhas of Tamil Nadu (the seventh century AD onwards) and Veerashaivas of Karnataka (the twelfth century AD onwards). The author of the Kural, Tiruvalluvar, a weaver by caste, had expressed himself against the caste system and was an inspiration for anti-caste movements in Tamil Nadu. Siddhas condemned bigotry and superficial symbols of religion, and emphasized universal love. The Veerashaiva Sharanas (devotees of Shiva) took into their fold people from all castes, from Brahmins to untouchables and also women on equal footing. In the zeal for erasing the caste system from the face of the society, they not only inter-dined but also encouraged inter-caste marriages. The marriage of the daughter of a Sharana who was earlier a Brahmin with the son of a Sharana who was formerly an untouchable, created tremendous commotion. Their leader, Basavanna, was a great visionary and clearly ahead of his time. Siddhas and Sharanas explicitly recognized that women were not a subordinate sex and women had equal access in philosophical discussions. The bhakti movements had quite a few women saints: Andal in Tamil Nadu, Akka Mahadevi in Karnataka, Meerabai in Rajasthan, Lalla in Kashmir, Janabai in Maharashtra, and several others who may not be as well known as those mentioned here. Similarly there were several eminent untouchables in Bhakti movements—Nandanaar in Tamil Nadu, Chokhamela in Maharashtra, and Ravidas in north India among them. There were even Muslims who were accepted as the sants of Bhakti movements—Pir Mohammed and Mastan Sahib in Tamil Nadu, Kabir in North India, Latib Shah, Shaikh Mohammed and Shah Muni in Maharashtra, and Shishunal Sharief in Karnataka. All of the sants condemned inequality in society and emphasized love of God as the only effective means of God realization.[8]

The sants were not merely saints and reformers, but also poets and mystics too. What is more, they composed in India's regional languages in a way accessible to all, avoiding Sanskrit, though quite a few of them like Jnaneshwar in Maharashtra knew Sanskrit very well. Jnaneshwar (1271–96) rendered the Gita into Marathi, which is more a commentary than an exact translation, known after him as *Jnaneshwari*. It became much more popular in Maharashtra than the original Gita. The poet-saints addressed themselves mainly to ordinary people, and had no inclination to elitist analysis of dharma or moral philosophy, though they made moral exhortations and tried their best to raise the moral level of ordinary people, leading a pious and simple life themselves. They mostly kept their occupations to make a living, being tillers, potters, weavers, washermen, cobblers, tanners and so on, and yet found time for *loka-hita*, welfare of people. A few verses by some of the sants, especially conveying their moral stance are presented below, to give a flavour of their works.

Nammalvar (880–930 AD approx.) born in a poor peasant family, wrote:

The four castes uphold all clans;
go down, far down, to the lowliest outcastes
of outcastes:
if they are intimate henchmen
of our Lord ...
then even the slaves of their slaves
are our masters.

(Tr. by A.K. Ramanujan 1993: 60)

Though protest against social injustice was one of the main themes in the literature of sants, other aspects of ethics, particularly the need for good conduct, truthfulness, equanimity and the like received equal attention. Akka Mahadevi (the twelfth century AD) was a prominent woman devotee, a Sharane, in Basavanna's movement, known for her detachment and equanimity. The following is my English rendering of one of her famous sayings (vachanas) in Kannada:

Having made home in a forest,
how can one be scared of wild beasts?
Having made home on the sea-shore,
how can one be scared of the waves of the sea?
Having made home in a market place,
how can one be scared of din and noise?
Once born in this world,
shunning anger,
one has to be at peace
both with praise and reproach,
Oh, Lord, Pure as Jasmine! [9]

Tukaram (1598–1650), respected as the greatest of the sants in Maharashtra, is known for his piety and prolific compositions (*abhangs*). He came from a non-brahmin family of grain dealers and broke through his caste barrier. Apart from expressing his intensity of love for Vithoba, his God, Tukaram's songs emphasize virues of self-control, simple living, freedom from hatred, softness of speech, kindness, integrity, and truthfulness. Here is an example of his abhang though translated into English:

I would bow to his feet,
who acts as he speaks,
I will sweep his courtyard
and accept his serfdom.
Like a slave I would stand
with folded hands before him.
Tuka says, God, my heart goes to his feet.

Chokhamela (the fourteenth century), an untouchable sant from Maharashtra, shows in his poems intense love and faith in God, but also strongly protests against inequity and disparity in the world. Here is an example of his Marathi poem rendered into English by Rohini Mokashi-Punekar:

You know, Keshiraj,[10] on the other hand,
I am filled with surprise.

A throne for one, a hovel for another.
Yet one other wanders bare,
one half-fed, another feasting,
for some not a scrap for the asking;
high glory for one, good posts for a few,
others beg from village to village.
Such, it seems, is the law of your world,
Says Chokha,
Hari, my fate lies in this.

(Tr. by Mokashi-Punekar 2002: 21)

Sant Kabir (1440–1518), a Muslim weaver in sant tradition, made fun of differentiating beween Hindus and Muslims, and between castes:

If caste was what the Creator had in mind,
　　why wasn't anyone born
　　with Shiva's three-lined sign?
If you are a Brahmin,
　　from a Brahmin woman born,
　　why didn't you come out some special way?
And if you are a Muslim,
　　from a Muslim woman born,
　　why weren't you circumcized inside?
Says Kabir, no one is lowly born.
　　The only lowly are those
　　who never talk of Ram.

(Tr. by Hawley and Juergensmeyer 2004: 54)

Samartha Ramdas (1608–1618), known to be the guru of the Maratha Emperor, Shivaji, is also well known for his two works—*Daasabodh* and *Manaache Shlok* in Marathi. Both show his ethical concerns and emphasis on *bhakti*, and and do not reflect any political beliefs or any dislike of Muslims, though Shivaji resisted Muslim rule. Both his works are free from any narrow or parochial feelings. Though an ascetic himself, Ramdas did not preach asceticism to others but emphasized that God realization is possible for ordinary people engaged in worldly affairs, provided that that they are devoted and ethical in conduct. One of his verses from *Manaache Shlok* is as follows in English rendering by me:

Compassionate to the meek,
Tender at heart,
Affectionate and gracious,
Protective of the poor,
How can anger torment him?
He is a blessed servant of God.

The contribution of bhakti movements in further promoting a sound ethical basis for Hinduism on non-sectarian and non-caste basis is of great importance. Every sant put emphasis on integrity and character. These ethical values have been there in Sanskrit texts referred to in the earlier sections. But the distinctiveness of bhakti movements was in transmitting ethical values to people in their own language through songs that reached their hearts directly.

In spite of this ethical teaching, social evils did continue in India, particularly the oppression of lower castes and discrimination against women. Their cause was taken up again by modern reformers, beginning with Raja Rammohan Roy (1774–1833). Roy laid the road map for the modernization of both Hinduism and India. He could see the advantage of Indians taking up science education on Modern Western lines in English in contrast with traditional learning, and gave great support to the British government in promoting it. He is also remembered in connection with resolute efforts to get *sati* finally abolished. He drew support for his stand from Hindu scriptures themselves, particularly the Gita. He fought against idol worship and superstition, again referring to Hindu scriptures. Similarly he fought against polygamy and child marriage. He started the Brahmo Samaj for carrying on the task of reforming Hinduism and making its practice more rational and ethical. The stimulus he gave to reform created a powerful mood for it which continued well after his death. His task was taken up later by several others—Swami Dayanand Saraswati (1824–1883), Mahatma Jyotiba Phule (1827–1890), Ramakrishna Paramahamsa (1836–1886), Mahadev Govind Ranade (1842–1901), Shri Narayan Guru (1854–1928), Rabindranath Tagore (1861–1941), Swami Vivekananda (1863–1902), Mahatma Gandhi (1869–1948), E.V. Ramaswamy (1879–1973), and B.R. Ambedkar (1891–1956), being some eminent persons among them in chronological order.

While some reformers reviled Hinduism as a whole, most sought to eradicate social evils within the framework of Hinduism, arguing that these social evils are not consistent with it. Shri Narayan Guru brought up a whole community of Ezhavas in Kerala from out of the status of untouchables into the mainstream of Hindu society, by encouraging them take up modern education. Nadars in Tamil Nadu also rose in economic and social status like the Ezhavas within the framework of Hindu society, demonstrating that it is quite possible for lower castes to raise themselves significantly in status within Hinduism. Though a

238 Ethics for Our Times

bitter critic of Hinduism, Ambedkar made a very valuable contribution to it by trying to reform its society through required legislation. Sants of the medieval age could not succeed in social reform despite strongly advocating it, because they had no political backing. It was the modern phase and its legislative process in a secular frame that finally dislodged the *Dharmashaastras* from their legal authority. Sardar Panikkar observed that social evils had persisted in Hindu society for ages, not because of lack of dynamism on the part of Hinduism but because India had lost political power for nearly eight hundred years (Panikkar 1953: 328). But the legislative process alone could not have worked in the absence of support from religious reformers. Forces of modernization and economic development also helped social reforms. With the breakdown of *jajmani* system, and with urbanization, the ritual rigidity of the caste system very much weakened, and the role of rituals declined. Priests and even heads of *Mathas* (monasteries) are now emerging from the so-called lower castes. Sophisticated practices like meditation and yoga are no longer the monopoply of higher castes. Devotional songs or bhajans are sung in mixed gatherings without botheration of caste and class. Cinema, the Press, and the electronic media have also played crucial role in giving easy access to religion and its moral instruction, for the masses.

Social service to fellow human beings got huge impetus as never before. During earlier phases, virtues of charity, hospitality, and helping fellow humans and even non-human beings were certainly eulogized, but implementation of this did not take any organized or institutional form. It was mostly at the individual level. During the modern phase, many Hindu institutions and philanthropists, either under the banner of Hinduism or not, took to social service in a big way.

Women also have started getting new opportunities as never before and begun to occupy public space occupied by men earlier. The enactment of the Hindu Law made it possible for Hindu women to obtain divorce and claim alimony. It enforced monogamy, made dowry illegal, and gave rights of inheritance to women. The task however is not over, since the dowry system is yet to vanish and women's status is not yet equated with that of men in the public space. With mandatory reservation of seats to women in village panchayats, the situation is improving slowly now even in rural areas. India is still behind several other developing countries in human development and gender indexes. It is hoped, however that with a faster pace of economic development and improvement in education, health and infrastructure envisaged, the socio-economic situation will considerably improve. Hinduism cannot and will not, be an obstacle in this process of improvement.

Concluding this essay, it may be observed that Hinduism aimed at an all-round human being, a complete human being. Ethics was certainly an important part of this vision, but not the whole of it. Hinduism celebrated aesthetic enjoyment of life, but also insisted that it be in a morally acceptable way. Though spiritual progress was highly regarded, dharma was a pre-requisite for it. J.N. Mohanty insightfully says, 'Aurobindo, unlike Gandhi but much like Tagore, did not regard the ethical person to be the highest person. A perfect individual for him, must make his entire life beautiful. The spiritual man, in his estimation, integrates the ethical, the aesthetic and the cognitive in a harmonious unity' (Mohanty 1999: 303).[11]

NOTES

1. Translated with the help of M.R. Kale (1971: 126).
2. This is in Mahabharata, Udyogaparva 40.12, quoted in Herur ed. (2001: 243).
3. See Hattangdi (2002: 133–6) for quotations from the *Rigveda* using the word, *satyam*.
4. As quoted by Sharma (2000: 165). His source is S.V. Oka (1957) *Uttara-gita with a translation into English and Appendices*, Poona: Bhandarkar Oriental Research Institute.
5. For a detailed documentation of this, see Nadkarni (2008: 77–129).
6. For an exposition of *Raajadharma*, see Michael ed. (2005).
7. Some of these have been quoted in the second section of this chapter.
8. For a detailed discussion of Bhakti Movements in India, see chapter 5 in Nadkarni (2008: 219–79).
9. This is my translation, as this vachana is not in Ramanujan (1973). Akka Mahadevi ends her vachanas, addressing her Lord as 'Chenna-Mallikarjuna', a name of Shiva. Ramanujan translates it as 'Lord, White as jasmine' in her other vachanas.
10. Keshiraj is one with lovely hair, a name of Krishna.
11. For a detailed account of modern religious leaders-cum-reformers, see chapter 6 in Nadkarni (2008).

Part IV

Some Contemporary Concerns

10 Ethics in Business

In a free society, there is one and only one social responsibility of business –
to use its resources and engage in activities designed to increase its profits
so long as it stays within the rules of the game, which is to say, engages in
open and free competition without deception and fraud.

—Milton Friedman
(Friedman 1962)[1]

Making profit is no more the purpose of a corporation than getting enough
to eat is the purpose of life. Getting enough to eat is a requirement of life;
life's purpose, one would hope, is somewhat broader and more challenging.
Likewise with business and profit.

—Kenneth Mason (1979)[2]

STAKEHOLDERS IN BUSINESS

Milton Friedman has been lambasted by quite a few for asserting that
making profits and serving the interests of shareholders is the only social
responsibility of a corporation. However, Friedman does not advocate
indulging in deception and fraud, and breaking the law in order to make
profits. To that extent, even Friedman concedes the importance of ethics
in business. He does not also appear to support unethical practices within
the purview of law, which are quite possible and even rampant, since
the law differs from country to country in being strict about business
ethics, and particularly about preventing environmental destruction.
The difference between Friedman and business ethicists is thus narrower

than normally presumed. But the difference is still there, as one can make out from Kenneth Mason's comment, cited earlier.

There is now a large degree of consensus even in the management circles that shareholders are not the only stakeholders in business, and that there are also other equally important stakeholders—customers, employees, suppliers, creditor banks, the state, and the community at large, or the environment. The management is equally or even more responsible to them as to shareholders. It is by genuinely caring for the interests of all the stakeholders that businesses will be following the principles of business ethics. In the following sections, we take up each stakeholder to identify which interests are vital for each of them and what a business enterprise can do about it. However, we are not, discussing the interests of the state and the obligations of business to it separately. The state has a vital interest in ensuring that not only businesses obey the law, they should also cause no damage to the well-being of other stakeholders, including environment, even if such damage is not presently covered by law. In caring for the interests of these stakeholders, it is not enough for business enterprises to obey the law; they have to show real concern to satisfy the stakeholders, at least to see that no harm is done to them by their business activities, and their well-being is increased to the greatest extent possible. Often, the process of tightening up the law follows a flagrant infringement of ethical principles. For example, laws governing the liability for damage to the employees, customers, and the public were often tightened up only after major disasters were caused by laxity and indifference. Business enterprises do not have to wait till they cause public outrage and violent protests, resulting in damaged reputation of the enterprises concerned, to wake up and follow ethical practices.

It may seem, if superficially viewed, that the interests of shareholders clash with those of stakeholders. Businesse organizations may have to spend more in the short run when they care for other stakeholders, which may seem to be at the expense of profits that would have gone to shareholders. But this is a very narrow and short run view. If a business is caught doing illegal things or causes a damage to workers' safety, cheats consumers, or causes destruction to the environment, the expenses that the business have to incur in litigation, fines imposed, and compensation paid for damages done, will far outweigh the money they may have saved in the short run by ignoring their just obligations.

Trevino and Nelson (2007) have presented in detail an example of the classic case of Pinto cars manufactured by Ford Motor Company in 1971, which I narrate briefly here. In the final stage of crash tests before launching the product, it was known that Pinto's tank often ruptured by rear-end impact, requiring a safety device costing $11 for each car. But the car had met the then prevailing official standards of safety, and it was thought to be too late to introduce the device. Moreover, the safety device could be introduced only at the cost of reducing the trunk space, which would have made the car less attractive in the market. Lee Iacocca, then President of Ford, thought, 'Safety doesn't sell', and that buyers in any case accepted some risks while buying cars. The company nevertheless did a cost–benefit analysis in which they compared the total cost of introducing the safety device in all the Pinto cars with the benefits from averting accidents in terms of various costs saved like the productivity losses from likely injuries and deaths, medical costs, funeral costs, litigation expenses, and cars burnt. On the basis of this analysis, the company decided that it was not worthwhile spending more money on the safety device. Trevino and Nelson add that by early 1973, there were field reports about the susceptibility of Pinto cars to exploding in rear-end collisions at very low speeds of under 25 miles per hour, but no recall of cars was initiated in spite of the mounting evidence. However, a victim filed a civil suit against the company and the jury awarded $125 million against Ford in 1978 in punitive damages. The judge took particular note of the fact that Ford knew about the susceptibility of Pintos to crashes and explosions before introducing the car, which was only confirmed by field reports later, and yet Ford did not order their recall. Apart from paying a huge penalty, which was not reckoned in the cost–benefit analysis, Ford had to recall all the 1.5 million Pinto cars built between 1970 and 1976. The example eloquently brings out the limitations of shortsighted cost–benefit analyses, and of concentrating on profits at the expense of safety considerations (ibid.: 115–18).

Even more disasters may await corporations if a morally wrong step and consequent loss of reputation damage their brand value, causing a sharp and prolonged fall in stock prices. It is misleading to assume that brand value is determined only by profit rates and dividends declared. The reputation of a corporation for its concern about taking due care of product quality leads to confidence among customers and improves its market share. Similarly, concern for employees' security and safety improves the corporation's image among workers, which can improve productivity and prevent costly strikes. Prompt payments to suppliers, without expecting bribes from them, inspire confidence in the company and improve the quality of their service. Concern for environment and interests of the community at large also adds very much to the brand value. A high reputation on all the fronts improves the credibility of the company with the banks and the state at large, which would be a great asset, particularly in tiding over unexpected difficulties. It is this overall moral reputation, which can assure an unenviable position in the stock market as well, and help shareholders especially in the long run. Moral reputation never goes waste; inevitably it gets capitalized.

CUSTOMER CARE

Customer care needs to be tailored to the specific requirements of the customer in different types of businesses. For example, in the case of doctors, lawyers, and auditors providing service to their patients or clients, it is important to maintain confidentiality of information about customers apart from assuring the quality of service. In the case of manufacturers of products, it is important to ensure both product quality and safety, and desist from misleading or making false claims in advertisements or product information literature. In the case of pharmaceuticals, it is also necessary to caution consumers about possible side effects and contra-indications. In packaged foods, it is essential to indicate nutrition values and mention all the ingredients so that customers can judge what foods they have to avoid or use only moderately. Such information is vital particularly when some ingredients can cause serious allergies, even death. It is the moral duty of business enterprises to provide such information to customers and take the customer into confidence, even where it is not mandatory by law to do so. This would greatly improve the prestige of the company and customers would develop trust in it. It is the duty of the government to make it mandatory to provide such information, and give the customer the right to sue the company if the required information is not given and if the product is defective or unsafe. All producers should have a system of recall of their products from the market, at least the concerned batch of the product, if the product is defective or unsafe.

Two of the examples given by Trevino and Nelson illustrate respectively how a pharmaceutical company cared for its customers and recovered from a disaster, and how another could not do so and consequently faced ruin. The former case took place in 1982, involving Johnson & Johnson, when it was informed of the death of seven people after ingesting its product, Tylenol—a painkiller. The company immediately pulled all Tylenol bottles (31 million, with a retail value of $100 million!) from the area where deaths occurred, and informed doctors, hospitals, and distributors. An investigation revealed that a batch of the tablets was laced with cyanide poison, in an act of external sabotage. Though there was some panic in the immediate aftermath, within a month the public understood not only that the company was not to blame for the deaths, but also that it responded immediately and took effective steps to prevent any further damage, thus showing that it cared by shouldering its due responsibility promptly (ibid.: 225–6).

While the example above is one of controlling what could have become a major disaster, the next one is one of allowing it to happen. A. H. Robins, a small pharmaceutical company purchased the ownership of Dalkon Shield, a new intrauterine device (IUD) in 1970, and at the time of purchase, did not know it had purchased a 'time-bomb'. It should have done the required testing and hired a gynecologist on its staff. Its ignorance was avoidable. Adding to this moral irresponsibility, 'Robins aggressively marketed it [the device] any way', and 'by 1975 there were more than 4 million Dalkon Shields all over the world' (ibid.: 227). The Shield had a defective design from the beginning, having a multi-filament tail (provided for the doctor to pull out the device). It was made up of hundreds of pieces of plastic that created a breeding ground for bacteria, causing massive infection that could lead to miscarriage and death. But 'A H Robins stonewalled at every opportunity. Its executives falsified medical data, lost or destroyed key company files and records related to the IUD, and completely denied knowledge of the danger under oath' (ibid.: 227). Only in 1975, the company alerted 120,000 doctors, but did not recall the IUD until 1984, when it launched a campaign asking women to get the device removed at company expense. But the damage had already been done. Fifteen women had died of pelvic inflammation, 60,000 women suffered miscarriages, and hundreds of women gave births to children with severe handicaps such as blindness, cerebral palsy, and mental retardation. The company had no funds enough to pay damages, and filed for bankruptcy in late 1985 (ibid.: 226–8).

Callous disregard of the customer proves counter-productive and hardly helps business enterprises to make profits sustainably. On the other hand, a culture of genuinely respecting the customer pays both in the short and long runs. It is not just a moral obligation. But often, when a customer visits, he or she is not even greeted with a smile in many places. Mahatma Gandhi had said:

> A customer is the most important visitor on your premises.
> He is not dependent on us.
> We are dependent on him.
> He is not an interruption in our work.
> He is the purpose of it.
> He is not an outsider in our business.
> He is part of it.
> We are not doing him a favour by serving him.
> He is doing us a favour by giving us an opportunity.[3]

ADVERTISING

Advertising is more than giving the necessary information about the product and the precautions to be taken, to doctors, equipment handlers, or even directly to consumers. It is often just publicity to promote the sales of the product or service. Is it morally justifiable? It depends. When a new product or brand is introduced, it is justifiable that the producer advertises the product to make the market aware of it. It can be beneficial not only to the producer, but also to the consumer, and even the world at large. An example is advertising a solar lamp or a solar heater, claiming that it saves electricity. The claim is truthful and entails no cheating, provided that the product is good and satisfies the specified standards.

However, advertising usually involves, what economists call product differentiation, and creates imperfections in competition, or monopolistic competition. Different producers produce practically the same product but under different brand names, and each producer has a monopoly of producing a particular brand. Advertisements are aimed at creating brand loyalties, enabling producers to raise the price above what would have obtained under pure competition and to make monopoly profits. There is competition here, no doubt, but it may not necessarily be on the basis of price alone, but on impressing the consumer that the advertised brand is the best. Advertising often creates a world of make-believe, because exaggerations are inherent in such advertisements, and consumers cannot easily surmise how much is reality and how much is an exaggeration. Normally, consumers are aware that there is exaggeration in advertisements and mentally discount the claims. But children are particularly vulnerable, and even in the case of adults, oft-repeated advertisements drill the message into the subconscious and almost seduce the customer. To make matters worse, sometimes advertising is done in subtle forms, like paid news, or articles meant to advertise but published in a way that appear as genuine, with the fact that they are advertiser's feature shown only in small print. In a TV interview, a film star may incidentally or most casually inform that she uses a particular product to maintain her skin health. The claim that advertising is educative is itself an exaggeration. Economist Stephen Leacock has characterised advertising as 'the science of arresting human intelligence long enough to get money from it', and that for the purpose of selling, 'advertising is superior to reality'.[4] Besides exaggerating, advertisements often promote wrong values. For example, fair-complexioned models endorsing fairness creams subtly create a colour complex prejudicing dark complexion. A bank, launching a savings drive, calling upon parents to save for daughter's wedding and son's higher education, is implicitly promoting a gender bias, which discourages girls' higher education and encourages dowry payments and lavish weddings. Advertisements promote harmful energy drinks, creating distaste for homemade healthy drinks. They tempt children into eating marketed junk foods, in place of healthy ones. In general, advertising makes the consumers buy more than what is good for them, not only draining their purse but also burdening the environment.

Yet there is no case for banning all such advertisements. Product differentiation under different competitive producers can provide incentives for constantly improving and maintaining quality, and for research and development. The business world will be dry and boring without witty, sometimes hilarious, and generally, colourful and even glamorous advertisements. But they can also lead to the exploitation of the consumers. That is why, in some countries, including India, a balance is tried between allowing generic drugs to be produced under careful watch for quality, and permitting some patented drugs with brands under product differentiation. It is understood in such cases that a patented drug would be allowed to be produced as a generic drug allowing others also to produce it, after a reasonable time period during which the innovator can recover expenses incurred on developing the product and make reasonable profits. In any case, there is need for self-restraint and moral responsibility on the part of both advertisers and media, so that the state is not compelled to impose draconian restrictions or, worse still, to make laws to censor all advertisements.

WORKERS' WELFARE

Workers in a business enterprise have actually much greater stake in its long run, health, and progress than shareholders. Shareholders may easily sell their shares and wash their hands off it, but workers or employees cannot. Shareholders normally hold the stocks of several enterprises, but employees are normally dependent on only one employer for making their living. Employees' interests cannot, therefore, be lightly taken. At the same time, it is equally necessary to provide incentives to enterprises to invest in business and employ as many people as they require. Otherwise, investors may simply divert their funds and invest in real estate or gold, and both job opportunities and national income would be reduced. Every country and every enterprise has to strike a constructive balance between the interests of both the employee and the employer.

There is a strong feeling that laws in India are loaded in favour of permanent employees in the organized sector, to the detriment of not only employers' interests but also to the interests of contract and casual workers engaged in unorganized sectors. Labour relations are still governed by the Industrial Disputes Act, 1947. The Act recognizes the rights of workers to form trade unions and declare strikes with due notice, and that of employers to declare lockouts. The Act provides for an elaborate mechanism consisting of several layers to settle industrial disputes. It protects job security and provides for industrial adjudication of unfair dismissals and discharges. An enterprise employing more than a hundred workers has to obtain prior permission of the government for resorting to layoffs or closure. This is not insisted in the case of smaller enterprises, but they have to give fifteen days' pay for each year of completed service to retrenched employees. The Act permits the removal of a person for *proven* misconduct, non-performance, habitual absenteeism or disablement due to ill health or serious injury, subject to due procedure as per law and payment of severance pay where applicable. The Contract Labour (Regulation and Abolition) Act was passed in 1970 to deal with the problem of contract labour and outsourcing.[4] According to the Act, contract work is not permitted if found to be of perennial nature, and the workers involved in it have to be either absorbed in regular employment or discharged. For casual labour, minimum wages are prescribed and raised from time to time, following inflation. The Factories Act, 1948, as amended in 1986, aims at ensuring safety of workers in factories. The Act requires appointment of safety officers in factories employing 1000 or more workers. It provides for independent inspecting staff and medical surveillance also. The Act is applicable to any premise wherein ten or more persons with the aid of power, or twenty or more persons without the aid of power are employed. (Kumar 2013: 121–37). Thus the Act has a wide coverage.

There is a clamour to 'liberalize' labour laws, permitting greater flexibility and incentives particularly to employers, and making settlement of industrial disputes simpler and more expeditious. Even though the labour laws in India look like pro-labour, there are some features of workers' situation, which are not pro-labour. First, not all business enterprises, particularly those employing 100 or less than 100 persons on records, have trade unions, and workers can be discharged practically without prior notice. Second, there is allegedly a lot of discrimination, nepotism, corruption, or favouritism in recruitment and promotions, and the laws are ineffective in dealing with the problem. Third, though there are laws to ensure workers' safety, the level of safety is believed to be far below what is obtained in developed countries.

It is, therefore, necessary to take the overall situation into account and review the choices available with due awareness of their implications, before a 'liberalization' or a reformation of the labour laws are considered. Particular note has to be taken of the United Nations' Universal Declaration of Human Rights, Article 23.1, which mentions: 'Everyone has the right to work, to free choice of employment, to just and favourable conditions to work and to protection against unemployment.'[5] Though the right to property is considered as a fundamental right, everybody does not have the privilege of having property, and many have to resort to work as the means of living. Equity principle demands, therefore, that the right to work is also considered as a fundamental right. Neither property right, nor the right to work, however, is absolute, and both have to be reconciled in the context of a business enterprise that hires workers.

A basic issue determining workers' welfare is the security of employment. We can even say that the right to work implies security of work too. There has to be some amount of certainty that we can get work tomorrow and the days after to make our living, if our right to work has any significance. Theoretically, the terms of hiring a worker can range from casual work on hourly or daily basis to life tenure. Close to casual hiring on daily basis, comes 'hire and fire' or 'employment at will' (EAW) under which an employee can be terminated with little or no advance notice and without giving any reason for it. On the other side of the spectrum, before assured life tenure, comes employment that can be terminated only for a just cause, following a just procedure, and with due severance pay. The just causes include two types: first, individual-level causes like misconduct, habitual absenteeism, proven incompetence, permanent disablement; and second, enterprise-level causes like 'downsizing' due to an economic downturn for the enterprise, restructuring for improving efficiency, or technological change requiring modernization. Which is the best policy that strikes a balance between employers' and employees' interests? The question requires some discussion about the comparative merits of the options. We leave aside the two extremes in the spectrum, namely, casual hiring and life tenure, and focus on 'EAW' and termination only for a 'just cause'.

'Employment at will' is defended mainly on three arguments: (a) the right to property and the freedom of contract, which it requires for its operation; (b) that EAW is necessary for ensuring efficiency or higher productivity; and (c) it is fair to both employers and employees. According to the first argument, a property owner has a right to regulate and even prevent access to property as desired, and should have, in all fairness, the autonomy and freedom to enter into a contract of hiring or ending it as per the owner's will and convenience. Otherwise, the right to property has no meaning. According to the second, a freedom of contract assures incentives to invest and hire, promotes efficiency in the enterprise both on the part of the employer (as it allows more productive allocation of resources) and the worker (since the person knows that immediate firing would follow any lack of dedication). 'Employment at will' is argued to be necessary for correcting any misjudgement about the employee's quality, which is not always known in advance at the time of recruitment, and can be known only on the basis of experience gained from employing the person. The improved efficiency owing to EAW in turn, results in improved overall employment and economic growth, which enables the terminated workers to get alternative employment within reasonable time. If EAW is not allowed, it is argued that the employer will either divert his/her funds to unproductive and speculative investments like buying real estate and gold, or seek loopholes such as outsourcing, subcontracting, or hiring on casual basis. The result is not beneficial to workers themselves in the long run, as employment opportunities are reduced and economic growth is stunted. Under EAW, the workers too would have a right to leave the job with little advance notice, when they get better opportunities in a growing economy. It is, therefore, contended to be fair to both employers and employees.

Defenders of the 'Just Cause' approach, like John J. McCall (2010), do not accept these arguments. First of all, the Just Cause rules do not deny property rights nor do they ease owners' control over corporate property; 'they merely alter the right to control at the margins' (ibid.: 224). Shareholders can buy and sell shares of the company as earlier. McCall also says that there is no evidence of Just Cause rules reducing the rates of profit or depressing the share prices of the company. Further, there is no substantiation that countries adopting just cause rules show lower rates of economic growth or lower labour productivity than countries under EAW rules. On the other hand, by acknowledging the stake of workers in the enterprise, Just Cause rules may improve their productivity. There is scope to terminate the services of employees on the grounds of misconduct, and so on, under Just Cause rules. However, if such action needs to be taken, it has to be done, not in a whimsical way, but with the due procedure of building the case against such employees with care, so that it respects the rights of employees and encourages good work on the part of other workers.

Thus, while the Just Cause rules ensure the incentives for efficiency, EAW rules discourage efficiency on the part of workers. The notion of efficiency under EAW is one-sided and narrow, while it is not so under Just Cause rules. The assumption that workers are removed under EAW only on the ground of efficiency is not correct; they may be removed for reasons unrelated to productivity, say, an attempt to organize a trade union, or just to make way for a favourite or a relative of the employer.

As to fairness, EAW is quite unfair to workers. There is no level-playing ground between employers and employees in the so-called free market. By putting some fair restrictions on the employer to fire workers at will, a level-playing ground may be created under Just Cause rules. McCall (ibid.: 224–5) points to a blatant exploitation of workers under EAW, which arises because normally workers are paid much lower than their productivity in the initial years of work, and their pay increases to a fair level only after several years. By cutting their years of work under EAW, the workers are deprived of benefits, which accrue only later. Employers' main motive in resorting to EAW could thus be to appropriate these exploitative and unjust savings at the expense of workers. Exploitation of workers can arise under EAW also because unreasonable demands may be imposed on them, for instance, unofficially asking them to work for longer time than is allowed under the law, or demanding higher productivity than can be reasonably expected within the hours provided by the law, and any one protesting against such exploitation may be fired at will. It is not unusual of supervisors asking for sexual favours from women workers on the pain of firing them if refused. McCall observes: 'Workplace productivity demands that have seriously damaging impacts on family and social existence are, on any account of a decent human life, demands that are unreasonable' (ibid.: 227).

It is argued that Just Cause rules can be bypassed by hiring workers on a casual basis or outsourcing work on contract under unorganized or informal industries. This is of course true, but the solution does not consist in casualizing all employment, as happens under EAW. Disallowing contract labour where the nature of work is perennial, and mandating the payment of minimum wages for non-regular workers are some of the ways of addressing this problem. Subsidized health insurance schemes, offering food security to all under a public distribution system or food coupons to the poor, and free education to all at least up to the high school level are in any case needed, which can help the casual workers. But the EAW rules would put an extra and unviable burden on the state to address unemployment and deprivation on a larger scale.

The Just Cause rules by themselves cannot guarantee workers' welfare and interests. There has to be a proper way to address sexual harassment at the workplace (discussed in Chapter 11), ensure workers' safety, insure against their illness and disablement, and provide for retirement benefits.

ENVIRONMENTAL CONCERNS

We have already discussed environmental issues emerging from the nature of economic development in Chapter 4. In abating air pollution and in reducing the rate of depletion of natural resources, business enterprises have a significant role to play. The state can do it only with the co-operation of business enterprises, because in the first instance they are in the forefront of generating and aggravating environmental problems, not to undermine the role of privately owned cars and households consuming electricity and heating gas. The problem is serious enough to need the urgent attention of all the actors involved. For example, the International Agency for Research on Cancer, a part of WHO, found recently that in 2010, as many as 223,000 deaths worldwide were due to lung cancer caused by air pollution. The Agency observed that the air that we breathe is laced with cancer-causing substances, classified as carcinogenic to humans.[6] The very survival of humanity is at stake. Industrial enterprises face two types of environmental problems. The first, though a prolonged one (not meaning one that can be postponed), nevertheless, includes important issues such as global warming, increasing concentration of carcinogens in the air, and accelerating depletion of potable water. The second refers to environmental disasters caused either by negligence or accident, such as the Bhopal gas leak disaster in India in 1984 and oil spills in the oceans from huge oil tankers running aground. It is not merely the global concerns but also concerns about the community around, which are involved in environmental problems. Both legal and moral obligations of enterprises need to be respected sincerely. Failure to do so can irreparably damage the image of the enterprises concerned.

To deal with the first case, industrial enterprises have not only to comply with environmental regulations in respective countries in an honest way, but also to constantly innovate to reduce pollution, consumption of energy, and depletion of potable water resources. Often such innovations help the enterprises to reduce their costs, increase productivity, improve working environment, establish leadership in the line, and create a good image about them in the community around and with the state. In suitable cases, the innovating firms should be given some extra incentives by the state in the form of public recognition and awards and tax remissions.

An example from India is given in what follows to illustrate the first type. The Coca-Cola company, a multinational, has a production plant at Plachimada village in Palakkad district of Kerala. There were serious allegations against the company of overexploiting the groundwater resources in the area to the detriment of local population, leading to scarcity of drinking water. Though it was complained that the company was using about 9 litres of water for every litre of the beverage, the company claimed that it was using less than 4 litres. The local panchayat (village local body) suspended the license of the company to use local water claiming prior right to drinking water for local population before any industrial use in any situation of scarcity. The matter was taken to the Kerala High Court, which after analysing the evidence available, observed that the scarcity was due to failure of rainfall in the year, rather than over-exploitation of water, and ordered the company to limit its drawal to 500,000 litres per day and release 75,000 litres per day to the village panchayat. This was in April 2005. The Kerala Pollution Control Board took up the matter, thereafter, and in August the same year, decided to cancel its consent given earlier to the plant to operate on three grounds—(a) the company was not supplying drinking water to the village; (b) bio-solids generated by the plant contained high levels of cadmium, some 400 to 600 per cent above permitted levels; and (c) the company had not installed Reverse Osmosis system for treating waste water. The company refuted all these allegations, but took some significant steps to resolve the problem, apart from supplying drinking water to the villages around and setting up a wastewater treatment plant as per global standards, which it had already begun earlier. The new steps were: (a) Through technological innovations, it reduced the use of water per litre of the beverage by 30 per cent, bringing it down to 3.12 litres. (b) It set up 200 rainwater harvesting structures both within the plant and in the vicinity to step up the rate of recharge. (c) It set up a fund of a million rupees to fund local development projects for the welfare of the local community. The matter was, however, taken to the Supreme Court by the village council in November 2005. The plant has remained closed since 2004 and the Supreme Court Decision is pending. There is a controversy about the product itself. Drinking Coca-Cola is alleged to cause acidity, tooth decay, obesity and diabetes, especially if consumed excessively. The company is alleged to have shifted from the use of sucrose to low-cost fructose derived from corn syrup, which makes cola consumers prone to obesity and diabetes.[7] The beverage, however, continues to be popular, exposing many including children to health hazards. The company on its part has been claiming that its conduct is safe and meets stringent Ell standards. (See 'Case Against Coca-Cola Kerala State: India' available at http://www.righttowater.info/?s=India. Accessed on 23 March 2014).

As for the second type of cases, both promptness and adequacy of measures are absolutely necessary to deal with disasters. Of course, safety precautions and measures to prevent disasters have to be fully taken before they happen. Industrial enterprises have also to keep themselves prepared with disaster management plans to manage disasters and arrange medical attention, when they take place in spite of precautions taken. An example from Indian experience is given in what follows to illustrate the second type of environmental cases.

The Bhopal gas-leak case of 2–3 December 1984 is considered as one of the world's worst such cases. The concerned plant was owned and operated by Union Carbide India Limited (UCIL), a subsidiary of Union Carbide Company (UCC) of USA. While the government banks and the Indian public held 49.1 per cent of the shares of UCIL, the majority holding (50.9 per cent) was by the Union Carbide. On the fateful night, over 40 tons of methyl isocyanate (MIC), a lethal chemical used in the production of pesticide Sevin, leaked from a storage tank, formed a toxic cloud, and caught unawares hundreds of thousand people in Bhopal and around. The impact was not confined to the immediate neighbourhood of the plant, but covered large parts of the city, particularly many slums where poor people lived. Within hours of the gas leak, the streets of Bhopal were littered with thousands of human corpses, and carcasses of cows, buffaloes, goats and chicken owned by the poor, not to mention street dogs and birds. Immediate human deaths were estimated to be 3800, but another fifteen to twenty thousand people died a slow premature death in the subsequent two decades owing to the exposure to the gas. According to the Bhopal Gas Tragedy Relief and Rehabilitation Department, compensation had been awarded by the end of October 2003 to 554,895 people for injuries and 15,310 survivors of those who were killed. The average compensation per family of the dead was only $2,200. It took a long time to clean up the toxic waste. There are reports of still continuing contamination of both soil and aquifers, a legacy left behind by Union Carbide for the people of Bhopal, as Edward Broughton bitterly observes (2005).

According to Trevino and Nelson, the parent company, Union Carbide, immediately sent medical supplies and a doctor who was an expert in dealing with the impact of chemicals, to Bhopal, and its CEO, Warren Anderson, flew to India the next day of the disaster to inspect and lend support to local officials of UCIL (ibid.: 245). However, Anderson was arrested on 7 December, and was flown back within six hours in a government plane, probably to save him from public anger. The assessment, of the role of Union Carbide, however, especially from Indian scientists is not very complimentary. On the basis of investigations by Indian scientists, Broughton (2005) observes: 'At every turn, UCC has attempted to manipulate, obfuscate and withhold scientific data to the detriment of victims'. The company did not even reveal what exactly was in the cloud that engulfed the city on that night. Degraded MIC contains hydrogen cyanide (HCN), which is even more dangerous than MIC. But UCC did not want to admit that the cloud carried it. Initially, UCC had recommended the use of sodium thiosulphate to treat the victims, which was effective for cyanide poisoning, but later it withdrew its statement to cover up the presence of cyanide. Doctors found that the colour of blood and viscera pointed to cyanide poisoning, and many injured victims responded better to sodium thiosulphate. UCC tried to mislead by claiming that all the safety systems were in place and the disaster was due to sabotage. This claim was impugned by subsequent investigations. Considering the extent of the tragedy, UCC would have had to pay damages to the tune of $10 billion to victims, had such a disaster taken place in the USA (ibid.). But UCC haggled almost interminably over a reasonable settlement, and finally, was ordered by the Supreme Court of India in 1989 to pay $470 million in damages. The company discontinued operating its Bhopal plant, and failed to clean up the site satisfactorily. It was taken over by Dow Chemical Company in 2001, but the new company also disowned any responsibility to clean up the site in Bhopal. Union Carbide Company, which suffered a severe setback in the US stock market following the disaster, recovered after the settlement in 1989, as the payment for damages was much lower than what was originally feared.

Was the disaster purely an unsuspected accident? The UCIL is said to have been warned by American experts as early as in 1981 of the potential of a 'runaway reaction'. In 1982, a MIC leak reportedly had affected eighteen workers. There were further leaks of MIC and other chemicals in 1983 and 1984. Lethal gas was stored in huge tanks, instead of more safely keeping it in smaller tanks to diversify risks of leak, and the large tanks were also filled up beyond recommended levels. Tank refrigeration systems, which could have mitigated the tragedy, were not in place. Overall maintenance of particularly safety systems was reported to be poor. There was more dependence on manual operations than was desirable, which delayed automatic corrective steps. It was thus a tragedy waiting to happen. To make it worse, there were no emergency or catastrophe action plans. Trevino and Nelson (2007) concede, in spite of their otherwise sympathetic assessment of the role of the parent company, that Union Carbide's 'original mistake was to allow a foreign facility to operate with lax controls and poor links to the mother corporation' (ibid.: 246). However, UCIL was a separate company with its own management and cannot escape blame. Moreover, what was the government's factory inspectorate doing? Why could it not compel the company to take all the safety measures? Both the state and central governments responded to the tragedy in a rather leisurely manner. It took some twenty-five years to finally pay compensation to all, and that too, not to the satisfaction of the victims.[8]

Musing over the lessons learnt from the Bhopal disaster, Broughton (2005) observes that speeding up industrialization in developing countries without a proper concurrent evaluation of all aspects, especially of safety, can have catastrophic consequences. He points out to double standards of multinationals operating in developing countries, and also questions how, in the first instance, the state government allowed such a dangerous industry in an urban area. Why, after all, was there a need to produce a dangerous pesticide? Were safer and environmentally benign pest controls not feasible at all? Did the corporate sector, especially multinational, learn a lesson from Bhopal? Broughton points out that 'in March 2001, residents of Kodaikanal in southern India caught Unilever red-handed when they discovered a dump-site with toxic mercury waste from thermometer factory, run by its subsidiary, Hindustan Lever. The 7.4 ton stockpile of mercury-laden glass was found in stacks spilling on the ground in a scrap-metal yard located near a school' (ibid.). Can companies be allowed to get away with such callousness?

ETHICS IN BUSINESS FINANCE

Robert Shiller, one of the three Nobel Prize winners in economics in 2013, believes that finance in the contemporary world 'can be the strongest force for promoting the well-being and fulfilment of an expanding global population – for achieving the greater goals of the good society', and that 'there is nothing in financial theory that specifies that control of capital should be confined to few "fat cats"' (Shiller 2012: 8–9). Shiller may be right, and finance can be the engine to drive economic development and encourage entrepreneurship among the non-rich, but in the actual capitalist world there is a tendency to concentrate the control of capital in a few hands. That is why, Shiller also emphasizes the need to 'humanize' and 'democratize' financial capitalism (ibid.: 5–6). For similar reasons, India under Indira Gandhi had taken steps to nationalize the leading banks in the country in 1969, prodding them to step up financing 'priority sectors' like agriculture and small industry. The setting up of a co-operative bank exclusively for the self-employed poor women in Gujarat by Ela Bhatt in May 1974 was an unprecedented adventure, formed by pooling Rs 10 from each woman towards membership. The Mahila (Self-employed Women's Association) (Co-operative Bank strengthened their entrepreneurship, and gave self-confidence and autonomy to them. And that is again the reason why Muhammad Yunus started the Grameen Bank in Bangladesh in 1983, which stimulated the growth of micro-finance or micro-credit institutions in the whole subcontinent.

There are several ethical issues in financial dimensions of business enterprises, particularly in the corporate sector. Issuing equity shares to the public is not only a way of getting finance for the company, but also one of broad-basing and democratizing its ownership. But, there is generally such a strong prejudice against shares as being undependable, that academic institutions like universities and even charitable trusts in India are barred from holding any part of their corpus funds in the form of shares and bonds of private corporations or investing in mutual funds. First, the public is not quite sure how far the Boards or the CEOs of corporations are committed to protect the interests of shareholders, most of whom are normally too dispersed to act in cohesion to demand their rights;[9] second, the part played by speculation in the market for securities is a serious deterrent to those who expect a minimum income from their financial assets, leaving the field only to the relatively rich who can afford to take risks. No doubt, risk taking, or, rather, bearing uncertainty[10] is an essential part of entrepreneurship, but in the case of a corporation, risk taking is done by shareholders too, and not by the promoter-entrepreneur alone (who also invests only a part of the capital). Those who want to avoid risky investments may do so, but those who are expecting to reap a handsome reward and willing to take some risks for it, should be free to invest in shares, provided it is their own money which would be at risk. A society, which is absolutely risk averse and shy of any uncertainty, will not progress; on the contrary, it is a recipe for stagnation and decline.

Though this appears true, will promoters and the management allow shareholders to claim their due share in the profits accrued? Shareholders expect two types of gains from their investments—dividends declared by the company and capital appreciation from selling their shares when in need of money. On both counts, there has to be some assurance to shareholders, that there is fair play and no frauds are committed either by the managements of the companies or by share brokers.

India has taken an important step recently, by passing The Companies Act, 2013, which replaced the old Companies Act of 1956. Thereby, the Act attempts to modernize, tone up, and, more effectively, regulate the conduct of companies in India, and to prevent fraud and embezzlement of funds by anyone in the companies.[11] It provides that at least one director of a company shall be elected by its shareholders. Further, it provides for a 'Class Action Suit' by a shareholder, or a group of them, against errant companies. The Act requires that at least one-third of the directors will be independent, who are not nominees of the management.

To prevent 'conflict of interest' situations, which tend to compromise one's decisions or judgment (a discussion of which is taken up in the next section), Section 166 of the Act lays down: 'A director of a company shall not involve in a situation in which he may have a direct or indirect interest that conflicts, or may possibly conflict, with the interests of the company'. To ensure that there is no conflict of interest regarding auditing, the accounts of the company have to be audited by an independent auditor who is not part of the management or the board of director or a consultant of the company. Section 195 of the Act takes care to prevent insider trading, which prohibits it explicitly. For the purpose of the Act, 'Insider trading' means: (a) an act of subscribing, buying, selling, dealing or agreeing to do any of these by any director or key managerial person or any other officer of the company who has access to any non-public 'price-sensitive information', or (b) an act of counselling about procuring, or communicating directly or indirectly to a company (or, presumably, to any relative or associate), which if published is likely to materially affect the price of securities of the company. The Act provides for stringent punishment in terms of hefty fine or imprisonment or both, for any violation. The Act provides for an institutional support to monitor and help its implementation through the creation of bodies like the National Financial Reporting Authority, Serious Fraud Investigation Office, and National Corporate Law Tribunal. These provisions of the law are expected to ensure that shareholders get fair treatment and to prevent any evil temptations on the part of company managements.

Shareholders expect fair play not only by the companies in which they hold shares, but also in the securities market where they trade their shares. They may be willing to face risks of unforeseen economic forces, such as changes (actual as well as expected) in demand or entry of a newly innovated product in the market at the micro level, and changes in macro-economic and political factors like tax policy, foreign exchange rates, and interest rates, which affect the share prices at the aggregate level. But shareholders, particularly the small and dispersed, would not like to be victims of moral turpitude on the part of any one who may be in a position to manipulate or rig share prices for personal advantage, or corner the market denying them thereby the chances to buy or sell securities. In the absence of unethical machinations or manipulations, the long-term value of the shares of a company tends to reflect its brand value, which is a composite outcome of several factors like leadership in innovations, reputation for product quality and after-sale services, fair treatment of employees, environmental concern, willingness to help communities around and even to undertake broader social responsibility, and, of course, a reputation for a sustained and fair rate of dividends, declared over the long run. If a share market works well without manipulations and rigging, dealing in shares would not certainly be like gambling, and would instead reflect the intrinsic worth of the company.[12] Share prices of individual companies would then act as efficient guides for allocation of capital, assuring a fair return to the investors in the long run. The attempt of regulators of shares and share markets has been to precisely restore this role to these markets.

The provisions in the new Companies Act of 2013 in India, regarding conflicts of interest and insider trading and overall attempt to improve the transparency of companies, certainly contribute towards improving the efficiency and moral reliability of share markets as well. They will help strengthen the already functioning Securities and Exchange Board of India (SEBI), which came into being as a result of the SEBI Act of 1992. The SEBI intends to protect the interests of investors, promote the development of securities market on a healthy footing, and regulate the functioning of these markets so as to prevent fraudulent and unfair trade practices. The SEBI Act prohibits deceptive devices, insider trading, and any substantial acquisition of securities or control. The Act requires the registration of all share brokers, sub-brokers, and short transfer agencies. If found guilty of manipulative practices like rigging share prices, registration can be cancelled and the concerned persons will be barred from the market, apart from being punished otherwise too. Price rigging, which takes place in unregulated markets, involves artificially inflating share prices, setting off a speculative bubble, and then, selling the shares at very high prices. Such an action bursts the bubble subsequently, leading to a crash in prices, which can set off another bubble, now in the direction of falling prices. When speculators decide that prices have crashed sufficiently enough, they would purchase the shares in big quantities, turning the circle upward once again. The fluctuating market prices bear no indication to the dividends paid or profits made by the company or its brand value in such cases. But when share markets are closely monitored and activities of traders and brokers are watched vigilantly by regulating bodies like the SEBI, such speculators can be identified and dealt with. Regulation is necessary for markets to function efficiently.

CONFLICTS OF INTEREST

Conflict of interest constitutes an ethical problem not merely in corporate affairs, but in many other cases involving the conduct of public officials and professionals. The problem is hardly new. Norman and Macdonald (2010) cite an instance from the pages of history: 'one can surely not understand why a sultan would have insisted on having his harem attendant castrated, without imagining him being keenly aware of the mostly unsupervised attendant's potential conflict of interest' (ibid.: 444). In the Preface to his 1906 play, *The Doctor's Dilemma*, George Bernard Shaw draws attention to this problem prevailing in the medical profession, by observing that we do not make the hangman the judge of whether the accused be hanged (while paying hangman's fees according to the number of hangings); yet, this is what precisely we do to a surgeon seeking advice on the need for a surgery. A conflict of interest situation arises typically when a professional or a public official has a potential personal gain or benefit from the concerned case, which comes in the way of the person's judgement in meeting fiduciary and professional obligations to her or his client. An example of particular relevance to a corporate enterprise is when it offers to hire a member of its auditing team as a consultant to the company. To deal with this problem, there are often laws that prohibit an auditing firm from offering consulting services.

Norman and Macdonald (ibid.: 451–62) offer a conceptual analysis of conflict of interest at three levels—micro, middle and macro. At the micro level, questions arise about identifying the duties and rights of individual professionals or officials, and what to do when the individual sees a conflict-of-interest situation. At the middle level, the key question is how to structure an institution or profession so that these institutions and their members can successfully avoid or ethically manage a conflict-of-interest situation. At the macro level, the concern is mainly about how the government, or the society at large, or the regulatory bodies like the SEBI or the Reserve Bank of India, or professional organizations like the Medical Council, should evolve appropriate laws, rules and regulations, and policies and procedures to tackle the problem. Policies may be necessary to decide at what level self-regulation would suffice and where the laws and their implementation need to be tightened up.

John Boatright (2007) has suggested a few methods for managing conflicts of interest, which have been listed with brief explanatory comments by Norman and Macdonald (2010: 457). A few of them are reproduced below by way of illustration:

*Avoidance (Avoiding acquiring any interest that would jeopardize one's judgment.)
*Alignment (The arrangement of incentives such that the decision-maker's interests are aligned with those of the persons being served.)
......
*Disclosure (Disclosing conflict of interest to those who would be affected.)
*Independent Judgment (Seeking to obtain the judgment of an objective third party.)
......
*Structural Changes (Ways of arranging operations so as to make conflicts of interest less likely, such as separating the auditing and consulting functions of accounting firms.)

What ultimately matters is an individual's own moral integrity and commitment to one's professional and moral duty, though there are upper layers of concern (at mid- and macro-levels). A doctor who recommends a cesarean instead of normal delivery surely knows in his/her mind what is best for the patient and is expected to behave with professional as well as personal integrity. Rules like disclosure of interests on the part of the company directors or consultants to a company may not necessarily help, as shown by Cain et al (2005: 104–25), if the person concerned plays a dirty game. A dishonest expert, who gives an advice based on narrow short-run personal interest rather than on the call of professional and fiduciary obligations, will inevitably be exposed sooner or later. Even in terms of long-term personal gains to make a good career, it is far better for one to be honest and establish a moral reputation.

CORPORATE CULTURE AND REPUTATION

Aristotle's concept of virtue ethics can be applied to organizations, including business enterprises, particularly the corporations. How would a corporation like to be known in the public? What image would it like to have and promote for itself? A moral reputation cannot come automatically, but only by cultivating a corporate culture of respecting ethical values in all matters of business, particularly on the part of the management. By creating an environment conducive to accepting *and* following moral values in all dealings with all stakeholders of the company, can such an image be promoted. Thinking merely in terms of taking care of the interests of stakeholders alone is not enough. It is the clear commitment to a comprehensively or holistically moral approach, which imparts a moral distinction to a company and should constitute its culture.

To acquire such a moral distinction, every business enterprise has to ask itself in introspection certain questions. These questions are of two types—Type One concerns with the responsibility to stakeholders and Type Two concerns with the responsibility to the society at large.

Under Type One we have: Does the company ensure the quality and safety standards of its produce? Does it promptly recall from the market all batches of its produce, which have been found to be defective or hazardous? Is there nepotism and corruption in recruitment? Does the company ensure safety in workplace and respect its workers and their rights? Does it have policies and procedures in place to promptly and effectively deal with cases of sexual harassment to its employees? Does it care for the community around and prevent any undue pollution of environment or depletion of community resources? Does it, in its actual behaviour, respect human rights, and fairly compensate and rehabilitate people displaced by its projects? Does it care for shareholders' rights to honest, transparent and fraud-free management, and try to ensure payment of a steady stream of dividends through innovations and efficiency in business operations?

Under Type Two, we have: Does the company avoid any discrimination against women and promote their employment particularly in top positions? Does it take its social responsibility seriously, say, by deliberately diversifying the social background of its employees particularly at the middle and top levels, and give some preference to physically challenged persons in employment? Does it directly contribute to projects for enhancing social welfare and environmental improvement? Does it, as a part of its corporate culture, encourage employees to undertake voluntary social service in their spare time and reward them for it?

To ensure a positive answer to these questions, it is desirable for corporations to evolve a clear policy to respectively deal with both types of responsibilities—to the stakeholders and to the society at large. In the primary task of meeting the responsibilities to the stakeholders, one requirement that should dominate the policy and conduct of an enterprise is to totally avoid deception and fraud, and to take measures that meet the interests of stakeholders wholeheartedly. Formulating a code of conduct, both for the management and employees, helps immensely in this task. A prompt and fair inquiry into all cases of misconduct and fraud, even if it involves those in the management and reasonable punishment, is an essential part of creating a proper corporate culture. Nobody should feel complacent that one can get away with unethical behaviour. At the same time, instituting incentives and rewards for leadership, initiative, honesty, and efficiency, would also be a part of the corporate culture. The code of conduct would have a commanding influence only if it is honestly followed by the management in the first instance. If the management itself turns out to be hypocritical in its implementation, the code would not be worth even the paper it is written on. If on the other hand, there is a formal code, evolved in consultation with all in the management and employment of the company, and made known even to shareholders and the public, it will greatly enhance the prestige and brand value of the company. To ensure strict adherence to the code of conduct and observance of principles of ethics, there is now a trend in developed countries of employing full-time ethics officers. It is their job to be not only vigilant but also to be available for advice when any ethical problem or dilemma emerges. Codes of conduct are usually designed to ensure what can be called as 'minimum morality' of protecting stakeholder interests. It is like setting up the base camp before climbing the Mt Everest. Ambitious companies can also go beyond the base camp and aim at the higher peak of more comprehensive morality of commitment to social justice at large. Even this minimum morality is a great help in establishing a moral reputation, bringing its own economic rewards. However, it calls for moral vigilance to constantly protect and enhance this reputation, and the management should take care that it does not fall into the trap of moral smugness. This is where the role of whistle blowers becomes relevant.

One of the dilemmatic questions that corporations face is what policy needs to be adopted in the case of whistle blowers. Whistle blowers are the persons who report on the wrong doings in the corporation or in any of its departments. They can be considered as conscience keepers in the organization, who do this out of moral compulsions, usually at a risk to themselves. Often companies feel greatly embarrassed by whistle blowers, and try to ignore or suppress the information given by them (which the management may already be knowing, or worse still, be a part of the problem). In such cases, the management tends to victimize whistle blowers, even terminating their services on some other excuse. However, conscientious corporations which are serious about following an ethical code of conduct, welcome such whistle blowers, and establish a set procedure for reporting any wrong doing or instance of moral turpitude. Such a constructive policy forms a part of the corporate culture.

The usual procedure may require the whistle blower to first report to his or her department head, who has to look into the complaint and report to the higher up and inform the whistle blower about the action taken. The whistle blower would be free to follow up the case, and if nothing is done by the department head, the whistle-blower may approach any top cell or committee created to look into such cases, or even to the CEO. If the whistle blower has grounds to suspect that even the CEO is involved in the wrong doing, or, if nothing is done by the management to correct the wrong, he or she may even go to the public or media. Some of the corporations are so considerate, that the whistle blower is rewarded if his or her complaint is found to be true, and is not punished even if the complaint is finally found to be based on wrong information.[13] Thereby, they ensure that whistle blowing is not discouraged, and that any possibility for moral turpitude is prevented. This only adds to the moral prestige of the company.

Corporate responsibility does not end with operating without deception and fraud in the interest of the shareholders. A corporation functions and makes profits within a society and has to do justice to its social responsibility too. This is not mere charity; it helps a corporation to improve its brand value, an intangible asset of high value. An improved brand value gets reflected inevitably in capitalization of reputation on a sustainable basis, which can tide over short-run pitfalls in the market. This is not all. A company active in social work also has smooth and respectable relations with the state and society, which is a great help in any period of unexpected crisis. Social responsibility of corporations in India is no longer a matter of sweet choice. The recent Companies Act 2013 stipulates in Section 135 that every company having a net worth of 5000 million rupees or more, or a net profit of 50 million rupees or more, shall spend at least 2 per cent of its net profit (averaged over the preceding three years) on social welfare as its Corporate Social Responsibility (CSR). Such a company shall constitute a CSR Committee of three or more directors, with one being independent, to formulate and recommend to the Board policies to eradicate hunger and poverty; promote education, gender equality, and empowerment of women; reduce child and maternal mortality; combat HIV and other diseases; and contribute to Prime Minister's National Relief Fund or respective State relief Funds, or like activities which may be *prescribed*. Sachin Pilot, who piloted the Bill as the concerned Union Minister, observed that India is the first country in the world to legally mandate corporate spending on social welfare. This was an attempt to putting Mahatma Gandhi's concept of trusteeship in operation (see Chapter 1 for an explanation of the concept). The Minister estimated that companies together are expected to spend between 150–200 billion rupees every year on CSR. Azim Premji, a leading IT industrialist and eminently generous philanthropist, reacted to the CSR mandate in the Act by saying that CSR has to be spontaneous and not forced (NDTV, 26 September 2013). But all industrialists are not like Azim Premji, and 2 per cent of net profits cannot be very burdensome for rich corporations. Spontaneity can be exercised above 2 per cent! Nevertheless, it would be desirable to give more freedom to companies to choose the social work for which they are best suited, with the understanding that it would not be mainly for the rich in the society. For example, a company may choose to create rainwater harvesting structures and help recharge aquifers in villages or even towns; help organize collection and recycling of municipal waste in an eco-friendly and efficient way; distribute wheel chairs to the physically challenged who are needy; organize classical music concerts and other cultural events to support artistic talents; or engage in several other socially beneficial activities. A company can be creative and innovative in more ways than the government may 'prescribe'.

There is some encouraging news for Indian business enterprises. According to a recent report of the Transparency International,[13] Indian companies have performed best among BRIC countries, in terms of transparency in management and information given. Three Tata companies were placed in top positions among the companies covered by the study. Chinese companies were reported to be at the bottom in this regard. Domestic legal requirements led Indian companies to provide more extensive financial information, including subsidiaries. They also reported on their subsidiaries in other countries.[14] This recognition should stimulate Indian corporations to maintain high standards of ethics in business, comparable with the best in the world.

NOTES

1. As cited in Milton Friedman's *Capital and Freedom*, quoted by him in his famous article 'The Social Responsibility of Business is to Increase Profits', *The New York Times Magazine*, 13 September 1970, reproduced in Newton et al, (2010: 56–61).

2. In his article on 'Responsibility For What's On The Tube', *Business Week*, 13 August, 1979, p. 14, as cited in Newton et al (eds) (2010: 55).

3. Google's cache of http://www.goodreads.com./quotes/128116-a-customer-is-the-most-important-visitor-on-our-premises. Downloaded on 11 October 2013.

4. Cf. S Leacock (1924).*The Garden of Folly.* New York: Dodd Mead, pp. 124–31. As quoted in Newton et al. (eds) (2010: 255).

5. www.un.org/en/document/udhr.

6. The above account of the Industrial Disputes Act is largely based on Kumar (2013) and Lalit Bhasin's article on 'Labour and Employment Laws of India'. (Source: http://www.mondaq.com/08/24/2007, downloaded on Oct. 15, 2013).

7. Sourced from Google News, US edition, dated 17 October 2013.

8. This account is based on www.blacksmithinstitute.org/does/coke1.doc, downloaded on 17 October 2013.

9. The account of the Bhopal disaster is based on Broughton (2005), and www.earthmagazine.org/article/benchmarks-bhopal-gas-leak-kills-thousands, downloaded on 18 October 2013.

10. A pioneering book by Berle and Means (1932), pointed out this fact publicly for the first time. Ever since then, one of the objectives of corporate law and regulations in all the countries in which share markets operate, has been to uphold the rights and interests of shareholders.

11. Economists make a distinction between risk—the probability of which can be estimated and insured—and uncertainty, which is not amenable to such calculation and is therefore, not insurable. The special role of the entrepreneur is said to be one of bearing uncertainty.

12. See The Gazette of India Extraordinary, Ministry of Law and Justice, dated 30 August 2013. www.mca.gov.in/Ministry/pdf/CompaniesAct2013.pdf.

13. Transparency International is an international NGO founded in 1993, which monitors and publicizes corporate and political corruption in international development. See www.tranparency.org/country for country profiles.

14. The remarks in this paragraph that in the long run share prices tend to reflect the intrinsic worth of shares and their companies is supported by the work of Nobel Prize winners in economics in 2013, awarded for their contribution to understanding why share prices change. They are Eugene Fama, Robert Shiller and Lars Peter Hansen. Fama believes that share markets are basically efficient, but difficult to predict in the short run because they constantly assimilate new information into asset prices. According to Shiller, though share prices tend to fluctuate widely around their intrinsic value in the short run, they tend to revert to the mean in the long run. Thus, the work of both complements each other, and suggests that it is more sensible to hold shares for long periods rather than only for short periods. Another insight from Shiller is that shares are not like consumer goods, demand for which falls when prices rise. In the case of shares, demand rises when prices rise, because it feeds expectations of further rise in prices, and investors like to buy shares expected to appreciate in value. Hansen's work focuses on the relation between asset prices and macro-economic variables (See Economic Leader—'A Very Rational Award', *The Economist*, 19 October 2013, Vol. 409, No. 8858, pp. 12 and 14.)

15. Trevino and Nelson (2007: 280) mention an example of such a firm. They quote a *Fortune* magazine report of Chairman of Bear Stearns issuing a memo to all directors, including the managing director:

...we welcome every suspicion or feeling that our co-workers might have about something they see or hear that is going on at Bear Stearns that might not measure up to our standards of honesty and integrity. ...

We want people at Bear Stearns to cry wolf. If the doubt is justified, the reporter will be handsomely rewarded. If the suspicion proves unfounded, the person who brought it our attention will be thanked for their vigilance and told to keep it up.

Forget the chain of command! That is not the way Bear Stearns was built. If you think somebody is doing something off the wall or his/her decision stinks, go around the person, and that includes me...'.

16. Based on Google News, Indian Edition, dated 17 October 2013.

11 Gender Justice*

Any practical concept at enhancing the well-being of women cannot but draw on the agency of women themselves in bringing about such a change.

—Amartya Sen (2000: 190)

THE PROBLEM

The violation of gender justice is one of the oldest and the most universal forms of injustice in the world and, in a sense, perhaps also the most complicated. Gender justice means a fair treatment of women without discrimination against them, recognizing their rights as human beings, and avoiding inequality in law and custom between women and men, and between girls and boys. It also means giving the same opportunities to women as to men in realizing their fullest potential in the development of their personalities, pursuit of happiness, and in the attainment of material and spiritual success. It also means that men and women have the same freedoms in all the spheres of life.

The concept of gender justice covers all genders, as it is now conceded that while sex is biological, gender is psychological (and also social), requiring recognition of other forms of gender also such as trans-sexuality and homosexuality, apart from female and male. The existence of multiple forms of gender is one of the complications in rendering gender justice. Trans-sexuality and homosexuality may be deviations from the normal majority, but they do not have to be treated as necessarily immoral or illegal for that reason. Persons with such genders also have to be treated as human beings, with equal rights. Nevertheless, discrimination against women can be taken to be the dominant and basic form of gender injustice, which extends even to the world of homosexuals and trans-sexuals. For example, gays may be more tolerated in the society than lesbians. Men who prefer to become women (like *hijras* in India) are accepted more than women who prefer to be treated as men, the latter being suppressed (Mohan 2013: 82–3). A woman going against the norm is less acceptable than a man doing the same. This essay, therefore, is basically and mainly concerned with discrimination against women, without denying the need for justice to homosexuals and trans-sexuals.[1] In any case, 'gender' is a broader term than sex, because 'gender' takes into account the social context of sex, in which sex discrimination takes place. For example, when a girl is expected to be coy and a boy is expected to be pushy, we are in the realm of 'gender', and not differences in biological sex. This essay is concerned with gender in this sense.

In terms of the degree of complexity, injustice between economic classes can be said to be the least complex, because the criterion of differentiation here is only economic, in terms of income and wealth. However, social disparities are hardly ever so simple. Injustice as between social groups in terms of race or castes is more complex than the former, because it involves both economic and social discrimination. Social customs, barring free social interaction and upward mobility, are as relevant as economic distance. The social distance is determined by birth, as taking birth in certain groups imparts inferiority or superiority, making it difficult or even impossible to bridge it. In contrast, economic distance between classes is relatively much easier to overcome at least at the individual level. A peasant can hope to become even a president or prime minister, just as mere foot soldiers could become kings in the past. A factory worker can dream of becoming an industrialist and realize her or his dream, though the division between a worker and a capitalist may not vanish. However, it was more difficult to breach the race and caste barriers, at least, till the recent past.

Discrimination against women is even more complex, difficult, and subtle than discrimination based on class, race, and caste. A part of the complexity arises from the fact that discrimination against women is superimposed on other forms of discrimination, making it difficult to identify and compounding it. For example, landlords from dominant castes routinely raped Dalit women from peasant and agricultural labour classes and castes, mainly to make these social groups submissive through humiliation. Historically, rape has been a favourite weapon for oppression and domination in a variety of situations. Second, discrimination against women is much more deeply rooted in the social and, hence, the individual psyche and custom than other forms of discrimination. This psyche is cultivated since childhood almost everywhere, even in cities, making males feel superior to females in all respects to such an extent that fathering is considered as superior and more respectable than mothering! While girls behaving or dressing like boys is tolerated or looked upon with amusement, boys behaving like girls are scorned even by parents. Boys are told: 'Don't cry like a girl!' 'Don't be timid, are you a girl?' Not only the physical, but also the mental make-up of women is considered to be fundamentally different from that of men. The difference is considered as 'natural', though much of it is the result of deliberate cultivation. I have observed a *mother*—a woman after all, telling her little son when he was hit by another little boy—'Hit him back! Are you a girl to take it meekly?' Third, discrimination against women is superimposed on kinships. This often makes women themselves a party to discrimination against women. For example, when a traditional marriage is arranged and terms are being negotiated before the formal engagement, the boy's mother is no less demanding than his father in asking for dowry and jewellery. In most of the tragic cases of 'dowry deaths' and suicides by young wives, the role of the husband's parents inclusive of the mother is no less nefarious than that of the cowardly husband.

Unfortunately, the role of religions hardly helped in reducing discrimination against women. On the contrary, all religions approved and even aggravated it. For example, in Hinduism, only the eldest son, and not the daughter even if she is the eldest of the children, can perform the last rites of any of the departed parents. If the deceased has no son, despite having a daughter, a brother or a paternal nephew or a nearest male relative of the same *gotra* (lineage) has to perform these rites. This has been one of the factors behind son-preference among the orthodox Hindus. Some of the orthodox spokesmen of Hinduism deny the right of reciting the sacred Gayatri mantra to women, let alone opening the doors of priesthood to them. Priesthood is denied to women in mainstream Hinduism on the ground that women menstruate. So what? Women priests can wear leak-proof modern sanitary napkins! How can a normal physiological function disqualify women? God is not a misogynist after all! In Hinduism, God is worshipped in both gender forms, and cannot therefore, have any gender preference. Modern reforms in the Hindu society, however, have reduced the rigours of many such restrictions on women.

Though gender injustice has been observed to be the most complicated for reasons stated in the preceding lines, in one sense, it is simple—there are practically no ethical dilemmas or ethical values conflicting in this case. It is injustice or discrimination, pure and simple, unmitigated by justification on any ground.

Discrimination against women is clearly due to male dominance in society owing to patriarchy. Patriarchy refers to a social system where the families are headed by the eldest males, or by the eldest sons if the father is very old. The descent is determined through the father, and the family property is owned and managed by males and inherited from the father to the sons. Women had practically no rights in the system, except for personal jewellery as in the case of *stree-dhana* (women's personal wealth) in Hindu societies. Patriarchy is considered to be a more universal form, and an outcome of greater aggressiveness of men, which replaced the woman-dominated matriarchal system. Arguably, this replacement may have occurred due to the greater ability of patriarchal societies to survive in a world of militancy. Men took unfair advantage of it, ignoring women's role in managing homes and nursing the children. In a typical patriarchal family, husband and wife are not considered as equal partners and friends; the husband has to be dominant. It is only the wife who, in most cases, has to compromise to save the marriage, when any strain develops between the two. Women, however, are becoming more assertive in recent times, modifying the patriarchal system and democratizing it.

Eventually, however, 'patriarchy' became an analytical term in the new discipline of Women's Studies and feminist movements both to describe and comprehend the world (Geetha 2007: 5). It is a system which 'automatically privileges men over women' in which women can 'lay claims to material, sexual and intellectual resources only through fighting for them' (ibid.: 5). Rights to property, to education, to choose their partners in life, to vote, and such other rights have not come automatically but only through fighting for them in patriarchal systems. When women do not contest the dominance and privileges of men, men reward women by glorifying the role of the mother and the wife, and protect them. But if they contest it, women would be humiliated, rejected, turned out of the house, and punished (ibid.: 6). In other words, the system is one of grave gender injustice.

Sources or causes of gender inequality have been:

1. Women are seen mainly in terms of their sexuality and motherhood, as if they have no other dimensions to their personality as human beings; However, this is not so in the case of men.
2. Even when it comes to sexuality, there is conspicuous asymmetry. Chastity has double standards, stressed in the case of women, but not in the case of men. If a man philanders, it is taken lightly and spoken of with amusement. But if a woman does it, she attracts contempt and punishment.
3. The female is considered as the weaker sex, not only physically but also as coy, timid, less capable and intelligent, and never a man's equal in any field except in nursing children, taking care of domestic needs and chores.
4. This led to a sexual division of labour, confining women to certain tasks or jobs only, and barring their entry to others. The important tasks assigned to women, such as home management, cooking, taking care of children, cleaning, and so on are not reckoned in terms of economic value, which therefore, tend to be taken for granted and ignored. A woman doing only the domestic chores is not even counted as a worker and is considered as a 'dependent'. This attitude has lowered the status of women. Sexual division of labour ensured that most of the 'earning' jobs (bringing money income) were monopolized by men. Even where women were allowed, they were paid lower wages for the same jobs, on the ground that women's productivity is lower. Sometimes, a subtle differentiation is made between tasks or jobs as those assigned specially for women where lower wages are paid, though explicitly there is no discrimination in wages.

The sad part of the story is that women themselves accepted this unfair discrimination. They almost agreed with the patriarchal assumption of their being the weaker and less competent sex and that the sexual division of labour was 'natural' or God-given. But this age-old tradition of the system faced a serious challenge by the rise of feminism and feminist movements, not only in the West but also in India. The movements increased the awareness of women to their social and economic status and made them fight for a change. Discrimination against women in jobs and promotions, as well as atrocities against women in the form of dowry demands, sexual harassment, and assaults have not, of course, ceased as a result of feminist movements, but have at least forced the state to be more serious than before about addressing these problems.

FEMINIST SCHOOLS OF THOUGHT

Considering the influence of the *Manusmriti* (of around 100 CE) on the Hindus, Vatsyayana's *Kamasutra* (around 300 CE) had 'surprisingly modern ideas about gender' as Wendy Doniger puts it (2013: 314). While the *Manusmriti* is notorious for its prejudice against women, the *Kamasutra* gave much more control to women on household funds, and permitted divorce and widow remarriage. The wife is to have a lot of freedom in running the household and decision making as per the *Kamasutra*, but Manu denied any freedom to women. The *Kamasutra* recognizes women's right to property, education, and even to sexual pleasure. If the wife is not satisfied with her husband, she can renounce him and marry another. However, the text is balanced enough to emphasize the need to be faithful and gives several reasons why a wife should hesitate to start an affair, – reasons like the need to cultivate conjugal love, regard for children, security of home and dharma, and so on. But the *Kamasutra* does not appear to expect similar faithfulness on the part of the husband, and even permits men to visit courtesans.[2] It means that even the *Kamasutra* can be accused of supporting gender inequality to that extent, though much less than the *Manusmriti*. Vatsyayana cannot be regarded as a 'feminist' proper, but considering his times, he was outstandingly bold and progressive.

The feminist movements of the modern times could be said to have started with Mary Wollstonecraft's book, *A Vindication of the Rights of Women*, published in 1792 in England. She challenged the idea that women existed mainly for the pleasure and convenience of men, and advocated the same opportunities to women as men in education, work, and politics.[3] With modernization, more and more women were entering the education stream by then, and as the capitalist development gained momentum, more and more women were joining factories and working outside home. This spurred women's movements, but initially, at least in the nineteenth century, they gave more attention to getting the right to vote and greater opportunities in the public space like politics than to other pressing problems affecting women.[4] By the end of the nineteenth century, three main schools of feminist thought emerged in Europe, continuing into the next century too.

The first school of thought was that of liberal feminism, which developed mainly in Europe and the USA. The publication of John Stuart

Mill's book, *Subjection of Women*, in 1869, greatly strengthened and furthered the cause of this school. It did not challenge the whole system— either capitalism or patriarchy—and pointed to the scope for enormous improvement in the position of women within the existing system. The solution to the problem of women lay simply in giving the same rights and opportunities that men enjoyed. Mill believed that marriage and motherhood did not pose any problem in this, and that in any case women's role and activities should not be bound and restricted by marriage and motherhood (Krishnaraj 2002: 105). It implied that when wives worked outside home and participated in public affairs, the husbands too should share equal responsibilities in domestic chores and looking after children. This did not require ending either capitalism or patriarchy, though gender justice showed the possibilities of significantly modifying and improving both the systems.

Liberal feminism influenced and shaped women's movement and feminist thought in India too. India's contribution to liberal feminism can be said to have started in the early part of the nineteenth century itself, which continued with force in the twentieth century. The pioneer was Raja Rammohan Roy (1774–1833) who was instrumental in getting the *Sati* system outlawed in 1829, and also in getting the Sarda Act (Prohibition of Child Marriage Act) passed in the same year. He started encouraging remarriage of widows too, but died early before completing his tasks on hand. His work was carried forward by Ishwar Chandra Vidyasagar who was instrumental in the widow Remarriage Act of 1856. He worked hard for promoting women's education too. The boost to women's education, especially of there from lower castes, came however from Jyotiba (Jyotiba) Phule (1827–1890) who pioneered it in Maharashtra, starting a girl's school in 1851. Another prominent figure in women's education was Dhondo Keshav Karve (1858–1962). He started a college for women in Mumbai, which he transformed in to India's first women's University, the SNDT University, named after its donor. Both Phule and Karve also fought against Child marriage and encouraged widow remarriage. Shahu Maharaj of Kolhapur (1874–1922) also worked enthusiastically for women's education, especially those from lower castes. A pioneering woman in India's feminist movement is Tarabai Shinde (1850–1910) whose book in Marathi—*Stree-Purush Tulana* (comparing women with men) published in 1882, strongly condemned discrimination against women in the society. It was equally harsh on caste patriarchy and hierarchy. Phule, Shahu Maharaj and Shinde attacked the system itself (like Dr B.R. Ambedkar (after),—the system of caste hierarchy and patriarchy, and wanted to drastically reform it along with emancipating women. Mahatma Gandhi too was a strong advocate of gender equality and brought many women into the mainstream of India's freedom struggle.

Two other schools—the socialist feminists and radical feminists—did not believe that women's emancipation was possible within the existing system and focused on a struggle to end the system itself. While the emphasis of the socialists was on ending the capitalist system, that of the radicals was on ending patriarchy. Both were influenced by Friedrich Engels' seminal book—*Origin of the Family, Private Property and the State*—published first in 1884. Engels argued that there was a time in history when there was no monogamous family, no private property and state, and members of a group lived together in a communistic 'household' where everything was shared commonly. During this period of primitive communism, women had an overall control, and even sexual relationships were relatively free. Descent was from the mother. However, life began to turn from nomadic to settled conditions, after women discovered the possibility and importance of cultivating crops, and agriculture emerged as a major form of production instead of hunting. Exchange relations developed to deal with surplus crop production and to get other necessities of life on barter. This led to the custom of monogamous marriages and private property, and men began to have more control over women. Monogamy, however, was one-sided. While women could have only one husband, men could have more wives. When family and private property emerged as major institutions, the emergence of the state—to protect ownership of private property and regulate exchanges—was not far behind. Women's position was relegated to that of subordination, both under feudalism and capitalism. An important impact of capitalism on women was that they started working outside homes in factories. On the one hand, this placed greater burdens and hardships on women, and on the other, it generated incomes of their own. Engels argued that for their emancipation, women should join proletarian struggles to end capitalism itself. Under socialism, they can have communal kitchens and communal care of children, which liberated them from the burden of domestic chores and gave them the freedom to pursue their interests and realize the full potential of their personality.

However, quite a few women socialists themselves raised doubts about whether the ending of capitalism could by itself alter the deprived situation of women, even while they denounced 'bourgeois feminists'. A prominent leader among them was Alexandra Kollantai, who was not only a thinker but also an activist. She was involved in the revolution, which overthrew the Tzar in Russia, and was in the new Bolshevik government. As the People's Commissar for Social Welfare, she drafted several decrees for women's liberation, including those which nationalized pre-natal care of the mother, provided for community kitchens and childcare centres for working women, made marriage laws more egalitarian, and encouraged women's education at state expense. Yet, she was sceptical if all this could help in ending women's subordination. Even if the achievement of communism proper would end it, she doubted if women could or should wait that long. She felt the need to challenge the existing sexual ethics which favoured men over women and was clearly one-sided.[5] Kollantai got the support of other woman socialists like Rosa Luxemburg, who together raised the issue of sexual division of labour in proletarian homes (Krishnaraj 2002:106).

The origin of the third school of feminist thought, radical feminism, can be traced to Friedrich Engels and feminist socialists like Alexandra Kollantai who questioned the logic and fairness of patriarchal sexual ethics. Radical socialists criticized socialists for their overemphasis on class as the main form of differentiation and inequality, and asserted that patriarchy should be smashed in all forms if women are to be liberated and made equal to men. Some of them coming from France advocated freedom of love and sex. The system of family and living in family with monogamous ethics were attacked. It was argued that subordination of women within family preceded and even shaped subordination in other spheres outside home – be it in work or politics. Corresponding to the socialist call for unity of workers from all over the world, the radical feminists advanced the idea of universal sisterhood and called on all women to end their subordination through an united struggle.

Radical feminism has not been accepted by the majority of feminists, as is the case with socialist feminism. Instead, it is the 'bourgeois' or liberal feminism which is still the most popular and accepted school of thought, not only in tradition-bound societies like India, China, and other Asian countries, but also in Europe and the USA. The institution of family still survives, though it faces an uncertain future. Yet the influence of radical feminism on the youth—both men and women, particularly in elite classes—cannot be undermined. It has resulted in greater permissiveness in sexual relations, both pre-marital and extra-marital.

While one-sided sexual ethics is certainly unfair to women, one wonders whether the solution lies in making this ethics more balanced and fair to all, or in throwing out all restraint on sexual ethics. One shudders to think about the future of humanity, its society, its stability, and well-being, if the institution of family breaks down as a result of excess dose of radicalism. Can the state really replace the family as some socialists hoped? Can communes really be an effective and satisfactory alternative? Is sexual anarchy really desirable or needed for women's emancipation? Who will provide the loving care, security, and stability, which children need if family breaks down as an institution? What is the experience of single-parent households? What system can ensure security to women along with freedom to enrich their personalities? These are the questions which feminists cannot ignore, whatever be their school of thought.

The most recent school of feminists is 'post-modern'. In fact, it is problematic to call them as feminists as such, because they recognize not just two genders of women and men, but also 'sexual minorities' and fight for their rights. They have a broader agenda than the other feminists. For the same reason, they do not agree with the idea of 'universal sisterhood', in view of there being different kinds of women with different types of sexualities and facing different forms of problems. Even while post-modern feminists are concerned with ending discrimination against women, they are more bothered about gender justice in a broader perspective, which recognizes the rights of homosexuals, bisexuals, and transsexuals. They insist on a legal recognition of marriage between homosexuals, of a 'family' where the partners are homosexuals without bothering about the concept of 'husband' and 'wife', and on the right of such families to adopt and raise children. They also claim the right to get income tax concessions extended to families.

While these contentions appear reasonable and some countries have conceded these rights, there is certainly a problem with bisexuals, the problem of adultery being intrinsic to it. Can a husband in a heterosexual family indulge in homosexual relations with another man, claiming his right as a bisexual and still remain in his family cheating his wife? Similarly, can a wife in a heterosexual family have a lesbian relation with another woman and still remain in her family? It does involve an extra-marital adulterous relationship. In insisting on recognizing the rights of bisexuals, post-modern 'feminists' may inadvertently slip into supporting adultery. Adultery is a serious challenge to the stability and survival of the institution of family, its dignity, and functional efficacy. It is only in a family, where partners sincerely love and are committed to each other, that children's growth is assured in a healthy direction, physically and morally. No feminist can reasonably even imply that the future of children is not their concern at all. Homosexuality and marriages between such persons cannot by themselves threaten the future of family and humanity, so long as they do not become 'normal' in a statistical sense and do not support promiscuity and multiple partnerships. Homosexuals are and will remain a minority, since heterosexuality cannot but be normal, being needed for continuing the human species. However, just because homosexuals and transsexuals are deviations from the statistical normal and are in a minority, their rights cannot be ignored, and they too should be treated as human beings. The greater threat to the survival of the human species lies in mutual hatred and violence, moral irresponsibility, and disregard to environmental health, and not in the deviations in sexuality among a minority of people.

We may conclude this section by observing that gender justice cannot wait till capitalism and patriarchy are smashed. Reforms are possible within the system such that they lead to emancipation of women and also modify the system itself to the advantage of women. Gender justice, however, cannot be confined only to elite women but should include all women. The rights of *all* women to property, education, job opportunities, personal dignity and security, equitable access to politics and public space, and so on can be guaranteed within the existing system itself. It is necessary to review from time to time how far gender justice is achieved for all, and where and how it is violated, so that timely remedial measures are taken. This should make the whole—social, economic, and political—system more democratic, humane, and woman friendly, in which *all* people become equal partners in humane progress and development.

Though the problem of giving justice to women remains to be satisfactorily resolved, the awareness of the problem has improved both among women and men. Groups to safeguard the rights of women are active in almost all the states of India, and women themselves have started becoming active agents to solve their problems and to urge the state to implement the laws passed to guarantee women's rights and to amend or pass new laws where necessary. What is more, a new and independent discipline of studies and research—Women's Studies, has emerged in social sciences in its own right, with even separate departments devoted to the discipline in many universities in India. This discipline has attracted brilliant women scholars, resulting in insightful findings helpful for policy formulation and implementation.

MAGNITUDE AND FORMS OF GENDER INEQUALITY

The magnitude of gender inequality is measurable and even ranked for inter-country comparison. UNDP's Human Development Reports (HDR) have been publishing the related statistics for some years now, presenting gender inequality indexes and ranks for the bulk of 186 countries, for which human development indexes are calculated. The Gender Inequality Index, as the HDR explains, is a 'composite measure reflecting inequality in achievement between women and men in three dimensions—reproductive health, empowerment and the labour market'. The index values and ranks, and the components going in to the calculation of the index values, are presented below in Table 11.1.

Table 11.1:   Gender Inequality in India and Selected Countries

Indicators	India	China	Japan	USA	World
1. Gender Inequality (2012)					
Rank*	132	35	21	42	–
Index Value	0.610	0.213	0.131	0.256	0.463
2. Maternal Mortality (deaths per 100,000 live births) (2010)					
	200	37	5	21	145
3. Adolescent Fertility Rate (births per 1,000 women aged 15–19) (2012)					
	74.7	9.1	6.0	27.4	51.2
4. Seats in Parliament (% female) (2012)					
	10.9	21.3	13.4	17.0	20.3
5. Population with at least Secondary Education (% aged 25>) (2006–10)					
Female	26.6	54.8	80.0	94.7	52.3
Male	50.4	70.4	82.3	94.3	62.9
6. Labour Force Participation Rate (% of persons aged 15>) (2011)					
Female	29.0	67.7	49.4	57.5	51.3
Male	80.7	80.1	71.7	70.1	77.2

Note: The reference years are shown in brackets. *Ranks follow the inverse order of index values, a higher rank indicating lower gender inequality.

Source: UNDP Human Development Report 2013, Table 4.

Table 11.1 shows how India is behind the world as a whole in each of the indicators, let alone more developed countries like China, Japan, and the USA. India ranks 132nd in gender equality, and is among the lowest one-third of the countries included in the HDR. Its gender inequality index is as high as 0.610, above the world average of 0.463. In reducing the maternal mortality rate, India has made good progress, since only about a decade ago it was 450 per lakh of live births, which has improved to 200 now. But it is still much behind China where it is only 37. India's adolescent birth rate (per 1000 women aged between 15 and 19) is very high at 74.7, compared with China's 9.1. This indicates the continuing high prevalence of child marriage, depriving young girls of their education and forcing them nurse infants and do domestic chores. They are thus effectively discouraged from making their own careers. What is sad, the bulk of women in India are not able to even complete their secondary education, let alone higher education (see indicator 5 in Table 11.1), though the proportion of women completing it has been steadily rising over the years.

Table 11.1 also shows how women's participation in labour force is also quite low in India, compared with the world average. Employment outside home is an important indicator of women's empowerment. The labour force participation rate has been declining for women for over two decades now, mostly in rural areas.[6] One explanation for this is in terms of an increasing proportion of rural girls getting into the education stream at higher levels.[7] Another but a gloomy explanation is that this has been due to a stagnation in the growth of agriculture, which was the major source of employment for women in rural areas, and also due to a slow down in the overall economic growth (Kannan and Raveendran 2012). Between 2007–8 and 2009–10, there was an absolute fall in the number of female workforce by 21 million, which virtually offset a rise in the male workforce by 22.3 million.[8] Women had to bear the main brunt of the agricultural stagnation. Both explanations seem pertinent; one need not preclude the other. A third explanation for the decline in female labour force may be a subtle and not-so-subtle discrimination against women candidates for employment, a point taken up later for a more detailed discussion. All the three factors have operated to depress female work participation particularly in India, as Table 11.1 shows.

The impact of pushing down women is evidently seen in the proportion of women's representation in the Parliament, which was only 10.9 per cent in India. This by itself is much less than the world average of

20.3 per cent which again is much low than what it should have been. The issue of reservation of seats for women at 33 per cent in the Parliament is being indefinitely postponed on the excuse that most of the reserved seats may be taken by the more educated and advanced upper caste women. However, in Indian politics, the level of education has hardly been a very important expectation, and intermediate and lower castes have more significantly contributed to political leadership than the upper castes. Moreover, the device of reservations within reserved quotas is not new to India. As a step towards improving women's representation in the Parliament and the state Assemblies, political parties should at least decide on allocating one-third of their tickets to women for contesting in the elections. The hesitation seems to be more due to prejudice than any real or objective difficulty.

An important fact that emerges from Table 11.1 above as also from the HDRs is that gender inequality tends to decline with economic development and a general rise in the levels of human development. The HDR of 2013 shows that the index value of gender inequality has consistently declined from 0.578 for the least developed countries to 0.457 for the medium human development countries, and then down to 0.376 for countries with high human development and to 0.193 for countries with very high human development. It seems, therefore, that even prejudices against women can change with economic, particularly human development, though an exclusive focus on economic growth by itself will not help much.

There are more indicators of importance than what are presented in Table 11.1. Sex ratio is one such indicator. The sex ratio is unfavourable to women (known as the phenomenon of 'missing women') consistently over time and across states in India (subject to some exceptions such as Kerala). This is indicative of the preference of a son and a deep patriarchal prejudice against women, leading to female foeticide and infanticide, and neglect of girls' health, resulting in turn, into high female infant mortality. This was first reported as early as in 1857 by C.J. Brown. Census Reports later confirmed this phenomenon. It has shown no sign of disappearing. Even as late as in 2001, there were only 927 women per 1,000 males in India in the age group of zero to six years, and the ratio declined further to 914 in 2011 as per the census reports. The situation is worse in rural areas, and it has been observed that it is particularly prominent among farm families with large holdings, and less so in the case of landless rural households (Arokiasamy and Goli 2012: 89). Though the flag bearers of patriarchy are landlords and farmers with large holdings, the legacy of patriarchy has continued to influence others too, including the urban households who have migrated from the rural areas. India has taken steps to address this problem, including a ban on pre-natal sex determination tests to prevent abortion of female foetuses and also by making demands for dowry a criminal offence. But the implementation of such practices has not been satisfactory as reflected in the data on sex ratios.

The problem of dowry is to a great extent responsible for sex selection, but this problem is much less acute or even absent in the case of certain castes which are not by and large landholders, and also in the case of 'love marriages' in contrast with marriages arranged by parents. But most of the marriages in India are still being arranged by parents, and there is resistance to 'love marriages' particularly in landholding rural families. But dowry is not insisted nowadays where the bride has either a regular job or has a rich potential for such a job. Unfortunately, there is still some prejudice against women in the job market on the ground that women tend to take more leave due to domestic requirements, apart from maternity leave. Dowry is sometimes tried to be explained as some sort of a discounted present value of a future stream of expected expenditure on maintaining the bride in the marital family, which has to be paid by her parents who would have incurred this expenditure had she not married. This point of view completely ignores the economic value of woman's unpaid domestic work and her potential to bring monetary income into the family by working outside home. To the extent that the above explanation holds, the solution lies in opening the opportunities in education and jobs to all girls. The huge expenses of getting daughters married are often mentioned as one of the reasons behind the preference of a son, aggravated by demands for dowry. Women's movements have to launch a campaign to limit this expenditure, which should preferably be shared equally by both the parties, and encourage exposing dowry demands and providing support to the bride in such cases. It is when people will look upon girls as assets rather than liabilities that their preference for the son will end. The state has an important role to play in changing this attitude.

The same discrimination against women operates in the job market, both in recruitment and payment of wages. Not only is women's work participation rate lower than that of men, the nature of employment women get is also less paying. The nature of employment of women in India and changes therein are presented in Table 11.2.

Table 11.2:   Nature of Employment of Women and Men in India (Percentages to total employment under three categories given)

Category & Year	Rural		Urban		Rural + Urban	
	Male	Female	Male	Female	Male	Female
1. Self-employed						
1993–4	57.7	58.6	41.7	44.8	53.6	56.8
2009–10	53.5	55.7	41.1	41.1	50.0	53.3
2. Regular Workers						
1993–4	8.5	2.7	42.0	28.4	17.1	6.3
2009–10	8.5	4.4	41.9	39.3	17.7	10.1
3. Casual Workers						
1993–4	33.8	38.7	16.3	25.8	29.3	36.9
2009–10	38.0	39.9	17.0	19.6	32.2	36.6

Source: NSSO Rounds, as cited in Mazumdar and Neetha (2011: 119, Table 1).

It is evident from Table 11.2 that the proportion of women employed in regular work, which is more secure and paying, is only 10.1 per cent in 2009–10, having increased from 6.3 per cent in 1993–4, taking both rural and urban areas together. It is lower still in rural areas—2.7 per cent in 1993–4 and 4.4 per cent in 2009–10. This is worse than in the case of men, though even in the case of men regular jobs accounted for only 17.7 per cent of total employment in 2009–10. Self-employment is the major work provider both for men and women, but a little more so for women. But this self-employment is mostly in low-paid types of work in informal or unorganized sectors.

Ela Bhatt played an important role in organizing self-employed women, vastly improving their bargaining power, enhancing their self-respect and confidence, besides enabling them to earn more. She started SEWA in 1972 at Ahmedabad for the purpose. *Sewa* in Sanskrit (and Gujarati) means service, a very apt name for the organization she founded and guided. It covers different categories of self-employed women, such as small retail vendors, home-based producers like *beedi* and incense-sticks makers, weavers, potters, milk producers, tailors, cooks, and even agricultural labourers and construction workers employed on casual or daily basis. SEWA has reduced the difference between paid regular work and self-employment, even making it more attractive in some cases, in terms of both income and stature. She started a co-operative bank of their own for the purpose of mobilizing their savings and giving credit, and arranged training for them to improve their skills both in production and marketing.

Where self-employed women are not organized as in other regions, micro-finance agencies and self-help groups of women have been useful in meeting credit requirements and encouraging entrepreneurship among women even if on a small scale. Scheduled banks have been active in promoting these self-help groups, many of which are working fairly well. But there are also many cases where micro-finance organizations have emerged on a private initiative of the elite, calling themselves as NGOs (non-governmental organisations), which are little better than the traditional exploitative moneylenders. What is worrisome here is that there appears to be no effective institutional set-up to monitor and control these organizations. So the problems of self-employed women do not seem to have been satisfactorily solved in all the regions of India.

Even where women get employment, they do not get the same wages as men, especially in casual work; and within paid work, it is the casual work which is more prevalent. The problem of lower wages for women exists both in rural and urban areas, because it is taken for granted that men do more work per hour or day than women, and are therefore more productive. This discrimination is quite open and remorseless, and constitutes a grave injustice to the poor women. According to the NSSO data, the ratio of women's wages to that of men was as low as 0.70 for casual agricultural labour in rural areas in 2004–05, which improved only a bit to 0.75 in 2009–10. As for non-agricultural labour in urban areas, the ratio was even lower at 0.62 in 2004–05, which fell further to 0.59 in 2009–10 (Swaminathan et al., 2012: 60, Table 1). Ironically, the disparity is greater in urban areas and has been increasing.

In the organized sector offering regular work, discrimination against women is more in the form of barriers to entry than in salaries, except in some cases like nurses and school teachers where women are preferred. A common factor in the prejudice against women is that they tend to take more leave (maternity leave in particular) than men, and that men can be more easily asked to work overtime. Some employers even think it is more risky to employ women as it increases their responsibilities to prevent sexual harassment at the workplace and beyond. Such employers do not realize what grave injustice they do to women in the process, and even to the society at large, by confining women to homes, and depriving the society of the benefit of their talent. Besides, entry of women can make the workplace more pleasant, efficient, and respectable. Countries, which are more open to recruiting women, are not less successful in business or in ensuring safety to them and have much lower crime rate against women. There should be strictly implemented laws to prevent discrimination against women in recruitment on the ground that being women they are likely to go on maternity leave. A woman should have the guarantee that she will be reinstated in her job on return from maternity leave and should not be denied of her due promotions. It is ironical that women have to suffer deprivation for their valuable role in motherhood and taking care of home.

Even where women are employed as in the case of teachers, unaided private schools and colleges pay them much less than what is officially due despite getting hefty fees and compulsory 'donations'. Ironically, women teachers are preferred because they do not protest against low salaries. It is presumed that they treat teaching, not as a career but only as a source of a side income and as a way of spending their spare time. In other words, women are not taken as serious workers, thereby justifying their lower pay. However, it is to the great credit of grit and push of women in India that women's entry has been steadily improving into jobs hitherto monopolized by men, ranging from auto-rickshaw drivers in busy cities to airline pilots, from police to combat troops, from lawyers to High Court and Supreme Court judges, and from panchayat presidents to chief ministers. Several women CEOs and entrepreneurs have come into prominence in India. Yet, Indian women have still a long way to go in gaining their just representation in all job categories and professions.

Another way to empower women, besides giving them jobs, is to give them an equitable share in inherited property and a right to own land. Ancient Indian tradition recognized the right of women to own wealth in the form of *stree-dhana* (women's wealth), which consisted mainly of jewellery including gold and silver, though a share in other forms of wealth like land and residential property was normally denied. In matriarchal families on the other hand, women enjoyed ownership and control on all types of property and wealth, but such families were confined to small corners as in parts of Kerala and the Northeast, and even there they have disappeared by now. Patriarchal families have been denying the just share in property to women, though laws of inheritance have been changed in favour of women. Such deprivation is particularly seen in agricultural lands, where daughters are persuaded to give up their rights to land in favour of their brothers on the ground that parents spend a lot of money in getting their daughters married, including payment of dowry. Another justification is on the ground of preventing fragmentation of farm holdings into economically unviable sizes. This is not applied exclusively in the case of women, since sons on whose education a lot of money was spent and who are in good regular jobs in towns and cities, are also persuaded to forsake their demands. Demographic pressures have already reduced the average size of farms significantly enough to affect their viability, which again is one of the weaknesses of Indian agriculture. Nevertheless, women cannot be denied their right to land. Bina Agarwal (1994) has powerfully advocated land rights to women in her book, *A Field of One's Own – Gender and Land Rights in South Asia*. She is critical of the ironical fact that the state itself in its land distribution programmes and policies allotted land only to men as heads of households. She points out that owning land gives women the necessary stature to command respect both within the family and outside.

Through a sample survey of both rural and urban households, totalling 4110, across eight districts of Karnataka, Swaminathan et al. (2012) found a fascinating picture of the pattern of women's share in different forms of wealth. Table 11.3 below presents some of their findings for selected forms of wealth.

It can be seen from Table 11.3 that except in the case of jewellery, women's share in wealth is less than a quarter, which declines in most forms of wealth as we go from rural to urban areas, and further declines in the city of Bengaluru. The exception is in the case of vehicles and cell phones.

Table 11.3:   Women's Share (%) in Forms of Wealth

Forms of Wealth	Rural	Urban	Bengaluru (Bangalore)
Principal Residence	23	21	10
Agricultural Land	15	11	–
Other Rural Estate	22	13	–
Non-Farm Business	13	2	3
Jewellery	76	71	55
Vehicles	19	24	34
Cell Phones	24	33	33
TOTAL GROSS WEALTH	18	23	17

Source: Swaminathan et al. (2012: 65, Table 7).

Ironically, it appears that when the economic status of the household improves, women's share in wealth declines, instead of improving. Swaminathan et al. show that as we go from the poorest to the richest quintile of households, women's share in total wealth declines from 44 to 16 per cent in rural areas, from 51 to 16 per cent in urban areas, and from 50 to 24 per cent in Bengaluru. The decline is consistently smooth, without fluctuations, as we move from the poorest to the richer quintiles of households. (Swaminathan et al. 2012: Table 8, p.65). A puzzle here is that this pattern goes against what was observed above on the basis of inter-country comparison that gender inequality tends to decline as we go from the least developed countries to the more developed. I offer three explanations. The first is that the survey results of Swaminathan et al. focus only on one dimension of gender inequality, namely, the women's share in wealth, whereas the gender inequality index of UNDP is more broad-based covering three dimensions—reproductive health, empowerment as indicated by seats in parliament, and labour force participation. But why should even women's share in wealth go against the trend in the three dimensions in UNDP's index? It need not, and probably will not. Our second explanation is that the Swaminathan survey could not perhaps adequately include an important form of wealth in urban areas—financial assets like bank balances, fixed deposits, and shares. Households either tend to not report or underestimate this information. Unlike land and buildings, women tend to have a greater share in financial assets. Third, the differences between households in the survey data within a given country do not reflect differences in the character of the states. As a household improves in economic status, it may not be immediately reflected in an improvement in women's status. It also requires support measures from the state in the form of creating a woman-friendly environment, conducive legislation and its implementation, aided by equally supportive women's NGOs. There are important differences between country to country in supportive environment, and India as a country has much more to do in this regard. The findings of the survey data strengthen the view that economic growth by itself is not enough, whether it is at the household level or the nation, for the emancipation of women.

WOMEN'S HEALTH CARE

One of the main problems in women's health care is that women themselves tend to ignore it. This is particularly so in families facing economic hardships. Not only do they postpone going to a doctor for a checkup, but they also neglect taking medicines regularly. even when they finally go and get prescriptions. Even when pregnant, the expectant mother does not take adequate nutrition and care. In poor families, at least, mothers give less nutrition to girls than to boys. Unfortunately, the performance of the state is hardly ameliorative. For decades, governments in India, both at the centre and the states, focused mainly on population control in the name of family welfare, and did not look at women's health in all its dimensions. The role of the state in health care is quite limited as only about 17 per cent of all the medical expenditure in the country is estimated to have been met by the state, and the rest met by individuals and families concerned (Narayanan 2011: 40). The share of philanthropic organizations involved in health care seems to be much less than that of the state. When most of the burden of health care falls on families, women's health normally gets less attention unless and until it becomes serious.

A break from the earlier target-oriented approach focused on reducing fertility rates came in the late 1990s under the Bharatiya Janata Party (BJP) government's Reproductive and Child Health Programme (RCHP). Instead of targets, the RCHP adopted the Community Needs Assessment Approach, which intended to adopt a comprehensive approach to health care, particularly reproductive and infant health services. Nevertheless, Harini Narayanan reports, on the basis of field visits around Delhi, that RCHP staff 'talks to the patient about contraception from the time she first comes to the health centre'. Narayanan adds: 'The one thing that has changed over the years is that clients are now offered a choice of contraceptives' (2011: 44). The National Population Policy 2000 recognized, however, that for any effective programme of stabilizing population, reproductive health care must be made accessible to all, besides providing the basic amenities like safe drinking water and sanitation, and empowering women through education and job opportunities. The United Progressive Alliance (UPA) government announced the National Rural Health Mission 2005–12, allocating each year more than the earlier RCHP provided in five years. Though the Mission declared that the 'desirable outcome' of the Mission would be a reduction in fertility rate to 2.1 across the country, it also said that this would be achieved by strengthening primary health and environment (ibid.: 44–45). Narayanan points out that the country's total fertility rate has come down drastically from 3.43 in 1992–3 to 2.06 in 2005–6 already, as seen from the three successive National Family Health Surveys. The fertility rate, however, with the urban poor at 2.8 in 2005–6, was still behind, though it is expected to catch up with the total fertility rate soon. Narayanan implies that the state in India can certainly look more comprehensively at the women's health care now (ibid.: 46).

What is worrisome about the fertility rate is not the total fertility rate of women in India, but the adolescent fertility rate, which remains high (see Table 11.1). The latter is high because of child marriages. According to the third National Family Health Survey estimates, 47 per cent of women in India, aged between twenty and twenty-four, were married before the age of eighteen (53 per cent in rural areas and 30 per cent in urban areas). The National Population Policy 2000 states that over 50 per cent of the girls marry below the age of eighteen, resulting in early pregnancies and high infant and maternal mortality rates too. Teen pregnancies are a health hazard for girls, apart from causing other deprivations in education and lost childhood. Convention on the Elimination of all forms of Discrimination against Women (CEDAW), ratified by India in 1993, states clearly: 'The betrothal and the marriage of a child shall have no legal effect, and all necessary action, including legislation, shall be taken to specify a minimum age of marriage and to make the registration of marriage in an official agency compulsory' (cited in Gupta 2012: 49).

The minimum age for a girl's marriage has certainly been fixed by law as eighteen, but is hardly implemented strictly. Child marriages are not declared as illegal and are in fact recognized, though not registered officially. Women's groups have been resisting and trying to prevent child marriages, and a woman activist, Bhanwari Devi of Rajasthan, who played a leading role in combating this social evil, was gang raped in 1992 as a 'punishment' for daring to oppose the custom (ibid.: 50). As per law, a woman who was married before eighteen, can petition to nullify the marriage on this ground, but very few actually do it since the marriage would have been consummated and even children may have been born already. The Prohibition of Child Marriages Act 2006 declares child marriages as void in three cases—one, where the girl is enticed out of the keeping of the guardian, second, in the cases of compulsion or use of deceitful means, and the third, for the purpose of trafficking. The Act legitimizes children born of child marriages and ensures protection in the form of maintenance and custody of the child as also for the minor girl-mother (ibid.: 51).

The experience so far shows the limitations of relying on law alone for preventing child marriages. Steps like giving incentives to girls to enter the education stream on the condition that they do not marry till they complete eighteen; making not only primary but also secondary and pre-university (XI and XII standards) education compulsory and free; and improving the quality of education, particularly in government schools are necessary to control the evil practice of child marriages, not to mention other benefits of doing so. Girls should by all means be encouraged to make a career and to consent to marriages only when they become full adults. Even where child marriages cannot be declared as void, at least harsh penalties on the parents of both sides would be necessary.

Child marriages are prone to early risk of contracting HIV. Even adult wives find it sometimes difficult to persuade husbands on safe sex, and child wives even more so. They may not even be aware of HIV. India is reported to be having the largest number of HIV affected people (in absolute terms, though not as per cent of total population). Women are especially vulnerable to the disease, without any fault of their own. 'A woman is four times more likely to contact HIV from a man than vice versa. Women have a larger surface area of mucosa that is exposed to their partner's semen for longer duration during intercourse and semen contains higher levels of HIV than vaginal fluids' (Medhini et al. 2009: 382). All the state governments in India have launched massive campaigns for the use of condoms, which is showing limited success. The greatest hindrance is the reluctance of men to use it. Educated women, who also have some economic security of their own, are better able to have a control on their bodies and to insist on safe sex. There have been proposals to make HIV tests legally mandatory for men before marriage, but they have not been taken seriously by even the state. When women are marginalized, they or their parents cannot insist on such tests on grooms-to-be. The bride's side is traditionally an unequal partner in the negotiations that take place before the wedding. It is very unfortunate that women tend to become innocent victims of such a horrible disease.

Violence Against Women

The UN Secretary General Ban-Ki-moon has forcefully declared: 'There is one universal truth applicable to all countries, cultures, and communities: Violence against women is never acceptable, never excusable, never tolerable'.[9] Yet such violence is widespread, and continues to be a serious challenge to the task of ensuring the safety and security of women and giving them justice. It has been reported that worldwide, one in three women are beaten or sexually abused in their lifetime, and that the abuser is usually a member of her own family or someone known to her.[10]

Violence against women takes several forms—femicide (the murder of women because they are women), rape or sexual assault, female infanticide, sexual harassment (which is more than eve teasing but also includes it), trafficking, kidnapping and abduction, harmful practices like genital mutilation of girls (mostly in certain countries of Africa), pushing women to suicide, wife-beating, and verbal abuse. Child marriage (discussed in the previous section and taken up again later in the chapter) is also a form of violence against women and needs to be treated as being one. There are of course laws against almost all forms of violence against women, but their implementation is far from satisfactory especially in India.

The magnitude of crimes against women in India during the last decade as reported by the National Crime Records Bureau, is presented in Table 11.4.

What is particularly shocking in the statistics of crime against women in India is its increasing incidence in recent years. There is a sharp increase not only in absolute numbers, but also relative to population. The cases of rape have increased from 16,075 in 2001 to 22,172 in 2010, and further to 24,923 within the next two years. Of these, more than 10 per cent were perpetrated on girls less than fourtten years of age. More than 90 per cent of rapes were by relatives, neighbours or people already known. Nearly every form of crime against women has shown an increased incidence. Some have argued that this is due to increased reporting of crimes in recent years, and not an actual increase. But this explanation does not carry conviction with many who believe that the ground reality offers no scope for such a positive view. Though the rate of conviction in rape cases has improved from 17.1 per cent in 2010 to 24.2 in 2012, even the improved rate is not high enough to inspire confidence among rape victims to prevent under-reporting. Cases of cruelty by husband and relatives have more than doubled, which also continue to be under-reported. It is unlikely that kidnapping and abduction cases are under-reported, and they too have more than doubled in incidence. Those who perpetrate violence against women do not see them as human beings but as objects of sadism, and in the process become worse than animals themselves.

Table 11.4: Crimes against Women in India (Cases in numbers, unless otherwise indicated)

Type of Crime	2001	2010	2011	2012
1. Incidence of Crimes against Women				
In hundreds	1438	2136	2287	2442
Rate per 100,000 of population	14.0	18.0	18.9	20.1
Conviction rate %	na	14.2	13.2	–
2. Crimes against women as % of total crimes (under IPC)	7.4	9.2	9.4	10.2
3. Rape cases (u s 376 of IPC)				
Numbers	16075	22172	24206	24923*
Of which incest	427	288	277	396
Incest victims up to 14 years of age (numbers)	81	89	68	165
Rape cases, in which offenders were known to victims (%)	84.0	97.3	93.2	98.2
Conviction rate (%)	na	17.1	16.8	24.2
4. Kidnapping and abduction (numbers)	14645	29795	35565	38667
5. Dowry deaths	6851	8391	8618	8233
6. Cruelty by husband	49171	94041	99135	106527
7. Molestation	34124	40613	42868	45351
8. Sexual harassment	9746	9961	8570	9173
9. Immoral Traffic Prevention Act of 1956	8796	2499	2435	2563
10. Dowry Prohibition Act of 1961	3222	5182	6619	9038

Source: National Crime Records Bureau Reports. As published in *EPW* 48(4), 26 January 2013, p. 78 for the years 2001, 2010, and 2011.

na means data not available.

*Of these, in 3025 cases, victims were below fourteen years of age.

To make matters worse, the law against rape was not strict enough in India, and had significant loopholes. For example, sodomy was not considered as rape, and as a result, a ward boy who raped Aruna Shanbaug in 1973 in Mumbai escaped with only 7 years' RI (rigorous imprisionment), but the victim who was strangulated by a dog chain during the crime is still surviving in a permanent vegetative state since then. Her whole life was devastated. Similarly, inserting a rod into the vagina was not considered as rape. Some of these loopholes have been addressed by a new law now, which uses the term 'sexual assault' instead of rape, which includes all forms of assault including sodomy. The Delhi gang rape of a young woman in December 2012, against which the whole country rose in angry protests, involved a boy of 17 years, who was alleged to have brutally pushed a rod into the victim injuring the intestines of the victim, and she succumbed to the injury. While the other four involved culprits were awarded the death sentence, the so-called minor was remanded to three years' reformation facility. There were protests against his exclusion from the death sentence, contending that a boy who could make such a brutal sexual assault leading to death, should not be considered as a minor, and that for such purposes at least, the upper limit for a minor's definition should be brought down from eighteen to sixteen. The identity of the accused minor has been kept secret as per law. One only hopes that the compassion for his age is not misplaced. However, the trial was exceptionally speedy, taking only a few months. Normally rape cases take several years, which dissuade rape victims from reporting the crime. The attitude of the police is generally indifferent to complaints of crimes against women, and the tendency is to first suspect the character of the victim or the complaining woman. The police doctor used to do a 'two-finger' test to determine whether the woman was habituated to sexual intercourse, and if found positive, the victim would herself be suspected of a loose character, and the case used to be dropped. This was strange because, a married woman, habituated to intercourse, can also be vulnerable to rape. Following protests from women's groups, the test has been withdrawn now. With an environment of anti-woman sentiment prevailing in the investigation of crimes against women, it is no surprise that the conviction rate is low. It does not mean that there are no false complaints of rape at all, and that in all cases the accused should be convicted. It is necessary, however, to rid the investigative agencies of anti-women prejudices, to sensitize the police to the need for gender justice, and also increase the presence of women investigators particularly in crimes against women.

Child marriages pose a dilemma in implementing the law against rape. The minimum age for marriage is eighteen for girls, but the minimum age of consent for sexual intercourse is sixteen, below which it is considered as a rape even if there is consent. The problem is that in spite of the law, neither a child marriage is termed invalid, nor is the sexual intercourse within child marriage considered as rape even if the child wife is below sixteen years of age and she is claimed to be 'willing', that is, if she does not complain to the police. But is there any meaning in the willingness of a child wife? There are many cases where the child is forcibly subdued and even gravely injured during the sex act, and yet neither the child nor her parents dare complain to the police unless it has resulted in death. This is an instance of how a custom cannot be ended simply by law making. In the meanwhile, child marriages cry for justice. Let alone the problem of depriving the child of her childhood and schooling, even the physical violence on her is not prevented and is left to the good sense of the husband and in-laws.

Sexual harassment may not be as violent as rape, but it is distressing. It is of two types, one, here unwanted physical contacts are made or eve teasing is done (in the form of obscene remarks or gestures or petty mischief); two, where sexual favours are sought or expected from subordinate women and subtle advances are made. While eve teasing is practised against strangers or equals (or those who may not be subordinates), the second type is against subordinates who hesitate to protest until it becomes unbearable. Sexual harassment is a thoroughly unprofessional and unethical conduct. Every organization has to take effective steps to prevent it, as suggested in the next section.

THE SOLUTION

In addressing the centuries-old deprivation and suppression of dalits (outcastes and other oppressed people), Dr B R Ambedkar called upon them to shed their sense of inferiority, develop self-respect, aim high, and assert their rights unitedly. His mantra was 'Educate, agitate, organize. Have faith in yourself'. The same teaching is applicable in solving the problem of women's subordination and their securing equal rights. This does not of course mean that women have to spend their lives in an adversarial mode fighting with all the men around, but certainly includes developing awareness of their situation and try to improve it consciously and resolutely. Emancipated women also will continue to be as caring and loving as ever.

Sheryl Sandberg, is one of the most powerful persons in the business world and, 'the co-pilot' of Facebook, 'the biggest network of humans the world has ever seen' (Luscombe 2013: 36). She gave a TED talk (TED stands for Technology, Entertainment, Design) in 2010, said to have been watched 2 million times and continues to be watched. Her main message to women in this talk is that one important reason why so few women are at the top in business or politics, is that they systematically underestimate their abilities and do not aim high. Sandberg takes a simple example. At a roundtable seminar, women participants on their own take the chairs in the row behind, leaving the front row near the table to men. She exhorts: 'Lean in at the table' with confidence and participate on an equal footing with men! She advises women to make a career too, and not be content with being merely a homemaker; they should in the process make men share equal responsibilities in domestic work and bringing up children. 'Leaning in' has now become a metaphor for urging women to aim at top positions.[11]

Often, women themselves become obstacles not only in their own emancipation, but also in that of other women. Sandberg observes, 'When a man is successful, he is liked by both men and women. When a woman is successful, people of both genders like her less' (Sandberg 2013b: 45). The tense relationship between the mother-in-law and her daughter-in-law in quite a few families (though not in all), has become a subject matter of popular TV serials and jokes. But this matter is not always one of amusement. There are several cases where the mother-in-law, jealous of the daughter-in-law for 'stealing' the love of her son, or for not bringing enough dowry, has driven the daughter-in-law to suicide, or divorce where the latter is bold and confident enough to turn a new leaf in her life. Even in milder cases, where no crime as such is involved, a woman resents if her son helps his wife in housework, or say, in changing the diapers of her grandchild. There are opposite cases too when the daughter-in-law has the upper hand and poisons the mind of her husband against his mother. The point is, women themselves hate other women as women in many cases—a hate which needs to be overcome for women's emancipation.

It is equally or even more necessary for men to be aware of the extent of injustice done to women, consciously or unconsciously. It has been long acknowledged that men have achieved top positions in life, because of the unstinted co-operation and support of their wives, who have taken over the responsibilities of housework and childcare. Since it is unpaid work, it is taken for granted, and men developed a stake in women being confined to homes to do housework. Even where women started working outside home, it was expected that her primary responsibility is housework. It had a doubly adverse effect on women. At home, even a woman working outside home had to continue to do the same amount of housework as before. And outside home at workplace, she was paid less or denied of higher opportunities because her priority is assumed to be her home and less was expected of her than men. In an article in the *Harvard Business Review*, Herminia Ibarra and others have pointed out how even where women received positive comments from their superiors ('Excellent! Terrific! Stellar!...'), such women were not considered as potential for higher positions, because the standards applied to women's work were themselves low, based on lower expectations from them (Ibarra et al. 2013: 89). It is necessary for both men and women to be aware of even subtle and implicit prejudices and overcome them.

Women's groups and media have also an important role in rendering justice to women. I am not at all suggesting trials by media, but they have a role in exposing cases of injustice and bringing pressure on authorities to act promptly. Sometimes as in the case of preventing child marriages and dowry harassment, the law by itself is hardly effective. It is social pressure and the fear of ignominy, which is more effective in which women's group and media can greatly help, without indulging in character assassination based on mere guess. Bollywood has a great reach to the masses not only in India but also in its neighbourhood, and can play a constructive role by depicting the true lives of women who went against the stereotype. Can someone in Bollywood like Aamir Khan produce a film on Malala Yousafzai, the girl who received a bullet in her head from Taliban gunmen for daring to go to school, and lived to inspire all girls to go to schools and get education?[12] Women's groups have to increase their organizational reach to cover all women as far as possible, both in villages and urban areas, both among the poor and the rich.

Business enterprises, educational, and other social institutions can help in rendering justice to women, first of all by shedding their conscious and unconscious prejudices against employing women. There has to be a policy of having a greater representation of women at all levels up to the board of directors. An organization giving due representation to women will have greater prestige outside and greater efficiency along with a comfortable and tension-free environment inside. Second, the organizations employing women should ensure safety and security to women. It is desirable that each organization or enterprise has women's grievance cell having a majority of women members, where women employees can register complaints of sexual harassments by others. It should be the duty of these cells to properly investigate such complaints and report to the top bosses for suitable action, and even to take the matter to the police or media if the enterprise takes no action within a reasonable period of time. The very existence of such a cell can act as a deterrent to sexual harassment and will create a proper environment where women are duly respected. Third, a major gap in India is in providing quality childcare for working women, a deficiency which comes in the way of their contributing fully to their jobs. The employing organizations should ensure such a facility within their premises. Where they are too small to do so, womens' groups and states should help in providing quality childcare in common centres.

In enabling women to have gender equity and to make social and economic advancement at par with men, it is acknowledged that women ought to have three things—agency, autonomy, and empowerment. Women's well-being cannot come as a gift from others, be they men, the state, or philanthropic bodies, but by women's own agency. Women ought to have control on their own bodies and due say in running the affairs at home, including children, and even in governance and politics of the country. That is, they ought to have the freedom to exercise their own judgement, choices, and decision making. For this they need empowerment—social, economic, and political. They also need to have all the rights necessary for such empowerment—the right to life and dignity, right to happiness, right to own property including land, residence, and financial assets, right to worship at par with men, the right to vote, and so on.

The state has an important role in recognizing these rights and facilitating their due exercise. The quality and scope of the state's supportive role makes an important difference. But India has fared poorly in playing its role. A Vision Statement by Idea Watch on Women and Economic Equality in the *Harvard Business Review* (Vol. 91, No. 4, April 2013: 30–31), has categorized countries of the world into four types, seen in terms of two dimensions—economic success of women (degree of inclusion and advancement, equality of pay) on Y axis, and support for women (policies guaranteeing access to education, credit, and employment) on X axis. The countries are graphically presented in four quadrants or boxes—low Y and low X, low Y and high X, high Y and low X, and high Y and high X. India is in the unenviable quadrant of low Y and low X (along with Bangladesh, Chad, Egypt, Ethiopia, Indonesia, Jordan, Kenya, Kuwait, Lebanon, Morocco, Nigeria, Oman, Pakistan, Saudi Arabia, Senegal, Sri Lanka, Turkey, UAE, Yemen, and others). The comment of the Vision Statement on the countries in this quadrant is that they have made no systematic effort to improve the economic position of women by, say, raising their literacy and education status. India's inclusion in this quadrant comes as no surprise, considering its low rank in gender equality. The stature and ranking of a country is decided not so much by its military power, as by the extent to which it fulfils social justice – particularly gender justice.

It is, therefore, not only important but also urgent for India to improve its international ranking in gender equality. In providing support measures for this, special attention may have to be given to physically, economically, and socially deprived groups. Under the first category, come the visually and otherwise challenged women, while in the second come economically deprived women in poor classes and castes. Under the third category come separated or divorced,[13] and widowed women and elderly ladies with no near and dear ones to support and take care of them. Both the state and women's groups or NGOs have to ensure that these women get their rights and entitlements by providing legal support, training, job support, and homes where needed. The quality of shelters for widows, especially for the elderly among them, cries for vast improvement.

In improving the security of women, even small steps can go a long way. A significant number of sexual assaults are reported as taking place in rural areas because of the lack of toilet facilities, forcing women to go out in the dark in the fields. A mandatory condition for all houses in rural areas should provide for toilets in or near homes. Urban slums should have enough number of common toilets. The high ways should also have areas where night buses can halt, and passengers, especially women, can relieve themselves and have drinking water. Because of lack of these facilities, night buses stop at remote places to enable passengers to get down and relieve themselves on road sides in the dark, which is particularly risky for women, apart from being embarrassing.

In boldly countering attacks on women, there should be a nation-wide programme for training them in self-defense, if necessary through sudden counter-attack on the attackers. Such a training will also impact self-confidence and courage. According to a news report (in The Hindu dated March 26, 2014, p. 22, under the caption, 'Lightweight revolver "Nirbheek" launched'), the Indian Ordinance Factory at Kanpur has launched a lightweight revolver, 'Nirbheek', especially for women to defend themselves in cases of assault. But, unfortunately, weapons have no moral judgement or intelligence of their own, and nothing prevents a revolver from getting into the hands of men,—of even rapists who may try to force a woman to submit at gun-point. Considering also the high price of the weapon (Rs. 1,22,360 as reported), which is beyond the reach of most women, a better strategy is to start a nation-wide programme suggested above. In the most cases of assault on women, she may not have the time to open her handbag and take out the revolver. But the training in self-defense can enable her to defend herself and thwart the attacker more quickly. At the larger level, security for women can be enhanced only by a more effective law-enforcement and by creating an environment of respect for women's rights. Every country may have some pervert minds and a few rogues. But when we hear about rapes and murder of women every now and then, it suggests something very wrong with the country and its governance.

India is aware of the gender situation and has taken important steps to improve it. The National Commission for Women was set up by an Act of Parliament in 1990 to safeguard the rights and legal entitlements of women. The 73rd and 74th Amendments to the Constitution of India, passed in 1993, have provided for reservation of 33 per cent seats in the local bodies both in the rural and urban areas. A National Policy for the Empowerment of Women has been adopted in 2001 to create a positive environment for gender justice and to guide people, organizations, and government personnel about what is expected of them in this regard (Samaddar 2009, 4: 425–41). Rape laws and laws against sexual harassment have been tightened up subsequently in pursuance of this National Policy. Women's representation in various cadres of jobs and positions still needs to be improved significantly. The reservation of seats for women's is still a mirage. Child marriages continue to be a matter of concern. However, with a more sincere implementation of the National Policy, it is hoped that women's emancipation and gender equity will make further progress in India enough to make its women happy and feel secure, and make the country proud in international ranking. Women themselves will have to fight for achieving it, but the environment now is more favourable for their success.

NOTES

   *In writing this chapter, I had the benefit of discussions with Saraswati Naimpally and Subhashree Banerjee.

   1. For a brief but informative account of the problems of homosexuals, bisexuals, and trans-sexuals, see Mohan (2013).

2. This account of the *Kamasutra* is based on Doniger (2013: 314–73).

3. See *The New Encyclopedia Britannica* 1990, 15th Edition, vol. 12: 735.

4. Ibid.

5. This account of Kollantai's thoughts is based on Geetha (2007: 38–41). Geetha refers to Kollantai's book on *Women's Liberation* published in English in 1998 at London by Bookmarks, edited with an Introduction by Charnie Rosenberg.

6. According to the National Sample Survey Reports, the female labour force as a proportion of total labour force (rural and urban together), as per the principal status of work, declined from 32.7 per cent in 1972–3 to 26.3 per cent in 1993–4 and further down to 22.2 per cent in 2011–12. The same, as per the principal as well as the subsidiary work status, declined from 32.4 per cent in 1993–4 to 27.4 per cent in 2011–12. Most of the decline in the proportion has been in rural areas. (Abraham 2013: 101, Table 3).

7. For example, Rangarajan et al. (2011) have argued this point, showing among other evidences, that the proportion of rural girls, aged sixteen to twenty-five, entering the education stream increased from 13.7 per cent in 1983 to 23.8 in 2009–10, and that of the urban girls (same age) increased from 24.2 per cent to 25.6 per cent between the same years (Rangarajan et al., 2011: 105, Table 8).

8. As quoted from the NSSO sources in Mazumdar and Neetha (2011: 118).

9. www.unric.org/en/uk-a-ireland-news-active-keystatistics-on-violence-against-women-and-girls; last accessed on 15 September 2013.

10. The same source as in 9.

11. See Sandberg (2013a and b) and Luscombe (2013).

12. This point was suggested and stressed by my daughter, Saraswati Naimpally.

13. Kirti Singh's book (2013) is a useful further reading in this regard.

Bibliography

Abraham, Vinoj (2013). 'Missing Women or Consistent Defaminisation?' *Economic and Political Weekly*, 48(31), pp. 99–108.

Agarwal, Bina (1994). *A Field of One's Own and Landrights in South Asia*. New Delhi: Cambridge University Press.

Agrawal, Purushottam (2006). 'Decoding Ethics of Srimadbhagavad Gita'. *The Book Review*. January–February, p. 29.

Ahluwalia, Montek Singh (1995). *First Raj Krishna Memorial Lecture 1995: Economic Reforms for the Nineties*. Department of Economics, University of Rajasthan, Jaipur. Accessed from http://planningcommsission.nic.in.aboutus/speech/spesma/msa033.pdf on 21 April 2011

Allen, Douglas (2008), 'Mahatma Gandhi's Philosophy of Violence, Nonviolence, and Education', in Douglas Allen (ed.), *The Philosophy of Mahatma Gandhi for the Twenty-First Century*. New Delhi: Oxford University Press, pp. 33–62.

———(ed.) (2008). *The Philosophy of Mahatma Gandhi for the Twenty-First Century*. New Delhi: Oxford University Press.

Arokiasamy, Perinayagam and Srinivas Goli (2012). 'Explaining the Skewed Child Sex Ratio in Rural India – Revisiting the Landholding-Patriarchy Hypothesis', *Economic and Political Weekly*, 47(42), pp. 85–94.

Badrinath, Chaturvedi (2007). *The Mahabharata: An Inquiry in the Human Condition*. New Delhi: Orient Longman.

Berle, Adolf A., and Gardiner C. Means (1932). *The Modern Corporation and Private Property*. New York: Commerce Clearing House.

Bharadwaj, Krishna (1980). *Some Issues of Method in the Analysis of Social Change*. Mysore: Mysore University.

Bhargava, Rajiv (2000). 'Holism and Individualism in History and Social Science', in *Concise Routledge Encyclopedia of Philosophy*. London: Macmillan, pp. 359–60.

Bhave, Vinoba (1963). *Swaraj Sastra: The Principles of a Nonviolent Political Order*. Tr. by Bharatan Kumarappa. Varanasi: Sarva Seva Sangh Prakashan.

Bilimoria, Purushottama (2001). 'Buddha', in Joy Palmer (ed.), *Fifty Thinkers on the Environment*. London: Routledge, pp. 1–7.

Bilimoria, Purushottama, Joseph Prabhu, and Renuka Sharma (eds) (2008). *Indian Ethics: Classical Traditions and Contemporary Challenges*. New Delhi: Oxford University Press.

Blackburn, Simon (2008). *Oxford Dictionary of Philosophy*, Second Edition. Oxford: Oxford University Press.

Boatright, John (2007). 'Conflict of Interest' in Robert W. Kolb (ed.) *Encyclopedia of Business Ethics and Society*. Thousand Oaks: Sage.

Brenkert, George G. and Tom L. Beauchamp (eds) (2010). *The Oxford Handbook of Business Ethics*. Oxford: Oxford University Press.

Broughton, Edward (2005). 'The Bhopal Disaster and Its Aftermath', *Environ Health*, Vol.4(6), available at www.ncbi.nlm.nih.gov/pmc/articles/PMC 1142333, accessed on 18 October 2013.

Brown, C. J. (1857). *Indian Infanticide, Its Origin, Progress and Suppression*. London: W. H. Allen and Co.

Cahn, Steven M. and Peter Markie (eds) (1998). *Ethics: History, Theory and Contemporary Issues*. Oxford: Oxford University Press.

Cain, Daylian M., George Lowenstein, and Don M. Moore (2005). 'Coming Clean but Playing Dirtier – The Shortcomings of Disclosure as a Solution to Conflicts of Interest', in Don A. Moore, Daylian M. Cain, George Lowenstein, and Max H. Bazerman (eds), *Conflicts of Interest, Challenges and Solutions in Business, Law, Medicine and Public Policy*. Cambridge: Cambridge University Press, pp. 104–25.

Callicott, J. Baird (2001). 'Aldo Leopold', in Joy Palmer (ed.), *Fifty Thinkers on the Environment*. London: Routledge, pp. 174–80.

Capra, Fritjof (1992 [1976]). *The Tao of Physics: An Exploration of the Parallels between Modern Physics and Eastern Mysticism*. London: Flamingo.

Carr, E.H. (2008 [1961]). *What is History?* London: Penguin.

Carson, R. (1962). *Silent Spring*. Boston: Houghton Miffin.

Chapple, Christopher Key (2008). 'Action Oriented Morality in Hinduism', in Purushottama Bilimoria, Joseph Prabhu, and Renuka Sharma (eds), *Indian Ethics: Classical Traditions and Contemporary Challenges*. New Delhi: Oxford University Press, pp. 351–62.

Chapple, Christopher Key and Mary Evelyn Tucker (eds) (2000). *Hinduism and Ecology: The Intersection of Earth, Sky and Water*. New Delhi: Oxford University Press.

Chatterjee, Amita (1997). 'Truth in Indian Philosophy', in Eliot Deutsch and Ron Bontekoe (eds), *A Companion to World Philosophies*. Mass: Blackwell, pp. 334–45.

Chatterjee, Margaret (1983). *Gandhi's Religious Thought*. London: Macmillan.

Chatterjee, Margaret (2005). *Gandhi and the Challenge of Religious Diversity: Religious Pluralism Revisited.* New Delhi & Chicago: Promilla & Co. in association with Bibliophile South Asia.

Christiano, Thomas and John Christman (eds) (2009). *Contemporary Debates in Political Philosophy.* Chichester: Wiley-Blackwell.

Cohen, Gerald A. (2009). 'Facts and Principles', in Thomas Christiano and John Christman (eds), *Contemporary Debates in Political Philosophy.* Chichester: Wiley-Blackwell, pp. 23–40.

Cooper, David E. (2001). 'John Passmore', in Palmer (ed.), *Fifty Thinkers on the Environment.* London: Routledge, pp. 216–21.

Crawford, S. Cromwell (1982). *The Evolution of Hindu Ideals.* Hawaii: University Press of Hawaii (First Edition in 1974).

———(ed.) (1989). *World Religions and Global Ethics.* NewYork: Paragon House.

CWMG (Collected Works of Mahatma Gandhi) (1958–). New Delhi: Government of India, Ministry of Information and Broadcasting, Publications Division.

Dagger, Richard (2009). 'Individualism and the Claims of Community', in Thomas Christiano and John Christman (eds), *Contemporary Debates in Political Philosophy.* Chichester: Wiley-Blackwell, pp. 303–21.

Dalton, Dennis (1998). *Non-violence in Action: Gandhi's Power.* New Delhi: Oxford University Press.

Damodaran, A. (2010). *Encircling the Seamless: India, Climate Change and the Global Commons.* New Delhi: Oxford University Press.

Das, Arvind N. (1982). 'Peasants and Peasant Organisations: The Kisan Sabha in Bihar', in Arvind N. Das (ed.), *Agrarian Movements in India: Studies in 20th Century Bihar.* London: Frank Cass, pp. 48–87.

Das, Gurcharan (2009). *The Difficulty of Being Good: On the Subtle Art of Dharma.* New Delhi: Allen Lane (Penguin).

Dasgupta, Ajit K. (1993). 'Gandhian Economics', in Ajit K. Dasgupta, *A History of Indian Economic Thought.* London: Routledge, pp. 130–62.

Dasgupta, Surama (1961). *Development of Moral Philosophy in India.* Bombay (Mumbai): Orient Longman.

Datta, Amlan (1986). *The Gandhian Way.* Shillong: North-Eastern Hill University.

Dayananda, Swami (2007[1985]). *The Teaching of the Bhagavad Gita.* Delhi: Vision Books.

Desai, Narayan (2009). *My Life is My Message.* (Tr. from Gujarati by Tridip Suhrud). Four volumes. Hyderabad: Orient Blackswan.

Deutsch, Eliot and Ron Bontekoe (eds) (1997). *A Companion to World Philosophies.* Massachusetts: Blackwell.

Doniger, Wendy (2013). *On Hinduism.* New Delhi: Aleph.

Dumble, Lynnette (2001). 'Vandana Shiva', in Joy Palmer (ed.). *Fifty Thinkers on the Environment.* London: Routledge, pp. 313–21.

Dwivedi, O.P. (2000). 'Dharmic Ecology', in Christopher Key Chapple and Mary Evelyn Tucker (eds), *Hinduism and Ecology: The Intersection of Earth, Sky and Water*. New Delhi: Oxford University Press, pp. 3–22.

E.B. (*Encyclopedia Britannica*), Volume 13, 1973 Edn.

Ehrlich, Paul (2002). 'Human Natures, Nature Conservation and Environmental Ethics', *BioScience*, 52(1), pp. 31–43, accessed from http://www.jstor.org./stable/1314111.

Fischer, Louis (1998[1953]). *The Life of Mahatma Gandhi*, Mumbai: Bharatiya Vidya Bhavan.

FritzRoy, Felix R. and E. Papyrakis (2010). 'Ethics and Climate Change', in Felix R. FritzRoy and E. Papyrakis, *An Introduction to Climate Change Economics and Policy*. London: Earthscan, pp. 83–103.

Fromm, Erich (1955). *The Fear of Freedom*. London: Routledge.

Gadgil, Madhav and K.C. Malhotra (1982). 'Ecology of a Pastoral Caste: The Gauli Dhanagars of Peninsular India', *Human Ecology*, 10(2), pp. 107–43.

Gadgil, Madhav and Ramachandra Guha (1995). *Ecology and Equity*. New Delhi: Penguin.

Gadgil, Madhav and V.D. Vartak (1974). 'Sacred Groves of India: A Plea for their Conservation', *The Journal of Bombay Natural History Society*, 72(2), pp. 314–20.

Gandhi, M.K. (1927). *An Autobiography or The Story of My Experiments with Truth*. Ahmedabad: Navjivan Trust.

———(1959). *My Socialism*. Ahmedabad: Navjivan Publishing House.

———(1960). *My Non-violence*. Ahmedabad: Navjivan Publishing House.

———(1961) *My Philosophy of Life*. Mumbai: Pearl Publications.

Ganeri, Jonardon (ed.) (2002). *The Collected Essays of Bimal Krishna Matilal: Ethics and Epics*. New Delhi: Oxford University Press.

Ganguli, B.N. (1973). *Gandhi's Social Philosophy: Perspective and Relevance*. New Delhi: Vikas.

Gasper, Des (2004). *The Ethics of Development: From Economism to Human Development*. New Delhi: Vistaar.

Geetha, V. (2007). *Patriarchy*. Calcutta: Stree.

Giri, Ananta Kumar (2008). *Self-Development and Social Transformation? The Vision and Practice of Self-Study Mobilisation of Swadhyaya*. New Delhi and Jaipur: Rawat.

Glotfelty, Cheryl (2001). 'Susan Griffin', in Joy Palmer (ed.), *Fifty Thinkers on the Environment*. London: Routledge, pp. 295–302.

Goleman, Daniel (1995). *Emotional Intelligence*. New York: Bantam.

——— (1998). *Working with Emotional Intelligence*. New York: Bantam.

Govindu, Venu Madhav and Deepak Malghan (2005). 'Building a Creative Freedom: J.C. Kumarappa and His Economic Philosophy', *Economic and Political Weekly*, 40(52), pp. 5477–85.

Grand, Julian Le (1991). 'Equality as an Economic Objective', in Brenda Almond and Donald Hill (eds). *Applied Philosophy: Morals and Metaphysics in Contemporary Debate*. London & New York: Routledge.

Grayling, A.C. (ed.) (2000[1995]). *Philosophy 1: A GuideThrough the Subject*. New York: Oxford University Press.

Griffin, Susan (2000). *Woman and Nature: The Roaring inside Her*. San Francisco: Sierra Club Books.

Guha, Ramachandra (2000). *Environmentalism: A Global History*. New Delhi: Oxford University Press.

——— (2006). *How Much Should a Person Consume? Thinking through Environment*. Ranikhet: Permanent Black.

Gundappa, D.V. (2001). *Shrimad-Bhagavad-Gita Taatparya Athavaa Jeevana Dharma Yoga* (in Kannada). Mysore: Kaavyaalaya.

Gupta, Pallavi (2012). 'Child Marriages and the Law: Contemporary Concerns', *Economic and Political Weekly*, 47(43), pp. 49–55.

Hales, Steven D. (2000). 'The Problem of Intuition', *American Philosophical Quarterly*, 37(2), pp. 135–47.

Hattangdi, Gopal (2002). *Aphorisms from the Rigveda*. Mumbai: Gopal Hattangdi.

Hawley, J.S. and Mark Jurgensmeyer (2004). *Songs of the Saints of India*. New Delhi: Oxford University Press.

Hayek, F.A. (1960). *The Constitution of Liberty*. London: Routledge & Kegan Paul.

Herur, Suresh (ed.) (2001). *Subhaashita Manjaree* (selected *subhaashita*s with Kannada translation). Bengaluru: Kannada Saahitya Parishattu.

Hindery, Roderick (1978). *Comparative Ethics in Hindu and Buddhist Traditions*. Delhi: Motilal Banarasidass.

Ibarra, Herminia, Robin Ely, and Deborah Kolb (2013). 'Women Rising: The Unseen Barriers', *Harvard Business Review*, September, pp. 61–66.

Iyengar, Sudarshan (2006). *Liberty and Individualism in Gandhian Perspective: Implications for Society's Sustainability*. Gandhi Memorial Lecture at Mahatma Gandhi Institute, Moka, Mauritius.

Iyer, Raghavan (2000[1973]). *The Moral and Political Thought of Mahatma Gandhi*. New Delhi: Oxford University Press.

——— (ed.) (2007 [1993]). *The Essential Writings of Mahatma Gandhi*. New Delhi: Oxford University Press.

Jahanbegloo, Ramin (2008). *The Spirit of India*. New Delhi: Penguin.

Janaway, Christopher (2000). 'Ancient Greek Philosophy I: The Pre-Socratics and Plato', in Grayling (ed.), *Philosophy 1: A GuideThrough the Subject*. New York: Oxford University Press, pp. 336–97.

Jodha, N.S. (1986) 'Common Property Resources and the Rural Poorin Dry Regions of India', *Economic and Political Weekly*, 21(27), pp. 1169–81.

Jois, Rama (1997). *Dharma, the Global Ethic*. Mumbai: Bharatiya Vidya Bhavan.

Jordens, J.T.F. (1998). *Gandhi's Religion*. London: Macmillan.

Kale, M.R. (1971). *The Niti and Vairagya Shatakas of Bhartrihari*. Delhi: Motilal Banarasidass.

Kamath, M.V. (2007) *Gandhi: A Spiritual Journey*. Mumbai: Indus Source Books.

Kane, P.V. (1990 [1930]). *History of Dharamashastra*. Poona: Bhandarkar Research Institute.

Kannan, K.P. and G. Raveendran (2012). 'Counting and Profiling the Missing Labour Force', *Economic and Political Weekly*, 47(6).

Kant, Immanuel (1959 [1785]). *Foundations of the Metaphysics of Morals*. Tr. by Lewis White Beck. Indianapolis: Bobbs-Merril.

Kant, Immanuel (1998). *Critique of Pure Reason*. (ed. & trans. by P. Guyer and A. W. Wood). Cambridge: Cambridge University Press.

Kapp, K.W. (1963). *Hindu Culture, Economic Development and Economic Planning*. New Delhi: Asia Publishing House.

Katju, Markandey (2009). 'Why the Caste System is on its Last Legs', *The Hindu*, 9 January, p. 10.

Keene, Michael (2004). *Religion in Life and Society*. Dunstable: Folens Publishers.

King, Robert J.H. (1991). 'Caring about Nature: Feminist Ethics and Environment', *Hypatia* 6(1), Spring; accessed from http://www.jstor.org/stable/3810034.

Knight, Frank H. (1936). *The Ethics of Competition and Other Essays*. New York: Harper & Brothers.

Krishnaraj, Maithreyi (2002). 'Women's Studies: Emergence of a Discipline (With Special Reference to India', in M.V. Nadkarni (ed.) *Landmarks in the Development of Social Sciences in the Twentieth Century*. Delhi: Allied Publishers.

Kumar, H.L. (2013). *Labour Laws Everybody Should Know*. New Delhi: Universal Law Publishing Co.

Kumar, Satish (2006). 'E.F. Schumacher', in Palmer (ed.), *Fifty Thinkers on the Environment*. London: Routledge, pp. 205–11.

Kumarappa, J.C. (1945). *Economy of Permanence*. Varanasi: Sarva Seva Sangha.

——— (1951). *Gandhian Economic Thought*. Bombay (Mumbai): Vora.

Kurien, C.T. (1973). *Guide to Research in Economics*. Madras: Sangam Publishers.

Lama, H.H. Dalai and Howard C. Cutler (1998), *The Art of Happiness: A Handbook for Living*. London: Hodder and Stoughton.

Leacock S. (1924). *The Garden of Folly*. New York: Dodd Mead.

Leopold, Aldo (1949). *A Sand Country Almanac and Sketches from Here and There*. New York: Oxford University Press.

Luscombe, Belinda (2013). 'Confidence Woman', *Time*, 181(10), 18 March, pp. 34–42.

MacIntyre, Alasdair (2010 [1967]). *A Short History of Ethics*. London: Routledge.

Marcuse, Herbert (1964). *One Dimensional Man: Studies in the Ideology of Advanced Industrial Society*. London: Routledge & Kegan Paul.

Matilal, Bimal Krishna (2002). *Perception: An Essay on Classical Theories of Knowledge*. New Delhi: Oxford University Press.

——— (ed.) (1989). *Moral Dilemmas in the Mahabharata*. Delhi: Motilal Banarasidass.

Mazumdar, Indrani and N. Neetha (2011). 'Gender Dimension: Employment Trends in India, 1993–94 to 2009–10', *Economic and Political Weekly*, 46(43), pp. 118–26.

McCall, J. John (2010). 'A Defense of Just Cause Dismissal Rules', in Newton et al. (eds), pp. 218–34.

McFague, S. (2008). *A New Climate for Theology: God, the World and Global Warming*. Minneapolis, M.N.: Fortress Press.

Medhini, Laya, Dipika Jain, and Colin Gonsalves (2009). 'Gender: Women and HIV', in Samaddar (ed.), *State of Justice in India*, Vol. 4: Key Texts on Social Justice in India, pp. 377–424.

Michael (ed.) (2005). *The Concept of Rajadharma*. New Delhi: Sundeep Prakashan.

Michael P. Nelson (2001). 'Lynn White Jr.' in Palmer (ed.), *Fifty Thinkers on the Environment*. London: Routledge, pp. 295–302.

Milner, Andrew and Jeff Browitt (2003). *Contemporary Cultural Theory*, Third Edition. Jaipur and New Delhi: Rawat.

Milton Friedman (1962). *Capital and Freedom*. Chicago: Chicago Press.

Miri, Mrinal (2003). *Identity and Moral Life*. New Delhi: Oxford University Press.

Mohan, Sunil (2013). *Towards Gender Inclusivity: A Study on Contemporary Concerns around Gender*. Bangalore: Alternative Law Forumand LesBiT.

Mohanty, J.N. (1999). 'The Idea of the Good in Indian Thought', in Deutsch and Bontekoe (eds), *A Companion to World Philosophies*, Mass.: Blackwell, pp. 290–303.

Mokashi-Punekar, Rohini (2002). *On the Threshold: Songs of Cholkhamela*. New Delhi: The Book Review Literary Trust.

Mukherjee, Rudrangshu (1993). *The Penguin Gandhi Reader*. New Delhi: Penguin.

Murry, William R. (2007). *Reason and Reverence: Religious Humanism for the 21st Century*. Boston: Skinner House Books.

Nadakarni, Aravind (1998). *Shaastradalli Vaamana* (Collection of essays in Kannada). Bengaluru: Kannada Sahitya Parishattu.

Nadkarni, M.V. (1997). 'Broadbasing Process in India and Dalits', *Economic and Political Weekly*, 32(33), pp. 2160–71.

——— (2003). 'Ethics and Relevance of Conversions: A Critical Assessment of Religious and Social Dimensions in a Gandhian Perspective', *Economic and Political Weekly*, 38(3), pp. 227–35.

——— (2007). 'Does Hinduism Lack Social Concern?', *Economic and Political Weekly*, 42(20), pp. 1844–9.

——— (2008 [2006]). *Hinduism: A Gandhian Perspective*. Delhi: Ane Books India.

Nandy, Ashis in conversation with Ramin Jahanbegloo (2006). *Talking India*. New Delhi: Oxford University Press.

Narayanan, Harini (2011). 'Women's Health, Population Control and Collective Action', *Economic and Political Weekly*, 46(8), pp. 39–47.

Nehru, Jawaharlal (1994). *The Discovery of India*. New Delhi: Oxford University Press (first edition in 1946 by Signet Press, Calcutta).

Nelson, Michael P. (2001). 'Lynn White Jr.' in Joy Palmer (ed.), *Fifty Thinkers on the Environment*. London: Routledge, pp. 201–3.

Newton, V., Elaine Englehardt, and Michael Pritchard (eds) (2010). *Taking Sides – Changing Views in Business Ethics and Society*. (Eleventh Edn.). New York: McGraw Hill.

Norman, Wayne and Chris Macdonald (2010). 'Conflicts of Interest', in Brenkert and Beauchamp (eds), Ch. 15, pp. 441–70.

Osborne, Arthur (1992[1954]). *Ramana Maharshi and the Path of Self-Knowledge*. London: Rider.

Ostrom, Elinor (1990). *Governing the Commons: Evolution of Institutions for Collective Action*. Cambridge: Cambridge University Press.

Palmer, Donald (2001[1988]). *Looking at Philosophy: The Unbearable Heaviness of Philosophy Made Lighter*. Mountain View, California: Mayfield Publishing Company.

Palmer, Joy A. (ed.) (2001). *Fifty Thinkers on the Environment*. London: Routledge.

Pandit, V. (1990). 'Conflicts, Paradigms and Economic Development: Some Gandhian Perspectives', in K.D. Gangrade and R.P. Mishra (eds), *Conflict Resolution Through Non-violence*. New Delhi: Concept Publishing, pp. 131–46.

Pandurangi, K.T. (1999a). *Indian Thought on Human Values*. Bangalore: Gandhi Centre for Science and Human Values of Bhartiya Vidya Bhavan.

—— (1999b). *Vichara Jyoti* (Kannada). Hubli and Bangalore: Loka-Shikshana Trust.

Pani, Narendar (2001). *Inclusive Economics: Gandhian Method and Contemporary Policy*. New Delhi: Sage.

—— (2004). 'Gandhian Economic Method and the Challenge of Expediency', in Anant Kumar Giri (ed.), *Creative Social Research: Rethinking Theories and Methods*. New Delhi: Vistaar Publications, pp. 185–205.

Panikkar, K. M. (1953). *Asia and Western Dominance*. London: Allen & Unwin.

Parekh, Bhikhu (2007), 'Gandhi on Poverty Eradication and People's Empowerment', in Sharma (ed.), *Peace, Nonviolence and Empowerment: Celebrating Hundred Years of Satyagraha' (1906–2006)*. New Delhi: Academic Foundation, pp. 139–151.

—— (2010). *Gandhi*. New York & London: Sterling.

Parel, Anthony (2006) *Gandhi's Philosophy and the Quest for Harmony*. New Delhi: Cambridge University Press.

Passmore, John (1980 [1974]). *Man's Responsibility for Nature: Ecological Problems and Western Tradition*. London: Duckworth.

Payne, Robert (1997). *The Life and Death of Mahatma Gandhi*. New Delhi: Rupa. Penguin.

Plumwood, Val (1993). *Feminism and the Mastery of Nature*. London: Routledge.

Rabbin, Robert (1994). 'Koan of Leadership', in John Renesch (ed.), *Leadership in New Era: Visionary Approaches to the Biggest Crisis of Our Time*. New York: New Leaders Press, pp. 195–206.

Rachels, James (1998). 'Modern Ethical Theory: Introduction', in Cahn and Markie (eds), *Ethics: History, Theory and Contemporary Issues*. Oxford: Oxford University Press, pp. 469–77.

Radhakrishnan, S. (1994 [1953]). *The Principal Upanishads*. New Delhi: Harper Collins.

Radhakrishnan, S. (2000 [1923]). *Indian Philosophy,* Volume 2. New Delhi: Oxford University Press.

Rajagopalachari, C. (1999 [1965]). *Kural: The Great Book of Tiruvalluvar.* Mumbai: Bharatiya Vidya Bhavan.

Ramanujan, A. K. (1973). *Speaking of Shiva.* New Delhi: Penguin.

––––– (1993). *Hymns for the Drowning: Poems for Vishnu by Nammalvar.* New Delhi: Penguin.

Rambachan, Anantanand (2006). *The Advaita World View: God, World and Humanity.* Albany: State University of New York Press.

Rangarajan, C., P.I. Kaul, and Seema (2011). 'Where is the Missing Labour Force?', *Economic and Political Weekly,* 46(39).

Rangarajan, L.N. (ed. and tr.) (1992). *Kautilya: The Arthashastra.* New Delhi: Penguin.

Rao, V.K.R.V. (1970). *The Gandhian Alternative to Western Socialism.* Bombay: Bharatiya Vidya Bhavan.

Rawls, John (1971). *A Theory of Justice.* Cambridge MA: Harvard University Press.

––––– (2001). *Justice as Fairness: A Restatement.* Edited by Erin Kelly. Cambridge Mass. & London: Belknap Press of Harvard University Press.

Regan, Tom (1982). *All that Dwell Therein: Animal Rights and Environmental Ethics.* Berkeley: University of California Press.

Richter, Duncan (2008). *Why Be Good? A Historical Introduction to Ethics.* New York & Oxford: Oxford University Press.

Roemer, John E. (1996). *Theories of Distributive Justice.* Cambridge Mass.: Harvard University Press.

Rolland, Romain (2004). *Mahatma Gandhi.* New Delhi: Publications Division, Government of India (first published in 1924 in London by George Allen and Unwin).

Roy, Ramashray (1984). *Self and Society: A Study in Gandhian Thought.* New Delhi: Sage.

Russell, Bertrand (2009a). *Philosophical Essays.* London: Routledge.

––––– (2009b). *An Outline of Philosophy.* London: Routledge.

Ryan, Alan (1970). *The Philosophy of Social Sciences.* London: Macmillan.

Samaddar, Ranbir (ed.) (2009). *State of Justice in India: Issues of Social Justice* (4 Volumes). New Delhi: Sage.

Sandberg, Sheryl (2013a). *Lean In: Women Work, and the Will to Lead.* New York: Alfred A. Knoff.

Sandel, Michael J (2009). *Justice: What's the Right Thing to Do?* New York: Penguin.

Sartre, Jean Paul (2007 [1996]) *Existentialism as Humanism.* New Haven and London: Yale University Press.

Schumacher, E.F. (1973), *Small is Beautiful: A Study of Economics as if People Mattered.* London: Blond and Biggs (Indian Reprint 1978 by Radha Krishna)

Schweitzer, Albert (1960[1936]). *Indian Thought and Its Development.* Boston: Beacon press.

Scruton, Roger (1995). *Modern Philosophy: An Introduction and Survey*. New York: Penguin.

—— (2000). 'Modern Philosophy I: The Rationalists and Kant', in Grayling (ed.) *Philosophy 1: A GuideThrough the Subject*. New York: Oxford University Press, pp. 440–83.

Sen, Amartya (1985). *Commodities and Capabilities*. Amsterdam: North Holland.

—— (1987). *On Ethics and Economics*. Oxford: Basil Blackwell; New Delhi: Oxford University Press.

—— (2000). *Development as Freedom*. New Delhi: Oxford University Press.

—— (2005). *The Argumentative Indian: Writings on Indian History, Culture and Identity*. London: Allen Lane.

—— (2006). *Identity and Violence: The Illusion of Destiny*. London: W.W. Norton and Company.

—— (2009). *The Idea of Justice*. London: Allen Lane (Penguin).

Sethi, J.D. (1979). *Gandhian Values and 20th Century Challenges*. New Delhi: Publications Division, Government of India.

—— (1991). *International Economic Disorder (A Theory of Economic Darwinism)*. Madras (Chennai): Sangam Books.

Sharma, Anand (ed.) (2007). *Peace, Nonviolence and Empowerment: Celebrating Hundred Years of Satyagraha (1906–2006)*. New Delhi: Academic Foundation.

Sharma, Arvind (2000). *Classical Hindu Thought: An Introduction*. New Delhi: Oxford University Press.

Sharma, Subhash (2006 [1996]). *Management in New Age: Western Windows Eastern Doors*. New Delhi: New Age International Publishers.

—— (2007). *New Mantras in Corporate Corridors: From Ancient Roots to Global Routes*. New Delhi: New Age International Publishers.

Shiller, Robert J. (2012). *Finance and the Good Society*. Princeton: Princeton University Press.

Shiva, V. (2001). 'Staying Alive: Women, Ecology and Development', in Nellison *et al* (eds), *Classics in Environmental Studies: An Overview of Classic Texts in Environmental Studies*. New Delhi: Kusum Publishing, pp. 285–95.

Singer, Peter (1975). *Animal Liberation: A New Ethics for our Treatment of Animals*. New York: Random House.

—— (1985). *In Defense of Animals*. Oxford: Basil Blackwell.

Singer, Richard (2007). *Your Daily Walk with Great Minds:Wisdom and Enlightenment of the Past and the Present*. Ann Arbor: Loving Healing Press.

Singh, Kirti (2013). *Separated and Divorced Women in India: Economic Rights and Entitlements*. New Delhi: Sage.

Smith, Adam (1976). *The Theory of Moral Sentiments*. (Edited by D.D. Raphael and A.L. Macfie.) Oxford: Clarendon Press.

—— (1937 [1776]). *An Inquiry into the Nature and Causes of the Wealth of Nations*. New York: Modern Library.

Soros, George (2009). *The Crash of 2008 and What It Means: The New Paradigm of Financial Markets*. New York: Public Affairs.

Stiglitz, Joseph E. (2007). *Making Globalization Work*. New York: W.W. Norton.

Subramaniam, Kamala (2001 [1965]). *Mahabharata,* Mumbai: Bharatiya Vidya Bhavan.

Sundaram, P.S. (ed. & tr.) (1990). *Tiruvalluvar: The Kural.* New Delhi: Penguin.

Swaminathan, Hema, Rahul Lahoti, and J.Y. Suchitra (2012). 'Gender Asset and Wealth Gaps: Evidence from Karnataka', *Economic and Political Weekly,* 47(35), pp. 59–67.

Swarupananda, Swami (1982). *Srimad Bhagavad Gita.* Calcutta: Advaita Ashrama (13th edition)

Tagore, Rabindranath (1989 [1932]). *The Golden Boat* (A collection of short stories, translated from Bengali by Bhabani Bhattacharya). Bombay: Jaico.

Tiwari, K.N. (1983). *Comparative Religion.* Delhi: Motilal Banarasidass.

Toynbee, Arnold (1991). *A Study of History* (Abridged and Illustrated One-volume Edition). New York: Barnes & Nobles.

Trevino, Linda K. and Katherine A. Nelson (2007). *Managing Business Ethics: Straight Talk About How to Do It Right.* Fourth Edition. Hoboken: John Wiley & Sons.

Tyagisananda, Swami (2000). *Narada Bhakti Sutras* (with Sanskrit text, English rendering, and Explanatory Notes). Madras: Sri Ramakrishna Math.

UNDP (United Nations Development Programme) (2009). *Human Development Report 2009.* New York: Palgrave Macmillan

——— (2013). *Human Development Report 2013.* New Delhi: Academic Foundation.

——— (2010). *Human Development Report 2010.* New York: Palgrave Macmillan.

Vauderville, Charlotte (1987). 'Sant Mat: Santism as the Universal Path to Sanctity', in Karina Schomer and W.H. McLeod (eds), *The Sants: Studies in Devotional Tradition of India.* New Delhi: Motilal Banarasidass, pp. 215–28.

Vidyalankar, Pandit Satyakam (n.d.). *The Holy Vedas: A Golden Treasury* (selected hymns with translation). Delhi: Clarion Books.

Vidyatmananda, Swami (ed.) (2006 [1972]).*What Religion Is: In the Words of Swami Vivekananda.* Kolkata: Advaita Ashram.

Vivekananda, Swami (2001). *Universal Ethics and Moral Conduct (Selections from The Complete Works of Swami Vivekananda).* Kolkata: Advaita Ashram.

Weber, Max (1930). *The Protestant Ethic and the Spirit of Capitalism.* London: George Allen & Unwin, Second Edition, 1976.

——— (1958). *The Religion of India: The Sociology of Hinduism and Buddhism.* Hans Gerth and Don Martindale (eds). New York: The Free Press.

Weiss, Paul (1974). *Beyond All Appearances.* Carbondale: Southern Illinois University Press.

Whichner, Ian (1998). *Integrity of the Yoga Darshana: A Reconsideration of Classical Yoga.* Albany, New York: State University of New York Press.

Williams, Bernard (2000). 'Ethics', in Grayling (ed.), *Philosophy 1: A Guide Through the Subject.* New York: Oxford University Press, pp. 545–82.

——— (2002). *Truth and Truthfulness.* Princeton: Princeton University Press.

Williams, Paul (1998). 'Indian Philosophy', in A.C. Grayling (ed.), *Philosophy 2: Further through the Subject.* New York: Oxford University Press, pp. 793–847.

World Bank (2010). *World Development Indicators 2010*. World Bank: Washington DC.

Young, Iris (2009). 'Structural Injustice and Politics of Difference', in Christiano and Christman (eds), *Contemporary Debates in Political Philosophy*. Chichester: Wiley-Blackwell, pp. 362–83.

Name Index

Subject Index

About the Author

M. V. Nadkarni founded the Ecological Economics Unit (renamed later as the Centre of Ecological Economics and Natural Resources) at the Institute for Social and Economic Change, Bengaluru, in 1981 at the instance and initiative of Professor V. K. R. V. Rao. He presided over the Annual Conference of the Indian Society of Agricultural Economics in 1995 at the Institute of Rural Management Anand, Gujarat (IRMA), and was also the Chairman of the Editorial Board of the *Indian Journal of Agricultural Economics* of the same society for three years. His publications include *Poverty, Environment and Development* (co-authored) (2001); *Hinduism: A Gandhian Perspective* (2006, 2008); and *Handbook of Hinduism* (2013), amongst others.